The DECATHLON

A colorful history of track and field's most challenging event

Frank Zarnowski, DA
Mount Saint Mary's College

Leisure Press
Champaign, Illinois

GV
1060.7
Z36
1989

Library of Congress Cataloging-in-Publication Data

Zarnowski, Frank.
   The decathlon ROBERT MANNING
                 STROZIER LIBRARY

   Bibliography: p.
   Includes index.   SEP 1 1989
   1. Decathlon--History. I. Title.
GV1060.7.Z36 1989   796.4'2   88-27308
ISBN 0-88011-344-8 Tallahassee, Florida

ISBN 0-88011-344-8

Developmental Editor: June I. Decker, PhD
Copy Editor: John Wentworth
Proofreaders: Linda Siegel, Pam Johnson
Assistant Editors: Robert King, Holly Gilly
Production Director: Ernie Noa
Typesetters: Angela Snyder, Kathy Fuoss
Text Design: Keith Blomberg
Text Layout: Jayne Clampitt
Cover Design: Tim Offenstein
Printed By: Braun Brumfield, Inc.

Printed in the United States of America

10 9 8 7 6 5 4 3 2 1

Leisure Press
A Division of Human Kinetics Publishers, Inc.
Box 5076, Champaign, IL 61825-5076
1-800-342-5457
1-800-334-3665 (in Illinois)

I would like to thank my father and mother, who introduced sports to me and made them an important part of my life. This book is dedicated to them and to all the decathletes who added life and color to the legend of numbers that accompanies any decathlon. I would particularly like to thank those decathletes from Mount Saint Mary's College, who over the years have made my advocation enjoyable: Jim Deegan, coach; Tom Delmoor, Robert Ekpete, Mike Ellrich, Alvin Fernandez, Knut Harold Gundersen, Dan Hallinan, George Hearn, Rick Hoolko, Even Hytten, Jim Keegan, Gernot Kellermayr, Mark Kilby, Steve Long, Chris Lockett, Vin Lupo, Harry Marra, Ahmed Mahour Bacha, Rick Mori, William Motti, Carlos O'Connell, Gudmund Olsen, Tony Pauline, Jim Sharp, Barry Stebbins, Bob Stebbins, Trond Skramstad, Bill Walsh, Georg Werthner, Justin Whitfield, and Joe Zaruba.

Table of Contents

Foreword

As I walked from the practice track toward the Olympic stadium in Montreal on that first day of the 1976 Games, I sensed that it was my time in history to win the Olympic decathlon. I had long been interested in the history of my event because my college coach, L.D. Weldon at Graceland, had coached an Olympic medalist 40 years before. I had prepared for these Games as well as I could, I knew the strengths and weaknesses of my opponents, and I simply felt that this was my day. I am pleased about this book because it puts my Montreal effort and records into perspective. I had some knowledge of decathlon history, but much was second-hand. Some was inaccurate. Zeke's book sets the record straight.

I have a second major interest in this book. My Montreal score set both American and world records. The world record has been upped eight times since, but the American record has lasted over a dozen years. I have mixed feelings about that. Of course I'm happy to still be on the books. But on the other hand, no U.S. citizen has even approached the record, now 8634 points. I am anxious for an American athlete to break it, because that might signal a resurgence of U.S. decathlon efforts. America once dominated the world decathlon scene. No longer. My hope is that this book will create future interest and higher scores.

Bruce Jenner

Preface

In 1972, I had a bit part in a Disney movie, *The World's Greatest Athlete*. The movie was a spoof featuring a jungle boy, Nanu (Jan-Michael Vincent), who would win every track event he entered. The movie won no Oscar, but no film ever had a better cast of extras. On the set were a dozen great decathletes—Bill Toomey, Fred Dixon, Dave Thoreson, Paul Herman, Barry King, and others—many of whom left the set early to compete in the United States Olympic Trials in Eugene, Oregon. Those in the background of the film truly were the world's greatest athletes.

The movie just borrowed a phrase that had been used by track and field people for decades. Ever since Jim Thorpe won a new event called *decathlon* at the 1912 Stockholm Olympics, the decathlon champion has been bestowed the title "The World's Greatest Athlete." My earliest recollection of the event dates to 1960, when I watched television coverage of the Rome Olympic Games. In the darkness of the Estadio Olympico, two collegiate teammates contested the decathlon to exhaustion. The Rafer Johnson/C.K. Yang duel never left my memory. By 1968 I was organizing small decathlons and coaching. The National Collegiate Athletic Association (NCAA) included the event in their championship format by 1970 and I was an impromptu announcer for their first decathlon. An early highlight for me came in June of 1971 when I met Bill Toomey, the reigning Olympic champion, and Bruce Jenner, who was then an Iowa hitchhiker. Both were watching the NCAA championships in Seattle, Washington.

This book is the thorough history of track and field's most formidable event. Its purpose is to introduce athletes, coaches, and fans to the heritage and mystique surrounding the decathlon. It is my hope that the reader will develop a lasting affection for those men who run, jump, and throw in anonymity for most of their competitive lives, receiving only a quadrennial chance for stardom.

Chapter 1 introduces the event. Factual characteristics and ideological framework are presented by avid fan Bert Nelson, Coach Sam Adams, and me.

The concept of the all-around or multi-event athlete is traced to the ancient Olympic Games in chapter 2. The similarities in nature and structure of the Greek pentathlon and the modern-day decathlon are no coincidence. This chapter should help the reader appreciate the age and popularity of the notion of the all-around athlete.

Chapter 3 covers the almost complete disappearance of multi-event competition in the Middle Ages, when athletics for the most part became recreational and local, to the reemergence of track and field in the 19th century, when multi-event competitions regained popularity. The contributions of early American colleges, the all-around event, and the modern Olympic Games are detailed. The careers of several all-around greats are presented in portfolio form.

Chapters 4 and 5 cover the history of the event decade by decade from its first competition until the present. The year 1964 is a watershed date when the decathlon turned the corner; this date divides the chapters. In all, 23 of the greatest champions in the history of the decathlon are presented in portfolios.

The modern Olympic Games highlight and showcase the decathlon. Chapter 6 is a special attempt to describe Olympic decathlon competitions. Here readers will find the drama of duels between Lövland and Hamilton, Bausch and Järvinen, Johnson and Yang, Jenner and Avilov, and others. Also offered are photos, complete results, a section on trivia, quotes, and even a list of the best and worst Olympic performances.

Chapter 7 attempts to diffuse the problems of scoring. It has been said that scoring a decathlon is even more difficult than participating in one. Information on how to score competitions, as well as how to foul up scores, is presented.

The appendixes present the author's research. Included are a plethora of records, a list of all modern Olympic performers, and suggestions for additional readings.

Is the decathlon champion the world's greatest athlete? Is he the ideal of the versatile, all-around, Renaissance athlete? I think so. No other athletic test purports to measure so many basic athletic virtues: speed, strength, spring, style, and stamina. There is no other objective test. Triathlons certainly don't count, measuring only layers of endurance. The modern pentathlon comes closest but has little interest outside the military. Some claim that NFL linebackers and NBA power forwards are today's super athletes, but none would be able to outrun, outjump, outthrow, or outvault any of today's current world-class decathletes. Invented by the Swedes, dominated by Americans for years, and now raised to an art form by a Brit, the 2-day 10-eventer, is sports' purest and most objective all-around test.

Acknowledgments

For the past 2 decades I have gathered decathlon-related material. The preparation of the text spanned 24 months. My indebtedness to colleagues and friends in the decathlon world has become so vast that it is impossible to list all those who deserve credit. However, I must thank Bill Mallon, an Olympics researcher extraordinaire, for his suggestions, results, photos, and support. I unashamedly exploited his brain power. The following people also provided valuable information and guidance: Sam Adams, Hal Bateman, Pete Cava, Peter Diamond, Ken Doherty, Manfredini Gabriele, Anti Haapalahti, Hans-Torkel Halvorsen, Jon Hendershott, Erkki Kiilunen, Alan Lindop, Rooney Magnusson, Martin Mandel, Reinhard Muller, Bert Nelson, Fred Samara, David Wallechinsky, Georg Werthner, and Ture Widlund. I am indebted to Fred Kudu who was a major source of inspiration. His 1988 death left a large void in the decathlon world.

I am grateful to Justin Whitfield for encouraging me to get this project off the shelf and back on my desk and to Debbie Shaffer of the Mount Saint Mary's College Library for tracking down manuscripts for me. No small thanks to both.

I want to add my appreciation to John Gill and June Decker for their help in making the book more readable and to Mary Wivell, Kristine Eyler, Phyllis Staley, and, especially, Julie Moscatello for supplying secretarial assistance through numerous revisions of the text. Finally, I am particularly thankful for the advice of my friend, Bil Gilbert.

The primary sources for the Olympic records section were the *Official Reports* of the various Olympic organizing committees. In many cases they were unreliable, incomplete, or just incorrect. My initial sources for career records included *Annuals* of the Association of Track and Field Statisticians (ATFS) and issues of *Track and Field News*. Both were very reliable. Bill

Mallon was instrument in providing Olympic material as well as spellings and accent marks for names of Olympic competitors. I am particularly indebted to him as well as to Rooney Magnusson and Erkki Kiilunen, who provided data on many early Scandinavian greats, and to David Wallechinsky and Ture Widlund, who filled in Olympic result gaps.

The editions of *The Decathlon Book* (Nelson & Zarnowski, 1975, 1976, 1978, and 1980) and the annual *TAC Decathlon/Heptathlon Guides* (Zarnowski, since 1980) were valuable sources of statistical information.

1

The World's Greatest Athletes

Whoever wants to know the heart and mind of the Renaissance man had better learn decathlon. This assertion, lifted from Jacques Barzun, who said the same thing 30 years ago about baseball and the American male, is advice to those who want to know the sum and substance of track and field's most interesting and misunderstood event—the decathlon. The decathlon embodies the idea of diverse preparation and skill. It is a track meet in itself. Astute observer Ken Doherty (1985) believes that the decathlon most clearly reflects the ancient Greek ideal of all-around, balanced excellence in sports.

The decathlon is a menu of athletic events, testing an individual's speed, endurance, strength, skill, and personality. The word is of Greek origin (deka [ten] + athlon [contest]). The decathlon includes five events on each of 2 successive days. The first day schedules the 100-meter run, long jump, shot put, high jump, and 400 meters. It is a day of speed, explosive power, and jumping ability. Day 2 consists of the 110-meter hurdles, discus, pole vault, javelin, and 1500 meters. The emphasis this day is on technique and endurance. Performances in the 10 events are scored by reference to point tables. The individual accumulating the highest number of points after 10 events is the decathlon winner.

Doherty (1985), a two-time national champion and Olympic medalist himself, captures the sense of the decathlon: "I have always rejected sport as a violent struggle against antagonistic opponents. In the decathlon the struggle is against time, distance, fatigue, and one's inner fears of weakness or failure. Other decathletes are fellow competitors, helpful motivators to doing one's best, often ignored, often good friends, never hostile. Each concentrates on doing his utmost, without concern for diminishing the efforts of others. Whoever scores the most points on the tables is the victor" (p. 287).

Figure 1.1. Discobolus, a statue of an early Greek pentathlete. (From the Zarnowski collection)

Anatomy of a Decathlon

To ancient Greeks and modern Germans, the decathlon performer was and is the king of athletes. But to most of the track world, including the United States, the decathlete is a sometime hero, recognized and applauded only when he wins the Olympic Games.

Hero or forgotten man, the 10-event performer is a rare and unique breed. The United States, which must have at least 100,000 sprinters, has less than 1000 athletes who compete in two decathlons per year (the number is probably somewhere between 700 and 900). Interest, although growing, is limited to a few countries. Of the 100 best performers in 1983, 35 came from the Soviet Union, 18 from the United States, 12 from West Germany, and 10 from East Germany. The remaining 23 were scattered over 16 nations. Tiny Switzerland, which for some reason promotes the event, usually has a few representatives in the top 100.

Although American decathletes are improving in both quality and quantity, they are seldom seen except when competing in an internationai championship such as the Olympic Games. In 1986, for instance, 600 fans witnessed the national (TAC) championships in Eugene, Oregon. Even more remarkable was that not even 100 Canadians stayed around to see Bob Coffman's fine 8279 win over the Soviets in Quebec City in 1979. When the national anthem was played during the awards ceremony for Coffman only four spectators could be counted.

Even competition is limited. The average good decathlete competes at most three or four times a year, the less talented even fewer. Bill Toomey's nine great efforts back in 1969 undoubtedly were unusual. Decathlon has been the most orphan of all Olympic events.

The decathlete does not have to be outstanding in any event to be a champion in the 10 events. But he must range from adequate in his weak events to good or better in the other skills. Because he must do well in the four runs and six field disciplines, he has little opportunity to perfect any one talent. His training is necessarily different as he strives to improve all techniques, gain strength without sacrificing speed, and acquire the stamina to see him through a competition that runs from a minimum of 4 hours to the usual 10 to 12 hours per day during the Olympics.

The decathlon is the only event in which it doesn't really matter if the athlete finishes first, third, or worse in a particular event. The score is the thing, and for the most part decathletes compete against themselves, while keeping a wary eye on the opposition. It is the only event with an arbitrary scoring system and thus the only one in which personal performance and records can be updated as new scoring tables are adopted. Under the original scoring tables adopted in 1912, Akilles Jarvinen of Finland finished second in both the 1928 and 1932 Olympics, but the new scoring system introduced in 1934 gave Jarvinen higher converted totals than both the men he lost to. World-record holder C.K. Yang lost 1032 points when his 1963 performance was converted late in 1964 to the new tables first used in the 1964 Olympics. His top rivals lost only 287 and 172 points when their bests were converted, and Yang dropped from overwhelming favorite to third on the pre-Games ranking, finishing a disappointed and understandably bitter fifth.

The arbitrary nature of the scoring tables can work in the opposite direction as well. In 1984, at the Los Angeles Olympic Games, Great Britain's Daley Thompson missed the world record by one point on the then-used 1962/77 tables. The tables were changed a year later and Daley's score in Los Angeles converted to a best-ever mark.

The decathlon is the only men's multi-event competition in track, meaning the competitor must bring into play technique, strategy, and awareness not needed elsewhere. By the same token, the decathlon is the only contest that allows a performer a chance to catch up after a bad outing. Foul up in one event and there is still hope.

Different, too, is the reaction to completed competition. The decathlete never nears perfection, is seldom completely satisfied, almost always finishes a bit frustrated. No matter how well he does, no matter the win or the record, he can always find room for improvement in several of the events. There is always a "wait until next time" attitude.

Mental factors play a greater role in a decathlon than they do in other events. The biggest problems are in maintaining concentration throughout the 10 events and getting psyched up for each event.

The decathlon is the most social of track events and promotes a strong sense of camaraderie among contestants. There is a lot of time to visit during and between events, much of which is used in helping other participants. Athletes will give and take advice, analyze each other's technique, assist each other in locating and checking take-off points, and even use each other's personal equipment. Record-holder Rafer Johnson worked closely with teammate C.K. Yang, defeated him by only 58 points in the 1960 Games, and later lost the world record to him. Bill Toomey and Russ Hodge lived with other decathletes in their Santa Barbara decathlon colony while taking turns breaking the world mark in 1966. Athletes commonly help their chief rivals: Siggi Wentz advised Jürgen Hingsen on hurdle technique, Bill Motti tutored Jim Wooding on high-jump approach, and Mike Ramos and John Sayre worked together on discus form.

Finally, the decathlon has certain unique rules. The amount of wind that invalidates a performance for world-record purposes is twice that allowable for open events. In IAAF and TAC competition three false starts will disqualify a competitor from a running event. The NCAA rule is two. Only three trials are permitted in the throws and the long jump.

What type of man is the decathlete? He comes in various shapes and sizes, ranging from Jeff Bennett, 5-8 and 145 lb, who was fourth at the 1972 Munich Olympics, to Rick Wanamaker, a 6-9, 210-pounder who won AAU, NCAA, and Pan Am titles in the 1970s. But most of the really good decathletes are remarkably similar in size. Most of the 15 best performers of all time are over 6 feet tall, ranging from Igor Soboyevskiy's 5-11 to 6-7 Olympic silver-medalist Jürgen Hingsen of West Germany. Weights range from 183 lb to 215 lb for the massive Hingsen. Few top 200 pounds. Of these top 15 performers, the average height and weight are 6-2, 195 lb—exactly Bruce Jenner's dimensions.

All the world-class competitors have good speed. Daley Thompson, Bob Coffman, and Guido Kratschmer have all clocked in the 10.30-10.40 range for 100m with automatic timing. Only Jenner did not have exciting speed, but he made up for it with consistency, strength, and balance. Almost all decathletes have good spring. Of the world-class athletes, few jump less than 1.90m (6-2 3/4), and it is not rare to see 2.13m (7-0) clearances. They are strong, most putting the shot over 15.00m (49-2 1/2). Bill Toomey's best was just under 14.33m (47-0), whereas Russ Hodge reached 18.56m (60-10 3/4).

Skill enters into a number of events, of course, and here the range of performance widens. In the vault, for instance, Toomey managed just 4.27m (14 feet), whereas Jenner achieved 4.88m (16 feet). Thompson has cleared 5.25m (17-2 3/4) and, more recently, American Tim Bright cleared 5.70m (18-8 1/4). Bob Coffman was a 13.5 hurdler. East German Joachim Kirst never bettered 15.0. And there are individual strong suits. Toomey looks good on anybody's list with a 45.68 metric quarter and 7.93m (26-1/4) long jump. Thompson has recorded a 10.26 100m and an 8.11m (26-7 1/4) long jump. Hingsen has a jump of 2.16m (7-1) and has put the shot 16.42m (53-10 1/2).

But it takes more than speed and strength and skill to make a decathlon man. Alphonse Juillard, an American decathlon nut for almost 50 years, firmly believed that such intangible qualities as mental toughness, determination, and concentration are more important in a decathlon than in any other event. Listen to Juillard:

> What fascinates me about it is especially the psychological toughness it requires. You will notice very few successful decathlon men who do not have unusual intellectual abilities. My observation is that the decathlon man is probably a little more intellectually developed than the people in other events. It's not only natural talent, nor tactics, but it's strategy . . . the strategy to plan not only for the contest and the year, but to plan on a long term basis. And this takes considerable determination and consistency.

> Inevitably . . . in this country more than in Europe, [decathletes] are loners. Precisely because they need a special kind of training, because there is rather little interest, because they usually compete almost in a vacuum, because of the kind of requirements. A decathlon man becomes very individualistic. His is a solitary effort especially in training and preparation.

> I think every decathlon man has to be a bit of an introvert. An extrovert would not take the solitary effort for the long months and long

years when you have to go and throw by yourself. And an extrovert could not get his best effort in front of 30 people.

Toomey observes that even in a "lousy decathlon one good thing can happen. You get positive feedback that will help the next event, or next time. If you're a 100-yard dashman and you blow your event you've had it.

"But the big problem," says the 1968 Olympic king, "is getting up, mentally, for each event. To prepare yourself, to change your attitude as a person to what you are doing. When you are throwing the shot you are not a long-jumper anymore. You are almost a super-schizophrenic. You are a giant shot-putter when you are throwing the shot. In the high jump, you're like a, well, a ballet type."

Although ignored by many, the decathlon has completely absorbed a handful of athletes and fans. It began where the Olympics began, in Greece, some 7 centuries before Christ. The Greek pentathlon, five events much like the present seldom-contested pentathlon, was included in the Olympics of 708 B.C. and soon became the high point of the games. The ancient competition included a run, long jump, discus, javelin, and wrestling, whereas today's pentathlon includes the long jump, javelin, 200m, discus, and 1500m.

In the modern era, a 10-event, all-around competition to be completed in one day was inaugurated by the United States in 1884. Such an event was held in connection with the 1904 Olympics at St. Louis. The decathlon was invented by Scandinavians, who eventually settled on the present 10 events after years of experimentation. They derived the original scoring system, now referred to as the 1912A tables, by using the then-current Olympic records. Both the decathlon, which took its name from the Greek *deka*, meaning *ten*, and *athlos*, meaning *contest*, and the pentathlon were held in the 1912 Olympics in Stockholm. Both were won with outstanding marks by Jim Thorpe, but the American Indian's name on the Olympic rolls was a long time in coming. Because he had played summer baseball for pay, earning from $60 to $100 a month, he was judged guilty of professionalism and stripped of his wins, medals, and records. The records were not reinstated until 1984.

In recent years, the most-remembered names are Bob Mathias, Rafer Johnson, Bill Toomey, Nikolay Avilov, Bruce Jenner, Jürgen Hingsen, and Daley Thompson.

Mathias startled the track world in 1948 when he captured the Olympic title as a 17-year-old. After twice breaking the world record, he topped the global standard yet a third time in repeating his Olympic win, becoming one of two ever to win twice. Johnson too got off to a fast start, cracking Mathias's record as a 19-year-old freshman. He went on to break the record twice more, to place second while injured in the 1956 Games,

Figure 1.2. Daley Thompson, one of the greatest athletes of modern times. (Claus Andersen/Courtesy of *Track and Field News*)

and to win the 1960 Olympics. Bill Toomey won the Olympic title in 1968 in mile-high Mexico City and claimed the world record a year later in Los Angeles. After finishing fourth in 1968 behind Toomey, Soviet lawyer Nikolay Avilov stunned the multi-event world in 1972 by breaking Toomey's mark and grabbing the Olympic Gold in Munich. Avilov surrendered his world record in 1975 and his Olympic title in 1976 (in Montreal), both to Bruce Jenner. Jenner posted 8634 points (new tables) in 1976, a mark never before or since approached by an American. Britisher Daley Thompson won golds at both Moscow and Los Angeles, tying Mathias's mark. West German Jürgen Hingsen, although he has bettered the global standard three times, has had the misfortune of competing in Thompson's prime.

Today, the decathlete is truly popular only in Germany. The Soviet Union promotes the event systematically, as it does all events. Jenner, after winning Montreal metal, has acquired a bit of recognition in the United States through television exposure. But in both East and West

Germany, the 10-event man has social standing. For instance, West German veterans Hingsen and Kratschmer are recognized on the street. The Germans have staged special competition in single events, such as the pole vault, involving only decathletes.

It is hoped that the new emphasis, especially from this country's collegiate ranks, will provide many new decathletes. Certainly our country is loaded with big, fast, talented tracksters. If the United States begins to produce the quantity and quality of decathletes it should, the American track world will be enriched by the addition of a great and exciting event that has always deserved much more attention than it receives.

DECATHLON

Sam Adams was a thrower at the University of California in the 1950s and was once the best three-event thrower in collegiate history. He was fifth at the 1956 Olympic Trials decathlon and held American records for the shot and discus in decathlon competition. Cal mentor Brutus Hamilton, the 1920 Olympic Games decathlon runner-up, passed the decathlon torch to him. Sam now coaches at the University of California at Santa Barbara. He is a widely respected and knowledgeable decathlon coach and served as multi-event coordinator for the 1984 Olympic Games in Los Angeles. More important, he is a long-time friend and supporter of decathletes. Sam offers some thoughts and feelings of decathletes as they compete in each of the 10 events.*

1. *100 Meters*. Take your marks; get set; gun!!!—drive—pump your arms—now try to relax, get rhythm, get length—there's the tape—ungh!—what was it? Deep breath, stop shaking! Relax.

2. *Long Jump*. Get your step, concentrate on the intermediate mark. Get your knees up! Settle, drive the knee, ungh! No height! How far? Where was my step? O.K. Let go on the next one. Ungh! That pit is hard! No lift. Relax! Don't get out of control. Ungh! O.K. Now you're a shot putter.

3. *Shot Put*. Feels light today. Take a deep breath. Relax. Good position and blast it. Ungh! O.K. Good start! Legs, reverse hard, follow the shot. Ungh! How far? Last one, let her go, good rhythm. Ungh!! O.K. Calm down. Relax.

4. *High Jump*. Get your run-up. Too far out, adjust. Get erect, arms good, lead leg lift, good clearance. O.K. Trying too hard, let

Note. From *The Decathlon Book* (p. 93) by Frank Zarnowski and Bert Nelson, 1975, Emitsburg, MD: DECA. Copyright 1975 by Frank Zarnowski. Reprinted with permission.

it happen. O.K. Damn trail leg. Get your roll off the take-off. O.K. Ungh! Ungh! 400.

5. *400 Meters*. Bang!! I'm tired. No, feels good now. Man, is this straight long. 200 already? Work the curve. Where's the end? O.K. Now pick up the foot, keep your form, use your arms. Don't tight. There's the tape. There's the tape. Come here, tape. Unnnnggghhh! Fire! Move around. Huh! Stand up. Keep moving. Man!! How fast? Warm down good.

Drink, eat, sleep, wake up. I'm tired. Little stiff. Plenty of fluids. Eat. Time to go. Warm up good. Stretch.

6. *110-Meter Hurdles*. It's all wood! Take your marks. It's all wood! Set! Bang!! Drive! Run each one. Punch it. That must be five. Keep momentum. Damn trail leg! Get it up early! Damn, damn, damn!!! Go to the tape, ungh!!! Damn hurdles! I hate em!!! Quit shaking. How fast?

7. *Discus*. Not bad wind. Discus feels good. Legs feel snapless. Got to relax and slow down a little. Let the legs get into it. Relax, keep erect. Get thee behind me, discus. Ungh! Good starter! Ungh! Lost it. Ungh!! Finally!

8. *Pole Vault*. My hands are really sweaty. Step on! O.K. Drive the box, plant early. Ungh! Under, 'bout ripped my shoulder off. Ungh! Better, O.K. Don't force. Good plant! Good. Good. Don't tighten up. Blagh! Flags out. Blagh! You're a butt. Relax. Last one, ah. Ungh! Good try, butt!

9. *Javelin*. This is my event. O.K. Keep your cool. Set it high. Drive right leg. O.K. Good openers. Keep it high. Finish the throw. Ungh! One more. Flight!! Relax. Keep the point where you want it. Ungh!! Not bad.

10. *1500 Meters*. What's my score so far? Should I run hard? Have to run hard. Should I warm up? Not much. Run steady pace. O.K. Set! Bang!!! Get relaxed and build. Where the hell do those guys think they're going? What lap is this? 880. Got to work this next lap. 1320—330 to go. Get it up!! Can't. Yes I can!! Thought I could. Where's the finish? No guts. Slow motion. 60 yards to go. Form! 10 to go. Unngh!!!! Crap, am I now here? Walk, you vegetable!! Where's the air? No legs. O.K. Now.

11. *Reflections*. Man, I sure can improve easy in six events. Next time I'll get that score for sure. Should have taken more fluids. I'd have been 200 points better on synthetic. Sure wasn't much of an aiding wind. Damn heat sapped me.

When's the next one?

2

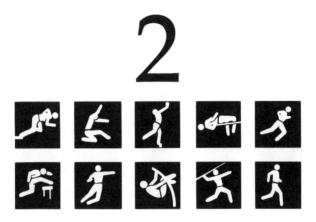

The Ancient Greek Pentathlon

Beginning in 1875, German archaeologists, while investigating the ancient Greek civilization, uncovered ruins of temples, statues, and playing areas near Olympia (Figure 2.1). The Greeks appreciated the athlete and believed that the body as well as the mind needed discipline, exercise, and an outlet for expression. We know a great deal about these periodic expressions, ceremonies for athletes that have come to be called the Olympic Games.

Figure 2.1.   Ancient Greek stadium today. Spectators stood or sat on the sloping embankment. (From Associated Press)

The Ancient Greek Olympics

One midsummer day in a year we calculate to have been 708 B.C. a multi-event contest was run in a rural area of what is now Southwestern Greece. A young Spartan named Lampis won the five-event pentathlon. It was an obscure event in an obscure spot but it earned Lampis fame: He is the first multi-event victor on record.

The place was Olympia, not far from Elis. Sixty-eight years before, the locals had initiated a race (about 192 yd) as part of an older festival to honor Zeus, the Greek's chief god. In 776 B.C., the locals embellished a religious festival with an athletic contest, and the Olympic Games were born.

Every 4 years for more than a millennium the Greeks gathered to celebrate, give honor to the gods, and watch athletic contests. Eventually spectators came from across the ancient world. The Olympic Games attracted tens of thousands of people willing to make an uncomfortable trek to an out-of-the-way sanctuary. Upon arriving, visitors got a good look at a 40-foot-high ivory and gold statue of Zeus in his temple, one of the seven wonders of the ancient world.

The program of sports reached its final form around 500 B.C. The contests were for males only. But the Olympics were neither the first nor the only organized Greek games. Book XXIII of the *Iliad* contained the funeral games celebrated in honor of the slain Patroclus. Historians have dated Homer's story of the siege of Troy to about 1250 B.C., the Greek Bronze Age. Mycenaean excavations confirmed the historical reality of Homer's epic. Homer's heroes were aristocratic warriors. Almost 700 lines of the *Iliad* describe in detail the sporting events organized by Achilles in honor of his dead companion, Patroclus. Winners (and second and third places!) received female prisoners, horses, mules, bulls, tripods, cauldrons, and gray irons for chariot racing, boxing, wrestling, running, discus throwing (where the implement was the prize), archery, and spear throwing. There were no multi-event contests in Homer's epics. But the Greeks certainly were involved in athletic contests long before the Olympic Games began in the 8th century B.C. Incidentally, Greek mythology attributes the father of Achilles, Peleus, as the winner of the first pentathlon.

The Greek physical contests were religious affairs. Those who took part did so to glorify a deity. And common belief was that the prizes came from a god.

The games at Olympia were not the only games to have their roots in religion. By the 6th century B.C., major games were held in Corinth, in honor of Poseidon, and in Delphi and Nemea, both for Apollo (Table 2.1).

The time and place of Greek festivals was sacred. After three full summer moons the heralds went forth to announce an Olympic truce. After 10 months of training, athletes gathered at a nearby town, Elis, and spent 30 more days in final preparation before traveling to the actual site on the river Eurotas.

Over time, the games expanded from a simple *stade* race (one length of the stadium) in 776 B.C. to an elaborate program. To the Greeks, winning was everything. There were no second or third prizes. And they did not go in for sportsmanship. Losers were jeered at and left quietly in shame. Sportsmanship was an invention of the 18th-century British. Greek winners publicly exulted their victories.

Greek record keeping, too, was almost nonexistent. In ancient Greece there wasn't a way to say "set a record" or "break a record." The Greeks were interested in firsts. We have no pentathlon marks, but we do know the names of many winners.

The Greek games were not without their feuds, boycotts, bribes, and commotion. Some things never change. The athletes were by no means "amateur" in the modern sense. When a potential wreath winner appeared, cities bid for his services, taking great pride in their athletic champions. By the end of the Classical Age, Olympic victors were paid bonuses and prize money by hometowns or sponsoring cities, the purchasing power of which, in modern terms, rivals our own professionals.

Greek society valued physical excellence. Athletes were honored in the form of statues and poetry. Socrates scorned those who took no pride in their bodies. He admired physical excellence and participated in

Table 2.1   Greek Athletic Festivals

Festival	Site	God honored	Branch/wreath	Interval	Founded
Olympic	Olympia	Zeus	Olive	4 years	776 B.C.
Pythian	Delphi	Apollo	Bay	4 years	582 B.C.
Isthmian	Corinth	Poseidon	Pine	2 years	582 B.C.
Nemean	Nemea	Apollo	Parsley	2 years	573 B.C.

Note. Pentathlons were held at each major festival, much like decathlons are held today, spaced 2 or 4 years apart.

Corinth's Isthmian Games. In *The Republic*, Plato insisted upon the importance of gymnastic exercises for both men and women. Even less known is that Plato won prizes as a wrestler at the Pythian, Nemean, and Isthmian games.

As shown in Figure 2.2, the Olympic Games were held like clockwork, every 4 years, down to A.D. 261 when an invasion threatened the area. The games were then discontinued briefly but were soon reinstated and remained until Roman Emperor Theodosius I, a Christian, closed all pagan sanctuaries in A.D. 393. Other games survived. The games of Antioch, for example, lasted until 520 A.D. The Olympic site was abandoned and left over the centuries to nature and earthquakes. In the late 19th-century, German archaeological teams began a systematic excavation of the ancient site. Soon thereafter, the Greeks and the Baron Pierre de Coubertin promoted a modern Olympic movement.

The Pentathlon

Between the Greek's Bronze Age and Classical Age, myth and fact get blurred. Greek mythology tells us that before Jason invented the pentathlon, field events (long jump, discus, and javelin) were treated separately and had their own prizes. The following story is told by Philostratos. During his quest for the Golden Fleece, Jason held games for his men. Lynkeus was the best man in the javelin, whereas Telamon was superior in the discus. Zetes and Kalais, the two sons of Boreas, were best at running and jumping. Peleus was second best in all of these, but could defeat everyone in wrestling. In a desire to honor his companion, Jason combined the five events, allowing Peleus to earn the victory. The pentathlon was born.

The fact is that the Greeks institutionalized only two sports that Homer did not mention in either the *Iliad* or the *Odyssey*. One was the pankration (a combination of wrestling, boxing, strangling, and gouging) and

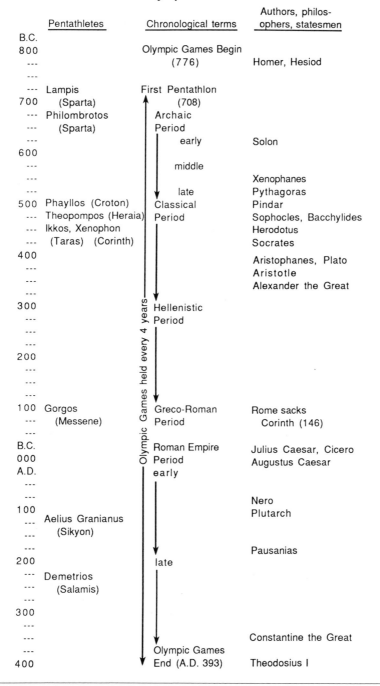

Figure 2.2.   Time line of Olympic pentathlon winers.

the second, the pentathlon. The pentathlon appeared on the Olympic program in 708 B.C., the 18th Olympiad. It stayed until the games were discontinued over 1000 years later.

The five events were always the same: long jump, discus, javelin, a sprint, and a wrestling match. It is worth noting that the first three "field" events were never contested individually. Rather, they were always events within the pentathlon. The pentathlon was held at other major festivals and at many minor meets throughout the Aegean. It was possible for athletes to do numerous pentathlons in local meets and to aim for a major festival wreath annually. But the ultimate goal was to win the Olympic olive wreath. Table 2.2 reveals the names of many Olympic pentathlon winners from records remaining from antiquity. The Spartans, because military preparation gave them an advantage in running, wrestling, and spear throwing, dominated the early contests. Philombrotos of Sparta won three consecutive Olympic pentathlons from 676 to 668 B.C. The ancient record, as we know it, is held by Gorgos of Elis with four Olympic pentathlon victories. Although the dates of his wins are unknown, it's obvious that even then there was a home field advantage. Table 2.2 shows that pentathletes from Elis won 15 of the 43 known ancient pentathlon titles.

Let's have a closer look at each of the five Greek pentathlon events.

The details of the long jump are a matter of controversy. A number of vase paintings depict jumpers practicing with hand weights (halteres) that are held in front of the athlete and then thrown back just before landing. Modern physics suggests this is not helpful for distance.

The Greeks threw the javelin with the use of a thong looped over the fingers. Elderwood was used for athletic javelins that were thrown for distance, although some scholars believe accuracy was important as well.

The discus is a peculiarly Greek event. Works of art suggest the Greeks used a rotary movement a la today. But the weight of the discus was not constant and remaining ancient discs are considerably heavier than today's.

The sprint traveled the length of the stadium (stade) or about 200m. Before a starting gate (hysplex) was introduced (probably in the 5th century B.C.), runners who false started were flogged before having to step back to give competitors a head start on the next signal.

The wrestling match was the best of three falls and, because there were no weight classes, favored the heavier athlete. Wrestlers used oil and then powder before contests. After the match, dust, oil, and sweat were scraped off with a bronze strigil. Wrestlers started on their feet, facing one another. Trips, holds, and technique throws are illustrated on numerous vases (Figure 2.3).

One suspects that the popularity of the pentathlon blew hot and cold. Aristotle apparently respected pentathetes. He called them the best

Table 2.2   Known Pentathlon Winners of Ancient Olympic Games

Date	Winner/city	Date	Winner/city
708 B.C.	Lampis of Sparta	444 B.C.	Ikkos of Taras
676 B.C.	Philombrotos of Sparta (1)	384 B.C.	Hysmon of Elis[a]
672 B.C.	Philombrotos of Sparta (2)	376 B.C.	Stomios of Elis[a]
668 B.C.	Philombrotos of Sparta (3)	332 B.C.	Kallippos of Athens
500 B.C.	Akmatidas of Sparta	312 B.C.	Alexibios of Heraia[a]
492 B.C.	Hieronymos of Andros[a]	296 B.C.	Timachos of Mantineia
488 B.C.	Euthykles of Lokroi[a]	252 B.C.	(. . .) of Elis[a]
484 B.C.	Theopompos of Heraia (1)[a]	232 B.C.	Gorgos of Messene[a]
480 B.C.	Theopompos of Heraia (2)[a]	200 B.C.	Timon of Elis[a]
476 B.C.	(. . .) of Taras	72 B.C.	Aristonymidas of Kos
472 B.C.	(. . .)amos of Miletos	A.D. 137	Aelius Granianus of Sikyon (1)[a]
468 B.C.	(. . .)tion of Taras	A.D. 141	Aelius Granianus of Sikyon (2)[a]
464 B.C.	Xenophon of Corinth	A.D. 197	Aurelius Metrodorus of Kyzikos
456 B.C.	(. . .)nomos of (. . .)	A.D. 229	Demetrios of Salamis (1)[a]
452 B.C.	Pythokles of Elis	A.D. 233	Demetrios of Salamis (2)[a]
448 B.C.	Keton of Lokroi	A.D. 241	Publius Asklepiades of Corinth

Pentathlon Victors of Unknown Date

Ainetos of Amyklai (Lakonia)
Aischinos of Elis (twice)
Gorgos of Elis (four times)
Klearchos of Elis
Kleinomachos of Elis
Menalkas of Elis
Theodoros of Elis
Lykos of Messene (uncertain)

Note. A list of many Ancient Olympic winners, including the pentathlon victors above, can be found in the once rare Sextius Julius Africanus (Edited by I. Rutgers) *List of Olympic Victors* by Ares Press.
[a]Date is uncertain.

athletes because of their speed and strength. But Plato believed the pentathlon was for the minor-league performer. Modern researchers have conflicting opinions about the quality of pentathletes. Not so with the poet Bacchlylides, who had this to say about a Nemean Games' pentathlon winner, Automdedes:

He shone among the other pentathletes as the bright moon in the middle of the month dims the radial the stars; even thus he showed his lovely body great ring of watching Greeks, as he threw the round discus and hurled the shaft of black-leaved elder from the grasp to the steep heights of heaven, aroused the cheers of the spectators by his lithe movements in the wrestling at the end. (McNab, 1971).

Figure 2.3. Vases depicting early Greek athletic events.

The order of the events and how the pentathlon winners were determined are controversial subjects among archaeologists and philologists today. Ample evidence clearly shows that wrestling was the final event, but there are numerous hypotheses concerning the order of the first four. A 1972 movie, *The Ancient Games*, written by Eric Segal, postulates that the sprint was the initial event, followed by the long jump, discus, and javelin. Most others contend that the field events (jump, discus, and javelin, in that order) were followed by the stade, a sprint one length of the stadium.

Despite the efforts of scholars, rules to determine the pentathlon winner remain unsolved. It seems clear the Greeks were concerned only with event winners. Apparently, second and third places did not matter. Scoring tables were not in existence. Harris (1972) believes that the pentathlon winner had to win one of the field events and that three individual wins were necessary for victory. The phrase, "winner of the first triad" occurs on numerous inscriptions. It is possible that the pentathlon ended when one athlete won three events, the remaining events being unnecessary. If no competitor won all three, a fourth event (a stade) was held. If there was still no competitor with three wins, a wrestling match was held. Several scholars, including Harris (1972) and McNab (1971), go to great lengths to explain how winners were determined. They speculate that the pentathlon was contested much like a five-set tennis match. The version of determining a winner I like best (but which is just as questionable) has contestants first competing in a jumping event, with the best finishers advancing to the spear (javelin) throw. The four best in the spear throw advance to the sprint, where another athlete is eliminated. That leaves three for the discus, where another athlete is dropped. Finally, the two best wrestle for the pentathlon championship.

The fact is we do not know how the pentathlon was contested. Mandel (1984) claims that each competitor did each field event five times and that tallies were kept. The problem of how the winner was decided remains unsolved. Rules may have been altered over time. Remember, the pentathlon was contested for over 1000 years.

The pentathlon was always contested on the 3rd day of the Olympic festival. Casson (1984) reports that the spectacular horse events of the 2nd day and the popular body-contact bouts of the 4th day sandwiched the pentathlon. Mandel (1984) disagrees and suggests the pentathlon was held on the 2nd day, when spectators would move to the grassy banks to watch the pentathletes after the horse races were completed. Most scholars do agree that the victory ceremonies for all events were held on the 5th and final day of the festival.

As it happens, we know a great deal more about the ancient world pentathlon. We have names of winners spanning 950 years. A boy's pentathlon was held in *only* the 38th Olympiad, 638 B.C. and on no other occasion. Other festivals held boy's and intermediate-division pentathlons.

We know something about the payments for pentathlon winners. David C. Young (1984), the most authoritative source of information about the Ancient Greek Olympics, notes that a single athletic victory in the pentathlon paid considerably more money than a full year's work. Pentathlon victors earned 60 amphoras (jars) of olive oil for a victory at the Panathenaic Games at Athens in the classical period. The going price per amphora was about 12 drachmas, so the pentathlon victor earned a prize worth roughly 720 drachmas—enough to buy three or four medium-priced slaves, a flock of 60 sheep, or a very nice house in Athens. In this period workmen normally made one to two drachmas a day. Pentathletes earned about as much as boxers and wrestlers but not as much as sprinters or chariot racers. A single victory brought them the equivalent of over $40,000 in today's money.

Athetes in the Olympic Games and other ancient Greek contests were not necessarily aristocrats. Young (1984) suggests that numerous "commoners" were Olympic champions and complains much of shoddy scholarship on this point. It was not necessary to be of noble birth to enter the Greek games or the pentathlon.

Pentathletes could also be specialists. In 464 B.C. Xenophon of Corinth won both the pentathlon and the stade. Ample evidence exists that pentathletes competed in "open" events as well. Some famous pentathletes, such as Ikkos of Taras, winner of the 444 B.C. pentathlon, turned to coaching when their competitive careers ended. Plato notes that Ikkos abstained from sexual activity while training.

Pentathletes were hardly amateurs in today's sense, nor were they above suspicion. Even bribery did not phase them. Reportedly, when an Athenian pentathlete was fined for trying to bribe his way to a win, the Athenians sent a top advocate to plead his case. When that failed they paid the fine themselves.

Athletics played an unusually strong role in several of the Greek colonies, especially Sicily and Croton (on the west coast of Italy). One Crotonian, Phayllos, won the pentathlon at the Pythian Games three times. One source credits him with a 16.76m (55 feet!) long jump. Obviously something was lost in translation. Scholars suggest the mark could have been for a combination of several jumps, (e.g., three running jumps or five standing jumps).

Knab (1934) reports that no pentathletes achieved the *periodoniken* of ancient athletes, a win at all four major festivals (victories in Olympic, Pythian, Isthmian, and Nemean Games), the ancient grand slam.

The Olympic pentathlon winner last recorded was Publius Asklepiades of Corinth, who won the wreath in A.D. 241 (see Table 2.2). More than 15 centuries would pass before we recorded another multi-event track and field winner.

The Greek pentathlon was a blend of speed and strength. Technique was a lesser factor, and endurance also played a small part. Much like the first day of a modern decathlon, the Greek pentathlon was power oriented. According to tradition, wrestling was the climax. Suspense among the spectators increased if the pentathlon was not decided early and the athletes had to fight for victory up to the last event. Ah, were it so today. The 1500m pales in comparison.

RE-CREATION OF ANCIENT GREEK PENTATHLON

Veteran ABC commentator Jim McKay (1973) tells a funny story about the production of a show written and narrated by Eric Segal, a professor at Yale, and produced by Dick Ebersol in June, 1972. The show featured two Olympic decathlon champions, Rafer Johnson and Bill Toomey, re-creating an ancient Greek pentathlon competition at Delphi, the site of many pentathlons of antiquity.

It seems that when they came to the foot race, Toomey false started. Segal, insisting that the competition be filmed accurately, called for the ancient Greek penalty for a false start—whipping. Toomey winced when Segal provided a whip, but he went along with the penalty.

The judge, wincing a bit himself, cracked the whip on Bill's bare back, raising several welts on Toomey's skin. Unfortunately, the take was no good. Sheepishly, director Lou Volpicelli informed Bill he must be rewhipped! This time the judge tried too hard to be careful and wrapped the whip around Bill's face. Bill was not amused. On this take the picture was fine, but the sound was bad.

Volpicelli was for whipping Toomey a third time, but Toomey had had enough and refused. A young Greek boy had been hired as a gopher for a few drachmas a day and someone suggested that they whip him instead, but the production crew decided to stick with what they had.

THE REALLY ANCIENT GAMES

Although the Greek Olympic Games date back 26 centuries, they are not the oldest of organized athletic events. The Tailteann Games were Irish national games of great antiquity held in memory of Queen Tailta. The games originated in Telltown, County Meath in what we now believe to be 1829 B.C. They survived with regularity at least until A.D. 1100. Thirty centuries!

Although there was never the renaissance of Irish culture in Western Europe, a la Greek culture, we do know some things about the Tailteann Games. As in the Greek Olympics, contests were held in athletic events, but there were also competitions in poetry, drama, prose, art, music, and dancing. Legends tell us of the Celtic hero Cu Chulainn, who gripped a chariot wheel by its axle, whirled it around his head, and hurled it away. Wheel-hurling was replaced by throwing a large stone attached to the end of a wooden handle.

This evolved into the modern hammer throw. The Tailteann Games, although worlds apart from the Greek Olympics, developed similar running and jumping events. They also included vaulting with a pole, an event that escaped the Greeks.

The Tailteann Games have been temporarily revived several times in the 20th century.

3

A.D. 400-1910

When Greek and Roman civilization declined, so did the importance of athletics and, for our purposes, multi-event contests. By A.D. 393, the Olympic Games had become a public nuisance. Thought pagan, they were abolished. The huge statue of Zeus was carried away to Constantinople, where it was later lost in a fire. Earthquakes and floods destroyed the Olympic site. But the idea of a versatile, all-around athlete was never completely lost in the 15 centuries the world went without the Olympic Games.

An Age Lacking Multi-Events, A.D. 400-1850

The five-event Greek pentathlon was designed to provide the ultimate challenge to well-coordinated athletes. But multi-event competitions disappeared from recorded organized sport between A.D. 393 and the middle of the 19th century. Very little organized track and field existed (except for a minor comeback in the 12th century), as numerous forces during the dark, feudal, Medieval times discouraged popular forms of recreation. A Protestant ethic, Victorian influence, and Puritan and evangelist movements inhibited the growth of sport. For most of this period in Western Europe, and later in the American colonies, sport was class-conscious and very local. Certain sporting activities flourished among "commoners" in the rural villages. Leaping, wrestling, and lifting, as well as some stick and ball games, were popular.

At the other end of the social spectrum, wealth, gallantry and polished manners were part of English gentry sport. In England, pastimes emerged from the upper-class traditions of the Middle Ages. Although examples of multi-event contests are difficult to find, the notion of multifaceted contests did not die during this extended era.

In the Viking era (ca. A.D. 800 to 1250), Norsemen had to exhibit a number of skills that were paramilitary in nature. Contests for Vikings included running, wrestling, throwing heavy spears, and running over oars.

Knights periodically tested their skills in tournaments. Some historians claim that the real sport of medieval aristocracy was war and that tournaments served as ceremonial preparation. As with Homeric contests, the outcomes of these ritual battles were chronicled by paintings and poets. Also, records are available from heralds, the scorekeepers of royal tournaments. A major collection of 16th-century scorecards at London's College of Heralds gives us such information as who broke a lance and who lost a mount.

As early as 1185 Frederick Barbarossa staged an imperial festival in Mainz (now a major decathlon training site) at which an alleged 40,000 knights participated. And in Tallinn, an Estonian city also famous in modern days for decathlon training, the citizens and knights initiated a tradition of equestrian tournaments beginning in 1440. Knights were asked to excel in multiple physical and martial skills.

The Renaissance provides us with examples of the idea of all-aroundness, although there were few examples of actual all-around competition. Leon Battista Alberti (1404?-1472) was the classic versatile Renaissance man. An accomplished architect, composer of music, scientist, inventor, theologian, linguist, and athlete, he was said to have been able to jump the height of a man from a standing position and throw a javelin to pierce the thickest of breast-plates. Alberti may well be an influence for many modern-day decathletes.

Treatises on educational reform in the middle of the 16th century called for youths to know how to ride in armor, vault on horseback, practice weight lifting, swim, row, run, wrestle, broad jump, and high jump. By the early 17th century, an English lawyer, Robert Dover, reinstated the Olympic Games with a well-documented festival of contests that would be the forerunner of its modern counterpart. In 1612 Dover sponsored the Olympick Games of the Cotswolds near Gloucestershire. Dover's Olympicks were so popular that he was held in the same esteem during his day as the Baron de Coubertin was 3 centuries later.

Thousands came annually to watch or contest events. A notable spectator, from nearby Stratford, may well have been William Shakespeare. References to Dover's games appear in *The Merry Widow* and *As You Like It*. As Shakespeare and Dover had common acquaintances, it seems probable that Shakespeare was a 17th-century Olympic spectator.

Dover's Olympicks were held on the Thursday and Friday after Whitsun (seventh Sunday after Easter), and consisted of wrestling, leaping, dancing, pitching the bar, throwing the hammer, music, leapfrog, shin-kicking, running races, horse racing, and hunting the hare. Chess and card games were held in tents. Sadly, there is no mention of an all-around contest at these games. The games were established with the permission of James I and held during the reign of 14 different monarchs. They were discontinued in 1852.

A superficial check of nonwestern cultures reveals no reference to multievent or all-around contests. Little is accomplished by examining literary evidence regarding the athletics of Japan, China, India, the Mayas, the (playful) American Indians, or the Islamic cultures. All of these cultures were sporting active, but a hasty check suggests none contained multievents.

We can conclude that recreation and games during this long period of European history were generally without combined contests that determined an all-around winner. Games were generally class-conscious and local. But during this period the notion of all-aroundness was not lost. The Renaissance did much to foster versatility in life, not just in games. The Enlightenment (new ideas about physical education and advances in technology and economics) would have its impact later in the 19th century.

Multi-Events Return, 1850-1910

Track and field games evolved into formal affairs by the first half of the 19th century. In both the United States and Europe weights and distances became standardized. No longer were there just stone throws. In 1857 in Dublin, 16 lb became the norm for the shot put. Races of 100 yards or 1 mile replaced runs across or around fields. With standardization came the concept of *records*. The German *turner movement* (gymnastics in unison) fostered by German educators encouraged participation over merely watching. Guts Muth (1778-1839) developed scoring tables for his pupil's performances in running, jumping, and swimming. The students' marks were recorded weekly and evaluated with his scoring tables. Much of today's decathlon was represented by Guts Muth and 19th-century German reformers. They stressed training techniques, equipment, and statistics.

The most popular and frequently contested games of the middle part of the 19th century were the Caledonian Games, sponsored by the Scots. Originally professional, these games fostered and developed many of the individual events later found in multi-event contests. The Caledonian Games had their roots in the Celtic Tailteann Games of ancient Ireland. The Caledonians developed clubs, codified rules, and showed the world the pole vault, race walking, the shot put, hurdle racing, and the hammer throw. Caledonian Games were popular on both sides of the Atlantic.

Many upper-class Englishmen were caught up in the organized sports movement and formed clubs around a modern concept of amateurism. Remember, this concept was foreign to the ancient Greeks, who did not even have a word for *amateur*. The London Athletic Club (1863) and the New York Athletic Club (NYAC) (1866) were two of the earliest notable amateur clubs. At the collegiate level, Oxford and Cambridge promoted "meetings" as early as 1864. In the United States, track and field began with races at regattas and evolved into field days, dual meets, relay carnivals, and, later, championship events.

Multi-Events in Europe

Italian expert Roberto Quercetani (1964) reports that all-around competitions were held in Ireland during the middle of the 19th century, but results of the first multi-event contests of modern times are found in accounts from Swedish newspapers (Pariente, 1979). In 1792, Stockholm papers chronicled young-adult multi-event contests (running, swimming, throwing a stone), with overall winners determined via a scoring system. An early (but certainly not the first) multi-event contest was held at yet another English Olympic revival, the 1868 Much Wenlock Olympics. A pentathlon was designed to test versatility. It included a high jump, long jump, putting a 36-lb (!) shot, an 880-yard run, and climbing a 55-foot (16.76m) rope. By 1880, the Germans presented a multi-event contest as part of their national gymnastics championships. It consisted of a stone throw, pole vault, and long jump and was won by Muller. His 28 points indicates that the overall winner was based on the sum of individual places. This affair was an outgrowth of the German turner (gymnastics) movement. It did not include a race, as the turners long resented running. But by 1889 the Germans had incorporated a 200m run into their all-around contests.

By the early 1890s Norway was hosting an annual pentathlon of ancient Greek format (Figure 3.1). A pentathlon (long jump, javelin, 190m, discus, and wrestling) was held in Tjalve in June 1891. Many individual marks remain from the Norwegian pentathlons. Other European nations, including Sweden and France, presented multi-event meets around the turn of the century. Notably, Great Britain did not.

Figure 3.1. Early Norway meet.

The American All-Around

One comprehensive study (Redmond, 1971) concludes that the spread of the Caledonian Games during the middle of the 19th century was part of the phenomenal rise of sport that occurred in the United States and Canada. They were the first organized track and field events to appear on the North American continent.

One early Caledonian all-around performer was George Goldie, the father of the pole vault. Goldie held (from 1869 to 1885) the 3-year and 5-year all-around athletic championships of the United States, a title earned by high showings at individual events. A Canadian, Goldie became the first physical education director of Princeton (1869) and later coach of the New York Athletic Club (1885). He demonstrated his athletic talents in 1873 at the Boston Caledonian Club's (20th) annual games. He won the standing broad jump, vaulting with the long pole, and the standing high jump. He also placed in seven other events, winning $33 for his efforts.

It is not difficult to discern the development of the United States' multi-event history. Titles such as Goldie's "all-around athletic champion" were earned by placing high in individual events at major meets. A fairer way of determining the top all-arounder would be to have the athletes go head-to-head in a series of athletic events. The all-around was inevitable. In 1884 it arrived formally in the United States, when the National Amateur Athletic Association of America (N4A) offered an all-around championship at New York's Washington Park. The one-day affair did not use scoring tables. Rather, points for place (one point for first, two points for second, etc.) were used. W.R. Thompson of Montreal won with a low score of 14 points (nine events).

The original American All-Around consisted of nine events: 100-yard dash, shot put, broad jump, 100-yard hurdle race, hammer throw, high jump, 56-lb weight throw, pole vault, and running hop-step-and-jump. It was quickly standardized to 10 events that included the 880-yard walk and the mile run. The triple jump was eliminated. The 440-yard dash made occasional appearances but was also deleted. Five minutes rest was given between events. For the first few years, standards for each event had to be achieved by each athlete in each event (e.g., 19 seconds in the hurdles). If a contestant did not meet the standard in three events, he was dropped from the scoring and places were rescored as if he had not competed. The procedure was meant to discourage specialists, but it resulted in much confusion. Indeed, in one AAU (the Amateur Athletic Union, which replaced the N4A) All-Around, all athletes failed to meet the required standards on three occasions. Confusion. Enter scoring tables. First developed by the AAU in 1894, they awarded points for each performance. The all-around winner accumulated the most points after all 10 events. The tables were based on the world-record marks of 1893. A thousand points were given for equaling the 1893 world record. Points were subtracted from 1000 for performances below the world record. The all-around was a popular affair; regional as well as national meets were conducted.

Among those who succeeded at this Pantagruelian (Quercetani, 1964) menu were Malcolm Ford, the Carl Lewis of his day (world-record holder in both the 100m and the long jump); Alexander Jordan, who won three national championships; and Irish-American thrower/jumper, Martin Sheridan. Jordan was the first to surpass 6000 points on the scoring tables (1891 when rescored) and Sheridan, the finest athlete of his time, became the first to score over 7000 points (1907).

Ellery Clark, in his insightful *Reminiscences of an Athlete* (1911), recounts the early American All-Around days. Clark, himself an Olympic champion in several individual events, a national all-around champ twice, and a New England titlist on four occasions, was in awe of Sheridan. He recounts how his heart dropped the first time he saw Sheridan pole vault (remember, this was 1905) and he knew that he no longer had a chance to win the all-around.

When St. Louis hosted the 1904 Olympic Games, the AAU All-Around was 20 years old. Huge Irishman Thomas Kiely became the first Olympic 10-event winner when he declined an "offer" from British officials to compete for England (he was living in London), paid his own expenses to St. Louis, and won the gold medal for Ireland.

The American All-Around was the initial multi-event contest with scoring tables. It enjoyed popularity well into the 20th century. The decathlon borrowed many of the all-around events. Like its predecessor, the decathlon started with a sprint and finished with a distance race. In between, both contests included three jumps, three throws, and a hurdle race. The similarities were striking. After the turn of the century, many American all-arounders made the easy transition to the decathlon.

American College

Students from the upper classes brought track and field from the clubs to the college campuses. In the United States, collegiate dual meets were held in the early 1870s and the Intercollegiate Amateur Athletic Association of America (IC4A) conducted annual championships beginning in 1876. But multi-event competitions were not numerous at the collegiate level. Versatile collegiate athletes found their way to all-around meets. They included Harvard's Clark and Penn's Truxtun Hare. One college that offered an annual multi-event contest was Mount Saint Mary's of Maryland. The Mount's Barbeque Day was held as early as the 1880s and crowned an all-around winner each fall with a simplified point system. The 1897 Barbeque Day scoresheet is displayed in Figure 3.2.

Barbeque Day All-Around Track Contest

	Putting 16-lb. shot	Throwing baseball	High jump, standing	High jump, running	100-yards dash	Pole vaulting	Broad jump, standing	Broad jump, running	Hop, step, and jump, standing	Hop, step, and jump, running	Standing high kick*	Running high kick*	Total number of points
Ahearn	—	—	3	3	3	2	3	3	3	3	—	—	23
Kittrick	—	1	1	1	1	3	2	2	2	2	—	—	15
Duggan	3	2	—	—	—	—	—	1	1	—	—	—	7
Prendergast	1	3	—	—	—	—	1	—	—	—	—	—	5
Walsh	2	—	2	—	—	—	—	—	—	—	—	—	4
Levert	—	—	—	—	2	1	—	—	—	—	—	—	3
Casey	—	—	—	2	—	—	—	—	—	1	—	—	3

*Owing to the lack of time, the high kick was not tried.

Figure 3.2.   Barbeque Day scoresheet, 1897. (Courtesy of Mount Saint Mary's College/Zarnowski)

The Decathlon

The term *decathlon* was first applied to early Swedish 10-event contests. Soon after the turn of the century, multi-event meets much like the American All-Around were conducted in Sweden, often in one day. In 1909 the Swedes held their first decathlon championship. Scoring tables were used. The events were normally the 100m, 1500m, 100m hurdles, long jump, pole vault, high jump, triple jump, shot put, discus, and javelin. Athletes threw implements with both hands and the total distance (left plus right) was tallied. "Both hand throws" were common; the Swedes saw them as a measure of versatile throwing ability. An early winner of Swedish decathlons was Karl Hugo Wieslander. By 1912 he would challenge the American Indian Jim Thorpe at the Stockholm Olympic Games.

After discussions with Olympic officials in Luxemburg in 1910, a pentathlon and decathlon were added to the 1912 Olympic program. Both had been held in various forms in Sweden for a number of years. A paramilitary event, the *modern pentathlon*, was also added in 1912. It included riding, pistol shooting, fencing, swimming, and cross-country running. Lt. George Patton, who was to become a WWII hero, was the American entrant.

Early United States Olympic reports charged the Swedes with designing contests that prevented American track and field specialists from dominating the medals. This was not so. The pentathlon was simply a return of the ancient counterpart, with the 1500m replacing a wrestling match. And the modern decathlon, with its present order of events and single-handed throws, was a natural outgrowth of earlier and similar Swedish decathlon versions.

Early Olympic Games

Although modern Olympic Games began in 1896 in Athens, no multi-event competitions were held until the 1904 games at St. Louis. A triathlon and an all-around were contested 2 days apart. The former was part of the gymnastics program and a reflection of the German *turnverein* influence. It included a long jump, shot put, and 100-yard dash. One

Table 3.1   Summary of Early Olympic Multi-Event Contests

Year	Site	Multi-event contest	Competitors/ nations	Winner	Nation	Points
1896	Athens	None				
1900	Paris	Pentathlon[a]				
1904	St. Louis	Triathlon[b]	118/4	Emmerich	United States	35.7
		All-around[c]	7/2	Kiely	Ireland	6036
1906	Athens	Pentathlum[d]	26/12	Mellander	Sweden	24
1908	London	None				

Note. Early Olympic gymnastic competition included all-around contests combining track and field with gymnastic events. In 1900 (Paris) an all-around gymnastics meet included the pole vault, long jump, and stone heave among 11 events. A six-event gymnastics competition in 1904 included the long jump, shot put, and 100-yard dash.
[a]The Paris "pentathlon" was actually a *four*-event contest and athletes were to have a choice of events as follows: 100 *or* 400; 800 *or* 1500; high jump, long jump, *or* pole vault; shot put *or* discus. Scoring was uncertain. It was included in the official program but never contested. [b]The St Louis "triathlon" included the long jump, shot put, and 100-yard dash. [c]The all-around events, contested on a single day, were the 100-yard dash, shot put, high jump, 880-yard walk, hammer, pole vault, 120-yard hurdles, 56-lb weight throw, long jump, and mile run. [d]The Athens "pentathlum" was a re-creation of the ancient event.

hundred and eighteen athletes competed. Irishman Tom Kiely, mainly a thrower, captured the all-around over a small field.

Two years later, at the interim Olympic Games in Athens, 26 athletes contested the ancient pentathlon, called *athletic pentathlum*. It included a standing long jump, discus throw Greekstyle, javelin, stade race, and Greco-Roman wrestling. Points were awarded for place in each event with the low score winning, à la today's cross-country scoring. Martin Sheridan was an easy favorite but was injured and withdrew. A 34-year-old Swede, Hjalmar Mellander, won over Istvan Mudin of Hungary, 24 to 25.

Malcolm Worthington Ford

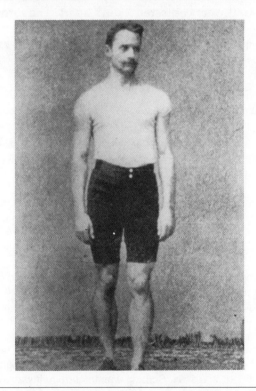

Figure 3.3.   Malcolm Ford, pre-1913. (From the Bill Mallon collection)

Before the turn of the century, Malcolm Ford was, with Lon Myers, one of America's two greatest track and field athletes, but his story is not a happy one.

Malcolm Worthington Ford was born in Brooklyn on February 7, 1862, the scion of a well-known American literary family. He first became prominent in national athletics in 1883, when he won the national title in the high jump and long jump. He also took the Canadian championship in the high jump. But later that year he had a falling-out with his family and was disowned by his father, who felt it beneath any Ford to take part in sports—amateur or professional.

Ford continued competing, however, and in 1884 won the long jump and 100 at the nationals and finished second in the all-around event. In 1885 he won what has recently come to be known as the "Carl Lewis triple" (100, 220, and long jump); he was also national all-around champion and won the 220 and 440 at the Canadian nationals. In 1886 Ford won the triple again, both at the United States and the Canadian championships, adding another United States all-around championship for good measure. He won American championships with marks of 10.4 (100 yds), 23.2 (220 yds, straight), 1.74m (5-8 1/2") high jump, and 6.72m (22-3/4") long jump.

In 1887 Malcolm Ford was suspended for professionalism, and, although he was later reinstated and won two more national championships in the long jump and all-around, his amateur status was revoked for good in 1890. The next year he toured Europe, performing athletic feats in a circus. On his return to the States, he took up the family profession of writing and married a wealthy New York heiress.

Late in 1891, Ford's father died from typhoid fever. The will split his huge estate among the other six children, but left Malcolm nothing. A few years later, Ford's wife divorced him. Ford was left penniless, forcing him to borrow from his brothers and sisters, who became increasingly irritated with his scheme, especially his best-known brother, novelist Paul Ford. Malcolm sued his entire family for a share of the family fortune, but lost a bitter court struggle.

In late 1901, Paul Ford, who was an invalid, told Malcolm he would support him no further. May 8, 1902 was a beautiful, crisp spring day in New York. Malcolm Ford called on Paul at his office, remarking to the doorman that "The better the day, the better

Table 3.2   Career Record of Malcolm Ford

All-Around	Competition	Site	Place	Points	Score	100 yds (order of events altered year by year)									Mile
May 10, 1884	NAAAA All-Around	New York	2	22	(4941)	@11.0	939+ sp	677 l j	?H	1877 hm	168 h j	?wt	213 pv	1345 t j	
Sept. 30, 1885	NAAAA All-Around	New York	1	33	(5045)	11.2	1041 sp	171+ h j	19.8 H	2134 hm	631+ l j	244 pv	57.6 q	549 wt	5:44
Sept. 18, 1886	NAAAA All-Around	New York	1	45	(5899) WR	10.4	?wt	167+ h j	54.2 q	1117 sp	282 pv	?H	2326 hm	635 l j	dnr
‚1888	NAAAA All-Around				(5161)										
Sept. 7, 1889	AAU All-Around	Brooklyn	1	30	(5186)	10.4	528 wt	168 h j	?q	1065 sp	2540 hm	@17.2 H	274+ pv	664 l j	dnr

Note. The events and order of events in the early All-Around changed annually.

Legend: sp = shot put, l j = long jump, h j = high jump, pv = pole vault, H = 120 yd hurdles except in 1984 when distance was 100 yds, hm = hammer, wt = 56 lb weight, t j = triple jump, q = 440 yds.

Score: Official score calculated by 5 pts for 1st place, 3 for 2nd, 1 for 3rd, with highest total winning. Score in ( ) calculated on later tables. Note that 13.45m (44 − 1 3/4) triple jump in 1884 meet was world best.

the deed.'' He then walked into the office and, in front of his brother's secretary, pulled a gun and shot Paul in the chest, mortally wounding him. He then turned the gun on himself. A few minutes later, Malcolm Ford's sad saga was over forever.

He competed in five all-arounds, breaking the world mark by over 500 points in 1886. In all, he won 10 individual national championships.

Ford portfolio written by Bill Mallon

Martin J. Sheridan

Figure 3.4. Martin Sheridan, 1906. (From the Bill Mallon collection)

A 1918 *New York Times* obituary proclaimed Martin Joseph Sheridan the greatest all-around athlete ever known in the United States (the *Times* has been known to exaggerate)—greater even than Jim Thorpe. Yet Sheridan never won the Olympic decathlon and is virtually unknown today.

Sheridan did win the discus throw at the 1904 and 1908 Olympics and also at the 1906 Intercalated Olympics. Counting 1906, he won five gold medals and nine Olympic medals, marks surpassed among American Olympians by only Ray Ewry and Mark Spitz. Besides his discus efforts, he won medals in the shot put (gold in 1906), the discus throw (Greek-style) (gold in 1908), the stone throw (silver in 1906), and the standing jumps (two silvers and a bronze). In 1906 Sheridan was entered in the unheard-of number of 14 events. In addition to the weight events, he entered the two standing jumps, the pentathlon, wrestling, weight lifting, and the tug-of-war. Mercifully, he competed in only half of these.

He did compete in the pentathlon, which was at the time called the pentathlum. It was an event based on the ancient Greek pentathlon and consisted of the standing broad jump, a stade race (a sprint of about 190m), the discus throw Greek-style, the javelin throw, and Greco-Roman wrestling. Sheridan had recently aggravated a knee injury, however, and it bothered him throughout the Olympics. After finishing second in the first event, the standing broad jump, he was forced to withdraw. He later called this his greatest athletic disappointment.

Sheridan almost certainly would have won that pentathlon had he finished. He was a superb weight thrower and jumper, and his other abilities had been amply demonstrated in the all-around championship. Three times, Sheridan entered the national championship in the all-around (1905, 1907, 1909) and three times he ran away from the field. In 1904 the record for the all-around stood at 6360 points, but Martin Sheridan successively broke the record by 460, 310, and 255 points, finally leaving it at 7385, a mark Thorpe broke by only a few points in 1912.

Sheridan's best event was easily the discus. He is listed with six world records with the disc, the first set at only his third try at the event in 1902. He eventually raised this 120'-7 mark to 141'-7 just before announcing his retirement in 1911. But in leafing through old meet results it is easy to see that Sheridan threw further than this and probably broke the world record several more times (most likely nine). He often competed on weekends in various club meets and the papers on Monday would report "another Sheridan world record," only to write the next day that the mark

Table 3.3   Career Record of Martin Sheridan

All-Around	Competition	Site	Place	Score	100 yd	sp	h j	880 w	hm	120 H	pv	56 wt	l j	mile
July 8, 1905	AAU All-Around	New York	1	6820 WR	@11.1	1221+	168	3:50.0	3419	17.2	320	825+	613	5:37.8
,1907	AAU All-Around	New York	1	7130 WR	10.8	1310+	173	3:51.2	3313	17.0	322	848	628+	5:42.4
,1909	AAU All-Around	New York	1	7385 WR	10.6	1313+	170	3:43.0	3836	17.2	328	913	628+	6:05.0

Pentathlon	Competition	Site	Place	Score	s l j	dis	192 m	jav	wrestling
April, 27, 1906	Olympics	Athens	--	dnf	2.855	(3),	inj, withdrew		

would not be accepted by the AAU because it had been achieved in a nonsanctioned club meet.

In 1908 Martin Sheridan made his most famous statement. In the opening ceremonies of the Olympics that year the flag bearer was the great shot-putter, Ralph Rose—not Sheridan, as often reported. Rose refused to dip the flag when he passed the king of England's box, a tradition that United States flag bearers at the opening ceremonies continue to this day. Rose held the flag aloft because the night before he, Sheridan, and a few other American athletes, many of them Irish immigrants, were holding aloft a few beers and venting their dislike of the English. They decided that, as Sheridan so aptly told the press afterward, "This flag dips to no earthly king!"

Little is known of Sheridan's life off the field. He was an Irish immigrant who crossed the Atlantic in 1897. He made a living as a policeman, as did many of New York's Irish athletes, and his fame led him to be the personal bodyguard for the governor of New York whenever the governor visited the city. Sheridan never married. On March 27, 1918, 7 years after he retired from athletics, he was dead of pneumonia at the age of 37. In his eulogy he was called the world's greatest athlete.

Sheridan portfolio written by Bill Mallon

4

Early Decathlon History, 1911-1964

A decathlon was added to the 1912 Olympic program in Stockholm. After experimentation, the following sequence of events was chosen: 100m run, long jump, shot put, high jump and 400m run on the first day; 110m hurdles, discus, pole vault, javelin and 1500m run on the 2nd day. The Swedes also developed a set of scoring tables, based on the Olympic records set by 1908, to evaluate each decathlon performance. After the 1912 Stockholm Games the tables were updated to include many new Olympic records.

1911-1919

Several decathlons were held in Sweden prior to the 1912 Olympics. Using the chosen sequence of events and scoring tables, the first competition was held on a single day, October 15, 1911, at Goteberg. Ironically, this was not technically the first decathlon, but one of the first two, as the Germans also contested a decathlon (same order of events but with a different table) on the very same day! So, the first decathlon world-record holder was the winner of the first completed meet. Karl Hugo Wieslander, a Swede, and Karl Ritter von Halt, a German, were the victors. The former received credit for four world records. The latter became president of the German Olympic Committee and a confidant of Adolf Hitler when Berlin hosted the Olympic Games 25 years later.

The 1912 Olympic decathlon has become legend because of the presence of Jim Thorpe. Five-eighths American Indian, Thorpe was born in Shawanee, Oklahoma, in 1888, one of twin boys. He spent his boyhood hunting, fishing, working, and playing. Thorpe's actual name, Wa-Tho-Huck, meant "Bright Path." At the age of 8 his twin, Charlie, died of pneumonia. In 1905 Jim found his way to the Carlisle (PA) Indian School, where he played a number of competitive sports and fashioned a national reputation on the gridiron. A legendary football hero, Jim fit track into his schedule during the baseball season. He left Carlisle in the spring of 1909 but returned in the fall of 1911 at the urging of coach Glenn "Pop" Warner.

Jim had a terrific 1912 spring track season, winning as many as six events per meet. He made the Olympic team in four events: decathlon, pentathlon, high jump, and long jump. In Stockholm he was ready. "I may have an aversion to work," Thorpe admitted, "but I also have an aversion for getting beat. I was always in condition, and I never left my best performance on the practice field."

The Russian czar had donated a viking ship as a prize for the decathlon winner. A bust of the king of Sweden was offered as a prize for the pentathlon. Thorpe easily captured the pentathlon, winning four of five events. A week later he took the decathlon by almost 700 points over his nearest opponent, Hugo Wieslander of Sweden. Because of the unexpected large number of entries, the decathlon was held over 3 days. Thorpe's 8412 points convert to 6564 points on the current tables, still a very respectable score three quarters of a century later. His Stockholm marks were outstanding for the time: 11.2 100m, 6.79m (22-3 1/4) long jump, and 12.89m (42-3 1/2) shot put on the first day; 1.87m (6-1 3/4) high jump, 52.2 400m, 36.98m (121-4) discus, and 15.6 110m hurdles on the second day; 3.25m (10-8) pole vault, 45.70m (149-11) javelin, and 4:40.1 1500m! Swedes (Wieslander, Charles Lomberg, and Gösta Holmer) captured the next three spots.

Upon his return to New York Thorpe won the AAU All-Around with a new world record, ending his track and field career. But Thorpe's epic at Stockholm had a sad postscript. An American newspaper revealed that he had played baseball for pay in the summer of 1909, then a common practice among collegians. He had earned a paltry sum. But after a hasty investigation, the AAU sanctimoniously deprived Thorpe of his amateur status. The International Olympic Committee then decided to strip him of his medals and prizes. His name was struck from the recordbooks. To their credit, both Wieslander and Norway's Ferdinand Bie (pentathlon runner-up) refused to accept Thorpe's medals, although both were subsequently listed as Olympic winners.

Thorpe went on to make a name in professional baseball and football, but he died virtually penniless in 1953. His body was buried in Mauch Chunk, Pennsylvania, a town which then changed its name in his honor to "Jim Thorpe." But the story of Jim Thorpe doesn't end there. Several years ago the IOC, after years of appeals, reversed its ruling and returned Thorpe's medals to his children and his name to the recordbooks.

Figure 4.1.   Avery Brundage—American decathlete, pentathlete, and past president of the International Olympic Committee.

Thorpe's score was not surpassed for 15 years. In his absence, there was little decathlon activity for the remainder of the decade. Only in Sweden was the decathlon often contested. The Swedes managed to stay neutral during World War I, which forced the cancellation of the games of Berlin in 1916. Interestingly, decathlons were held as part of the Far Eastern Games (forerunner of the Asian Games) in 1913, 1915, 1917, and 1919.

In the United States the decathlon event did not immediately replace the AAU All-Around. The latter remained popular for the remainder of the decade and found a new champion, Avery Brundage of Chicago (Figure 4.1). In Stockholm, Brundage was an "also ran" in both the pentathlon and decathlon. But he captured three United States All-Around titles in an event that favored strength and race-walking ability over the speed of the decathlon. Brundage once compared the pain of race walking to the pangs of childbirth. He later served as president of both the United States Olympic Committee (USOC) and the International Olympic Committee (IOC). Brundage is remembered largely for his dogmatic stand on amateurism. Interestingly, in his latter role, he insisted on personally presenting the medals to all Olympic decathlon winners. By the time he bowed out of the IOC in 1972 he was, in some way, connected to every Olympic decathlon from Thorpe's to Avilov's.

Only in 1915 did the AAU offer a decathlon. It was won by former Brigham Young high-jumper Alma Richards. In 1919, Norway's Helge Lövland ran up the decade's second highest score in Kristiania (now Oslo). Because Thorpe's name had been removed from the recordbook, Lövland's total of 7786 (6035) was considered a world record.

Figure 4.2. Jim Thorpe.

The decathlon made its big-time international debut in the 1912 Olympic Games at Stockholm and the run-away winner was Jim Thorpe. The fabled American Indian athlete tallied 8412.955 points (the first over 8000) on the 1912A tables.

Young Thorpe (often and according to official school records spelled "Thorp") arrived at Carlisle in February 1904, but it was not until 3 years later that he was discovered. His first track competition took place when he was 18 and is chronicled in the *Arrow*, the Carlisle Indian School paper. The competition was an annual class contest and took place on the Carlisle fields on April 20, 1907. Jim, competing for his sixth-grade team, won the 120m high hurdles in 19 seconds flat and the high jump at 1.60m (5-3). He also placed second in the 200m low hurdles and third in the shot put. He was 18. By the end of his first varsity season Jim had scored nine varsity points and was awarded his "C."

The 1908 Carlisle team was undefeated and placed two men on the USA Olympic team (long-jumper, Frank Mount Pleasant and distance ace, Louis Tewanima), but it was Thorpe who had developed a reputation as the team's versatile star. He won the Penn Relays high jump at 1.83m (6-0) and scored in at least five events in every dual meet, but he returned to his home in Oklahoma before the 1908 Olympic Trials. By 1909, Jim may have been the finest all-around track man in America. Now 1.81m (5-11) and more robust, Jim dominated track competitors. He won the Middle Atlantic AAU title with five firsts, including 7.16m (23-6) in the long jump. Soon after he left Carlisle, apparently with little intention of returning. It was during this 2-year absence that Jim played semipro baseball in North Carolina, which later resulted in the loss of his Olympic medals.

Jim returned to Carlisle in the fall of 1911. Because of his pigskin exploits he was already being called, "the athletic marvel of the age." If Jim had any doubters, the 1912 track season convinced them he was for real. He enjoyed a successful indoor campaign, overcame Lafayette in a duel with six firsts, and won the Olympic Trials pentathlon and high jump at 1.96m (6-5), 5/8 of an inch off the world record. He made the Olympic team in four events.

In Stockholm Jim captured the pentathlon with 7 points (points-for-place system) and the decathlon by a whopping 688 points. Even though the decathlon was a new event and not widely contested yet, his mark lasted 15 years. If there had been world rankings in 1912, Jim would have been listed among the world's elite in five individual events (long jump, shot put, high jump, and both hurdles). In September he returned to New York to set a world record in the all-around in spite of spending 3 days in the hospital with ptomaine poisoning.

Thorpe's name was struck from the official recordbooks in 1913 when it was discovered he had played semipro baseball for a few dollars. In what must have been the rawest deal in the history of the games, he was stripped of his medals. Voted as the "Athlete of the First Half Century," he was subsequently elected to the Professional and College Football Halls of Fame. In October 1982, 29 years after Thorpe's death, the IOC lifted the ban and Jim's medals were presented to his children on January 18, 1983. Thorpe died in Lomita, California on March 28, 1953. In a 35-meet career, his verified records included marks of 11.2, 7.16m (23-6), 14.10m (46-3 1/4), 1.96 (6-5), 52.2, 15.6, 36.98m (121-4), 3.25m (10-8), 46.72m (153-3), and 4:40.1.

Table 4.1 Career Record of Jim Thorpe

Pentathlon	Competition	Site	Place	Score	1985 Tables	lj	jav	200	dis	1500
May 18, 1912	Eastern Olympic Trials	New York	1	7	3098 WR	661	4150	23.4	3506	4:49.8
July 7, 1912	Olympic Games	Stockholm	1	7	3371 WR	707	4671	22.9	3575	4:44.8

Decathlon	Competition	Site	Place	Score	1985 Tables	100	lj	sp	hj	400	dis	110H	pv	jav	1500
July 13-15, 1912	Olympic Games	Stockholm	1	8412 WR	6564 WR	11.2	679	1289	187	52.2	3698	15.6	325	4570	4:40.1

All-around	Competition	Site	Place	Score	1985 Tables	100y	sp	hj	880yW	ham	pv	120yH	56wt	lj	mile
Sept. 2, 1912	AAU all-around	New York	1	7476 WR		10.6	1349	186	4:37.0	3744	290	16.4	797	708+	5:26.0

Hugo Wieslander

Figure 4.3.   Hugo Wieslander. (From the Official Report of the Organizing Committee of the 5th Olympiad, Stockholm)

Karl Hugo Wieslander was 23 (born June 11, 1889) when his nation hosted the games of the fifth Olympiad of Stockholm. He was the Swedish champion and, although unheralded as such in those days, a three-time world-record breaker in the decathlon. The Swedes, who had experience with multi-events, designed today's modern decathlon, and it was Wieslander who won the early meets. In Stockholm he placed second to Jim Thorpe, about 700 points behind (although 500 points ahead of his own previous best score). A year later he was moved to the top spot (and given the global standard) when Thorpe's mark was erased for professionalism.

Wieslander had competed in a total of 12 decathlons before Stockholm, a trio of international versions and nine Swedish versions. The Swedish decathlon included the 100m, 1500m, 110m hurdles, high jump, pole vault, long jump, triple jump, and both-hand throws of shot, discus, and javelin. Special Swedish scoring tables were used. Wieslander won 12 of his 15 career decathlons, losing only the 1912 nationals, the Olympic title, and the 1913

Table 4.2   Career Record of Hugo Wieslander

Date	Competition	Site	Place	Score	1985 Tables	100	lj	sp	hj	400	110H	dis	pv	jav	1500
Oct. 15, 1911	Pre-Olympic trials	Goteborg	1	6903 WR	5386	11.6	615	1125	167	55.6	18.2	2974	300	4889	4:59.4
June 5-6, 1912	Olympic trials	Stockholm	1	7099 WR	5493	12.0	604	1144	165	55.6	18.0	3629	300	4838	4:47.2
June 20-21, 1912	Warm-up	Stockholm	1	7244 WR	5583	11.9	628	1232	165	54.7	17.8	3517	320	4635	5:02.0
July 13-15, 1912	Olympics	Stockholm	1	7724 WR	5965	11.8	642	1214	175	53.6	17.2	3629	310	5040	4:45.0
Aug. 31-Sept. 1, 1912	Swedish champs	Stockholm	2	6876	5318	12.4	616	1141	165	56.4	18.2	3387	300	4945	4:54.4
Sept. 7, 1913	National Cup meet	Karlskrona	1	6726	5058	12.5	595	1237	170+	59.5	18.3	3867	312	4730	5:46.0

Note. The six decathlons listed used the now-common 10 events, usually in today's order. The 1912 tables were used. The 1911 meet was the first decathlon using the standard events and order. The 1912 Olympics were held over 3 days. Wieslander also competed in 9 other "Swedish-version" decathlons, using similar but not identical events. He won 8 of them: 1908 Malmo, 1909 Malmo, 1909 Orebro (1st Swedish Champs), 1910 Malmo, 1910 Karlskrona, 1911 Halmstad, 1911 Stockholm, and 1912 Karlskrona. He also competed at Eskilstuna in 1911 but did not win.

Pentathlon	Competition	Site	Place	Score	1985 Tables	lj	jav	200	dis	1500
July 7, 1912	Olympics	Stockholm	7	32	2970	627	4956	24.1	3074	4:53.1

Note. Wieslander competed in other pentathlons and won Swedish championships in 1910 (10 pts) and 1911 (6 pts).

nationals to Charles Lomberg, Wieslander also won the 1907 Swedish high-jump title at 1.70 m (5-7) and national pentathlon crowns.

Wieslander is perhaps most famous for his refusal to accept Thorpe's gold medal, which was offered to him by the IOC after Thorpe returned it in 1913. He declined to accept the medal claiming, "The medal belonged to the best man." Wieslander's personal records were 11.6, 6.56m (21-6 1/4), 13.65m (44-9 1/2), 1.80m (5-10 3/4), 53.6, 17.0, 39.00m (127-11), 3.33m (10-11), 54.10m (177-6), and 4:45.0. He competed for IF Kamraterna Club.

In 1971 Wieslander revealed to decathlon expert Rooney Magnusson that he visited the United States in 1925 and attempted to find Thorpe. The Swede was on tour with a Stockholm choir. Then 37, Thorpe had been released by a New York football team and Wieslander was unsuccessful.

1920-29

Americans and Scandinavians so dominated the decathlon during the 1920s that they claimed 24 of the first 30 Olympic places. The decathlon became an annual championship event in the United States beginning in 1920, as the all-around lost its importance.

Evert Nilsson of Sweden set a world mark in 1920 only to see fellow Scandinavian Alexandr Klumberg (Figure 4.4) of Estonia surpass it a day later. In 1922 in Helsinki, Klumberg gained the first International Amateur Athletic Federation (IAAF) world record, 7481 (6087) points. It was, however, Norwegian soldier Helge Lövland who won the 1920 Antwerp Olympics, with a score of 6804 (5804). Lövland won by a scant 36 points in the final event, passing Brutus Hamilton of the University of Missouri. Hamilton was to become one of America's most famous coaches and head of the 1952 USA Olympic team. While coaching at the University of California in the 1950s, he introduced the 10-eventer to Sam Adams, who is now recognized as America's most outstanding decathlon coach.

In the 1924 Olympic Games at Paris, American Harold Osborn of the Illinois Athletic Club was an easy winner, setting a world record of 7711 (6476) points. Alexandr Klumberg and American Emerson Norton claimed the remaining medals. Osborn became the only man to win an individual event and the decathlon at the Olympic Games. He won the high jump at 1.98m (6-6) 5 days before and had set the world high jump standard of 2.03m (6-8) months earlier. The University of Illinois grad had fancied himself an 800m runner and had good all-around credentials. He won three AAU decathlon titles and his world mark, although inferior to Thorpe's, stood until 1926.

Half a century after his Paris victory, Osborn, then an osteopath in Champaign, Illinois, reflected on the conditions of track and field in his day. He noted that tracks were normally six narrow lanes wide and that lanes for the sprints and hurdles were marked off by ropes as well as by chalk on the ground. High jumpers and vaulters landed in shallow, virtually ground-level, sawdust pits. Jump runways and throwing circles were either grass or dirt. They were easily chewed up so that throwers often wore spikes, too. And starting blocks had not become legal, so sprinters and hurdlers started from footholes dug in the track.

Despite the differences, Osborn felt that athletes haven't changed much between then and now. He felt today's athletes were as dedicated, determined, well trained, and knowledgeable in technique as athletes of old.

A pair of decathletes who knew what they wanted to achieve dominated the remainder of the decade. Finns Paavo Yrjölä and Akilles Järvinen claimed the top two medals at the 1928 Olympic Games in Amsterdam. Yrjölä trained alone on his farm, made his own implements from the nearby forests, and kept track of his competitors via newspapers. He broke

Figure 4.4.   Alexandr Klumberg. (Fred Kudu/Mitme-Volstlus)

the world mark no less than four times. American Ken Doherty, a two-time AAU winner (1928 and 29), claimed the bronze medal in Amsterdam, finishing ahead of two other Americans, James Stewart and Thomas Churchill. Doherty was to become one of this nation's outstanding coaches (Michigan and Pennsylvania), meet directors (Penn Relays), and writers (*Track and Field Omnibook*) in a distinguished career that led to his election to the National Track and Field Hall of Fame in 1976.

Järvinen, who hailed from a distinguished family of Olympic athletes, was second in two editions of the Olympic Games. He would later garner the silver medal at Los Angeles. On both occasions the winner bested the listed world record under the then-current tables, but had the present tables been used, Järvinen would have won both Olympic contests. The subjectivity of the scoring system relegated a potential champion to a historical footnote.

A pentathlon was held at both Antwerp and Paris, with Finn Eero Lehtonen winning both affairs. The event was discontinued after 1924.

The success of the Scandinavians in multi-events needs examination. There is little evidence that the Swedes, Finns, Norwegians, or Estonians adopted a systematic decathlon training system. The Americans did not. Some believe that the Scandinavians, generally less gifted in the natural events (sprints and jumps), tended to specialize in the technical (field events and hurdles). This too is doubtful. Their decathlon success is probably better explained as a reflection of a well-rounded view of physical education in northern European nations. In Scandinavia, physical fitness and versatility were common elements for young students and were appreciated as a way of life. On the other hand, American decathlon success is attributed to talented collegiate specialists who attempted multi-events every 4th year.

Helge Lövland

Figure 4.5.   Helge Lövland. (From the Zarnowski collection)

Table 4.3 Career Record of Helge Lövland

Date	Competition	Site	Place	Score	1985 Tables	100	lj	sp	hj	400	110H	dis	pv	jav	1500
July 19-20, 1919	District Champs	Kristiania	1	7786 WR	6033	11.4	657	1203	167	54.5	16.1	3812	306	5161	5:01.4
July 26-27, 1919	National Champs	Drammen	1	7063	5529	11.6	630	1154	159	58.9	16.0	3585	283	4964	5:06.0
July 10-11, 1920	National Champs	Kristiania	1	6754	5886	11.5	664	1116	165+	54.3	15.9	4104+	258+	4502	4:54.0
Aug. 20-21, 1920	Olympics	Antwerp	1	6803	5803	12.0	628	1119	165	54.8	16.2	3734	320	4801	4:48.4

Note. The 1912A tables were used for Lövland's 2 meets. The latter 2 used 1912B tables. The Norwegian town of Kristiania was later renamed Oslo.

Pentathlon	Competition	Site	Place	Score	1985 Tables	lj	jav	200	dis	1500
Oct. 8, 1916		Kristiania	1	8						
Aug. 22, 1917		Kristiania	1	8						
June 6, 1918	District Champs	Kristiania	1	3506						
July 7, 1918	National Champs	Kristiania	1	3946 WR	3169	648	5042	24.3	3924	4:55.3
Sept. 29, 1918		Kristiania	1	3808						
June 18, 1919	District Champs	Kristiania	1	4146 WR	3345	692	5070	23.4	3908	4:56.7
July 13, 1919	National Champs	Kristiania	1	4193 WR	3344	659	5512	23.5	3888	4:52.8
Aug. 6, 1920	Olympics	Antwerp	5	27	3262	632	5313	24.0	3951	4:45.8

Note. The 1912A tables were used.

Norwegian Helge Lövland was, at 30, the oldest Olympic decathlon champion. He went undefeated in four career 10-eventers. He also posted a world decathlon record in 1919 of 7786 (6044) points, although it was inferior to Jim Thorpe's unrecognized Stockholm mark. He also held a trio of world records (by later scoring methods) in the pentathlon.

A career military man, Lövland defeated 20-year-old Missourian Brutus Hamilton at the seventh Olympic Games at Antwerp in 1920 in the closest finish in Olympic history. The Norwegian came from behind, outdistancing Hamilton by 11 seconds in the final event to win by a whisker of 32 points. I interviewed Lövland in Oslo in 1980. He was 90 then but had a remarkably clear memory and an even more remarkable spring to his step. (He took the bus to our meeting.) He recounted the Antwerp affair, event by event, and recalled several announced scoring errors that confused both him and Hamilton. He recollected Hamilton with kindness and respect.

Lövland was both a humble and proud man, if that is possible. I asked if he could have defeated Thorpe (who was 2 years older) in his prime. "Oh, no. No. Thorpe was too good," he replied. But he proudly displayed his gold medal, a bit worn after 60 years, which he carried in a paper envelope.

Lövland was also fifth in the 1920 Olympic pentathlon. He later became president of the Norwegian Athletic Federation (NIFF) and was an avid hunter and cross-country skier. He served as a fitness role model, and, up to his death in 1984 (at age 94), could be seen on Norwegian television doing calisthenics. His lifetime bests include marks of 11.4, 7.03m (23-3/4), 12.53m (41-1 1/2), 1.76m (5-9 1/4), 53.4, 15.3, 44.51m (146-0), 3.20m (10-6), 60.44m (198-3), and 4:42.6.

Harold Osborn

Figure 4.6. Harold Osborn. (Courtesy of University of Illinois)

Track history would have found a secure spot for Harold Osborn had he never won a decathlon. He was an outstanding high-jumper, setting a world record of 2.03m (6-8) in the 1924 United States Olympic Trials. In the 1924 Olympics he captured the high jump with an Olympic record of 1.98m (6-6). Adding the decathlon title, Osborn became and remains the only man ever to win the decathlon title and an individual event.

Osborn's career was far longer than most. He graduated from the University of Illinois in 1922 and as late as 1936, at age 37, high jumped a personal best of 2.04m (6-8 1/4). That same year he standing high jumped 1.68m (5-6), still one of the highest on record. He also established indoor world bests for the high jump

Table 4.4   Career Record of Harold Osborn

Date	Competition	Site	Place	Score	1985 Tables	100	lj	sp	hj	400	110H	dis	pv	jav	1500
Sept. 11, 1922	AAU champs	Newark	2	6798	5929	11.5	669	1119	188	55.9	16.7	3314	320	4293	4:49.0
Sept. 3, 1923	AAU champs	Chicago	1	7351	6247	11.5	655	1144	195	52.9	15.6	3365	320	4612	4:53.1
June 10-11, 1924	Olympic Trials	Southfield	1	7377 AR	6248	11.9	691	1176	188	53.9	15.8	3462	335	4757	4:49.0
July 11-12, 1924	Olympic Games	Paris	1	7710 WR	6476	11.2	692	1143	197	53.2	16.0	3451	350	4669	4:50.0
July 5-6, 1925	AAU champs	San Francisco	1	7706	6375	11.6	653	1171	198	53.2	15.8	3747	366	4712	5:06.0
July 6-7, 1926	AAU champs	Philadelphia	1	7188	6021	11.8	680	1103	188	53.6	16.4	3434	335	4676	5:07.4
July 3-4, 1927	AAU champs	Lincoln	dnf	(714)	-----	11.8									

Note. Osborn competed in several other multi-event contests. In 1922 he won an all-around championship at an indoor relay carnival (6 events) in Illinois. In 1924 he won a multi-event contest at the ancient Tailteann Games in Ireland (it was not a full decathlon). The 1912B scoring tables were used during his career.

and standing hop-step-jump. He competed in 33 national AAU meets in 20 years, winning 18 titles in six different events and taking 35 medals in nine events.

Osborn competed at 1.78m/78 kg (5-10 and 172 lb). He perfected the technique of using his lead shoulder to pin the high-jump bar back against the standards while clearing in the days before the bar could fall off from both front and back.

Osborn was born April 13, 1899, practiced osteopathy, and was a keen supporter of his alma mater's track program (serving a term as assistant coach) until his death on April 5, 1975. He competed for the Illinois Athletic Club most of his career.

There are seven decathlons on Osborn's record. He won all but the first and the last. In between, he won three AAU titles, set an American record in winning the 1924 Olympic Trials, and established a new world mark of 7710.775 (6476) in gaining Olympic gold. His best marks in decathlon competition were 11.2, 6.92m (22-8 1/2), 11.76m (38-7), 1.97m (6-5 1/2), 52.9, 15.6, 37.47m (122-11), 3.66m (12-0), 47.57m (156-0), and 4:49.0

Paavo Yrjölä

Figure 4.7. Paavo Yrjölä, 1928. (From the Official Report of the Organizing Committee of the 9th Olympiad, Amsterdam)

The claim to fame of the great Finnish decathlete Paavo Yrjölä is without question. He dominated the event during the late 1920s, winning the 1928 Olympic Games and breaking the world mark no less than four times, an achievement equaled only by Daley Thompson. He topped the world list three times and was second three times from 1925 through 1930.

Born in Hameenkyro, Finland, on June 18, 1902, Yrjölä debuted 3 days after his 20th birthday. He placed ninth at the Paris Olympic Games. A year later he was second best in the world. In 1926, Paavo started a run of 3 straight years of topping both the world list and the old world record, culminating this impressive streak with his Olympic win.

Table 4.5   Career Record of Paavo Yrjölä

Date	Competition	Site	Place	Score	1985 Tables	100	lj	sp	hj	400	110H	dis	pv	jav	1500
June 21-22, 1922	National champs	Tampere	3	6149	5300	12.2	601	1182	165	56.3	18.6	3223	280	5112	4:47.4
July 28-29, 1923	National champs	Helsinki	3	6573	5563	12.1	631	1292	170	56.9	18.1	3446	290	5136+	4:51.4
May 28-29, 1924	Olympic Trials	Tampere	1	6617	5580	12.3	629	1350	165	54.2	19.7	3543	280+	5583	4:49.3
July 11-12, 1924	Olympic Games	Paris	9	6548	5742	11.8	631	1328	160	54.6	18.8	3814	273	5293	5:08.6
July 18-19, 1925	National champs	Helsinki	1	7671	6324	12.0	645	1369	180	52.8	17.6	3940	320	5761	4:34.8
July 17-18, 1926	National champs	Viipuri	1	7832 WR	6460	11.8	654	1397	185	52.4	16.9	3731	330	5670	4:41.1
July 16-17, 1927	National champs	Helsinki	1	8018 WR	6586	11.7	673	1427	185	52.8	16.8	4076	320	5740	4:41.8
June 9-10, 1928		Kuopio	1	7695	6317	11.9	661	1437	180	54.2	16.8	4108	310	5718	4:56.1
July 7-8, 1928	Olympic Trials	Helsinki	1	7846	6361	11.7	642	1428	187	55.0	17.1	4198	320	6140	4:53.9
Aug. 3-4, 1928	Olympic Games	Amsterdam	1	8053 WR	6587	11.8	672	1411	187	53.2	16.6	4209	330	5570	4:44.0
Sept. 1-2, 1928	National champs	Turku	1	7465	6105	11.8	669	1389	180	54.1	16.6	4087	310	6215	5:59.0
July 20-21, 1929	National champs	Helsinki	1	7607	6296	11.7	653	1320	175	55.1	16.4	4078	320	5515	4:42.7
July 9-10, 1930		Aalborg, Den	1	8117 WR	6700	11.6	676	1472	185	53.2	16.1	3966	310	5888	4:37.5
July 18-19, 1931	National champs	Tampere	2	7529	6285	11.8	642	1354	170	53.6	16.4	4076	315	5324	4:37.3
Aug. 1-2, 1931		Inkeroinen	1	7781	6465	11.7	664	1385	180	51.9	16.6	4172	315	5193	4:44.3
June 25-26, 1932	Olympic Trials	Viipuri	1	7565	6319	11.9	646	1346	170	52.5	15.9	3882	320	5648	4:49.5
Aug. 5-6, 1932	Olympic Games	Los Angeles	6	7687	6385	11.8	659	1368	175	52.6	17.0	4077	310	5612	4:37.4

Pentathlon	Competition	Site	Place	Score	1912B Tables	1985 Tables	lj	jav	200	dis	1500
Aug. 16, 1925	National champs	Viipuri	1	8 pts	3816	3309	663	5695	24.1	4090	5:02.8
Aug. 15, 1926	National champs	Tampere	1	10 pts	3702	3231	656	5592	23.8	3949	5:10.7
Aug. 21, 1927	National champs	Turku	1	12 pts	3440	3007	665	5835	25.1	3907	5:42.8
Aug. 26, 1928	National champs	Helsinki	2	11 pts	3991	3437	659	6195	24.0	3980	4:49.8
Aug. 17, 1930	National champs	Tampere	3		3863	3406	660	5428	23.8	3955	4:38.4
Aug. 16, 1931	National champs	Helsinki	2		4067 WR	3542	653	5789	23.8	4120	4:28.5
Sept. 27, 1931	National champs	Kaustinen	1		3737	3242	649	5466	24.0	4199	5:08.4

Yrjölä was a self-made decathlete, living and working on a farm. He made his own equipment from the local woods, fashioned a running area on the pastures, and trained alone while keeping track of his opponents in the newspaper. Although he was unsure of the correct height, he built his own hurdles. He was confident before the 1928 Olympic Games in Amsterdam, where he broke the world record and beat countryman Akilles Järvinen and American champion Ken Doherty.

Yrjölä broke the record again in 1930, but it was not ratified— probably because Järvinen improved on Yrjölä's new record just a few days later. Paavo wound up his career with a sixth place finish in the 1932 Los Angeles Games. He also claimed a world second-best in the pentathlon, where there were no records at the time, scoring 4061 (3542 on the 1985 tables) in 1931.

Yrjölä's career extended over 11 years and encompassed 17 meets, both remarkably numerous for the era. His nine straight wins have been topped only by Bob Mathias, Bill Toomey, and Daley Thompson. His lifetime bests include marks of 11.6, 6.76m (22-2 1/2), 14.72m (48-3 1/2), 1.87m (6-1 1/2), 51.7, 15.4, 43.34m (142-2), 3.30m (10-10), 62.15m (203-11), and 4:28.5. He died on February 11, 1980 at age 77.

1930-39

American decathletes dominated the 1930s by winning both Olympic titles, as a worldwide depression had little impact on decathlon scores. Six times the world record was improved, three by Americans.

Yrjölä and Järvinen set world marks within the space of 10 days in July 1930. America revealed a number of new faces, mostly young post-collegians. Jim Bausch, of Kansas, upped Ken Doherty's national mark at the 1931 Kansas Relays in his first-ever decathlon. Two months later he lost the mark to Jess Mortensen of Los Angeles. Bausch regained not only the national but the global standard, 8462 (6735) points, at the 1932 Los Angeles Olympic Games. The 210-lb football and basketball star clubbed a great field that included four past or future world-record breakers. Bausch won four of five career 10-eventers. He was basically a thrower who managed to lift his bulk over 4.00m (13-1 1/2) in the vault in the 1932 games. Järvinen won the silver medal and Germany's Wolrad Eberle the bronze.

The United States was blessed with multi-talented athletes during the decade. Wilson Charles, an Indian from the Haskell Institute, won the 1930 AAU meet and placed 4th at the Los Angeles Games. Pennsylvania's bulky Barney Berlinger won three Penn Relay titles, the 1933 AAU, and a Sullivan Award. San Francisco's Bob Clark captured two (1934-35) AAU crowns.

In Europe, a new decathlon genius emerged. The German giant, Hans-Heinrich Sievert, honed his skills early in the decade and, by 1934, he was ready. In July the German, renowned for his shot-discus distances, upped the world record to 8790 (7147) points. He took the first European decathlon crown by over 300 points, despite running 5:55.2 for the 1500m. According to one study which compares decathlon performances with the specialist's world records of the day, few decathletes are better. The Nazi propaganda machine ballyhooed Sievert's decathlon chances, establishing him as the favorite for the 1936 Olympic Games in Berlin. Unfortunately, the brilliant Sievert was injured during the 1936 Games. To be just, it is doubtful he could have defeated the newest American giant.

Glenn Morris was a little-known intermediate hurdler from Denver, Colorado, who, like others before him, turned to the decathlon during the Olympic year. He set an American mark at the 1936 Kansas Relays (his very first decathlon!) and a new world record at the combined AAU/Olympic Trials in Milwaukee. In Milwaukee he defeated Bob Clark, Jack Parker, and Clyde Coffman. Clark used a 7.90m (25-11) long jump to put himself on the team.

In Berlin, the Sievert/Morris matchup was one of the greatest duels that never happened. Morris competed like a man possessed. His aggressiveness and grim determination, matched in later Olympics only by Bruce

Jenner, was captured by Leni Riefenstahl's film, *Olympiad, Festival of Nations*. Morris literally ran himself into exhaustion and into the record books with yet another world record, 7900 (7254) points. A new set of scoring tables were now in force. Nearly 14 years would pass before his world mark would be topped. Clark and Parker completed an American sweep. The latter, from Sacramento Junior College, was coached by young L.D. Weldon, who would soon move to Graceland College in Iowa. Four decades later, Weldon uncovered a new decathlon talent named Jenner.

Morris, undefeated in a three-decathlon career, immediately retired. He went on to star as Tarzan in one Hollywood film and also had a fling as a running back in the National Football League (NFL), but he made little of either career.

Akilles Järvinen

Figure 4.8. Akilles Järvinen. (From the Official Report of the Organizing Committee of the 10th Olympiad, Los Angeles)

Table 4.6   Career Record of Akilles Järvinen

Date	Competition	Site	Place	Score	1985 Tables	100	lj	sp	hj	400	110H	dis	pv	jav	1500
Sept. 6-7, 1926	Club champs	Tampere	2	7172	6057	11.4	649	1242	170	53.4	16.8	3386	320	5345	4:53.6
July 16-17, 1927	National champs	Helsinki	2	7124	6023	11.7	664	1282	170	53.6	17.0	3525	300	5413	4:52.0
July 7-8, 1928	Olympic qual	Helsinki	2	7495	6345	11.3	691	1345	170	52.6	15.6	3676	300	5490	5:09.0
Aug. 3-4, 1928	Olympic Games	Amsterdam	2	7931	6645	11.2	687	1364	175	51.4	15.6	3685	330	5558	4:52.4
Sept. 1-2, 1928	National champs	Turku	2	7141	5982	11.6	680	1305	170	53.5	16.0	3446	330	5784	5:59.0
July 19-20, 1930	National champs	Viipuri	1	8255 WR	6865	11.1	689	1314	180	50.0	15.4	3647	360	5815	4:54.2
July 18-19, 1931	National champs	Tampere	1	8160	6771	11.2	699	1305	180	50.9	15.8	3794	355	5621	4:52.6
Aug. 5-6, 1932	Olympic Games	Los Angeles	2	8292 WR	6879	11.1	700	1311	175	50.6	15.7	3680	360	6100	4:47.0
Aug. 7-8, 1936	Olympic Games	Berlin	--	dnf		11.4	669	1353	175	50.7	withdrew				

Pentathlon	Competition	Site	Place	Score	1985 Tables	lj	jav	200	dis	1500
Aug. 21, 1927	National champs	Turku	2	3260(15)	2927	664	5391	24.4	3559	5:42.8
Aug. 26, 1928	National champs	Helsinki	1	3717(9)	3325	670	5583	23.6	3441	4:45.3

None of the other great decathletes came from an athletic heritage as rich as the Järvinen's. Three sons of Werner Järvinen, Finland's first Olympic gold medal winner (1906 Greek-style discus), competed in the 1932 Olympic Games. Best known is Akilles's brother, Matti, who won the Los Angeles Olympic javelin competition and set 10 world records between 1930 and 1936.

Sometimes overshadowed by countryman Paavo Yrjölä, Aki placed second in two Olympic decathlons, 1928 and 1932. Under the present (1985) scoring system, he would have won them both. In 1930 in Viipuri he bettered the world decathlon record with 8255 (6865) points. At the 1932 Olympics he again upped the world record to 8292 (6879), holding it for all of the 30 seconds it took Jim Bausch to finish the 1500m with an even higher score, 8462 (6735).

Aki was born September 19, 1905 and competed for Club Tampereen Pyrinto. During World War II he flew against the Russians as a bomber pilot. He died in an air crash over Tampere on March 7, 1943. His personal records include marks of 11.1, 7.00m (22-11 3/4), 13.64m (44-9), 1.80m (5-10 3/4), 50.0, 15.4, 37.94m (124-6), 3.60m (11-9 3/4), 61.00m (200-1), and 4:47.0.

Figure 4.9. Jim Bausch. (From the Zarnowski collection)

Jim Bausch's decathlon career lasted less than 16 months, but it was long enough for him to earn trackdom's two most-coveted awards: an Olympic title and a world record. They came to him in the 1932 Olympics, where he rolled up 8462 points on the 1912B tables (6738).

A native of Wichita (born on March 29, 1906), Bausch was considered the greatest all-around athlete in the illustrious sports history of the University of Kansas. He started in football (all-American) and basketball as well as track, making good use of his 210 lb.

Jim's decathlon debut was a headline maker. He won the 1931 Kansas Relays with an American record of 7847 (6329). Later that

Table 4.7   Career Record of Jim Bausch

Date	Competition	Site	Place	Score	1985 Tables	100	lj	sp	hj	400	110H	dis	pv	jav	1500
Apr. 17-18, 1931	Kansas Relays	Lawrence	1	7847 AR	6329	11.5	641	1518	165	54.9	16.4	4376	380	5328	5:21.0
July 3-4, 1931	AAU champs	Lincoln	6	7208	5813	11.5	668	1476	160	56.8	16.1	4425	354	5550	dnf
Apr. 22-23, 1932	Kansas Relays	Lawrence	1	8017	6445	11.4	655	1533	169	54.4	16.2	4618	365	5618	5:35.7
June 24-25, 1932	AAU/Olympic Trials	Evanston, IL	1	8103	6431	12.1	646	1483	170	54.2	16.1	4634	376	5944	5:22.2
Aug. 5-6, 1932	Olympic Games	Los Angeles	1	8462 WR	6735	11.7	695	1532	170	54.2	16.2	4458	400	6191	5:17.0

Note. The 1912B tables were used during Bausch's career.

year, at the AAU meet, he suffered his only decathlon loss. The year 1932 was all-conquering. In the Kansas Relays Jim achieved a new personal best of 8017 (usually reported as 8022), which fell short of Jess Mortensen's recent AR of 8193. Jim improved again at the combined AAU-Olympic Trials.

Bausch was one of America's best all-around throwers, making national lists in the shot, discus, and javelin. He was also an excellent vaulter. In Los Angeles, he manhandled a strong field, winning the Olympics by 170 points. He turned back Akilles Järvinen, the world-record holder and second-place finisher in 1928; Paavo Yrjölä, the defending champ and four-time world-record holder; and Hans-Heinrich Sievert, who eventually succeeded Jim as world-record holder. Jim broke four lifetime decathlon bests on his way to winning and tied two others. His 15.32m (50-3 1/4) shot compared favorably with the Olympic champion's put of 16.00 (52-6). Bausch's decathlon bests were 11.4, 6.95m (22-9 3/4), 15.33m (50-3 1/2), 1.70m (5-7), 54.2, 16.1, 46.34m (152-0), 4.00m (13-1 1/2), 61.91m (203-1), and 5:17.0. In an era when decathletes struggled with the vault, Jim's 4.00m vault, achieved in the Olympics, was particularly noteworthy for his size. The 1932 Olympic pole vault champion's record was barely a foot higher.

Bausch was a Sullivan Award winner. He spent a career with the United States Department of Agriculture. He died on July 9, 1974 in Hot Springs, Arkansas.

Figure 4.10.   Hans-Heinrich Sievert. (Das Sportbild von Schirmer/Courtesy of *Track and Field News*)

Hans-Heinrich Sievert gained attention in 1927 when he posted excellent shot results at age 18. In 1929 he tried his first decathlon while a student in Halle, now part of East Germany. He was fourth with 511 points, using the German's own tables. His performance was worth 5803 on the current scorebook.

In 1931, while making a reputation as one of the world's best shot/discus men, Sievert won the German decathlon title with a new national record. A year later he was fifth at the Los Angeles Olympic Games, injuring himself in the vault. Injuries plagued the strapping youth, but he recovered to set in 1933 the first of his two world records. The IAAF never ratified his 8467 at Hamburg, when it was learned that he was awarded 1.825m (5-11 3/4)

Table 4.8 Career Record of Hans-Heinrich Sievert

Date	Competition	Site	Place	Score	1985 Tables	100	lj	sp	hj	400	110H	dis	pv	jav	1500
July 21-22, 1929	National champs	Breslau	4	511	5803	11.7	629	1319	167	55.2	17.1	3869	330	5205	5:24.0
Aug. 24-25, 1929	National champs	Halle	1	531	5949	11.8	653	1435	171	54.2	17.0	3878	291	5238	5:15.0
Aug. 1-2, 1931	National champs	Berlin	1	7875	6492	11.3	708	1423	170	53.0	16.8	4393	300	5939	5:10.2
Aug. 5-6, 1932	Olympics	Los Angeles	5	7941	6515	11.4	697	1450	178	53.6	16.1	4454	320	5391	5:18.0
July 22-23, 1933	Club meet	Hamburg	1	8460 WR	6833	11.4	709	1455	182	54.0	16.2	4666	340	5958	4:59.8
Aug. 12-13, 1933	National champs	Köln	1	8435	6828	11.2	678	1531	185	53.8	15.8	4575	330	5832	5:06.0
July 7-8, 1934	Club meet	Hamburg	1	8790 WR	7147	11.1	748	1531	180	52.2	15.8	4723	343	5832	4:58.8
July 27-28, 1934	National champs	Nürnberg	1	8498	6870	11.2	710	1492	180	52.1	15.9	4725	350	5812	5:26.0
Sept. 8-9, 1934	Euro champs	Turin	1	8103	6667	11.2	700	1477	180	49.6	16.0	4503	330	5547	5:55.2
July 16-17, 1938	National champs	Stuttgart	1	7467	6895	11.1	705	1460	180	52.0	16.0	4559	330	5579	4:56.4
Sept. 4-5, 1938	Euro champs	Colombes	–	dnf	(2820)	11.3	668	1439	175	withdrew					

Pentathlon	Competition	Site	Place	Score	1985 Tables	lj	jav	200	dis	1500
Sept. 9, 1933		Turin	1	4163 WR	3565	699	5754	22.6	4406	5:10.0

Note. The 1929 meets were scored on the German system. Using the IAAF system then in use (1912B tables), the score would have been 7117 for the Halle meet and 7007 for the meet in Breslau. All Sievert's meets used the 1912B tables until 1938, when the 1934 tables were used.

in the high jump and rules counted only centimeters (1.82m). So the world mark remained with American Jim Bausch (8462) until the following year when the German decided not to cut it so close. This time, in Hamburg, Hans exploded for 8790 (7147), a mark that left no doubt about his all-around greatness. Later that year, in spite of again sustaining a vault injury, he won the first European championship in Turin.

Injuries again held Hans out of the decathlon in 1935, 1936, and 1937. He would have certainly been one of the favorites at the Berlin Games, but a potential battle with American Glenn Morris went uncontested. Sievert made a comeback in 1938, scoring 7467 (6895), but injuries again prevented him from defending his European title later that year. He retired in 1940 with World War II already in progress. During a 14-year career, he won four German decathlon titles and a pair of national crowns in the shot and discus. His lifetime bests include marks of 11.1, 7.48m (24-6 1/2), 15.89m (52-1 3/4), 1.85m (6-3/4), 49.6, 15.8, 49.32m (161-10), 3.50m (11-5 3/4), 62.63m (205-5), and 4:56.4. He was born on December 1, 1909 in a Northern Rhine village of Grittern. For most of his career he competed for the Eimsbutteler Trunverband, a Hamburg Club. He died on April 6, 1963.

Figure 4.11. Glenn Morris. (From the Zarnowski collection)

A versatile track man at Colorado Agricultural College in Fort Collins, Glenn Morris first tried the decathlon when he was out of school. His top collegiate achievement had been a 54+ seconds in the intermediate hurdles. Three times in 1936 Morris tackled the 10 events. All three times he came away with a notable record.

Representing the Denver Athletic Club, Morris made his debut at the Kansas Relays and came away with an American record. But the track world hadn't seen anything yet. At the AAU/Olympic Trials he brought home a new world record of 7880 (7213) points. Off to Berlin, Morris won the Olympics with still another world mark of 7900 (7234) points.

Table 4.9   Career Record of Glenn Morris

Date	Competition	Site	Place	Score	1985 Tables	100	lj	sp	hj	400	110H	dis	pv	jav	1500
April 17-18, 1936	Kansas Relays	Lawrence	1	7576 AR	7109	10.6	697	1349	180	50.9	15.2	4114	339	5546	4:52.3
May 26-27, 1936	AAU/Olympic Trials	Milwaukee	1	7880 WR	7213	10.7	686	1445	187	50.7	14.9	4310	345	5606	4:48.1
Aug. 7-8, 1936	Olympic Games	Berlin	1	7900 WR	7254	11.1	697	1410	185	49.4	14.9	4302	350	5452	4:33.2

Note. The 1934 tables were used in all of Morris's career meets.

Undefeated in a three-decathlon career, Morris immediately retired. He had a brief Hollywood career, playing Tarzan opposite
Eleanor Holm in a 1937 film entitled *Tarzan's Revenge*. After that
he went on to be a running back in the National Football League.
One can only wonder what Morris would have done to the recordbook had he maintained an interest in the decathlon. He was born
in Simla, Colorado on June 18, 1912. He died in 1973 in a Palo
Alto, California veteran's hospital.

1940-49

War in Europe and the Pacific caused the cancellation of both the 1940 and 1944 Olympic Games, which were to be held in Tokyo/Helsinki and London. One can only speculate how the decathlon competitions would have turned out if the games had been held. In 1940, former University of Michigan star William Watson would have been a heavy favorite. He dominated the event in the United States. At the 1940 AAU meet he strung together some stunning performances, including a 10.8 sprint, a 7.43m (24-4 1/2) long jump, a 15.28m (50-1 3/4) shot, and 46.10m (151-3) in the discus. His 7523 (6904) point score was the best in the early war years. Watson was the first American black to excel at the decathlon, winning a pair of AAU titles. He may have been a good bet for 1944 as well. Another American athlete who reached his peak during the war years may have pushed Watson. Irv Mondschein was a formidable jumper who captured three national decathlon crowns (1944-46-47). He later became a well-known coach at the University of Pennsylvania and was named the decathlon coach for the 1988 United States Olympic team.

In 1948 the Olympic Games were renewed, with London as host. Up to this time, the decathlon had been viewed as an event for the mature athlete. Indeed, Mondschein became infamous for reminding us, "This event is not for kids." Then a 17-year-old American, Robert Bruce Mathias, competing in only his third decathlon, changed that view by winning the gold medal at Wembley Stadium.

Bob's interest in sports was kindled by his father, a physician and surgeon who had starred at football at the University of Oklahoma. In high school in Tulare, California, Bob starred at basketball, football, and track. His track coach, Virgil Jackson, suggested the decathlon as a new challenge in the spring of 1948. Neither was certain of the decathlon's 10 events, but Bob won the Southern Pacific AAU Games with 3 week's practice and the AAU/Olympic Trials meet in Bloomfield, New Jersey, a few weeks after that.

Cold, rainy conditions kept scores down in London, but tribute must be paid to this high school boy who showed competitive spirit and maturity of purpose against the world's best of the day. He trailed Argentine Enrique Kistenmacher and France's Ignace Heinrich after the first day. On the 2nd day he used his hurdles, discus, and javelin prowess to win a meet that lasted almost 12 hours. After he dragged his body over the finish line of the 1500m, he told his parents, "Never again. No more decathlon. I never worked for anything so hard in my life." Heinrich captured the silver medal and North Carolina's Floyd Simmons, the bronze. Mondschein placed 8th.

There is an interesting postscript to the 1948 London decathlon. A new magazine, *Track and Field News*, ranked Heino Lipp (Figure 4.12), the huge

Figure 4.12.   Heino Lipp. (Fred Kudu/Mitme-Volstlus)

(1.92m/6-3 1/2, 102 kilos/225 lb) Estonian decathlete, as tops in the world for 1948. His best score led the world by over 500 points. But the Soviets were not part of the Olympic movement in the early post-World War II era, preventing a match-up between the Russian and the American teenager. Lipp's coach, Fred Kudu, would guide numerous Soviet decathlon champions (including Nikolay Avilov in 1972). But in 1948 Lipp and Kudu stayed home. A year later, Mathias won the AAU title in his hometown of Tulare, a small farming community of 12,000. This time, Lipp and Iceland's Orn Clausen followed the 18-year-old in the world rankings.

William Watson

Figure 4.13. William Watson, second from left, back row.

Bill Watson, born in 1916, was America's premier all-around athlete in the World War II era. A 1940 Michigan grad, Watson was a world-class performer in several events and tried his hand at the decathlon on only three occasions. He won a pair of AAU crowns and would have been the odds-on favorite had the 1940 Olympic Games been held. His major opponents in those games might have been Fritz Muller and Ernest Schmidt of Germany.

In 1940 Bill turned in a performance in Cleveland that made him the fourth highest performer of all time, with 7523 (6904) points. His marks included a 10.8 sprint, 7.43m (24-4 1/2) long jump, and 15.28m (50-1 3/4) shot. Watson won by over 600 points. Even a dozen years after, his score still stood as the ninth best score of all time.

Bill was thickly built, standing 1.78m (5-10) and weighing 86 kilos (190 lb). He represented the Detroit Police AA and spent most of his career performing individual events. In 1939 he barely lost two AAU titles: long jump of 7.66m (25-1 3/4) and shot put of 16.31m (53-6). He lost the AAU meet to Bill Terwilliger in 1942,

Table 4.10   Career Record of William Watson

Date	Competition	Site	Place	Score	1985 Tables	100	lj	sp	hj	400	110H	dis	pv	jav	1500
June 15-16, 1940	AAU champs	Cleveland	1	7523	6904	10.8	742	1528	178	52.2	16.8	4612	357	4417	4:53.8
June 26-27, 1942	AAU champs	Chicago	2	6076	5536	11.6	670+	1469	178	54.3	17.7	4517	278	4408	dnr
June 26-27, 1943	AAU champs	Elizabeth	1	5994	5449	11.3	674	1486	175	55.7	18.6	4337	289+	4469	dnr

but regained it a year later in Elizabeth, New Jersey. In both meets Bill declined to run the 1500m—a common practice in those days.

Bill's individual record is outstanding. From 1938 to 1945 he placed in four different events at AAU meets a total of 14 times. At the NCAA championships he was in the top six in three different events on seven occasions. At the 1937 NCAA championships he finished fourth in the shot. He won the Big-10 long jump the same year. In 1938 he won the Big-10 long jump, shot, and discus and won second, third, and fourth at the NCAA. In 1939 he again won all three events at the Big 10 and finished second, second, and fourth at the collegiate championships. His lifetime bests include marks of 10.8, 7.76m (25-5 1/2), 16.62m (54-6 1/2), 1.78m (5-10), 52.2, 16.8, 49.84m (163-6), 3.57m (11-8 1/2), 44.69m (146-7), and 4:53.8.

1950-59

Improving steadily, the youthful Mathias arrived at Stanford University in 1950, the same year a new set of scoring tables was approved. Mathias, in his hometown, won the AAU title after a tussle with North Carolina sophomore Bill Albans in a meet illustrating two styles of performances. Albans's highlights included a 10.6 100m, 7.48m (24-6 3/4) long jump, and 14.1 hurdles—all spectacular. Albans, age 25, led Mathias by 210 points after six events. On the other hand, Mathias, who was now 19, did not have one super event, but came through with 10 balanced efforts and a world-record score.

The top Europeans were Russians Lipp and Pytor Denisenko. Both missed the European championships at Brussels, where Heinrich bested Clausen under the 1934 tables. The places would have been reversed if the 1950 tables (first used in 1952) had been in force.

In 1950 Mathias stayed clear of the decathlon because of a bad back, and Bob Richards, later of *Wheaties* fame, posted the three best American scores and won the AAU title. Few remember the "Reverend" as a great decathlete, but during the 1950s he was world ranked six times. The University of Illinois vaulter won three national decathlon titles, plus a pair of Olympic pole vault wins in 1952 and 1956.

The top performance in Europe in 1951 was another duel between Heinrich and Clausen. Under the old tables, the Frenchman triumphed once again. And, again, the finish would have been reversed had the newer tables been used.

To rectify this anomaly, new tables (approved in 1950) were widely adopted in 1952. At the United States Olympic Trials in early July, Mathias returned to active competition and broke his own world record with a 7825 (7543) point performance. In second was a great high school prospect, Milt Campbell of Plainfield, New Jersey. Floyd Simmons edged Bill Albans for the third spot. At Helsinki, the three Americans swept the medals. Mathias became the first to win the Olympic decathlon twice. In the 4 years since 1948 he had captured the Sullivan Award as the nation's outstanding amateur athlete and had become an outstanding fullback at Stanford. Now 21, he was 191m/93 kg (6-3/205 lb). At Helsinki, where the weather was infinitely better than in London, Mathias finished more than 900 points (!) ahead of Campbell, the largest margin in Olympic decathlon history. It was the third world record for Bob, who immediately retired, having completed nine 10-eventers.

A promising 20-year-old Russian, Vasiliy Kuznyetsov, won the first of many national titles in 1953. A year later, Bob Richards had total success, winning the AAU over, among others, yet another high school boy of great promise, Rafer Johnson of Kingsburg, California. In July, at Kiev, Kuznyetsov erased Sievert's 20-year-old European mark and had no trouble taking the European crown in Berne, Switzerland, where bad weather kept scores down.

The first major competition of 1955 was the Pan American Games in Mexico City. Johnson, now a frosh at UCLA, held off the challenge of the more-experienced Richards, who, down 100 points, declined to run the final event (a common practice in the 1950s). Improving week by week, Johnson returned to his hometown to set a world record; he then passed up the AAU meet. In the latter, Richards bested University of Southern California star Bob Lawson. Kuznyetsov was a one-man European show, winning the Warsaw Youth Festival and the Russian championship with yet another European record.

Johnson won his first national title the following year at the combined AAU/Olympic Trials meet in the red-brick town of Crawfordsville, Indiana, making the boat to Melbourne. His final score included a 4640-point (world best) first day. Milt Campbell, now stationed at the San Diego Naval Training Center, made an expected comeback to clinch the second spot ahead of Richards. Highlights included a 47.9 400m by Johnson, a 14.1 hurdles by Campbell, and a 4.57m (15-0) vault by Richards. Twice, prior to the Olympics, Kuznyetsov upped the European record. And, setting the stage for Melbourne, German vet Walter Meier and novice Martin Lauer, later a hurdles world-record holder, scored well. Lauer had marks of 14.1 (hurdles) and 47.7 (400 meters) in his first-ever decathlon. As a sideline, it is interesting to note that Marine Lt. Bob Mathias won an interservice decathlon in 1956 with 7193 points. Mathias did not run the 1500m but had his best weight triple: 15.35m (50-4 1/2) shot, 48.82m (160-2) discus, and 62.20m (204-1) javelin.

Unfortunately, Johnson injured a knee before the Olympic Games (held "down under" in November), putting him at a disadvantage to Campbell and Kuznyetsov. But even in top condition Johnson would have had his hands full with Milt, who ran up the second highest total ever. Campbell ran a super 14-flat in the hurdles and would have broken the global standard but for a 3.40m (11-1 3/4) vault clearance. "I could have made the pole vault if I had taken a longer run. It was a stupid mistake," he said after the meet. "I had my heart set on making the [Olympic] team as a hurdler. When I came in fourth [in the Olympic Trials] I was stunned. But then God seemed to reach into my heart and tell me he didn't want me to compete in the hurdles, but in the decathlon. This win was for my mother . . . she never gave up on me." Johnson was 450 points back at the end, finishing with the silver medal. Kuznyetsov collared the first of two bronze medals. Leaving the Melbourne cricket grounds, Johnson prophetically announced, "I'll be like Milton and look ahead 4 years. I'd sure like to win at Rome in 1960."

In 1957 Kuznyetsov defeated Yuriy Kutyenko at the Soviet championships. Russia's "Mr. K" continued his fine form into 1958. At Krasnodar in May he bettered Johnson's world record with 8014 (7653) points, showing general all-around consistency instead of big events. More latent talent was discovered at the Asian Games in Tokyo, where Formosan Yang Chuan-kwang (Americans knew him as C.K. Yang) won. Later, Yang traveled to the United States and placed second to Johnson at the AAU championships.

In Moscow in 1958 the American and the Soviet track teams met in their first duel ever, seen as a way to diffuse the cold war. Athletes and spectators did not find the raw and damp July weather at Lenin Stadium conducive to record breaking, but it did not matter. Rafe and Mr. K overshadowed all other events in the match. Johnson built a first-day lead and, surprisingly, increased it on the second day. A 49.07m (160-11) discus and 72.60m (238-2) javelin helped the 22-year-old American regain the world record with 8302 (7789) points. Kuznyetsov ran up his second best total ever, and American Dave Edstrom from Oregon edged Kutyenko for third.

Later in 1958 Kuznyetsov captured yet another European crown in Stockholm. He also won a Soviet title, winning over Estonian Uno Palu and Armenian long-jumper Igor Ter-Ovanesyan.

In May 1959, Kuznyetsov and Kutyenko tangled again in Moscow's Lenin Stadium. Again a world record resulted, as Kuznyetsov chalked up 8357 (7839) points. Back in the United States the new AAU champ was Yang, who won the event by five points over Edstrom. Hometown favorite Johnson sat in the stands, the victim of an auto accident. Later in the year Yang improved to 7835 (7494), a fantastic rate of progress for such a short career. Johnson, still injured, was unable to compete in Philadelphia against the Soviets. On the second day at Penn's Franklin Field Kuznyetsov was in great form in spite of bad weather. He missed the world record by only seven points with 8350 (7838). And in Chicago Dave Edstrom claimed the Pan American title, although he was not in shape following an appendectomy.

The great talent Martin Lauer returned to the decathlon for the first time since 1956 and took away the 1959 German title and record. He ran a windy 10.2 100m and a legal 13.8 hurdles for all-time decathlon bests. As the decade closed, European standards improved. The world mark was improved seven times in the 1950s, five by Americans and twice by a Russian. In 10 years of world rankings (10 deep per year) American decathletes had 36 spots, the Soviet Union 30, and the rest of the world 34.

Bob Mathias

Figure 4.14. Bob Mathias. (From the Zarnowski collection)

Bob Mathias's place in decathlon history would have been secure if he had done nothing but win the 1948 Olympics. After all, he was but 17-years-old, then and now the youngest male track winner in modern Olympic history. Exhausted, cold, and hungry after a long, drawn-out contest held in incredible conditions, the big youngster vowed "never again." But he thought better of it and went on to reach even greater heights.

Bob was off to a sickly start as a young boy in Tulare, California (born November 17, 1930), but grew large, strong, and athletically gifted. A star discus thrower and hurdler in high school, Bob was urged by coach Virgil Jackson to try the decathlon. "Work hard at it and I'll bet you make the Olympic team . . . in 1952," Jackson told him. Bob overcame bad conditions and bad luck. By the end of the year, he was the reigning Olympic king.

After a year at Kiski Prep, Bob captured the AAU title in June, 1949—this time before hometown folks. He entered another meet that year (although the usual was one or two decathlons per year) and won against Scandinavia in Oslo. After entering Stanford, Bob was back in Tulare for the 1950 AAU. He was extremely ready, poured it on all the way, and achieved personal bests in seven of the events. The result was a new world record.

It was now time to take a rest from the decathlon, and Bob didn't compete again until 1952. But he honed his skills and improved his strength with multi-event performances on the Stanford varsity. At 21, Bob went back to Tulare for his last decathlon appearance in California's great Central Valley. He rewarded the enthusiastic home crowd by winning the combined AAU/Olympic Trials with another world record. So great was his improvement that he chalked up bests in eight events. And at Helsinki, for his second Olympic win, Bob overcame an injury to score his third world record.

Mathias retired undefeated, a world-record breaker on three occasions and the first person ever to win two Olympics in the decathlon. His four AAU wins constituted a record. But there was an encore. In 1956, now a professional after having starred in a movie version of his life, *The Bob Mathias Story*, the Marine officer competed in the interservice championships at Los Angeles. With 3 years of little competition or training, Bob nevertheless scored 7193 (6747)—without running the 1500. Had he run 4:50.9, as he had in his last decathlon, Mathias would have been close to the scores posted by Rafer Johnson and Milt Campbell as they earned berths on the 1956 Olympic team. Natural maturity resulted in PRs in all three throws.

In his 10 decathlons Bob had bests of 10.8, 7.14m (23-5 1/4), 15.34m (50-4 1/2), 1.90m (6-2 3/4), 50.2, 14.6, 48.83m (160-2), 4.00m (13-1 1/2), 62.20m (204-1), and 4:50.8. In nondecathlon competition he long jumped 7.44m (24-5), spun the discus 52.84m (173-4), ranking seventh in the world in 1951, put the shot 15.60m (51-2), and ran the metric highs in 13.8, a time that had been bettered by only eight men.

A 1953 graduate of Stanford, Bob had a television career, established a successful High Sierra camp, and served several terms in Congress before losing out in the Democratic sweep in 1974. He was also director of the United States Olympic Training Center in Colorado Springs. He was named one of the 13 best trackmen of all time by Cordner Nelson in his book *The Great Ones* (1970).

Table 4.11   Career Record of Bob Mathias

Date	Competition	Site	Place	Score	1985 Tables	100	lj	sp	hj	400	110H	dis	pv	jav	1500
June 10-11, 1948	Southern Pacific AAU	Pasadena	1	7094	6609	11.3	651	1313	178	52.1	15.7	4268	358	5345	4:59.2
June 26-27, 1948	AAU/Olympic Trials	Bloomfield	1	7224	6713	11.2	656	1296	183	51.0	15.1	4255	351	4793	4:55.2
Aug. 5-6, 1948	Olympic Games	London	1	7139	6628	11.2	661+	1304	186	51.7	15.7	4400	350	5032	5:11.0
June 28-29, 1949	AAU champs	Tulare	1	7556	6944	11.3	682	1379	183	51.3	15.0	4598	350	5424	4:58.2
July 28-29, 1949	vs Scandinavia	Oslo	1	7346	6786	11.4	679	1357	183	51.8	15.3	4289	370	5252	5:02.0
May 30-31, 1950	Practice	Stanford	1	7542	6926	10.8	668	1513	178	51.9	15.0	4086	366	4958	4:54.1
June 29-30, 1950	AAU champs	Tulare	1	8042 WR	7287	10.9	709	1448	185	51.0	14.7	4462	398	5559	5:05.1
Aug. 5-6, 1950	Swiss champs	Berne	1	7312	6746	11.1	651	1398	180	52.7	15.3	4552	360	4886	4:57.6
July 1-2, 1952	AAU/Olympic Trials	Tulare	1	7825 WR	7543	10.8	715	1521	189	50.8	14.6	4815	375	5909	4:55.3
July 25-26, 1952	Olympic Games	Helsinki	1	7887 WR	7592	10.9	698	1530	190	50.2	14.7	4689	400	5921	4:50.8
June 15-16, 1956	Interservice champs	Los Angeles	1	7193	6747	11.0	691	1534	182	51.9	14.9	4883	364	6220	dnr

Note. Mathias had marks of 11.08, 50.38, 14.91, and 4:51.11 auto timed in Helsinki in 1952. During his career the IAAF scoring tables were changed twice. The1934 tables were used for his first 8 meets. The 1950 tables were used for the 1952 AAU. The tables were then slightly revised and called the 1952 tables; these were used for his last 2 meets. All marks have been converted to the 1985 tables.

Figure 4.15.   Milt Campbell. (Ace Lane/Courtesy of *Track and Field News*)

Milt Campbell lost more decathlons than he won. In fact, he only won two. But his record needs no apology, only understanding.

Milt was 18 and had another year at Plainfield (NJ) High School when he first tried the 10-eventer. It was the 1952 Olympic Trials and AAU at Tulare, California. As the hometowners cheered Olympic champ Bob Mathias to a world record, they took to heart this young novice who reminded them so much of Mathias's amazing prep feats of 4 years before. Campbell made the Olympic team, defeating 1948 bronze-medalist Floyd Simmons with 7055 points on the 1950 tables. The score was good enough for seventh on the all-time list.

Table 4.12   Career Record of Milt Cambell

Date	Competition	Site	Place	Score	1985 Tables	100	lj	sp	hj	400	110H	dis	pv	jav	1500
July 1-2, 1952	AAU/Olympic Trials	Tulare	2	7055	6997	10.7	691	1356	189	50.7	14.4	4052	338	5338	5:14.1
July 25-26, 1952	Olympic Games	Helsinki	2	6975	6948	10.7	674	1389	185	50.9	14.5	4050	330	5454	5:07.2
July 3-4, 1953	AAU champs	Plainfield	1	7232	7040	10.5	681	1415	185	49.3	14.3	4091	365	4770	5:22.1
July 13-14, 1956	AAU/Olympic Trials	Crawfordsville	2	7559	7292	10.7	692	1414	190	49.2	14.1	4331	366	5196	5:06.8
Nov. 29-30, 1956	Olympic Games	Melbourne	1	7937 OR	7565	10.8	733	1476	189	48.8	14.0	4498	340	5708	4:50.6

Note. The 1952 tables were used.

At Helsinki, Milt was no threat to the high-flying Mathias. But once again he was second, scoring 6975 (6948). The next year, just out of high school, Milt tallied 7232 (7040), third on the all-time list, in annexing the AAU in his first decathlon win. Then he put the decathlon on the closet shelf, concentrating on the high hurdles at the University of Indiana. Among other successes, Campbell tied the world record of 13.4 in 1957.

Returning to the 10-event wars in 1956, Campbell again ran into a world-record holder. This time he took second to young Rafer Johnson in the AAU/Olympic Trials. But Milt's 7559 (7292) was the fourth best ever and presaged strong competition in the Melbourne Olympics. Unfortunately for Johnson and for track fans, Rafer was at less than his best with a knee injury and couldn't really press Campbell. Had Johnson been sound, there might have been a decathlon classic. Milt was superb. Facing nearly 10 hours of competition daily, he achieved the second highest score ever and came within 48 points of Johnson's world record. Milt's new Olympic record was 7937 (7565) and included no less than seven decathlon PRs. The win gave him a gold and silver in Olympic decathlons, a record bettered only by Mathias and Daley Thompson.

The second great black decathlete (and first Olympic winner), Campbell was in the classic mold, checking in at 1.91m (6-3) and 94 kilos (208 lb), with speed to spare. He was born December 9, 1933. He was an all-state fullback and an all-America free-style swimmer at Plainfield High. His best marks in a decathlon were 10.5, 7.33m (24 1/4), 14.76m (48-5), 1.90m (6-3), 48.8, 14.0, 44.98m (147-7), 3.66m (12-0), 57.08m (187-3), and 4:50.6.

Rafer Johnson

Figure 4.16.   Rafer Johnson. (From the Zarnowski collection)

At age 16 Rafer Johnson traveled 25 miles from his home in Kingsburg, California to Tulare. There he saw Olympic champion Bob Mathias set a world record in qualifying for his second Games. Concluding that he could have beaten most of the 26 contestants, Johnson decided then and there to become a decathlon man. Three years later he broke Mathias's mark and owned the world record. He broke the record twice more, finished second in the 1956 Olympics, and capped a remarkable career by winning the 1960 classic. In 7 years he competed only 11 times in the 10-eventer, but he left an indelible mark.

Johnson was handicapped by numerous injuries before and during his athletic tenure. At age 12 (he was born on August 18, 1935) he caught his left foot in a cannery conveyor belt, requiring stitches and weeks on crutches. A knee injury and torn stomach muscles hampered his first Olympic challenge in Melbourne. Three years later he suffered leg trouble and a serious

Table 4.13 Career Record of Rafer Johnson

Date	Competition	Site	Place	Score	1985 Tables	100	lj	sp	hj	400	110H	dis	pv	jav	1500
July 2-3, 1954	AAU champs	Atlantic City	3	5877	6316	11.1	627	1208	177	51.5	15.5	3736	345	4992	5:29.6
Feb. 18-19, 1955	Pan Am qualifying	Los Angeles	1	7055	7020	10.6w	730w	1320	183	49.3	15.2	4130	365	5202	5:23.0
Mar. 18-19, 1955	Pan American Games	Mexico City	1	6994	6946	10.8	719	1343	189	50.9	14.9	4383	370	5358	5:47.5
June 10-11, 1955	Central California AAU	Kingsburg	1	7985 WR	7608	10.5	749	1380	185	49.7	14.5	4720	387	5909	5:01.5
July 13-14, 1956	AAU/Olympic Trials	Crawfordsville	1	7755	7420	10.6	707	1516	185	47.9	14.4	4554	350	5559	5:12.4
Nov. 29-30, 1956	Olympic Games	Melbourne	2	7587	7422	10.9	734	1448	183	49.3	15.1	4217	390	6027	4:54.2
June 24-25, 1958	Invitational	Kingsburg	1	7780	7415	10.6	709	1537	160	48.7	14.2	4812	335	6393	5:02.0
July 4-5, 1958	AAU champs	Palmyra, NJ	1	7754	7432	10.6	684	1531	177	48.3	14.8	4721	381	6149	5:14.7
July 27-28, 1958	vs USSR	Moscow	1	8302 WR	7789	10.6	717	1469	180	48.2	14.9	4907	395	7260	5:05.0
July 8-9, 1960	AAU/Olympic Trials	Eugene	1	8683 WR	7981	10.6	755	1585	178	48.5	14.5	5198	397	7109	5:09.9
Sept. 5-6, 1960	Olympic Games	Rome	1	8392 OR	7901	10.9	735	1582	185	48.3	15.3	4849	410	6976	4:49.7

Note. The 1952 tables were used for Johnson's entire career.

back injury in a head-on auto collision enroute to his sister's high school graduation. Rafer could not even jog until February 1960, took his first sprint starts in April, and long jumped for the first time since his accident in June, 1960. Then, in July, Johnson scored his third world best. Rafer Johnson was the most gifted all-around athlete of his, and perhaps any other, era.

He won 9 of 11 decathlons, losing only his initial meet, as a recently graduated high school senior, and the 1956 Games in Melbourne, which he participated in while injured. Though Rafer was a four-sport star at Kingsburg High School, his coach, Murl Dodson, recalled the difficulty he had convincing Rafer to take up the decathlon. "I had to talk with him like a Dutch uncle. I finally convinced him." Rafer won the state high school decathlon in both 1953 and 1954. He enrolled at UCLA and, although he played basketball for the frosh team, won the Pan American Games in 1955. Later that spring he rewarded his friends and neighbors in Kingsburg with an unexpected world record.

Rafer captured the Olympic Trials in 1956 with ease, then collared the silver medal in November at Melbourne. Humble, Rafer said of Milt Campbell, "I lost to a good man." In 1958 Rafer achieved two big victories: His classmates elected him president of the UCLA student body, and, in July, he reclaimed the decathlon world record from Vasiliy Kuznyetsov at Moscow, scoring 8302 (7789) points.

By 1958 Rafer was training with soon-to-be UCLA teammate C.K. Yang of Formosa. Both made considerable progress under innovative Ducky Drake, the Bruin mentor. "In our own way we established our own United Nations on the UCLA campus," Rafer later said. Both surpassed the world record at the 1960 AAU/Olympic Trials in Eugene and battled fiercely at the Rome Olympics. Drake recalled, "Even though I was coaching both boys I was for them both doing the very best they could. I could not have a favorite." Rafer won a close struggle by outthrowing C.K. and staying close enough in the remainder of events to score 8392 (7901) points. That was the end of a decathlon career that saw him produce event bests of 10.5, 7.55m (24-9 1/2), 15.85m (52-0), 1.89m (6-2 1/2), 47.9, 14.2, 51.98m (170-6), 4.10m (13-5 1/2), 72.59m (238-2), and 4:49.7. In open competition he ran 10.3, jumped 7.76m (25-2 3/4) (making the United States Olympic team in the long jump in 1956), put 16.75m (52-11 1/2), hurdled 13.8, threw the discus 52.50m (172-3), and hurled the javelin 76.75m (251-9).

As the individual marks testify, Johnson would have been a great success had he never heard of the decathlon.

He won the 1960 Sullivan Award, symbolic of the top amateur athlete in the nation. Beginning in 1961, he recruited volunteers for President John F. Kennedy's Peace Corps. Perhaps Rafer is best remembered for his struggle to tear the gun from the hand of Sirhan Sirhan moments after presidential candidate Robert F. Kennedy was shot at the Ambassador Hotel in Los Angeles on June 5, 1968. Today Rafer is a true ambassador of sport. In 1984 he carried the Olympic torch its final leg during the opening ceremonies at the Los Angeles Games. He also serves as a spokesman for the Special Olympics.

Vasiliy Kuznyetsov

Figure 4.17. Vasiliy Kuznyetsov. (Courtesy of *Track and Field News*)

In 1962, *Track and Field News* called Vasiliy Kuznyetsov the "most consistent decathlonist of all." Indeed, Kuznyetsov's 14-year career included two Olympic medals, three European titles (still the most ever), a pair of world records, five European records, and seven national records. He won 30 competitions in 43 decathlons. Eight times he was the Soviet national champion.

Although Kuznyetsov ran into such runaway trains as Milt Campbell and Rafer Johnson in Olympic meets, he always impressed followers with his competitiveness. Ten thousand people sat in the stands through a downpour at Philadelphia's Franklin Field in 1959 to watch Kuznyetsov's attempt to break his own world record. He speared 63.79m (209-3) in conditions so soggy that the specialists could not better 63.56m (208-6), so treacherous was the footing after an hour of rain. He then needed 5:02.4 to

Table 4.14   Career Record of Vasiliy Kuznyetsov

Date	Competition	Site	Place	Score	1985 Tables	100	lj	sp	hj	400	110H	dis	pv	jav	1500
Aug. 8-9, 1953	World Youth	Bucharest	6	6784	6386	11.1	642	1226	170	52.3	16.1	4368	330	5309	5:01.8
1953		Odessa	1	7001		no marks available									5:01.8
Oct. 3-4, 1953	USSR champs	Nalchik	1	7205	6696	11.0	654	1300	169	51.7	15.8	4361	350	6076	5:01.8
Nov. 7-8, 1953		Ashkabad	1	6862	6411	11.1	693	1304	168	53.2	16.4	4453	340	5434	5:23.2
July 6-7, 1954		Kiev	1	7292 ER	7227	11.0	671	1370	180	51.0	15.4	4985	390	6082	4:54.4
Aug. 26-27, 1954	Euro champs	Bern	1	6749	6881	11.2	690	1288	170	50.7	15.4	4473	380	5620	4:58.6
Sept. 14-15, 1954	USSR champs	Kiev	1	7026	7063	11.2	693	1419	175	50.4	15.3	4521	370	6110	5:03.2
Aug. 4-5, 1955	World Youth	Warsaw	1	7264	7209	10.9	715	1350	178	50.3	15.2	4541	370	6418	5:07.2
Nov. 15-16, 1955	USSR champs	Tbilisi	1	7645 ER	7427	10.9	728	1430	183	51.0	14.9	4738	390	6533	5:11.4
July 3-4, 1956		Moscow	1	7694	7468	10.7	716	1451	183	49.6	15.4	4686	410	5961	5:02.4
Aug. 14-15, 1956	Spartakaide	Moscow	1	7733 ER	7429	10.7	710	1371	175	50.8	14.4	4921	390	6498	5:11.0
Nov. 15-16, 1956	USSR champs	Tbilisi	1	7647	7427	10.9	728	1430	183	51.0	14.9	4738	390	6533	5:11.4
Nov. 29-30, 1956	Olympic Games	Melbourne	3	7465	7330	11.2	704	1449	175	50.2	14.9	4433	395	6513	4:53.8
Aug. 31-Sept. 1, 1957	USSR champs	Moscow	1	7379	7269	11.0	709	1373	182	50.5	15.2	4762	400	5981	5:08.0
Sept. 28-29, 1957		Plzen	1	7369	7232	10.8	710	1368	180	52.2	15.1	4602	401	6556	5:18.6
May 17-18, 1958	Regional meet[a]	Krasnodar	1	8014 WR	7653	11.0	730	1449	175	49.1	14.5	4750	400	6616	4:50.0
July 27-28, 1958	vs USA	Moscow	2	7897	7596	10.8	749	1390	185	49.6	15.1	4717	400	6539	5:04.0
Aug. 20-21, 1958	Euro champs	Stockholm	1	7865	7563	10.9	734	1427	180	48.6	14.8	4857	400	5942	5:00.0
Sept. 8-9, 1958		Moscow	1	7068		no marks available									
Oct. 31-Nov. 1, 1958	USSR champs	Tbilisi	1	8042	7658	10.8	711	1463	181	49.7	14.7	4814	410	6755	5:00.8
May 16-17, 1959	Regional meet[a]	Moscow	1	8367 WR	7839	10.7	735	1468	189	49.2	14.7	4994	420	6506	5:04.6
July 18-19, 1959	vs USA	Philadelphia	1	8350	7838	10.8	740	1548	190	49.6	14.6	4981	411	6379	5:03.8
Aug. 12-13, 1959	USSR champs	Moscow	1	8006	7616	11.1	710	1434	185	49.7	14.9	5053	430	6659	5:11.0
Oct. 11-12, 1959		Yalta	1	7467	6936	10.9	708	1403	185	50.9	15.2	4912	400	6677	dnr
July 17-18, 1960	USSR champs	Moscow	1	7737	7514	10.9	703	1415	184	50.4	14.7	4561	370	6773	4:45.2
Sept. 5-6, 1960	Olympic Games	Rome	3	7809	7527	11.1	696	1446	175	50.2	15.0	5052	390	7120	4:53.8
Oct. 18-19, 1960	Ukrainian champs	Kiev	1	7845	7559	11.0	704	1551	185	50.2	14.8	5081	380	6415	5:02.8
May 28-29, 1961	Regional meet[a]	Kiev	2	7672	7011	10.7	708	1501	183	49.6	14.4	4873	390	5790	dnr

Date	Competition	Site	Place	Score	1985 Tables										
Aug. 15-16, 1961	Universaide	Moscow	1	7761	7502	11.0	710	1468	180	50.0	15.0	4899	400	6581	5:03.7
Aug. 31-Sept. 1, 1961	USSR champs	Sofia	1	7918	7603	10.9	729	1394	183	49.7	15.0	4773	410	6703	4:59.0
Oct. 8-9, 1961		Tbilisi	--	dnf		withdrew, injury, no marks available									
July 21-22, 1962	vs USA	Palo Alto	1	7825	7475	10.9	700	1448	180	51.2	14.6	4737	420	6966	5:20.0
Aug. 12-13, 1962	USSR champs	Moscow	1	7891	7556	10.8	694	1452	185	49.6	14.8	4660	420	6370	5:04.2
Sept. 13-14, 1962	Euro champs	Belgrade	1	8026	7653	10.8	691	1432	175	49.3	14.5w	4808	390	6808	4:41.0
July 20-21, 1963	vs USA	Moscow	1	7666	7479	11.0	713	1360	188	51.1	15.4	4691	410	6712	4:53.6
Aug. 14-15, 1963	USSR champs	Moscow	1	7854	7609	10.8	705	1427	186	51.4	15.3	4669	390	6819	4:33.2
July 25-26, 1964	vs USA	Los Angeles	1	7842	7488	11.0	708	1353	180	50.8	15.0	4691	447	6821	5:09.2
Aug. 29-30, 1964	USSR champs	Kiev	3	7673	no marks available										
Oct. 19-20, 1964	Olympic Games	Tokyo	7	7569	7454	10.9	698	1406	170	49.5	14.9	4381	440	6787	5:02.5

Pentathlon	Competition	Site	Place	Score	1985 Tables	lj	jav	200	dis	1500
Sept. 3, 1959	Universaide	Turin	1	4006 WR	4051	718	7279	22.2	4950	4:59.5

Note. Of 43 career meets 39 are listed. The 1934 tables were used by Russians before 1954. The 1962 tables were used in the 1964 Olympic Games.
aThe 3 Regions meet was an annual affair: Leningrad/Moscow/Ukraine.

break the world record. Bandaged, he could not quicken the pace in the final sprint and finished gamely in 5:03.8, missing the standard by seven digits. For the tremendous ovation he received, he might as well have broken the record. The crowd let him know he was a worthy champion. An hour later in the dressing room he expressed in broken English his disappointment. "Javelin no good. Can do better," he apologized as he drew "72.64" (238-4) on the floor with his finger, indicating his best jav result.

The 1.85m (6-3/4), 84 kilo (185 lb) Russian was born in the village of Kalikino on February 7, 1932. He was virtually the same age as Bob Mathias (15 months younger), yet his entire career came after Mathias retired and included four times as many meets. His finest hour may have been the 1962 European championships in Belgrade. His closest competitor, Werner von Moltke, had finished all 10 events with a score of 8022, leaving Vasiliy the task of running a 4:41.3 1500 (a 4-second lifetime best) in the final heat to overtake the German. Normally in the 5-minute range, he got 4:41.0 to win by four points (8026) and gain a third continental crown.

Because of Vasiliy's consistency, frequent competitions, and world rankings, Soviet coach Alexandr Ushakov in 1979 called him the greatest decathlete of all time. A bit of an overstatement, but Kuznyetsov was world ranked for 12 (!) consecutive seasons and led the world lists in both 1957 and 1959. He also claimed the world mark for the pentathlon in 1959. He was third, third, and seventh in three Olympic tries. After his retirement, he published an excellent training manual for the event. His career PRs include marks of 10.5, 7.49m (24-7), 15.51m (50-10 3/4), 1.93m (6-4), 48.6, 14.4, 52.00m (170-7), 4.50m (14-9), 72.79m (238-9), and 4:33.2.

1960-69

By 1960, UCLA coach Ducky Drake was preparing Johnson and new student C.K. Yang for the Rome Olympics. In July, Eugene, Oregon, hosted the combined AAU/Olympic Trials decathlon, where Johnson and Yang battled it out. Johnson recaptured the world record with a staggering 8683 (7981) points, marking the third time he broke the world mark and heralding a return to the decathlon after a severe injury in 1959 threatened to cut short his career. Both Johnson and Yang bettered Kuznyetsov's mark, but Rafer needed only nine events to wipe out the record. His first javelin throw sailed 71.10m (233-3). When the measurement was announced and that Johnson had set a world record, the Eugene crowd broke into a standing ovation. Rafer, in the middle of the infield, knelt on one knee and said a prayer. As an anticlimax, the 25-year-old plodded through the 1500, then waited until C.K. finished his 1500 in a later heat. Edstrom and Phil Mulkey, placing third and fourth, made the trip to Rome.

In Rome, Johnson would not only have to beat three other 8000-point men, he would have to conquer the tension and weariness that usually accompany an Olympic decathlon. His toughest opponents figured to be Yang and Kuznyetsov, but the latter was not in top condition. Yang beat Johnson in 7 of 10 events, yet lost the overall fight. Had he done better in the weights he probably would have won the gold medal. But take nothing away from Johnson. He set an Olympic record under the toughest conditions and came through when he had to. The UCLA teammates went into the final event, the 1500m, with Rafer leading marginally. C.K. needed to put 10 seconds between himself and Johnson. In the darkness of the Estadico Olympico, lap after lap, Johnson hung tenaciously to Yang's shoulder. A last ditch sprint by Yang couldn't shake the American, and Johnson dragged himself home in 4:49.7, less than 2 seconds behind Yang. It remains the most dramatic finish in Olympic decathlon history. Rafer said he knew he had about a 10-second working margin and that he was not going to let C.K. get away. He added "Victory obliterates fatigue. Phil Mulkey helped me with good words in the most difficult moments. I never want to go through that again, never. This is my last one and you can print that." Johnson's victory was the sixth consecutive American gold medal.

In the locker room after the competition, Johnson was mobbed with well-wishers. Nearby, Yang sat on a bench and wept. C.K. finally managed to struggle to his feet, seized Johnson's left hand, and muttered, "Nice going, Rafe." Kuznyetsov settled for his second bronze.

The Olympics of 1960 was the last won by an unbalanced decathlete. Because the 1950 tables did not reward many points for the 1500m, few decathletes worked on the event. In Rome, half of the athletes did not better 4:48.0. Neither Johnson nor Yang could run a 5-minute mile. Both were great athletes but incomplete all-arounders because, with little distance training, they totally lacked endurance. The tables were to blame.

The 1960s would be a new age for the decathlon. No longer would very talented specialists be able to dominate the event. Less-talented but better-balanced and well-trained decathletes would soon come to the fore. By the 1964 Olympic Games in Tokyo the decathlon had turned the corner.

C.K. Yang

Figure 4.18.   C.K. Yang. (Courtesy of *Track and Field News*)

Table 4.15   Career Record of C.K. Yang

Date	Competition	Site	Place	Score	1985 Tables	100	lj	sp	hj	400	110H	dis	pv	jav	1500
May 3-4, 1954	Asian Games	Manila	1	5457	5978	11.5	640	1056	187+	52.2	15.6	3310	321	4846	5:23.3
Nov. 29-30, 1956	Olympic Games	Melbourne	8	6521	6997	11.2	690	1156	195	51.3	15.0	3392	330	5788	5:00.8
Mar. 1-2, 1958		Taipei	1	7149	7080	10.8	718	1301	190	50.6	14.6	4009	340	5426	4:59.2
May 9-10, 1958		Taipei	1	7363	7182	10.8	735	1235	193	50.2	14.2	3968	360	5807	5:16.0
May 28-29, 1958	Asian Games	Tokyo	1	7101	7094	11.1	730	1268	185	50.1	15.0	4004	390	5741	5:06.1
July 4-5, 1958	AAU champs	Palmyra	2	7625	7407	10.9	730	1250	193	48.4	14.5	3794	365	6357	4:51.0
Aug. 14 & 21, 1958	SPA AAU	El Monte	1	7479	7304	10.7	700	1270	183	49.4	14.6	3828	364	6808	4:53.1
Aug. 27-28, 1959	SPA AAU	El Monte	1	7835	7494	10.6	724	1343	183	49.1	14.6	4028	431	5866	4:58.6
June 25-26, 1959	AAU champs	Kingsburg	1	7549	7246	10.6	731	1356	177	50.1	14.5	3795	433	5945	5:27.8
Apr. 22-23, 1960	Mt Sac Relays	Walnut	1	7892	7530	10.6w	721w	1332	187	49.1	14.4w	4035	425	5648	4:51.9
July 8-9, 1960	AAU champs	Eugene	2	8426	7778	10.7	775	1422	168	48.0	14.1	4221	423	7108	5:09.3
Sept. 5-6, 1960	Olympic Games	Rome	2	8334	7820	10.7	746	1333	190	48.1	14.6	3983	430	6822	4:48.5
June 29-30, 1962	AAU champs	Tulare	1	8248	7694	10.6	737	1385	188	48.0	14.3	4065	429	6632	5:18.0
Apr. 27-28, 1963	Mt Sac Relays	Walnut	1	9121 WR	8009	10.7	717	1322	192	47.7	14.0	4099	484	7175	5:02.4
Apr. 25-26, 1964	Mt Sac Relays	Walnut	1	8043	7342	10.9	691	1359	183+	50.0	14.6	4121	482	6144	5:31.4
June 26-27, 1964	AAU champs	Walnut	1	7853	7732	10.6	697	1340	193	49.0	14.4	4270	482	6508	5:18.8
July 31-Aug. 1, 1964	Invitational	Toronto	1	7646	7518	10.8	668	1333	188	48.7	14.8	4199	472	6689	5:18.4
Oct. 19-20, 1964	Olympic Games	Tokyo	5	7650	7599	11.0	680	1323	188	49.0	14.7	3959	460	6815	4:48.4

Note. The 1950/52 tables were used until May 1964, when the 1962 tables went into effect.

Born in Taitung, Taiwan, China on July 10, 1933, Yang Chuan-kwang (Americanized to C.K. Yang, pronounced *Young*) stood 1.84m (6-1/2) and weighed 81 kilos (180 lb). He became interested in track in 1954 and won the Asian decathlon that year at age 21. C.K. credits Bob Mathias, then visiting Taiwan on a United States State Department tour, for his interest in track. Mathias left a javelin with Yang.

Yang considers the Melbourne Olympic Games, in which he finished eighth, as his career turning point, as it was there, in 1956, that he met Rafer Johnson and his coach, Ducky Drake. He came to the United States 2 years later, knowing one word (*beefsteak*), enrolled at UCLA, and made rapid progress under Drake. By 1960 he was a serious challenger to training-partner Johnson. At the 1960 AAU meet in Eugene, Oregon, Yang topped the listed world record, but Johnson, running in an earlier heat of the 1500, was 200 points better. In Rome, Johnson's power made C.K. settle for the silver medal.

By 1963 Yang reached another goal, the world record. At April's Mount Sac Relays he shattered Johnson's mark by over 400 points. His mastery of the controversial fiberglass pole enabled him to clear 4.84m (15-10 1/2), higher than the tables had a score for. He actually broke the record after nine events and then became the first man to exceed 9000 points (on any table), with a 9121 (8009) score.

The year 1964 was not kind to Yang, who was now 31. He had become one of the world's premier vaulters (5.00m/16-4 3/4), but the IAAF altered the tables, reducing him from a premeet favorite to only a serious contender at the Tokyo Olympics. Injured, he finished a bitterly disappointed fifth.

Yang's career stamps him as an all-time great. He won 13 of 18 career decathlons, losing only at the Olympics and a pair of AAU meets to Johnson. He won two Asian titles and three AAU crowns. In Olympic competition he was eighth, runner-up, and fifth. He was world ranked on six occasions and topped the world in both 1962 and 1963. His career decathlon bests were 10.6, 7.75m (25-5), 14.22m (46-8), 1.95m (6-4 3/4), 47.7, 14.0, 42.70m (140-1), 4.84m (15-10 1/2), 71.75m (235-4), and 4:48.4. In open competition he had even better marks, including marks of 13.9 in the hurdles, 4:36.9 in the 1500, 5.00m (16-4 3/4) in the vault, and an unofficial 2.02m (6-7 1/2) high jump. He threw 44.59m (146-3) in the discus and 73.82m (242-2) in the javelin. He also recorded times of 23.2 and 23.5 for the 220-yard hurdles (straight and turn) and 53.0 for the 400m hurdles.

J. AUSTIN MENAUL
THE WORLD-RECORD HOLDER NOBODY KNEW

United States Olympic (pentathlon and decathlon) trials were regional in 1912. Eastern trials were held in New York, Central trials in
the Chicago area, and Western trials in Berkeley, California. In all
three cases the decathlon trials followed the pentathlon trials by a
week.

On May 18, with a points-for-place system in effect, Carlisle's famous Jim Thorpe dominated the Eastern meet with 7 points in a
four-man field. Chicago AA's Avery Brundage captured the Central
pentathlon over one other contestant, J. Austin Menaul. On the same
day, Jim Donahue competed alone in the west.

Two entries appeared for the eastern decathlon trials a week later,
Thorpe and one other. The event was cancelled and Thorpe was
added to the Olympic decathlon team on the basis of his reputation
and his pentathlon win. America's first decathlon then took place
at Northwestern University in Evanston, Illinois, on May 22 and 23.
A points-for-place system was again used, with the low score winning. Scoring tables had been used in Europe, the same tables that
would be used at the Stockholm Games. But American officials either
chose not to use them or did not have a copy. This unfortunate situation resulted in J. Austin Menaul's world record in the decathlon
going unacknowledged for over 75 years. His performances, when
calculated on the 1912A tables, were far superior to the best known
mark at the time, a 6903.920 by Sweden's Hugo Wieslander, set in
Goteburg the previous fall. The Swede's score, known at the time,
has been listed over the years as the event's first score—therefore,
its first world record (see record section). He later produced two
additional decathlon records in June 1912 that have also been considered world records. But, upon review of the new evidence from
the forgotten 1912 United States Olympic Trials, the Swede's scores
were inferior to Menaul's. Wieslander was later second to Thorpe
in Stockholm and got credited for yet another world record when
Thorpe's record was stricken from the record book a year later.

Here's how the Menaul story evolved. Searching for the American
results and using some tips by Olympic researcher Bill Mallon, I dug
up the meet results at the Library of Congress in 1987. I also checked
early German results with West German expert Reinhard Muller.
A microfilm check of Chicago's three dailies followed. The *Tribune*
was not helpful, but the *Daily News* and *Record Herald* provided summaries of the meet. The *Daily News* even ran a photo of the 1500m

start in its Saturday morning (May 24, 1912) edition. Five started: Menaul, Brundage, George Philbrook (Notre Dame), R. Leslie Byrd (Adrian College), and Eugene Schobinger (University of Illinois), who was incorrectly identified as the meet winner in a dissertation dealing with the life of Avery Brundage. Brundage later became International Olympic Committee President.

Menaul was born in Albuquerque, New Mexico; at age 24, he was a student at the University of Chicago. He won the first event (100m) in 11.4. In accordance with AAU All-Around tradition, only times of short-race winners were taken. The distance between the winner and each place was noted. Menaul could do no better than 19-10 1/2 in the long jump (fourth), but he won the shot with 41-8 1/2 and placed second in the high jump with 5-10 clearance. He ended the first day with a 53.8 win in the 400m and led with 9 points after day one. Had the then-current tables been used, his first-day score would have been 3928.26, 300 points more than Brundage and 600 more than Schobinger.

The little Maroon opened the second day with a close second to Schobinger's 16.4 hurdles. The *Daily News* reported that Menaul was only "inches back at the finish," whereas summaries in the *Record Herald* stated he was "four feet back." It conservatively gave him a 16.6. He placed fourth in each of the next three events (108-3 in the discus, 9-6 vault, and 132-10 javelin). So comprehensive were the newspaper summaries, that all three discus and javelin marks were given for all competitors. We now know that Adrian Byrd was the first American decathlete to "foul," recording one on his third discus effort. The *Record Herald* reported of Menaul that "his work yesterday was not as impressive as that on Thursday . . . the manner in which he performed leaves little doubt that he is the man most available in the west, if not the United States . . . and there is little doubt that he will be chosen to make the trip to Stockholm this summer. Perhaps most impressive about Menaul's performance was the wonderful fighting spirit he showed. Time after time when he seemed beaten he fought back on his last trial and secured himself better places." He ended with a terrific 4:37.2 1500m in a race that only two others finished. It was clearly Menaul's day. Table 4.16 shows the official results.

The 7414+ was the best score yet in the decathlon's early history. Yet J. Austin Menaul's marks produced no fanfare. His official mark was 24 1/2 points. He was named to the Stockholm team but, ironically, did not contest the decathlon. In Stockholm, only Thorpe and Wieslander topped Menaul's score. So dominating was Thorpe that no one thought to rescore Menaul's Evanston marks. Had anyone consulted the tables, they would have found Thorpe broke Menaul's world best by almost 1000 points. So Menaul's decathlon acclaim was lost in the elation of Thorpe's truly outstanding Stockholm meet. Menaul's score was buried for 75 years. Yet it was the world record in early 1912.

Menaul did compete in the Stockholm pentathlon, placing a credible fifth in a 26-man field. He finished behind Thorpe but topped both Brundage and Wieslander.

The story of the 1912 United States Olympic Trials does not end with Menaul's performance. The Western trials were held in Berkeley on May 24 and 25. Only James Donahue, 27, entered. At 5-6, 135, he was a versatile star from the Los Angeles Athletic Club. Still, the "decathlon trial" started with Donahue competing against specialists in each event. His first-day companions included Peter Gerhardt, runner-up in the Western Olympic Trials 100m. Donahue's marks, on a raw and windy day, included: 11.2, 22-3 5/8, 32-7/8, 5-8 1/4, and 51.0. The 2nd day was rainy and cold, so Donahue, according to the *San Francisco Chronicle* elected not to finish the event. He was subsequently named to the Olympic team and placed fifth (decathlon) and third (pentathlon) in Stockholm. Again, à la officials at the Central trials, scoring tables were either unavailable or unused. Donahue unbelievably (considering 2nd-day skills) was

Figure 4.19. J. Austin Menaul, number 11 on the 1910 University of Chicago track team. (Courtesy of University of Chicago Alumni Association)

on world-record pace when he dropped out. Had he continued and recorded his Stockholm 2nd-day marks he would have bested Menaul's 2-day old record by 46 points. It may have been the only time in history that an uninjured decathlete who was headed for a world record stopped after five events.

Table 4.16   Results of the 1912 Decathlon at Northwestern University

Place Winners	Score
1. J. Austin Menaul univ. of Chicago	24 1/2 points
2. Avery Brundage, Chicago AA	29 points
3. George Philbrook, Notre Dame	29 1/2 points
4. Euguen Schobinger, Illinois	30 points
5. R. Leslie Byrd, Adrian College/CAA	37 points

Manaul's Evanston performance would have been scored:

Menaul's performance				1912A Tables	1985 Tables
5/23/87	100m	11.4		857.20	732
	lj	6.06	19-10 1/2	652.10	600
	sp	12.70 +	41-8 1/4	790.00	649
	hj	1.78m	5-10	832.00	610
	400m	53.8		796.96	642
	1st-day total			3928.26	3224
5/24/87	110mH	16.6		848.00	641
	disc	33.00	108-3	678.52	524
	pv	2.89 +	9-6	557.20	331
	jav	40.48	132-10	605.375	449
	1500	4:37.2		797.20	698
	2nd-day total			3486.295	2643
	Final score			7414.555	5867

5

Decathlon: The Modern Era

Three early-decade developments, all of which altered the nature of the sport, culminated at the 18th Olympic Games at Tokyo.

The first concerned several revisions of Rafer Johnson's world record. A 1961 effort by American Phil Mulkey, 8709 (8049) points, was never ratified. It appeared that Mulkey was aided by pacers in the running events. As little a role as this may have played in the final total, Mulkey, who was the local AAU records chairman, never submitted his own mark for ratification. And a 1963 performance by Yang, who was now 3 months shy of his 30th birthday and a senior at UCLA, was the first to exceed 9000 points on any table. Yang was the first decathlete to take advantage of the new fiberglass vaulting poles, piling up over 1500 points in that event alone for 4.84m (15-10 1/2) at the Mount San Antonio College Relays. He literally vaulted off the tables, piling up 9121 (8009) points, a gaudy sum. He broke the world record before the 1500m event.

The IAAF was responsible for the second development. Recognizing the technical advancement in the vault, the IAAF approved a new scoring table in 1962. The new tables were implemented just before the 1964 Olympics, giving athletes very little time to strengthen point-weakened events. Hurt most of all was Yang. A favorite in Tokyo, he finished a disappointing fifth and retired soon after. The 1962 tables, with minor alterations in 1971 and 1977 for fully automatic timing (1/100th second), were used until the spring of 1985. They were the fairest set of tables the event has known.

West German coach Friedel Schirmer was responsible for the third alteration. Schirmer, who finished eighth at the 1952 Helsinki Olympic Games, raised coaching standards, emphasized training the "whole" decathlete, and insisted that specialists not be turned into decathletes. To Schirmer, the decathlon was an event in itself and not a collection of unrelated contests. The 10 events were still the same, but balance was the focus of the new tables and West German training. Schirmer believed that the decathlon could no longer be won by a few good events, but that it could be lost by one bad one. He promoted technical expertise and dual team competitions between nations. A surge in depth and quality by West Germans was the result of long years of planning.

The 1960s were dominated by Schirmer-trained decathletes. Even American champion Bill Toomey spent considerable time training with him. Counting two Olympic Games (1964 and 1968) and two European championships (1962 and 1966), Schirmer's athletes captured 10 of the 12 available medals.

At Tokyo, West German Willi Holdorf was the winner, with teammates Hans-Joachim Walde and Horst Beyer finishing third and sixth. Holdorf led from the fifth event but was never safe. Even during the 1500m the outcome was in doubt, and, ultimately, four athletes finished within 100 points of each other. Soviet Rein Aun, an Estonian coached by Fred Kudu, grabbed the silver medal. American Paul Herman was fourth. Yang was not in good form and dropped to fifth.

The remainder of the decade was dominated by a trio of personalities: Americans Bill Toomey and Russ Hodge and West German Kurt Bendlin, all of whom took turns setting the world mark.

By far the most impressive was Toomey, a product of a United States system rich with college clubs but poor in organization. Beginning in 1965, Toomey rarely lost, capturing every available title. He won five consecutive AAU titles, the 1967 Pan American crown, the World University Games, and the 1968 Mexico City Olympic title. In 1966, in Salina, Kansas, Toomey broke the world record, but it was never ratified because of a technicality. His 8234 (8096) points edged super-talented Russ Hodge, 8130 (7938). Hodge administered a rare defeat to Toomey in Los Angeles a month later, 8230 (8119) to 8219 (8082). Hodge's total then stood as the accepted world record because the IAAF did not accept the Salina score.

Hodge (Figure 5.1), a combination sprinter and thrower, was never able to maximize his awesome potential. At 1.86m (6-1 1/4) and 100 kilos (220 lb), he recorded lifetime bests of 10.2 in the 100m, 4:12.7 in the 1500, 18.54m (60-10) in the shot put, and 53.14m (174-4) in the discus. His fragile body was on the shelf more often than not and in 1972 he retired with three 8000-point performances to his credit.

Bendlin (Figure 5.2) was also the epitome of raw talent. He used speed (10.5 100m) and massive shoulders (a 78.40m/257-3 javelin) to capture the world record at Heidelberg in 1967. Bendlin dedicated himself to the event after a close friend was killed in an auto accident, and he made the world record his goal. The Schirmer-trained Bendlin claimed to eat several pounds of raw meat each day. He was world ranked on six occasions.

If Hodge and Bendlin had natural talent, Toomey was the model of dedication and competitiveness. He could concentrate when things were going badly. At the 1968 Olympic Games in Mexico City he missed twice at his opening height in the vault. "The Olympics were no games, Charley," Bill would say later. "When I missed those two vaults, oh my God. I've never been in anything like that before and never will again, unless maybe

Figure 5.1. Russ Hodge (768) of the USA, Werner Duttweiler (587) of Switzerland, and Hans-Joachim Walde (264) of West Germany compete in a 100m heat at the 1964 Olympics. (Courtesy of *Track and Field News*)

Figure 5.2.   Kurt Bendlin of West Germany. (From the Official Report of the Organizing Committee of the 19th Olympiad, Mexico City)

when somebody holds a gun at my head. It has to be my greatest effort ever. I could have lost the whole thing right there.'' He didn't of course. Digging deep, he cleared the bar on his final attempt and went on to set a new Olympic record of 8193 (8158) points. West Germans Walde and Bendlin grabbed the remaining medals.

After several unsuccessful attempts, Toomey finally broke Bendlin's global mark in Los Angeles in December 1969. He was the first over 8400 points, with 8417 (8309) in his 35th career decathlon. When he hung up his spikes for good, Bill owned 13 of the world's 33 8000-plus scores. From 1965 to 1969, Toomey competed in 24 decathlons. He was second to a world record, second when injured, third while ill, and failed to finish once. The other 20 times he was a winner. Witty and quotable (he once claimed he'd rather have a good case of diarrhea than sit through nine innings of baseball), he retired in 1970 for a career in broadcasting.

What a change from the '20s and '30s! Only two of the 100 world-ranked decathletes of the 1960s were Scandinavians. Eighty-eight came from the USA, the USSR, or West or East Germany. Central and Eastern Europeans showed a penchant for organization and planning. New stars Joachim Kirst of East Germany and Nikolay Avilov of the Soviet Union epitomized what was soon to be the future reign of Europeans.

Willi Holdorf

Figure 5.3.   C.K. Yang (right) congratulates new Olympic champion Willi Holdorf at the 1964 Olympic Games in Tokyo. (From the Official Report of the Organizing Committee of the 18th Olympiad, Tokyo)

West German Willi Holdorf had one of the shortest careers in the post-60s era. Coached by Bert Sumser of L.G. Bayer (Leverkusen), Holdorf made the top-10 world ranking (top ten) at age 21

Table 5.1   Career Record of Willi Holdorf

Date	Competition	Site	Place	Score	1985 Tables	100	lj	sp	hj	400	110H	dis	pv	jav	1500
Oct. 3-4, 1959		Lorrach	4	6204	6517	10.8	640	1231	173	50.0	15.9	4078	310	4552	4:39.0
Sept. 24-25, 1960	GER champs	Hamm	1	6619	6742	10.8	647	1344	170	49.6	15.3	4187	360	4861	4:58.3
Sept. 23-24, 1961	GER champs	Heilbronn	1	7238	7163	10.7	711	1346	170	48.8	15.0	4198	380	5478	4:53.4
June 23-24, 1962	GER champs	Hamm	3	7668	7427	10.6	706	1408	170	48.0	14.9	4285	390	5284	4:29.7
Sept. 13-14, 1962	Euro champs	Belgrade	5	7523	7355	10.5	708	1400	175	48.7	15.1w	4443	360	5098	4:30.0
June 1-2, 1963	vs Yugoslavia	Bad Reichenhall	3	7711	7473	10.6	702	1428	176	48.9	15.0	4380	400	5608	4:36.5
July 13-14, 1963	6 nations	Enschede	3	7059	7099	11.2	685	1436	170	48.2	15.8	4153	370	5641	4:32.9
Sept. 7-8, 1963	GER champs	Hannover	1	8085	7681	10.5	727	1468	179	48.6	14.5	4571	390	5393	4:33.5
Oct. 5-6, 1963	7 nations	Lubeck	2	7669	7427	10.6	680	1507	176	48.6	14.9	4271	390	5446	4:36.3
June 6-7, 1964	vs Switzerland	Liestal	2	7656	7490	10.6	710	1390	178	48.7	14.7	4467	410	5458	4:47.3
July 18-19, 1964	GER champs	Karlsruhe	3	7718	7581	10.6	731	1488	178	47.8	14.9	4228	430	5359	4:52.5
Aug. 29-30, 1964	All German trials	Jena	2	7869	7711	10.5	737	1480	183	48.2	14.9	4207	430	5734	4:48.8
Oct. 19-20, 1964	Olympics	Tokyo	1	7887	7726	10.7	700	1495	184	48.2	15.0	4605	420	5737	4:34.3

From. DECA, The Decathlon Association, and 1988 TAC *Decathlon Handbook.* Reprinted by permission.
Note. The 1952 tables were used for scores in 1959-63. The 1962 tables were used in 1964.

in 1961. He moved to eighth in 1962, to third in 1963, and to the top spot a year later. His career lists a dozen meets from 1959 to 1964, when he retired at 23 to try his hand at bobsledding.

In 1962 Holdorf placed fifth at the European championships in Belgrade. A year later, in Hannover, he topped 8000 (on the 1952 tables). With the IAAF scoring-table change due for 1964, he became a favorite for the Tokyo Olympics. The new scoring tables (approved in 1962 and put into effect in late spring of 1964) emphasized speed and reduced the influence of the fiberglass vaulting pole. While others, including world-record holder C.K. Yang, lost many points, Holdorf lost little to the new tables.

Holdorf had excellent speed (10.5, and never slower than 11.2 in his decathlon career), even making the 100m final at the 1964 West German championships. His Tokyo battle with Soviet Rein Aun was one of the closest in Olympic history. The West German literally ran himself off his feet in the final event and was still dazed during the awards ceremony.

Holdorf had decathlon bests of 10.5, 7.37m (24-2 1/4), 15.07m (49-5 1/2), 1.84m (6-1/4), 47.8, 14.5, 46.05m (151-0), 4.30m (14-1 1/4), 57.37m (188-2), and 4:29.7.

Bill Toomey

Figure 5.4. Bill Toomey. (Don Chadez/Courtesy of *Track and Field News*)

Bill Toomey stands apart from earlier prominent decathletes in two respects: He was considerably older at his prime and he competed a great deal more. His world record came just one month short of his 31st birthday. Compare that with Bob Mathias and Rafer Johnson, who were both record holders as teenagers. As a matter of fact, Bill didn't take the decathlon seriously until he was 24.

Bill was born January 10, 1939 in Philadelphia and high schooled in New Canaan, Connecticut. He started as a baseball player but switched to track when persuaded to compete in the state championships for small schools. He scissored over 1.73m (5-8) for the win and gave up baseball (''I can't stand it now''). Bill long jumped 7.04+m (23-1 1/2) in high school, then went to Worcester Academy in Massachusetts before entering the University of Colorado. Toomey won no real honors at Colorado, despite long jumping 7.53m (24-8 1/2) and running the intermediates in 51.7. Finishing school in 1962, Bill moved west to do graduate work at Stanford. He competed in numerous all-comer meets and won several AAU pentathlons.

"The turning point came in 1963," remembers Bill. "My ambition always had been to be the world's greatest quarter miler. But I was getting nowhere." Entering a local decathlon, he promised to become a decathlon man if his score justified an attempt. "If I could score over 6000 points I'd give it a try. If under, I would try the half mile. I made 6400. Then Bill Gairdner (Canadian Olympic decathlete) started talking up the event. In February 1964 I started becoming a decathlon man." Once underway, Toomey competed frequently. He put much into his training and preparation, working hard at the event for 6 years.

Fourth in the final 1964 Olympic Trials, Bill made up his mind not to be a spectator the next time. In between 1965 and 1966 AAU title wins, he spent 6 months in West Germany under the tutelage of Friedel Schirmer. The German experience was not a complete success, however. In 1966 Bill was hospitalized with infectious mononucleosis, a strength-sapping disease that threatened to end his career. "I can't understand it," Bill wrote at the time. "My friends drink and miss sleep and I get sick. Maybe I was cut out to be a spectator." But 1966 turned out to be a banner year. In the space of 3 weeks, Bill twice broke the world record. Unfortunately, neither counted. His 8234 (8096) at the AAU in Salina, Kansas was disallowed because of meet management irregularities (Bill has still not forgiven them). And an 8219 was good for only second place behind Russ Hodge's 8230.

From then on it was a chase after the record, with a stop along the way to capture the 1968 Olympics with a meet record of 8193 (8158) points. From 1966 through his world record in 1969, Bill competed in two dozen decathlons and won 20. He won virtually every major title open to him, even the British AAA title.

During the peak of his decathlon career Bill lived and trained in Santa Barbara, where coaches Sam Adams and Pete Petersons helped his progress. Russ Hodge was Bill's roommate, and the pair dominated the American scene during the latter 1960s. Despite an early accident that hampered his throwing, Bill's improvement was rapid. He severed a median nerve in his right wrist, lost almost all feeling, and the hand withered. He built it back with therapy, but the hand bothered his throwing throughout his career.

Table 5.2   Career Record of Bill Toomey

Date	Competition	Site	Place	Score	1985 Tables	100	lj	sp	hj	400	110H	dis	pv	jav	1500
1959	PA-AAU	Stanford	3	5349		no details available							256		
1962	PA-AAU	Stanford	1	6383		no details available							275+		
Apr. 27-28, 1963	Mt Sac Relays	Walnut	6	7057	6812	11.2	702	1167	172	48.5	15.4	3370	332	5606	4:24.9
June 28-29, 1963	AAU champs	Corvallis	5	7065	6939	11.0	726	1186	165	49.3	15.8	3495	350	6318	4:28.6
Apr. 25-26, 1964	Mt Sac Relays	Walnut	4	7466	7306	10.8	705	1194	184	47.8	15.6	3934	367	6172	4:27.8
June 26-27, 1964	Olympic Semi-Tr	Walnut	5	7571	7408	10.8	704	1172	183	47.5	14.9	3786	381	5870	4:17.8
Sept. 12-13, 1964	Olympic Trials	Los Angeles	4	7615	7466	11.0	738	1204	182	48.1	15.4	3905	381	6119	4:12.7
June 11-12, 1965	SPA AAU	Walnut	dnf	(6550)		10.6	752	1312	184	47.0	14.8	4176	395	injured	
June 30-July 1, 1965	AAU champs	Bakersfield	1	7764	7594	10.6	723	1321	183	47.7	15.1	4084	397	5722	4:24.3
July 31-Aug. 1, 1965	vs USSR	Kiev	2	7729	7563	10.7	731	1340	180	47.1	15.4	4020	400	5804	4:26.4
Aug. 11-12, 1965	vs GER	Augsburg	2	7584	7419	10.9	724	1292	184	47.6	15.4	4204	370	5751	4:28.0
Aug. 26-27, 1965	Universidade	Budapest	1	7565	7397	10.7	718	1258	180	48.5	15.6	4232	380	5936	4:26.7
July 2-3, 1966	AAU champs	Salina	1	8234 WR	8096	10.3	777	1394	195	47.3	14.8	4495	396	6063	4:30.0
July 23-24, 1966	International	Los Angeles	2	8219	8082	10.5	744	1351	190	46.8	14.7	4452	410	6419	4:20.3
Aug. 21-22, 1966	Invitational	Hamburg, WG	1	7990	7816	10.4	745	1425	190	46.8	14.5	4062	420	5036	4:35.6
June 10-11, 1967	AAU champs	Los Angeles	1	7880	7761	11.0	743	1405	191	49.0	15.0	4244	400	6703	4:32.3
July 8-9, 1967	vs British Com	Los Angeles	2	7779	7635	10.7	751	1329	189	48.4	14.9	3864	400	6053	4:34.1
Aug. 1-2, 1967	Pan Am Games	Winnipeg	1	8044	7926	10.8	759	1331	192	47.3	15.1w	4018	410	6762	4:23.3
Aug. 16-17, 1967	vs GER	Düsseldorf	1	7938	7783	10.8	736	1346	192	47.1	14.8	4176	400	5846	4:24.4
Apr. 27-28, 1968	Mt Sac Relays	Walnut	1	7800	7650	10.7	737	1355	195	49.0	15.0	4346	396	6085	4:45.3
June 6-7, 1968	AAU champs	Santa Barbara	1	8037	7900	10.6	754	1404	192	47.6	15.0	4097	410	6350	4:31.8
July 20-21, 1968	Invitational	Kassel, WG	3	7628	7442	10.4	739	1404	192	48.0	14.9	4185	370	5666	5:14.0
Aug. 9-10, 1968	British AAA	London	1	7985	7846	10.8	736	1359	195	48.4	14.7	4148	400	6426	4:21.2
Sept. 6-7, 1968	Olympic Trials	S Lake Tahoe	1	8222	8100	10.5	779	1390	200	46.4	14.95	4455	400	6419	4:47.2
Oct. 18-19, 1968	Olympic Games	Mexico City	1	8193 OR	8158	10.41	787	1375	195	45.68	14.95	4368	420	6280	4:57.18
Apr. 26-27, 1969	Mt Sac Relays	Walnut	dnf	(6509)		10.7	742	1407	195	48.3	15.2	4336	366	withdrew	
June 7-8, 1969	Special	Los Angeles	1	8169	8035	10.5	764	1375	195	47.6	14.7	4699	410	5870	4:33.0
June 27-28, 1969	AAU champs	Bakersfield	1	7818	7664	10.6	731	1399	195	48.2	14.8	4416	400	6105	5:04.4
July 18-19, 1969	International	Los Angeles	1	7938	7804	10.8	753	1406	194	47.1	15.3	4280	400	6391	4:42.9
Aug. 5-6, 1969	vs GER	Augsburg	1	8116	7990	10.5	740	1341	195	46.9	14.7	4514	380	6807	4:35.9

Date	Competition	Site	Place	Score										
Aug. 28-29, 1969	vs Poland	Warsaw	1	8075	10.5	766	1306	200	46.9	14.7	4140	398	6034	4:35.8
Sept. 13-14, 1969	Indian Summer G	S Lake Tahoe	1	8137	10.4	793	1415	185	47.0	14.7	4542	402	6879	4:58.7
Oct. 3-4, 1969	Invitational	Los Angeles	1	8277 AR	10.5	777	1406	190	47.0	14.5	4600	401	6404	4:28.9
Oct. 19-20, 1969	Special—UCLA	Los Angeles	1	8270	10.4	731	1392	190	46.4	14.2	4383	420	6438	4:30.4
Dec. 10-11, 1969	Special—UCLA	Los Angeles	1	8417 WR	10.3	776	1438	193	47.1	14.3	4649	427	6574	4:39.4
Aug. 23-24, 1970	Fresno St. University	Fresno	1	7728	10.6	729	1379	189	48.7	14.9	4206	400	5842	4:49.2
Sept. 25-26, 1971	Exhibition—UCSB	Santa Barbara	1	7244	11.0	742	1325	185	49.9	15.6	4049	379	5832	5:12.1
Aug. 21-22, 1971	Olympic qual—exhib	Santa Maria	4	7451	10.7	732	1239	190	51.4	15.2	4274	400	6388	5:07.5

Career Pentathlon Record

Date	Competition	Site	Place	Score	1985 Tables	lj	jav	200	dis	1500
July 4, 1959	PA-AAU	Stanford	1	2915	3384	696	4927	22.6	3196	4:37.2
July 16, 1960	AAU champs	Kansas City, M	1	3010	3402	675	4867	22.4	3246	4:29.9
July 8, 1961	AAU champs	Boulder	1	3484 AR	3703	711	5416	21.3	3390	4:30.4
Oct., 1961	PA-AAU		1	3165	no marks available					
July 7, 1962	AAU champs	Boulder	2	3177	3475	710	5510	21.7	2533	4:35.1
July 4, 1963	AAU champs	Seattle	1	3365	3658	739	5999	22.2	3263	4:43.8
July 25, 1964	AAU champs	Westbrook, ME	1	3687 AR	3882	725	5892	22.0	3804	4:21.4
Aug. 16, 1969	Invitational	London	1	4123 WR	4282	758	6616	21.3	4452	4:20.3

With the Olympic title safely tucked away, Bill went after the world record in 1969. He started 10 decathlons. The global standard finally came in December 1969 in Los Angeles, when Bill broke Kurt Bendlin's record with 8417 (8309) points. His numerous efforts proved that a well-trained athlete can compete frequently at a world-class level.

Bill stood 1.87m (6-1 1/2) and weighed 88 kilos (195 lb). His 4282 points in the pentathlon is the best ever and his individual marks total to an impressive 8774 points—10.41, 7.93m (26-1/4), 14.38m (47-2 1/4), 2.00m (6-6 3/4), 45.68, 14.2, 47.00m (154-2), 4.28m (14-1/4), 68.78m (225-8), and 4:12.7.

DR. TOM WADDELL, 1937-1987

Tom Waddell was born Tom Flubacher in Paterson, New Jersey. He was a gifted athlete, a paratrooper, a physician, and a world-class decathlete. At age 30, the Springfield College grad made the United States Olympic team and finished sixth at the 1968 Olympic Games in Mexico City. American Bill Toomey won the gold medal. Waddell scored 7720 points (1962 tables), placing him, at the time, in the top ten of all American performers. He recorded five lifetime bests in Mexico City.

A calm, rational man, Waddell gained notoriety during the 1980s as the organizer and prime mover of the Gay Olympic Games, an event designed to foster the Olympic notion and gay pride. Respected in track circles, Waddell fought numerous battles, including one for using the word *Olympic* in his Gay Games title. He lost that battle when the Supreme Court ruled five to four in favor of the USOC. He became a headliner again when in 1986 he contracted AIDS. He died 4 days after taking himself off all medication, on July 11, 1987. Soon after, he was the subject of a tribute held at the San Francisco City Hall.

1970-79

The 1970s produced a trio of dramatic competitions: the 1972 Munich Olympics, the 1975 USA/USSR/Poland team match, and the 1976 Olympic Games in Montreal. The decade's two brightest stars, Soviet Nikolay Avilov and American Bruce Jenner, competed in all three affairs, and each resulted in a new world record.

When Bill Toomey retired in 1970 no American was ready to fill his shoes. But the decathlon grew in popularity in the United States because Toomey had demonstrated that decathletes could compete more frequently than once or twice per year. The United States Track and Field Federation (USTFF) promoted decathlons and such collegiate organizations as the National Association of Intercollegiate Athletics (NAIA) and National Collegiate Athletic Association (NCAA) made the decathlon a scoring event at their championships. In 1969, diminutive Jeff Bennett of Oklahoma Christian was the initial NAIA winner. A year later, the NCAA held decathlons at both the college division and university division levels. Winners were Steve Gough of Seattle Pacific and Rick Wanamaker of Drake University, respectively.

A large crop of American collegians took a growing interest. John Warkentin (Fresno State) and Wanamaker won the decade's initial AAU titles. Wanamaker, a 6-9 basketball prospect who was drafted by the National Basketball Association and who had held UCLA's Lew Alcinder to his collegiate low, won the 1971 Pan American title in Columbia. Bennett, 5-9, 150 lb, won two AAU titles (1972-73). With four 8000-plus efforts, he remains the best little man in decathlon history.

In Europe, East German Joachim Kirst used first-day skills to claim the 1969 and 1971 European championships and was first in world rankings for the initial two seasons of the 1970s. His 8279 (8180) lifetime best and five 8000-plus scores stamped him as an Olympic favorite.

At the 1972 United States Olympic Trials in Eugene, Jeff Bannister, a rangy youngster from New Hampshire, put together an 8120 (7981) score to top Bennett's 8076 (7960). The trials also produced a new name, Bruce Jenner, then an unknown from Graceland College, Iowa. He grabbed the third spot from Gough, Oklahoma's Andrew Pettes, and Penn's Fred Samara. The 1500m settled everything. After nine events, Gough stood third with 7291 points, but was the slowest metric miler of the foursome. Samara was fourth at 7257 but injured. Jenner (7164) and Pettes (7156) had equal 1500 skills. Jenner, responding to the crowd, pounded home in 4:16.9 while listening to the public address announcer place him on the Olympic team. He surpassed Gough by a scant 24 points (Figure 5.5).

In Munich, Kirst led after the first day, but many were in the hunt. Nikolay Avilov was hot both days. The Odessa lawyer scored personal bests in nine events (considering auto timing), matched another, and ran

Figure 5.5.   Left to right: Bruce Jenner, Jeff Bennett, Steve Gough, Jeff Bannister, and Andrew Pettes in the 1500 meters at the 1972 Olympic Trials. (Don Chadez/From the Zarnowski collection)

up the best second-day total ever. The hurdles decided lots of things. Avilov ran the fastest time and took a lead he never relinquished en route to a world record 8454 (8466) points. Contenders Kirst, Bannister, and Poland's Ryszard Skowronek all fell in the hurdles to end their chances.

The 1500 decided the remaining medals. Leningrad soldier Leonid Litvenyenko leaped from eighth to second, thanks to a superior 4:05.9. But officials failed to place Bennett in the final heat with all the medal contenders. He had easily won an earlier heat but was denied the opportunity to race for the medal. All remaining contenders knew exactly how fast they had to run in the 1500 to surpass Bennett's score. Poland's Ryszard Katus, who later defected to the United States, edged Bennett by 10 points, running the 1500m one and one-half seconds faster than he needed to for the bronze. Jenner, still unknown, was a respectable 10th.

On the field, Avilov was both imposing and clownish. He moved with an easy grace, appearing relaxed, almost nonchalant. At times he kept a wary eye on his opponents while appearing to be napping. But his seriousness of purpose at Munich turned the games into a rout.

The second of the 1970s super competitions brought the American, Soviet, and Polish teams together in Eugene in 1975. It matched all the 1972 medalists with European champion Skowronek (he won in 1974), Jenner, and American find Fred Dixon (Figure 5.6). So deep were the great scores that Katus, third at the previous Olympics, placed 10th (!) with 8005 points.

Figure 5.6. Fred Dixon made two U.S. Olympic Teams and was ranked first in the world in 1977. (Don Chadez/Courtesy of *Track and Field News*)

Jenner, much improved, led the world list in 1974. He had recovered from nagging injuries, moved to San Jose with a new bride, and dedicated his life to the 10-eventer. He worked at the decathlon as no American had worked before. Not particularly swift or springy, Jenner's forte was consistency, technique, and stamina. Also, he did not have a bad event. He poured it on in Eugene, upping Avilov's world mark to 8524 points. It was a hand-timed performance, then acceptable as a world record. "I started thinking world record right after the first event. I never stopped thinking it," Jenner said as he recorded a smashing victory over all three Olympic medalists. Dixon also stamped himself as an Olympic threat, besting Avilov, Skowronek, Litvenyenko, Samara, Gough, Craig Brigham, and Katus. The six-man USA team averaged 8150 points, itself a world best. Some experts still refer to the Eugene team match as the finest decathlon of all time.

Jenner completed the 1975 campaign by edging Dixon for the Pan American title in Mexico City. The two Americans were ranked first and second worldwide for the season.

At the 1976 Montreal Olympics, Jenner and Avilov battled a final time. Using four personal bests, Jenner totaled a gaudy 8618 (8634) points for his third world record in 13 months.

Jenner felt that he would stand sixth or seventh after the first day, but found himself third behind young West German Guido Kratschmer and Avilov. Jenner did not take the lead until the pole vault, but pulled away with a career-best 1500 and bowed out with the gold medal and the record. Kratschmer, Avilov, and Sweden's Raimo Pihl claimed the next places. Dixon nearly fell in the hurdles and no-heighted in the vault. Samara placed 15th. Jenner's victory was one of will, of obsession. He had the good fortune to accomplish his feat in front of a prime-time viewing audience who sat up and took notice. His last lap in the 1500m (61 seconds) and the resulting victory lap were an experience none who watched will likely forget. Bruce walked away from competition on the spot, even leaving his vaulting poles in the stadium tunnel. He chose his offers carefully and made a career as a TV and movie personality.

The year 1977 saw Fred Dixon step into Jenner's shoes. After a close win over Warkentin at the AAU meet, Dixon beat new Soviet challenger Alexandr Grebenyuk at the annual USA/USSR team match. Short on training, Dixon still piled up 8393 (8397) points under very unfavorable conditions in Bloomington, Indiana. Hot (over 96 degrees both days), humid weather, headwinds, and a soft track prevented an 8500+ score (Figure 5.7). Dixon ended the season ranked first in the world.

A year later, Grebenyuk returned Dixon the favor at the 1978 USA/USSR match in the Ukranian town of Donetsk. The muscular Russian, a clerk from Rostov-on-the-Don, captured the European championship over injured Guido Kratschmer and a talented but brash Britisher, Daley Thompson, one of the also-rans behind Jenner at Montreal. While only 20, Thompson had recorded a 8467w (8470) score and won the Commonwealth Games in Edmonton, Canada. The 1978 Prague loss to Grebenyuk toughened the youngster psychologically and offered a lesson in big-meet preparedness. Daley was determined not to let losing happen again. He would not lose another decathlon for nine seasons. Kratschmer captured the West German title with 8498 (8496) points, then the second best score of all time.

The year 1979 saw Kratschmer again win his national title, while Thompson shunned 10-event competitions, content to work on individual events.

Figure 5.7. While Alexandr Grebenyuk looks on, Nikolay Avilov (r) congratulates Fred Dixon on a 8393-point performance at the 1977 USA versus USSR meet. (From the Zarnowski collection)

Many of America's best were injured. But Bob Coffman, a raw, rangy Texan, proved a pleasant surprise. He edged John Crist for the AAU crown, added the Pan Am title, then stunned the Russians with a 8274 (8248) performance in Quebec City. He was the last American to lay claim as the world's top-ranked decathlete.

The 1970s saw Americans claim the top individual ranking in four seasons. Soviets, Germans, and an Austrian shared the other six top individual spots. And only one man who had been a force at the beginning of the decade remained near the top at its close, Nikolay Avilov. The lanky lawyer was still a world-class competitor in 1980, but when he was unable to make the Soviet Olympic team (for a fourth time) for the Moscow Games, he subsequently retired, his Olympic accomplishments intact.

Nikolay Avilov

Figure 5.8. Nilolay Avilov. (Larry Crewell/From the Zarnowski collection)

A three-time Olympian, Soviet Nikolay Avilov was best when it really mattered. At 20, he finished fourth to Bill Toomey in Mexico City. Four years later he returned to the Olympics to eliminate Toomey's world record in Munich. In Montreal, Nikolay was third behind Bruce Jenner's new global standard. Fourth, first, and third in three Olympic tries. Only Daley Thompson can match that mark.

Born in Odessa on August 6, 1948, Avilov spent much of his youth playing soccer and basketball. He long jumped 7.01m (23-0) at 17 and tried the decathlon with junior implements a year later (6991 on 1962 tables). Nikolay attempted his first international decathlon 5 days shy of his 19th birthday, placing fifth in the Soviet championships.

Table 5.3 Career Record of Nikolay Avilov

Date	Competition	Site	Place	Score	1985 Tables	100	lj	sp	hj	400	110H	dis	pv	jav	1500
July 31-Aug. 1, 1967	USSR champs	Moscow	5	7266	7344	no marks available									
Sept. 16-17, 1967	vs GDR	Madeburg	6	7505	7768	10.9	720	1205	200	49.7	14.9	3964	390	5318	4:36.6
Aug. 17-18, 1968	USSR champs	Leninakan	3	7905	7905	10.8	746	1331	207	50.5	14.6	4474	410	5714	4:39.7
Oct. 18-19, 1968	Olympics	Mexico City	4	7909	7795	10.9	764	1341	207	49.9	14.5	4664	410	6012	5:00.8
May 31-June 1, 1969	vs GER	Heidelberg	1	7945	7814	11.4	752	1368	200	49.2	14.6	4088	400	6112	4:27.2
Sept. 17-18, 1969	Euro champs	Athens	4	7779	7648	no marks available									
Nov. 1-2, 1969	USSR champs		—	dnf		no marks available									
May 30-31, 1970		Nalchik	1	7764	7620	11.2	738	1339	204	49.1	15.0	4186	410	5876	4:28.9
June 27-28, 1970	vs GDR	Tallinn	18	7021		11.5	723	1333	205	50.2	14.3	4108	410	5003	4:32.0
July 23-24, 1970	vs USA	Leningrad	1	7685	7554	11.0	734	1298	204	50.5	14.4	4370	410	5617	4:37.4
Aug. 15-16, 1970	vs GER	Leningrad	2	7874	7741	11.3	748	1315	212	49.2	14.3	4386	420	5496	4:34.6
Sept. 4-5, 1970	Universaide	Turino	1	7803	7675	10.9	738	1373	209	49.5	14.8	4086	420	5556	4:33.5
May 30-31, 1971		Nalchik	2	8096	7958	11.7	706	1326	204	50.7	14.1	4443	400	5684	4:23.0
July 2-3, 1971	vs USA	Berkeley	4	7570	7434	11.81	688	1333	203	51.8	14.9	4475	440	5900	4:33.9
Aug. 11-12, 1971	Euro champs	Helsinki	—	dnf		11.1	744	1410	192	50.1	15.01	4299	430	withdrew	
June 9-10, 1972	vs GER	Moscow	1	8084	7976	11.1	741	1398	208	49.0	14.4	4606	455	5930	4:34.8
July 14-15, 1972	USSR champs	Moscow	1	8115	7996	11.00	768	1436	208	48.50	14.2	4420	440	5800	4:27.8
Sept. 7-8, 1972	Olympics	Munich	1	8454 WR	8466	11.39	721	1410	212	50.4	14.31	4698	400	6166	4:22.8
Aug. 18-19, 1973	Universaide	Moscow	2	7903	7869	11.58	711	1343	208	50.0	14.68	4374	440	6090	4:34.6
Sept. 22-23, 1973	Euro Cup f	Bonn	8	7677	7625	10.9	730	1453	204	49.5	14.55	4518	450	5858	4:37.1
June 7-8, 1975	USSR champs	Tallinn	1	8229	8126	11.0	735	1447	201	50.4	14.3	4532	450	6594	4:26.6
Aug. 9-10, 1975	vs USA/Pol	Eugene	3	8211	8121	11.35	733	1422	210	49.9	14.1	4424	440	6566	4:35.8
Sept. 6-7, 1975	Euro Cup	Bydgoszcz	2	7973	7947	10.9	752	1468	207	50.0	14.41	4430	445	5948	4:39.6
June 10-11, 1976	USSR champs	Kiev	1	8336	8248	11.23	752	1481	208	48.16	14.2	4848	420	6324	4:29.6
July 29-30, 1976	Olympics	Montreal	3	8369	8378	11.40	744	1445	214	49.85	14.20	4560	430	6228	4:26.26
July 16-17, 1977	Euro Cup f	Kishinyov	1	7934	7912	11.51	699	1457	209	50.07	14.86	4494	450	6140	4:38.8
Aug. 13-14, 1977	vs USA/Can	Bloomington	4	7880	7858	11.37	729w	1402	207	50.25	14.86	4710	440	6504	4:43.0
Sept. 17-18, 1977	Euro Cup	Lille	5	8053	8042	11.47	735	1418	207		14.35	4626	440	6124	4:31.0
July 29-30, 1978	vs USA	Donetsk	—	dnf					195	dnf	14.56	4694	440	withdrew	
Sept. 28-29, 1978		Odessa	1	8165	8053	10.9	732	1425	206	49.1	14.3	4550	440	6212	4:37.6
June 20-21, 1980	Olympic Trials	Moscow	7	8062	8067	11.33	737	1432	208	50.34	14.66	4648	440	6714	4:39.2

Note. The 1962 tables were used during Avilov's entire career.

At 24, in Munich, Nikolay was at his best. Standing 1.90m (6-3) and 86 kilos (190 lb), he put together the kind of meet decathletes dream about. The margin of victory was 400+ points and his second day was the best ever. At a postmeet interview, he commented, "I would prefer to have all the events in one day. The 400 and 1500 are my most difficult events. If they were not included I could start a decathlon every day." He was always a favorite of athletes and fans because of his confidence and good humor. A ready smile lighted up his strong bronze face.

Records indicate Nikolay finished 28 of 31 career meets, winning 11. A Ukranian (representing Dynamo of Odessa), he was coached nevertheless by Estonian Fred Kudu. A lawyer, he retired in 1980 after a chance at a fourth Olympics fell short. His PRs were 11.00, 7.79m (25-6 3/4), 14.81m (48-7), 2.14m (7-1/4), 48.16, 14.20, 48.48m (159-1), 4.55m (14-11), 67.14m (220-3), and 4:22.8.

Bruce Jenner

Figure 5.9. Bruce Jenner. (Dave Drennan/Courtesy of *Track and Field News*)

Late in the day on July 30, 1976, Bruce Jenner retired from the decathlon, pleased to have achieved all of his goals in an activity that had consumed his life for 3 years. He left the event with an impressive new world record of 8618 (8634), two previous world records, an Olympic title, and three straight number-one world rankings—the only decathlete to be so honored. A dozen years later, he is still the American-record holder.

Soon after his Montreal win, Bruce had this to say about the title that goes along with the Olympic crown: ''Am I the world's greatest athlete? I am if anybody is. That takes in such a great area. What I am, really, is the world's greatest decathlete. Many use the 10-eventer as an objective test of total athletic ability. It's

Table 5.4   Career Record of Bruce Jenner

Date	Competition	Site	Place	Score	1985 Tables	100	lj	sp	hj	400	110H	dis	pv	jav	1500
Apr. 22-23, 1970	Drake Relays	Des Moines	6	6991	6805	11.2	654	1162	191	53.3	16.3	3876	411	5861	4:39.0
June 3-4, 1970	NAIA champs	Billings	3	6808	6623	11.7	640	1283	189	54.0	16.4	3990	413	6037	4:58.6
Apr. 15-16, 1971	Kansas Relays	Lawrence	1	7330	7162	11.4	640	1377	183	51.5	15.6	4201	427	5971	4:25.6
Apr. 21-22, 1971	Drake Relays	Des Moines	2	7401	7257	11.4	678	1401	178	50.8	16.1	4221	449	6297	4:34.1
May 24-25, 1971	All Comers	Lawrence	1	7533	7389	11.2	680	1384	179	51.5	15.3	4395	447	5985	4:27.4
June 3-4, 1971	NAIA champs	Billings	1	7403	7266	11.2	683	1340	172	50.8	15.0	4245	442	5916	4:35.9
June 11-12, 1971	AAU champs	Porterville	21	5704	5788	11.6	660	1379	nh	51.0	15.5	4198	nh	6088	4:38.6
Apr. 20-21, 1972	Kansas Relays	Lawrence	3	7399	7254	11.4	667	1325	189	51.5	15.4	3900	442	6278	4:32.0
Apr. 26-27, 1972	Drake Relays	Des Moines	1	7678	7563	11.4	655	1326	193	50.9	15.3	4244	457	6948	4:24.7
May 31-June 1, 1972	NAIA champs	Billings	3	7422	7248	10.9	692	1362	196	51.0	15.0	3868	412	5574	4:52.4
July 3-4, 1972	Olympic Trials	Eugene	3	7846	7699	11.1	684	1374	195	50.4	15.3	4378	440	6318	4:16.9
Sept. 7-8, 1972	Olympic Games	Munich	10	7722	7664	11.35	653	1356	192	49.5	15.59	4224	455	6602	4:18.9
Apr. 25-26, 1973	Drake Relays	Des Moines	5	7253	7095	11.3	664	1362	190	51.2	15.4	3944	397	6404	4:50.8
June 1-2, 1973	USTFF	Wichita	2	7770	7621	11.0	698	1397	200	50.2	15.0	4460	412	6026	4:36.5
June 22-23, 1973	AAU champs	Porterville	5	7617	7477	11.0	648	1300	183	49.9	15.2	4392	450	6294	4:27.8
Aug. 4-5, 1973	WUG Trials	U Park, PA	dnf	(1347)	(1342)	11.4	615	(withdrew, pinched nerve in back)							
Apr. 17-18, 1974	Kansas Relays	Lawrence	1	8240	8127	11.0	722	1412	198	49.0	14.7	4650	457	6394	4:15.3
May 24-25, 1974	Late afternoon	Santa Barbara	1	7991	7843	11.0	697	1435	193	48.5	14.5	4348	425	6020	4:19.6
June 14-15, 1974	AAU champs	Richmond	1	8245	8202	11.15	732	1434	191	48.2	14.7	4410	480	6474	4:13.6
Aug. 3-4, 1974	vs USSR/W Ger	Tallinn	1	8308	8211	10.9	727	1437	198	49.0	14.7	4910	470	6350	4:22.7
Jan. 24-25, 1975	N.Z. Games	Christchurch	1	7665	7581	11.48	696	1404	192	50.1	15.53	4266	450	6242	4:30.4
Apr. 23-24, 1975	Drake Relays	Des Moines	1	8138	8021	11.0	696	1455	195	49.3	14.7	4518	450	6640	4:18.1
June 21-22, 1975	French champs	Colombes	1	8058	7985	11.0	705	1459	194	48.9	14.9	4440	450	6310	4:22.7
July 12-13, 1975	AAU champs	Santa Barbara	dnf	(6500)	(6392)	11.1	707	1443	198	48.8	15.1	4716	nh	6094	dnr
Aug. 9-10, 1975	vs USSR, POL	Eugene	1	8524 WR	8429	10.7	717	1525	201	48.7	14.6	5000	470	6552	4:16.6
Oct. 18-19, 1975	Pan Am Games	Mexico City	1	8045	8024	11.09	700	1523	197	49.12	14.95	4792	460	6400	4:42.9
Apr. 21-22, 1976	Drake Relays	Des Moines	1	8250	8163	11.1	712	1399	198	49.4	14.5	4808	460	6864	4:19.4
June 24-25, 1976	Olympic Trials	Eugene	1	8542w WR	8465	10.7	721w	1404	200	48.6	14.3	5170	460	6926	4:16.4
with unofficial auto timing:				8448	8459	10.93				48.72	14.57				4:16.60
July 29-30, 1976	Olympic Games	Montreal	1	8618 WR	8634	10.94	722	1535	203	47.51	14.84	5004	480	6852	4:12.61

Note. At Olympic Games 400 and 1500 were auto timed, but rounded. When 1977 adjustment to tables was made, the 47.51 400 made a one-point difference and the official score was adjusted to 8617.

a good test, superior to any yet devised,'' Jenner continued with modesty, ''But that doesn't help me when I stand up at a tee and try to hit a golf ball. Then I'm just another guy who can't hit straight.''

Born October 28, 1949, in New York, Jenner was a fine athlete in Connecticut schools. He enrolled at Graceland College in Lamoni, Iowa, as a left-handed quarterback but was soon introduced to the decathlon by L.D. Weldon, a veteran who had tutored Jack Parker, third-place finisher at Berlin. Bruce made his debut at the 1970 Drake Relays, finishing sixth. His progress was steady, one notable exception being the 1971 AAU meet, when he performed a rarity—no-heighting in both the high jump and the pole vault to finish 21st with a measly 5704 points. But most of the time Bruce was upward bound. He won the NAIA in 1971 and was a surprise third placer in the 1972 Olympic Trials, finishing a solid 10th in the Munich Olympics. The day after the 1972 trials, a headline in an Oregon newspaper screamed, ''Bannister, Bennett Make Team, But Who's Jenner?''

The year 1973 was down for Jenner, including some injuries. But in 1974 he started his inexorable move to permanent glory with 8308 points. He defeated the Russians and West Germans and clinched the first of his three top-spot world rankings.

Bruce at 1.88m (6-2), 88 kilos (194 lb), was even better in 1975. He did lose the AAU with another no-mark vault, breaking a seven-meet win streak, but he bounced back with a world record of 8524 points. And, of course, there was 1976—only three meets, but a pair of all-time highs in the trials and the Olympics.

During Bruce's Montreal victory lap my thoughts drifted back to a warm, August afternoon in 1973. Jenner had just walked off the Penn State track. I doubted that he'd ever compete again. The Graceland College senior had broken his foot during the season's first indoor meet and lost 2 months' training. He'd then injured his back throwing the javelin, resulting in an infected vertebra. At University Park, Pennsylvania, he had withdrawn dejectedly from the trials of the World University Games (WUG) after an 11.4 and 6.15m (20-2 1/4) for the first two decathlon events. Injured and discouraged, he returned home to Connecticut with lots to ponder. Three years later, to the week, he was the Olympic champion and world-record holder. I remembered the Penn State scene and did not know whether to laugh or cry. We laughed, of course. Everyone did. We also cheered like hell. I had a lump in my throat. A happy, emotional drama was being acted out before our eyes. Those of us who knew what difficulty the principal actor had in preparing for his part, how many obstacles he had overcome, found the entire Montreal decathlon tender and touching.

In his 7-year career, Jenner started 28 decathlons and finished 26 of them. He had 16 wins and won 11 of his last dozen matches. Scoring over 8000 points 10 times and over 8200 on 7 occasions, he averaged almost 8300 for his top-10 performances. His personal bests include marks of 10.7, 7.32m (24-1/4), 15.35m (50-4 1/2), 2.03m (6-8), 47.51, 14.3, 51.70m (169-7), 4.88m (16-0), 69.49m (227-11), and 4:12.61. His best nonflip long jump was 7.22m (23-8 1/4) and best auto times included 10.93 and 14.57 in the 1976 Olympic Trials.

AMERICAN COLLEGIATE INTEREST

The year 1970 was a watershed year for the decathlon in the United States. The NCAA followed the lead of the NAIA and offered the decathlon as part of their national championship event. The decathlon is now a mainstay of collegiate conferences and relay carnivals.

Before 1970 the decathlon was an occasional collegiate event. Eighteen American collegians, using 1962 tables, had surpassed the national class score of 7000 points a total of 55 times. Since 1970, more than 250 United States collegians have surpassed 7000 over 1350 times. Some universities have emphasized the event more than others. Table 5.5 lists the number of 7000-point performances and performers from various colleges and universities since 1970.

Table 5.5   Collegiate 7000-point Performances

School	Performances	Performers
Mount St Mary's	109	10
Brigham Young	77	17
Washington State	42	9
Washington	41	6
U.C.L.A.	37	10
Pennsylvania	37	5
Fresno State	35	9
Arizona State	30	8
L.S.U.	30	6
U.C.—Irvine	23	8
U.S.C.	23	5
Azusa Pacific	22	8
Houston	21	6
Penn State	20	4

School	Performances	Performers
Southern Illinois	20	2
U.C.S.B.	19	6
Tennessee	19	4
Oklahoma Christian	18	3
Abilene Christian	17	6
Arizona	17	5
Maryland	17	5
Nevada—Reno	16	3
Oregon	16	2
Kansas	15	4
George Mason	15	3
Virginia	15	2
Auburn	14	4
Fisk	14	1
Campbell	13	3
Eastern Michigan	13	1

Note. From DECA, The Decathlon Association, and 1988 TAC *Decathlon Handbook.* Reprinted by permission. Totals from 1970 to 1984 are scored on 1962 tables; all scores after 1984 are scored on new (1985) table.

1980s

So far, the 1980s have clearly been the Daley Decade. Despite increased interest, competition, and high-level performances worldwide, Britain's Daley Thompson has reigned supreme. For the decade's first 7 years Thompson claimed a pair of Olympic golds, set four world records, won three European and two Commonwealth crowns, and went undefeated. Daley was ranked first in the world for 1980, 1982, 1983, 1984, and 1986. He did not compete in 1981 or 1985. Only in 1987 and 1988 did he experience defeat.

Thompson opened the 1980 season with a world mark at Gotzis, an Austrian village that could serve as a setting for *The Sound of Music*. He surpassed Bruce Jenner's 8617 (at Montreal) by 5 points, then lost the record a month later to Kratschmer, as the West German added another 27 points at Bernhausen. Sadly, both Kratschmer and American Olympic Trials winner Bob Coffman (Figure 5.10) (over Lee Palles and Fred Dixon) were victims of the Jimmy Carter–led boycott and unable to compete. In Moscow, however, later that summer Thompson won easily over Soviets

Figure 5.10.   Bob Coffman was the last American decathlete to be ranked first in the world (1979). (Jeff Johnson/Courtesy of *Track and Field News*)

Yuriy Kutsenko, Sergei Zhelanov, and a young Austrian, Georg Werthner.

Many of the big names took 1981 off. In the United States, Brigham Young's Tito Steiner, an Argentine, set a collegiate best of 8279w (8304). In 1982 the global standard fell on three occasions. Thompson again blasted the mark at Gotzis, now the site of early-season record performances. Thompson's 8704 (8730) was the first score over 8700 on the 1962 tables.

In August, young West German Jürgen Hingsen added another 19 points to the record at Ulm, setting the stage for the first of the great Thompson/Hingsen clashes. They met in Athens, amid 100 degree temperatures, with the continental crown at stake. Daley won this struggle and won the world record back with a gutty 1500 performance. Outside the new Athens stadium, hours after his record, we talked.

"It was great fun, eh? But the 1500 was ha-a-a-ard," he said.

"It looked like Kratschmer said something to you with a lap to go," I mentioned.

"Yeah," Daley replied. "He passed me going into the turn and said, 'Let's pick it up.' Pick it up! I glanced at him and he looked terrible. If he could look that bad and still wanted to run, I guess I could too. So we ran together."

"When you arrived at the finish line why didn't you collapse like everyone else?" I asked.

"There were bodies everywhere. I wanted to, but couldn't find room to lie down." Our conversation ended minutes later when young fans discovered him.

Hingsen was second at Athens, East Germans Siegfried Stark and Steffen Grummt third and fourth, and Werthner fifth. Later in the season, Daley claimed the Commonwealth crown.

In 1983 the West Germans left their mark, recording six of the world's top 10 scores. Hingsen, now called the "German Hercules," took back the world record at Bernhausen in June with 8779 (8825) points, a scant 61 better than his fast-improving young teammate, Siegfried Wentz. The veteran Kratschmer was third with 8457 (8462), and pity poor German, Andreas Rizzi. His 8369 (8331) score ranked no better than fourth nationally, leaving him off the world championship team.

But the real honors of 1983 went to Thompson, who claimed the first world championship over Hingsen and Wentz at Helsinki in August. Daley and I again got together to chat after his Helsinki win, this time in a TV booth.

"You didn't come here totally healthy, did you?" I asked.

"Did it show much?" he replied.

"Well, you fooled them all in the 400 and before they realized you weren't in peak shape it was too late. Right?"

"I was trying so-o-o hard," he smiled.

I continued, "One day it's going to catch up with you, and you'll have to run like hell in the 1500."

"Never happen," he said.

Later in 1983, Canadian Dave Steen captured the World University Games and Grigoriy Degtyarov upped the Russian record to 8538 (8580) in Moscow.

Both Thompson and Hingsen spent much of their winters training in Southern California. While Daley prepared in San Diego, the German used Santa Barbara as base. "Sometimes, at the end of a hard session, I do the last one for Daley," Hingsen once remarked. He did not need to be reminded of Thompson and the challenge of 1984. He went home in June and rebroke the world mark with 8798 (8832) points at Manheim.

Once again Thompson rose to the challenge. At the Los Angeles Olympic Games, where this time a boycott claimed the Soviets, East Germans, and Poles, Thompson came within an eyelash of the world mark (it was later given to him after a reread of the hurdles photo and a change in the scoring tables) in turning back Hingsen, Wentz, Kratschmer, and a talented young Frenchman, William Motti. Daley's postmeet antics were as noteworthy as his record. He had prepared several T-shirts. One worn during a victory lap exclaimed on the front, "Thanks L.A. for a great time and a Great Games . . . ." And on the back it continued, "But what about the T.V. coverage?" This was in reference to ABC's chopped coverage of his and other events that weren't red, white, and blue.

A second T-shirt was better. I handled interviews at the press tent until Daley was released from doping control. As he entered the tent and faced over 100 worldwide reporters and cameras, he revealed another T-shirt that read, "Is the World's Second Greatest Athlete Gay?" The tent stirred and a British type quipped, "Daley, is your shirt referring to Jürgen Hingsen or Carl Lewis?" "Take your pick," Daley quipped back. The interview was off and running.

John Crist (Figure 5.11), who finished sixth, was the first American at Los Angeles. Other Americans included Jim Wooding, who placed seventh, and Tim Bright, twelfth. Daley became only the second to win two Olympic decathlon gold medals. Unlike the other, Bob Mathias, he did not retire. Just 26 and enjoying the competition, he rested the following season.

The year 1985 was a case of the best of the rest. Hingsen failed to finish his only 10-eventer. Torsten Voss (Figure 5.12), who was second to GDR teammate Uwe Freimuth at Gotzis and himself the world junior record holder, won against the Soviet Union and also won the European Cup "A" Finals. And Mike Ramos, University of Washington, became the first American in 6 years to win an international affair. His World University Games win in Kobe, Japan resulted in a rank of 10th in the world. He became the first American in five seasons to make the list. No Americans appeared in the world rankings (by *Track and Field News*) from 1981

Figure 5.11.   John Crist won three U.S. national titles and the 1984 U.S. Olympic Trials.

to 1984. Also in 1985, a newly approved IAAF scoring table, which did little to alter top scores and much to confuse the decathlon community, was introduced.

Guido Kratschmer opened the 1986 season at Gotzis with a stunning 8519 win—at age 33! Thompson survived the Commonwealth Games in Edinburgh, Scotland (cold, rainy conditions and a third-attempt clearance at his opening vault attempt), winning over Canada's David Steen and New Zealand's Simon Poelman. Soviet Grigoriy Degtyarov won the Moscow Goodwill Games. He had upped the Soviet record in 1984 with 8652 (8698 on new tables), only to lose it to Alexandr Apaitchev (8709) when the tables changed. Dave Johnson captured the TAC crown and Ramos nudged William Motti's United States collegiate standard off the books.

For Daley Thompson, it was more of the same. At the European championships in Stuttgart he once again turned back Hingsen and Wentz (8811, 8731, 8676), running his head-to-head score versus Hingsen to 8-0.

In 1987 Thompson, now 29, had a down year. Injured, he competed anyway in the world championships at Rome, placing ninth. It was his first defeat in nine seasons. Hingsen, also injured, with broken ribs, did not finish. In their absence, East Germany's Voss, a 24-year-old mechanic, ran up a workman-like 8680 to hold off Wentz and Soviet Pavel Tarnovetsky. Daley, although appearing loose and relaxed on the infield,

Figure 5.12. In winning the 1987 World Championship, East German Torsten Voss became the first decathlete in 9 years to defeat Daley Thompson. (Theo Van De Rakt/Courtesy of *Track and Field News*)

was not talkative to the press in Rome. On the first day, an exchange with a reporter went like this:

"Do you have anything to say?"

"Nothing, thank you."

As the interviewer had no intention of going away, Daley added, "Are you deaf?"

"If you win, can I come back for an interview?"

"No, thank you."

At Rome, the first American was Gary Kinder, who finished 12th, one spot in front of Rob Muzzio. Siggi Wentz claimed the World University Games, whereas Voss and Motti won European Cup titles in 1987. Tim Bright was the TAC victor with a PR score of 8340.

1988 saw great depth of 8000 plus scores but no one threatened Thompson's world record. Even Daley had a down year. He arrived at the Seoul Olympic Games slightly injured and short on conditioning. Only Helge Lövland (1920) had won an Olympic decathlon title past his 30th birthday. East German youngster (23) Christian Schenk PRd in Seoul with

8488 points, 89 more than Voss. Dave Steen edged Daley for the bronze medal.

No other decade saw as much record action. The world mark was pushed up on eight occasions, the most in any decade. The improvement was a scant two and one-half percent, but there was an explosion of high-level scores. In the first 7 years of the 1980s, 103 performers bested 8000 points on 397 occasions, far more than all of the previous decades combined (the 1970s had 70 and 205, the 1960s, 12 and 31). The Soviets, with Fred Kudu providing much guidance, had incredible depth. In 1986 alone they claimed 13 performers and 19 performances over 8000! From 1980 to 1987 the Russians claimed 22 spots in the world rankings versus 17 for West Germany and 19 for the GDR. The rest of the planet combined for the remaining 22 spots.

For Americans, it was the worst decade yet, but not all the news was negative. John Crist won three TAC crowns and John Sayre opened eyes with a windy 8381 at the 1985 TAC meet. The years 1986 and 1987 provided a ray of hope, as nine Americans surpassed 8000 points, now judged to be a world-class cutoff.

Guido Kratschmer

Figure 5.13.   Jürgen Hingsen (left) and Guido Kratschmer. (Horstmuller/Courtesy of *Track and Field News*)

Guido Kratschmer is a man of few words. Quiet belies an inner drive that has made him the dean of present world-class decathletes and one of the most competitive of decathletes in modern years. "He is a good fighter," remarks West German national coach Wolfgang Bergman when asked to describe one of his prize pupils from USC Mainz. Well past 30, Kratschmer, a physical education teacher, has been a world-class decathlete for 15 years.

In 1986, at age 33, Kratschmer posted his second-best career performance in a career that has seen twenty-three 8000+ scores. Had it not been for a little bad luck, the West German (born on Jan. 10, 1953) would have been the first four-time Olympic decathlete. He was runner-up to Bruce Jenner in 1976 and fourth to

Table 5.6   Career Record of Guido Kratschmer

Date	Competition	Site	Place	Score	1985 Tables	100	lj	sp	hj	400	110H	dis	pv	jav	1500
May 12-13, 1972	Decathlon Day-DLV	Bonn	1	7550	7379	10.7	698	1433	188	50.6	14.7	3636	410	5668	4:38.7
June 2-3, 1973	vs POL/SOV	Weinheim	18	7488	7329	10.6	719	1428	185	49.7	14.8	3828	390	5392	4:49.1
July 7-8, 1973	Club meet	Hannover	7	7326	7157	10.9	712	1355	190	51.3	14.5	3576	390	5392	4:49.1
May 17-18, 1974	Club meet	Bonn	1	7888	7736	10.6	741	1424	198	49.6	14.4	3820	400	5946	4:36.5
July 13-14, 1974	WG Jr champs	Trostberg	2	7894	7763	10.8	745	1476	194	49.1	14.0w	3646	410	6162	4:41.5
Aug. 3-4, 1974	vs USA/SOV	Tallinn	4	7856	7713	10.7	748	1431	195	50.3	14.4	4234	380	6046	4:37.3
Sept. 6-7, 1974	Euro champs	Rome	3	8132	8108	10.83	760	1356	201	48.44	14.29	4210	420	6358	4:31.0
May 24-25, 1975	vs Rumania	Pliezhausen	1	8005	7866	10.5w	751	1468	192	50.7	14.0w	4470	410	6146	4:49.3
June 21-22, 1975	WG champs	Lubeck	1	7746	7600	10.8	736	1236	201	49.3	14.2w	4378	410	5318	4:48.9
July 19-20, 1975	EuCp Poiana	Brason	4	7697	7628	10.89	662	1414	198	48.78	14.72	4382	410	6168	4:54.96
Sept. 6-7, 1975	Euro Cup f	Bydgoszcz	9	7538	7467	11.01	716	1447	192	49.1	14.85	3172	400	5890	4:34.6
May 15-16, 1976	International	Gotzis	1	8381	8302	10.7	783	1468	195	48.5	14.1	4486	430	6908	4:31.9
July 29-30, 1976	Olympics	Montreal	2	8411	8407	10.66	739	1474	203	48.19	14.58	4570	460	6632	4:29.1
Sept. 4-5, 1976	GER champs	Hannover	1	8265	8148	10.5	742	1439	195	48.8	14.3	4560	440	6498	4:35.4
June 18-19, 1977	GER champs	Bernhausen	6	7852	7813	10.81	775	1326	191	49.92	14.31	4132	420	5822	4:40.2
Aug. 27-28, 1977	Euro Cup sf	Hannover	1	7972	7928	10.83	748	1474	194	49.34	14.49	4250	440	5644	4:38.8
Sept. 17-18, 1977	Euro Cup f	Lille	3	8086	8061	10.90	766w	1499	186	49.34	14.43	4574	440	5700	4:27.1
May 27-28, 1978	International	Gotzis	1	8410	8411	10.78	777	1606	188	47.98	14.08	4640	450	6084	4:26.46
July 29-30, 1978	GER champs	Bernhausen	1	8498 ER	8493	10.60	784	1656	191	47.64	14.01	4546	450	5880	4:28.3
Aug. 30-31, 1978	Euro champs	Prague	–	dnf		dnf, injured, withdrew									
June 15-16, 1979	GER champs	Krefeld	1	8484	8476	10.54	761	1518	196	48.44	14.17	4674	440	6580	4:24.7
Sept. 1-2, 1979	Euro Cup	Dresden	2	8053	8037	11.04	740	1490	198	48.67	14.46	4340	450	6368	4:48.2
May 17-18, 1980	International	Gotzis	2	8421	8425	10.87	781	1492	196	48.36	14.16	4612	440	6418	4:21.21
June 13-14, 1980	GER champs	Bernhausen	1	8649 WR	8667	10.58	780	1547	200	48.04	13.92	4552	460	6650	4:24.15
July 16-17, 1980	Liberty Bell	Philadelphia	–	dnf		10.91	724	1570	189	49.7	14.49	3f withdrew			
Sept. 6-7, 1980	vs USSR	Lage	1	8185	8175	10.86	723	1516	191	49.54	14.50	4356	450	6896	4:25.7
June 13-14, 1981	vs USSR	Leningrad	4	7847	7799	11.08	727	1482	190	49.83	14.71	4238	430	6044	4:33.86
Aug. 8-9, 1981	GER champs	Lage	3	8066	8029	10.90	683	1418	194	48.78	14.33	4676	450	6204	4:29.41
Aug. 29-30, 1981	Euro Cup f	Birmingham	5	8095	8069	11.13	739	1470	195	48.80	14.41	4558	450	5816	4:27.99

(Cont.)

Table 5.6 (Continued)

Date	Competition	Site	Place	Score	1985 Tables	100	lj	sp	hj	400	110H	dis	pv	jav	1500
June 27-28, 1982	vs USA	Baton Rouge	--	dnf		dnf 100 meters, injured, withdrew									
Aug. 14-15, 1982	GER champs	Ulm	3	8215	8194	10.80w	724	1519	191	49.25	14.31	4718	480	5746	4:29.55
Sept. 7-8, 1982	Euro champs	Athens	9	8015	8030	11.02	726	1477	191	49.03	14.65	4384	450	6154	4:24.24
June 4-5, 1983	WC Trials	Bernhausen	3	8457	8462	10.83	765	1596	200	48.81	14.37	4718	460	6248	4:26.91
Aug. 12-13, 1983	World champs	Helsinki	9	8096	8059	10.86	735	1499	194	48.61	14.29	4656	460	5224	4:36.43
Sept. 10-11, 1983	Euro Cup A	Sofia	11	7946	7905	11.06	729	1440	192	48.99	14.42	4494	450	5590	4:35.95
June 8-9, 1984	Olympic Trials	Manheim	3	8420	8429	10.63w	715	1667	198	49.07	14.15	4648	480	6752	4:45.75
Aug. 8-9, 1984	Olympics	Los Angeles	4	8326	8357	10.80	740	1593	194	49.25	14.66	4728	490	6940	4:47.99
July 13-14, 1985	GER champs	Ulm	2		8223	11.01	727	1627	188	49.13	14.37	4762	490	6372	4:45.53
Sept. 7-8, 1985	Euro Cup A	Krefeld	--	dnf	dnf	10.96	728	1105	withdrew						
May 24-25, 1986	Invt.	Gotzis	1		8519	10.82	776	1662	193	48.75	14.09	4842	460	6382	4:32.36
Aug. 27-28, 1986	Euro champs	Stuttgart	--		dnf	10.62	750	withdrew							
July 9-10, 1988	GER champs	Rhede	--	dnf		dnf, injured, withdrew									

Note. The 1962 tables were used until 1985. Kratschmer participated in youth decathlons in 1970 and 1971. His best scores were 7009 in 1970 and 7617 in 1971.

Daley Thompson and two teammates in 1984. He barely missed making the 1972 Olympic team (beaten by veteran Werner von Moltke) at age 19. And the boycott ruined his chances in 1980. Guido was injured and did not compete in Seoul in 1988.

Guido's promising career has been beset by bad luck. In 1978 he was the favorite at the European championships in Prague but was brought down by injury a few steps out of the 100m blocks. In 1980 he exploded for a world record of 8649 points (8667), but his nation joined the boycott and, instead of competing, he watched from the stands as Daley Thompson won the gold medal.

As his countrymen Jürgen Hingsen and Siegfried Wentz ran up higher scores, Guido stayed at it. 1988 marked his 17th at the event, but an Achilles tendon injury sidelined him once again. He has captured six straight national crowns (1975-80), competed in six European Cups, and in four European championships. He set four national records, two European marks, and one world record. Today no one commands more respect from fellow athletes.

Guido's PRs include marks of 10.54, 7.84m (25-8 3/4), 16.94m (55-7), 2.03m (6-8), 47.64, 13.85/13.6, 49.74m (163-2), 4.90m (16-3/4), 69.40m (227-8), and 4:21.21.

Jürgen Hingsen

Figure 5.14. Valeriy Kachanov leads Jürgen Hingsen, Daley Thompson, and Steffen Grummt in the 1500 meters at the 1982 European Championships. (Fionnbar Callanan/Courtesy of *Track and Field News*)

The tall German Jürgen Hingsen set world records in each of 3 successive years (1982-84) but lives in the shadow of Britain's Daley Thompson. Jürgen won the 1982 West German championships in Ulm with a new global standard 8723 (8741 on 1985 tables), only to lose the record to Thompson at the European championships in Athens later that year. Similar events occurred in 1983. Hingsen again upped the world mark, this time in Bernhausen, with a score of 8779 (8825), and again he was no match for Thompson at the world championships in Helsinki. There was more of the same in 1984. Jürgen improved the world mark to 8798 (8832) at Mannheim, but Thompson took the Olympic gold in Los Angeles. Interestingly, all of the German's records have come on home soil. None of Thompson's have been set in his homeland.

The "German Hercules" was born January 25, 1958, in Duisburg. He came to prominence in 1977 at 19 with a win over the

Table 5.7 Career Record of Jürgen Hingsen

Date	Competition	Site	Place	Score	1985 Tables	100	lj	sp	hj	400	110H	dis	pv	jav	1500
June 17-18, 1977	vs USSR Jr	Bernhausen	1	7464	7402	11.57	717	1325	209	51.12	15.01	3732	400	5638	4:34.09
July 23-24, 1977	vs France Jr	Pulversheim	1	7614	7483	11.5	732	1380	213	51.0	15.0 w	3716	400	5686	4:29.4
Aug. 19-20, 1977	Euro Jr champs	Donyetsk	3	7524	7465	11.65	721	1358	204	50.01	15.50	3808	400	5972	4:28.3
July 29-30, 1978	WG champs	Bernhausen	3	7966	7944	11.34	757	1382	218	49.50	14.87	3874	390	6190	4:19.0
Aug. 30-31, 1978	Euro champs	Prague	13	7640	7584	11.39	739	1394	198	50.22	15.33	3972	410	5866	4:28.6
June 15-16, 1979	GER champs	Krefeld	2	8240	8218	11.28	757	1506	216	49.64	14.79	4208	430	6022	4:12.3
Sept. 1-2, 1979	Euro Cup f	Dresden	10	7820	7790	11.49	762	1384	213	49.76	14.91	3870	420	5560	4:28.1
Sept. 10-11, 1979	Universaide	Mexico City	2	8034	8020	11.15	767	1404	213	48.95	14.32	4092	440	5618	4:42.2
May 17-18, 1980	International	Gotzis	3	8276	8277	11.18	783	1448	214	48.48	14.49	4198	420	6112	4:21.1
June 13-14, 1980	GER champs	Bernhausen	2	8407	8409	10.97w	788w	1506	212	48.78	14.78	4168	430	6500	4:15.6
July 16-17, 1980	Liberty Bell	Philadelphia	--	dnf	-----	11.30	738	1426		withdrew					
June 13-14, 1981	vs USSR	Leningrad	1	8051	8024	11.34	771w	1495	208	49.91	14.61	4222	420	5718	4:22.86
Aug. 8-9, 1981	GER champs	Lage	2	8168	8146	11.10	742	1480	206	49.27	14.52	4102	450	6150	4:22.47
Aug. 29-30, 1981	Euro Cup f	Birmingham	2	8138	8139	11.38	769	1458	204	49.25	14.71	4080	450	6394	4:21.31
May 22-23, 1982	International	Gotzis	1	8529	8541	10.95w	792	1595	211	47.86	14.52	4500	460	5810	4:23.87
Aug. 14-15, 1982	GER champs	Ulm	1	8723 WR	8741	10.74w	785	1600	215	47.65	14.64	4492	460	6310	4:15.13
Sept. 7-8, 1982	Euro champs	Athens	2	8517	8530	11.01	758	1552	215	48.10	14.61	4474	480	6042	4:22.22
June 4-5, 1983	World champs qual	Bernhausen	1	8779 WR	8825	10.92	774	1594	215	47.89	14.10	4680	470	6776	4:19.74
Aug. 12-13, 1983	World champs	Helsinki	2	8561	8599	10.95	775	1566	200	48.08	14.36w	4330	490	6742	4:21.59
June 8-9, 1984	OG qual	Mannheim	1	8798 WR	8832	10.70	776	1642	207	48.05	14.07	4936	490	5986	4:19.75
Aug. 8-9, 1984	Olympics	Los Angeles	2	8673	8695	10.91	780	1587	212	47.69	14.29	5082	450	6044	4:22.60
Sept. 7-8, 1985	Euro Cup A	Krefeld	--	dnf	dnf	dsq, withdrew									
June 14-15, 1986	GER champs	Bernhausen	2		8458	10.98	762	1657	200	50.05	14.42	4750	480	6378	4:25.94
Aug. 27-28, 1986	Euro champs	Stuttgart	2		8730	10.87	789	1646	212	48.79	14.52	4842	460	6438	4:21.61
Sept. 3-4, 1987	World champs	Rome	--		dnf	11.26	767	1533	nh	withdrew					
June 18-19, 1988	International	Gotzis	10		8133	11.17	765	1548	196	49.52	14.64	4484	440	6232	4:28.74
Aug. 20-21, 1988	Invt.	Lage	1		8360	11.26	744	1562	201	49.46	14.28	4680	480	6386	4:26.63
Sept. 28-29, 1988	Olympic Games	Seoul	--		dnf	dsq, withdrew									

Russian Juniors. He was third (to Thompson) at the 1978 European Junior championships, has a pocketful of silver medals, and has won 8 of 28 career decathlons, including two national crowns. But Hingsen has faced (and benefited from) major competition in West Germany from Siegfried Wentz and former world-record holder Guido Kratschmer. In Seoul Jürgen suffered the ultimate decathlon embarrassment. He was disqualified in the 100 meters for 3 (!) false starts and sadly withdrew.

Hingsen has not bested Thompson in 10 direct contests, but his best performances added up would take him over an unbelievable 9300 points (9323 to be exact)! He has been world ranked on seven occasions and posted several outstanding indoor septathlon marks. His PRs are 10.70, 8.04m (26-4 1/2), 16.57m (54-4 1/2), 2.18m (7-1 3/4), 47.65, 14.07/13.8w, 50.82m (166-9), 5.10m (16-8 3/4), 67.42m (221-2), and 4:12.3.

Figure 5.15.   Only Daley Thompson is left standing at the finish of the 1500 meters at the 1982 European Championships. (Knut Ed. Holm/Courtesy of *Track and Field News*)

Daley Thompson claims more decathlon honors than anybody before him. He is the only man in any event to win two Olympic golds and a world championship. Add four world records, three Commonwealth titles, and a pair of European crowns and you have Francis M. "Daley" Thompson.

Born of a Scottish mother and Nigerian father who named him Adodele (an African name shortened to "Dele" and by his friends to "Daley"), he is as ferocious on the track as he is amiable off.

Daley was born in Kensington, London, July 30th, 1958. He stands 1.84m (6-1/2) and weighs 88 kilos (194 lb). His athletic career started at boarding school, where he gave early notice of his all-around ability. He competed in his first decathlon when he was 16. A year later he won the AAA title and qualified for the Montreal Games, where he finished a little-noticed 18th. But Bruce Jenner noticed him and claimed later that Daley never stopped asking him questions. The next year, in his first match-up with Jürgen Hingsen, Daley won the European Junior title. He went on to score 8000 twice that year. And he was still a teenager.

His first major international win came in Edmonton, Canada, in 1978, the Commonwealth Games title. But he lost the European championships in Prague to Russian Alexandr Grebenyuk. It was his last defeat until 1987. A new world record of 8622 (8648) and the Olympic title in Moscow followed in 1980. In 1982 he trained in San Diego and London. Daley was rewarded with two more world records, the second coming in Athens, where he captured the European championships with 8743 (8774). In 1983, despite groin and back injuries, Daley went on to win the initial world championships in Helsinki with a score of 8666 (8714). But by 1984, Hingsen, the ever-present nemesis, had pushed the world mark up several notches, posing an Olympic threat. When Daley heard that Hingsen expected to leave Los Angeles with the gold medal in 1984, he grinned. ''The only way he'll do that is to steal mine,'' he said.

It was during the discus competition in Los Angeles that Thompson revealed the truest part of his character, the remarkable competitiveness that was to stamp his entire career. After two awful throws and a near lifetime best by Hingsen, Daley suddenly found himself trailing. ''It was like I went to the cliff and looked over the edge,'' he later remarked. But he never hesitated on his final toss. It went out low but with terrific force, landing at 46.56m (152-9), pushing him back to a lead he never relinquished. For Thompson's career, *that* was his moment of truth.

Commonwealth and European titles followed in 1986, the latter over Hingsen again. He was married in 1987. Injured, he stuck it out in the world championships in Rome before losing his crown to workmanlike Torsten Voss of the GDR—his first defeat in nine seasons. It was a similarly difficult year in 1988. A daughter arrived, and another injury reduced his effectiveness at the Seoul Olympic Games. Again an East German, this time Christian Schenk, replaced him as Olympic champion. Daley barely missed the bronze medal.

What's in the future for Daley? He shares with Bob Mathias the distinction of being the only two-time Olympic gold medalist

Table 5.8 Career Record of Daley Thompson

Date	Competition	Site	Place	Score	1985 Tables	100	lj	sp	hj	400	110H	dis	pv	jav	1500
June 28-29, 1975	Welsh AAA	Cwmbran	1	6685	6523	11.0	699	1074	197	50.2	16.8	3142	290	5188	4:31.0
Aug. 30-31, 1975	AAA Jr champs	Cwmbran	1	7008	6845	10.7w	721	1080	193	49.6	15.8	3220	330	5328	4:36.5
Oct. 4-5, 1975	vs France Sr	Cwmbran	2	7100	6935	10.8w	711	1177	190	49.3	16.0	3184	340	5704	4:30.9
Apr. 22-23, 1976	AAA Sr champs	Cwmbran	1	7684	7517	10.8	740	1279	198	49.1	15.5	3878	380	5692	4:20.3
June 26-27, 1976	vs Neth/Spain/Den	Copenhagen	10	6639	6649	10.6	726	1194	193	48.6	15.3	3646	nh	5134	4:41.2
July 29-30, 1976	Olympics	Montreal	18	7434	7330	10.79	719	1310	191	48.15	15.98	3636	420	4518	4:29.55
Sept. 4-5, 1976	International	Talence	4	7905	7748	10.5	757	1359	195	48.1	15.4	3770	440	5192	4:24.9
May 21-22, 1977	International	Gotzis	1	7921	7865	10.71w	772	1338	200	48.35	15.24	3728	420	5578	4:23.8
June 25-26, 1977	vs Spain/Den/Ita	Madrid	1	8190	8097	10.5	760	1385	207	47.4	15.1	3960	480	5032	4:29.0
July 30-31, 1977	Euro Cup sf	Sittard	1	8124	8082	10.70	754	1384	201	47.31	15.26	4170	470	5448	4:30.4
Aug. 19-20, 1977	European Jr champs	Donyetsk	1	7647	7568	11.02	725	1372	206	47.59	14.95	3822	380	4972	4:35.53
May 27-28, 1978	International	Gotzis	2	8238	8226	10.77	795w	1389	203	47.76	14.85	4140	460	5690	4:29.11
Aug. 7-8, 1978	Commonwealth G	Edmonton	1	8467w	8470	10.50w	811w	1443	203	47.85	14.92	4168	480	5660	4:25.78
Aug. 30-31, 1978	European champs	Prague	2	8289	8258	10.69	793	1469	204	47.77	15.28	4352	420	5980	4:22.80
July 28-29, 1979	GER Invt.	Flein	--	(6954)dnf	(6875)	10.45	760	1482	206	47.30	14.39	4314	nh	6192	dnr
May 17-18, 1980	International	Gotzis	1	8622 WR	8648	10.55	772	1446	211	48.04	14.37	4298	490	6538	4:25.5
July 25-26, 1980	Olympics	Moscow	1	8495	8522	10.62	800	1518	208	48.01	14.47	4224	470	6416	4:39.9
June 13-14, 1981	vs Canada	Saskatoon	1	7936	7797	10.47	784	1454	205	47.64	14.81w	4166	500	6254	dnf
May 22-23, 1982	International	Gotzis	1	8704 WR	8730	10.50w	795	1531	208	46.86	14.31	4434	490	6052	4:30.55
Sept. 7-8, 1982	European champs	Athens	1	8743 WR	8774	10.51	780	1544	203	47.11	14.39	4548	500	6356	4:23.71
Oct. 4-5, 1982	Commonwealth G	Brisbane	1	8410	8424	10.66	771	1517	204	47.59	15.00	4220	490	6298	4:43.98
June 7-8, 1983	vs Canada	Etobicoke	1	8509w	8529	10.44w	763	1538	209	48.73	14.46w	4220	510	6204	4:42.58
Aug. 12-13, 1983	World champs	Helsinki	1	8666	8714	10.60	788	1535	203	48.12	14.37w	4446	510	6524	4:29.72
May 23-24, 1984	UCLA	Los Angeles	--	(7938)dnf	(7806)	10.54	764	1566	187	48.17	14.26	4722	500	6334	dnr
Aug. 8-9, 1984	Olympics	Los Angeles	1	8798 WR	8847	10.44	801	1572	203	46.97	14.33	4656	500	6524	4:35.00
May 17-18, 1986	vs France	Arles	1		8667	10.56	781	1539	198	47.52	14.35	4762	490	6328	4:30.04
July 27-28, 1986	Commonwealth G	Edmonton	1		8663	10.37	770	1501	200	47.30	14.22	4372	510	6082	4:39.63
Aug. 27-28, 1986	European champs	Stuttgart	1		8811	10.26	772	1573	200	47.02	14.04	4338	510	6278	4:26.16
Sept. 3-4, 1987	World champs	Rome	9		8124	10.67	752	1509	201	48.61	14.87	4518	480	5414	4:48.78
Aug. 20-21, 1988	Invitational	Lage	--		dnf	10.84	697		198		14.79	4502		5934	dnr
Sept. 28-29, 1988	Olympic Games	Seoul	4		8306	10.62	738	1502	203	49.06	14.72	4480	490	6404	4:45.11

and with Austrian Georg Werthner the accomplishment of completing four Olympic decathlons. But he dearly loves the training and competition, feeling most comfortable on the field with other athletes. Don't be surprised to see the name "Thompson/GBR" on the Barcelona program in 1992.

Daley's competitive ability has brought him unparalleled decathlon success. He has won 19 of 31 meets and every major title open to him. Interestingly, despite having competed in four decathlons in Wales and one in Scotland, he has never done a 10-eventer in England. His lifetime bests add up to a stunning 9289 points: 10.26, 8.11m (26-7 1/4w), 16.10m (52-10), 2.14m (7-1/4), 46.86, 14.04, 48.62m (159-6), 5.20m (17-3/4), 65.38m (214-6), and 4:20.3.

Figure 5.16.   Christian Schenk. (duomo/Steven E. Sutton)

Born in Rostock, East Germany, on February 9, 1965, Christian now stands 2.01m (6-7) and weighs 92 kilos (203 lb). As a youngster he was primarily a straddle high-jumper (taking third at Spartakaid in the high jump when he was just 16), but he converted to multi-events at age 18. By age 23 he was the Olympic champion. Ironically he claimed the East German junior crown in 1983, then went 5 years without a decathlon win.

In 1983, then 1.96m (6-5) and 80 kilos (176 lb), he raised eyebrows by taking a runner-up spot to Soviet Walter Kulvet at the European Juniors. A year later, while still a junior, he posted an 8000+ score. At 20 (in 1985) he made surprising progress, placing fourth in the Euro Cup A and scoring over 8000 on three occasions. But he was consistently overshadowed by GDR

Table 5.9 Career Record of Christian Schenk

Date	Competition	Site	Place	Score	100	lj	sp	hj	400	110H	dis	pv	jav	1500
June 18-19, 1983	vs USSR	Moscow	24	7558	11.38	735	1286	206	49.85	15.27	3756	380	5990	4:19.91
Aug. 25-26, 1983	Euro Jr Champs	Vienna	2	7552	11.51	735	1336	213	49.51	15.10	3976	360	5434	4:22.52
July 20-21, 1984	Olympic Day	Potsdam	5	8036	11.54	728	1426	216	49.23	15.06	4474	420	6598	4:24.11
May 25-26, 1985	International	Gotzis	5	8163	11.21	761	1520	220	49.09	15.02	4020	400	6648	4:26.47
July 6-7, 1985	vs USSR	Dresden	8	7851	11.37	729	1482	200	49.24	15.04	4380	420	5740	4:22.11
July 20-21, 1985	Olympic Day	Potsdam	2	8092	11.23	751	1472	218	49.11	15.00	4094	400	6246	4:19.11
Sept. 7-8, 1985	European Cup	Krefeld	4	8141	11.30	757	1427	216	48.93	15.04	4002	420	6714	4:21.38
May 24-25, 1986	International	Gotzis	dnf	—	11.32	withdrew								
May 23-24, 1987	International	Gotzis	5	8147	11.31	769	1494	217	49.58	15.11	4614	420	6092	4:31.05
June 6-7, 1987	vs USSR	Dresden	2	8228	11.25	742	1435	212	49.24	14.91	4632	460	6254	4:25.88
July 4-5, 1987	European Cup	Basel	5	8161	11.43	757	1462	210	49.52	15.15	4322	460	6404	4:22.70
Sept. 3-4, 1987	World Champs	Rome	5	8304	11.42	763	1530	225	51.34	15.03	4726	450	6142	4:23.55
May 28-29, 1988	National Champs	Cottbus	3	8225	11.44	723	1477	220	49.13	15.16	4624	470	6106	4:25.77
June 18-19, 1988	International	Gotzis	5	8330	11.36	771	1476	220	49.23	14.99	4486	440	6138	4:16.02
July 16-17, 1988	International	Talence	2	8475	11.10	763	1517	222	49.50	15.09	4760	470	6008	4:21.41
Sept. 28-29, 1988	Olympic Games	Seoul	1	8488	11.25	743	1548	227	48.90	15.13	4928	470	6132	4:28.95

Note. All scores are on 1985 tables. Original scores for meets before 1985: Moscow (7614), Vienna (7552), Potsdam (8053).

teammates Uwe Freimuth and Torsten Voss. Freimuth remains the third-highest performer ever (8792 points in 1984), and Voss became the 1987 world champion.

Christian missed the entire 1986 season, withdrawing from the Gotzis opener after one event. But in 1987 he posted two additional lifetime best scores, a runner-up 8228 versus USSR and a fifth-place 8304 at the World Championships under atrocious conditions. It was in the latter meet in Rome that he dazzled the crowd as lightning from a coming storm danced in the skies. He leaped 2.25m (7-4 1/2), then passed 2.28m (7-5 3/4), a height that would have broken the world decathlon best, only to miss closely at 2.31m (7-7). In decathlon history no one has ever attempted such a height.

The year 1988 was even better for the single medical student. His coach, Dr. Klaus-Gerhard Schlottke of SC Empor Rostock (club) had Christian ready. He improved in each of four meets, getting three PR scores. After a third-place finish (8255) at the GDR nationals in Cottbus, Christian PRd at Gotzis with an 8330 fifth-place finish. One month later the tall German improved to 8475 behind another Christian, France's Plaziat.

He was primed in Seoul. Two days before the affair even Voss was picking him as a winner. He stood ninth after two events but got rolling with four PRs and equaled a fifth in the next six events to lock up the Olympic title. He scored another PR, 8488, to capture Olympic gold and equaled the decathlon world best in the high jump, 2.27m (7-5 1/2) in the process.

Christian has been world-ranked three times and has the following career bests: 11.10, 7.71m (25-3 1/2), 15.48m (50-9 1/2), 2.27m (7-5 1/2), 48.90, 14.91, 49.28m (161-8), 4.70m (15-5), new jav-62.54m (205-2), old jav-67.14m (220-3), and 4:16.02. Eight of the 10 marks were achieved in 1988.

6

The Olympic Games

France's Baron Pierre de Coubertin promoted a revival of the games banned by the Emperor Theodosius in A.D. 393. The modern version was first held in Athens in 1896. In the ancient games, wars were postponed so that the Olympics could go on. Today the reverse is true.

Each Olympiad brings a renewed interest in the decathlon. Indeed, the Olympic Games are the showcase for the event and it suffers when wars or boycotts prevent the world's greatest athletes from gathering. They first did so for a decathlon in 1912 at Stockholm.

Stockholm, 1912

JULY 13-15, 29 COMPETITORS, 12 NATIONS

Native American Jim Thorpe had already won the pentathlon, placed fourth in the open high jump, and taken seventh in the long jump. He had acquired a following and the crowds, which averaged over 20,000 daily, swelled on the morning of the first Olympic decathlon. Thorpe looked casual and relaxed. Jim was 1.80m (5-11), deep chested, with a thick neck. He was slightly bow-legged and rocked on his heels as he walked. Stockholm spectators, watching him dominate the competition, exclaimed, "Isn't he a horse!" as Thorpe lumbered around the infield, chest held high.

Because of the large number of entries, the decathlon was spread over 3 days. Americans (six) and Swedes (eight) combined to form almost half the field of 29. Three events were held on the first and third days and the hurdles and discus reversed on the second. Twenty-three athletes

Figure 6.1.   Jim Thorpe competed in three long jumps in the 1912 Olympics. He was seventh in the open competition, first in the pentathlon, and third in the decathlon. (Courtesy of Bob Wheeler)

began day 2, but only 16 started the final day. Only a dozen completed all 10 events. Partly because the decathlon was spread out over so many days, Thorpe had a mesmerizing effect on the crowds. Everywhere they looked, there he was breaking the tape at the finish line, hurling implements, or clearing crossbars. He led after the first day and was no worse than fourth in any event. Several of his marks, notably the high jump and hurdles, were world class. The final decathlon events were held on the last day of the fifth Olympiad and Thorpe's victories were instantly acclaimed by King Gustav and the crowd. Jim's two appearances before the Swedish monarch at the victory stand drew the loudest ovations. For his decathlon victory he was awarded a jewel-encrusted chalice from Czar Nicholas of Russia. His win in the pentathlon earned him a bronze bust of the king of Sweden. Presenting Thorpe the bust, Gustav exclaimed, "Sir, you are the greatest athlete in the world." "Thanks, king," Thorpe supposedly said.

Thorpe's victory over Sweden's Hugo Wieslander stretched almost 700 points. His world-best score would not be surpassed for 16 years. Jim also managed to somehow fit in a baseball game in Stockholm, going one for two as the rightfielder on a USA Olympic Exhibition Team.

Jim became a hero in the United States and was honored with a ticker-tape parade down New York's Broadway. Months later, however, he was declared a professional for playing baseball for money years before. His

Figure 6.2. Hugo Wieslander in the decathlon long jump. (From the Official Report of the Organizing Committee of the 5th Olympiad, Stockholm)

Table 6.1   Results of 1912 Olympic Decathlon, Stockholm

Results		100	lj	sp	hj	400	110H	dis	pv	jav	1500	1912A Total Points Tables	1985 Total Points Tables
1. Jim Thorpe	USA	11.2	679	1289	187	52.2	15.6	3698	325	4570	4:40.1	8412 WR	6564
2. Hugo Wieslander	SWE	11.8	642	1214	175	53.6	17.2	3629	310	5040	4:45.0	7724	5965
3. Charles Lomberg	SWE	11.8	687	1167	180	55.0	17.6	3535	325	4183	5:12.2	7414	5721
4. Gösta Holmér	SWE	11.4	598	1098	170	53.2	17.0	3178	320	4628	4:41.9	7348	5748
5. James Donahue	USA	11.8	648	967	165	51.6	16.2	2995	340	3709	4:44.0	7083	5701
6. Eugene Mercer	USA	11.0	684	976	165	49.9	16.4	2195	360	3232	4:46.3	7075	5825
7. Waldemar Wickholm	FIN	11.5	595	1109	160	52.3	17.0	2978	325	4258	4:33.9	7059	5676
8. Erik Kugelberg	SWE	12.3	620	999	165	55.7	17.2	3148	300	4567	4:43.5	6758	5346
9. Karl von Halt	GER	12.1	608	1112	170	54.2	17.7	3546	270	3982	5:02.8	6682	5286
10. Josef Schäffer	AUT	12.3	604	1150	155	58.2	18.9	3714	325	4106	5:05.3	6568	5049
11. Aleksandr Tschulz	RUS	12.3	575	1008	155	54.5	17.8	3134	270	3899	4:46.4	6134	4976
12. Alfred Alsebens	RUS	12.2	627	848	170	59.0	19.5	2921	nh	3734	5:08.6	5294	4823
-- George Philbrook	USA	12.4	634	1279	180	56.7	16.8	4156	250	4167	dnr		
-- Ferdinand Bie	NOR	11.7	669	1020	165	53.2	16.4	3165	290	4852	dnr		
-- Fred Lukeman	CAN	11.2	614	929	175	52.1	16.3	3052	270				
-- Avery Brundage	USA	12.2	640	1112	170	55.2	17.1	3407	290				
-- Georges André	FRA	11.6	560	990	175	54.4	16.4	2537					
-- Alfredo Pagani	ITA	12.4	583	967	165	56.1	17.2	3020					
-- Evert Nilsson	SWE	11.5	572	1283	170								
-- Otto Röhr	GER	11.3	643	981	170								
-- Skotte Jacobson	SWE	11.0	646	935	155								
-- Gunnar Rönström	SWE	12.3	599	1069	160								

--	Alex Abraham	GER	12.0	552	1129	150
--	Pierre Failliot	FRA	11.3	605	1054	
--	Harry Babcock	USA	11.6	629	1016	
--	Svend Langkjär	DEN	12.0	589	986	
--	Wiktor Hackberg	SWE	12.5	564	1030	
--	Manlio Legat	ITA	12.1	556	823	
--	Megerdich Magherian	TUR	13.3	543	1105	

name was removed from the recordbooks and his awards returned to the IOC. But for Thorpe's admirers over the years, the title he'd received from King Gustav was award enough.

GENERAL GEORGE S. PATTON

The legend of Four-Star General George Smith Patton, Jr. resulted from his tank campaign over Northern Africa and Western Europe during World War II, but he first made his mark as a multi-event competitor.

The Swedes added a "modern" pentathlon to the 1912 Olympic program, different from track and field's "ancient" pentathlon. The five military events were built on the idea that a Napoleonic soldier must deliver a message. He begins on the back of an unfamiliar horse. Encountering the enemy, he must duel with swords and use a pistol. Then he swims across a river and completes his assignment by running over varied terrain. Scoring was based on an athlete's placing in each event.

Patton, a 26-year-old army lieutenant and 2 years out of West Point, asked the war department to assign him to the 1912 Olympic team. He was a first-rate fencer. By highlighting his fencing skills and casting his limited athletic accomplishments in the best possible light, he received orders to go to Stockholm.

Patton was the only American in a field of 42. The host nation entered a dozen pentathletes. The first event began the day after Jim Thorpe won the track and field Pentathlon. Patton got off to a poor start in the pistol shooting, somehow missing the target completely in a pair of shots and placing 21st in the event. He rallied by finishing seventh in the 300m swim, fourth in epee fencing, sixth in riding, and third in the cross-country race. Had he not been such a poor marksman he certainly could have been a medalist. His fifth-place finish (41 points) trailed four Swedes. Gösta Lilliehook won the gold medal with 27 points.

Two years later, Patton, as the Army's Master of the Sword, gained a staff position with General John J. Pershing. When the United States entered World War I, Patton accompanied Pershing to France and set out to become a legend as a tank commander.

Antwerp, 1920

AUGUST 20-21, 23 COMPETITORS, 12 NATIONS

Belgium, devastated by World War I, found the general admission price for the Olympics, about 30 cents, too steep. The 30,000-seat stadium in Antwerp was almost empty for many of the track events. Later, it was thrown open free of charge to school children. They walked in and saw the first unfurled Olympic flag, with its interlocking multicolored rings. They also saw the tightest decathlon finish ever.

Norwegian soldier Helge Lövland won over Missourian Brutus Hamilton by a scant 32 points, a difference of but 6 seconds in the 1500m. Lövland, at 30, was the oldest ever to win an Olympic 10-event crown. He survived rain and scoring confusion to claim the gold medal. Hamilton, who had won the United States Olympic Trials 6 weeks earlier, was to become one of America's most respected and famous coaches. He was

Figure 6.3.   Helge Lövland in the discus. (From the Zarnowski collection)

Table 6.2 Results of 1920 Olympic Decathlon, Antwerp

Results		100	lj	sp	hj	400	110H	dis	pv	jav	1500	1912B Total Points	1985 Tables
1. Helge Lövland	NOR	12.0	628	1119	165	54.8	16.2	3734	320	4801	4:48.4	6803	5803
2. Brutus Hamilton	USA	11.4	632	1161	160	55.0	17.3	3614	330	4808	4:57.8	6771	5739
3. Bertil Ohlson	SWE	12.0	643	1107	165	55.0	17.0	3778	330	3989	4:50.6	6580	5639
4. Gösta Holmér	SWE	11.8	592	1106	170	56.5	16.6	3482	320	4762	5:01.6	6532	5551
5. Evert Nilsson	SWE	12.2	567	1139	175	55.7	20.0	3477	340	4928	4:45.6	6433	5371
6. Waldemar Wickholm	FIN	11.6	612	1144	160	52.8	16.8	3230	300	4276	4:45.6	6405	5630
7. Gene Vidal	USA	12.0	613	1116	165	55.7	17.1	3730	330	3532	4:46.6	6358	5489
8. Axel-Erik Gyllenstolpe	SWE	12.0	635	1069	165	55.8	16.8	3365	290	4931	5:01.4	6331	5482
9. Ernst Gerspach	SWI	12.0	600	1059	160	57.0	17.2	3278	310	4188	5:02.3	5947	5188
10. Constant Bucher	SWI	11.8	585	971	145	56.0	19.2	3243	290	3646	4:56.4	5273	4783
11. René Joannes-Powell	BEL	12.2	593	947	155	56.4	18.0	2829	290	2963	4:52.6	5091	4718
12. Noguchi Gensabulo	JAP	12.1	563	813	145	57.2	dnf	2197	260	3548	5:11.2	3668	3775
-- Harry Goelitz	USA	12.0	583	1081	165	53.9	16.4	3350	280	3730	dns		
-- Einar Räder	NOR	12.0	627	1099	165	55.7	17.0	2874	250	3574	dns		
-- Alexsandr Klumberg	EST	12.4	621	1161	170	56.2	18.0	3591	310				
-- Everett Ellis	USA	12.0	566	1145	160	54.6	16.2	3163	270				
-- Carlo Butti	ITA	12.6	574	1061	155	58.0	19.0						
-- Eero Lehtonen	FIN	11.6	655	1066	150	54.4							
-- Eduard Hasek	TCH	11.6	612	993	150	55.6							
-- P. Johansson-Jaale^a	SWE	12.4	604	1169	155	60.2							
-- Apost Nikolaidis^b	GRE	12.8	544	1139	165								
-- Andro Demetriades^c	GRE	12.6	552	992	155								
-- Hugo Lahtinen	FIN	12.0	623	1006	155								

aFull name: Paavo Johansson-Jaale. bFull name: Apostolos Nikolaidis. cFull name: Andronidas Demetrios Demetriades.

head United States Olympic coach in 1952. Fourth placer Gösta Holmér of Sweden also became a world-renowned coach.

It should be noted that the scoring table used in Antwerp and later is often termed the *1920 Table*. The correct designation is the *1912B Table*. The only difference from the original 1912A table (used in Stockholm) was the change in the 1000-point standard. A thousand points was now equal to the Olympic records as of 1912.

Figure 6.4. Norwegian Helge Lövland (center) is sandwiched by Finland's Waldemar Wickholm and Sweden's Bertil Ohlson in the 1500 meters. (Courtesy of Norsk Fri-Idrett)

Paris, 1924

JULY 11-12, 36 COMPETITORS, 22 NATIONS

In 1924, the French provided the first contemporary Olympic village for athletes. The Germans and Austrians were not invited. The stadium at Colombes held a 500m running track but was more like an inferno. Punishing heat sent temperatures soaring as high as 113 degrees on track dates.

Multitalented Harold Osborn won the decathlon with a world record, adding the title to his high jump victory. He is the only decathlete champion in Olympic history to have an individual title as well. The stocky 25-year-old Illinoisan had set the world high jump record in May with a jump of 2.03m (6-8 1/4). In Paris, he was no worse than ninth in any event, winning by 360 points.

Osborn's teammate Emerson Norton led after eight events but was 4 meters back of Osborn in the javelin and barely finished the 1500m. His 5:38.0 was the slowest in the history of Olympic medalists. Former world-

Figure 6.5.   Decathlon gold medal winner Harold Osborn displays the form that also won him the gold medal in the high jump. (Courtesy of Mrs. Harold Osborn)

Table 6.3   Results of 1924 Olympic Decathlon, Paris

Results		100	lj	sp	hj	400	110H	dis	pv	jav	1500	1912B Total Points	1985 Tables
1. Harold Osborn	USA	11.2	692	1143	197	53.2	16.0	3451	350	4669	4:50.0	7711 WR	6476
2. Emerson Norton	USA	11.6	692	1304	192	53.0	16.6	3311	380	4209	5:38.0	7351	6117
3. Alexandr Klumberg-Kolmpere	EST	11.6	696	1227	175	54.4	17.6	3679	330	5770	5:16.0	7329	6056
4. Anton Huusari	FIN	12.0	616	1202	170	53.4	16.6	3315	320	5365	4:37.2	7005	5952
5. Edward Sutherland	SAF	11.6	667	1086	180	56.0	16.6	3083	330	5101	5:19.0	6794	5928
6. Ernst Gerspach	SWI	11.4	646	1035	170	53.4	16.8	3391	340	4482	5:08.2	6744	5765
7. Helge Jansson	SWE	11.6	632	1222	183	54.2	17.8	3208	310	4720	5:22.0	6656	5633
8. Harry Frieda	USA	11.6	594	1101	160	54.0	19.0	3509	340	5490	5:02.6	6618	5541
9. Paavo Yrjölä	FIN	11.8	631	1328	160	54.6	18.8	3814	273	5293	5:08.6	6549	5547
10. Harry J.M. DeKeijser	HOL	11.4	600	1131	160	54.6	19.0	3841	350	4466	5:15.4	6510	5458
11. Adolfo Contoli	ITA	11.6	637	1054	165	55.8	17.2	3292	310	4693	4:56.0	6407	5543
12. Antoni Cejzik	POL	11.8	568	1187	170	55.4	17.8	3738	290	4623	5:15.4	6319	5375
13. Enrique R. Thompson	ARG	11.4	610	1034	170	52.0	17.8	3089	273	4337	4:32.4	6311	5615
14. Guido Jekkals	LAT	11.4	648	1041	170	54.2	17.8	3225	253	4302	5:11.6	5982	5377
15. Constant Bucher	SWI	11.4	612	971	160	54.0	18.4	3478	290	3941	4:57.2	5962	5267
16. Eugen Neumann	EST	11.8	649	963	165	55.4	17.0	2846	330	4069	5:19.0	5899	5186
17. Josse Ruth	BEL	11.8	631	874	170	51.8	16.8	2387	320	3228	4:36.4	5867	5384
18. Peroslav Fercovic	YUG	11.8	617	1056	150	55.0	20.4	2589	350	3659	4:37.0	5518	5026
19. William Shanahan	IRL	11.8	620	961	170	55.4	16.8	2506	280	3939	5:41.4	5427	4931
20. Edouard Médécin	MON	11.6	652	1129	160	53.0	18.0	2765	nh	3068	4:29.6	5348	5137
21. Elmar Rähn	EST	11.8	627	952	160	53.6	18.4	nm	280	3838	4:44.0	5293	4707

(Cont.)

Table 6.3 (Continued)

Results	100	lj	sp	hj	400	110H	dis	pv	jav	1500	1912B Total Points	1985 Tables
22. Tokushige Noto JPN	11.6	642	955	150	51.4	17.2	2361	230	3522	4:45.8	5248	5090
23. Edouard B. Armand HAI	11.6	638	865	160	53.0	19.0	2188	320	1164	4:42.4	5207	4740
24. Stylianos Benadis GRE	12.2	570	989	160	57.6	19.2	3056	290	4064	5:25.6	5189	4601
25. David G. Slack GBR	11.6	598	876	165	55.2	17.6	2432	260	3611	5:11.8	5148	4789
-- Gabriel Sempé FRA	11.4	608	1033	165	56.8	17.2	3204	280				
-- Arthur Percy Spark GBR	12.8	507	1086	140	59.0	dnf	3308					
-- Adolf Meier SWI	11.6	617	1000	?	55.2	17.0						
-- Denis V. Duigan AUS	11.8	603	973	175	52.0	dnf						
-- Iivari Yrjölä FIN	12.0	650	1308	180	54.0							
-- Bertil Fastén SWE	12.0	618	1141	165	54.6							
-- Valter Ever EST	11.8	645	1090	170	55.8							
-- Duro Gaspar YUG	12.6	530	1095	160	62.2							
-- Elemer Somfay HUN	11.6	640	1055	160								
-- Evert Nilsson SWE	12.2	640	1009	160								
-- Otto Anderson USA	11.8											

Figure 6.6.   Osborn wins a heat of the 100 meters, beating Harry Frieda of the USA (right) and Antoni Cejzik of Poland. (Courtesy of Mrs. Harold Osborn)

record holder Alexandr Klumberg-Kolmpere of Estonia missed the silver medal by 22 points. Klumberg-Kolmpere himself ran 5:16.0 but actually made up ground (!) on Norton. South African Edward Sutherland placed fifth and remains the only African ever to place in the top six.

It was the first Olympic decathlon in which all six continents were represented, but, interestingly, a two-time Olympic pentathlon champ, Eero Lehtonen of Finland, did not contest the 10-eventer. He retired in Paris at age 26. He'd won two Olympic golds in the pentathlon, but had *never* finished a decathlon.

Amsterdam, 1928

AUGUST 3-4, 38 COMPETITORS, 19 NATIONS

The 1928 Olympics in Amsterdam saw the first female track and field contestants (despite the protests of retired IOC president Baron Pierre de Coubertin and Pope Pius XI) in Olympic history. United States Olympic Committee president, General Douglas MacArthur, promised an invincible performance by the American track and field contingent. Unfortunately, the USA men suffered their most dismal performance, winning only 1 of 11 individual running events. On the field, decathlon champion Harold Osborn did not defend, although he did come back for a fifth place in the high jump.

Nations were allowed four individual entries and the decathlon, with 38 competitors, saw one of the biggest Olympic fields. Finnish duo Paavo Yrjölä, world-record holder, and Akilles Järvinen won over a trio of Americans, Ken Doherty, James Stewart, and Tom Churchill. Yrjölä, who

Figure 6.7. Jim Stewart and Barney Berlinger (back right) watch silver medalist Akilles Järvinen. (From *Athletes in Finland*, Martti Jukola, 1932)

won 4 of 6 contests with Järvinen, set a new world record, besting his teammate by over 100 points. Järvinen, 22, and four years younger than Yrjölä, would have been Olympic champion by 38 points under today's scoring tables.

The Amsterdam track was brick dust and newly laid, but hard rain on the 2nd day hurt all performances. Sixty years later, the back of Ken Doherty's track suit is still red, even after several dry cleanings. Doherty

Figure 6.8. Ken Doherty in the long jump. (Courtesy of Ken Doherty)

was the American champion and known for his consistency. He recalls a snafu in the hurdles. Yrjölä fell and failed to finish. When officials checked the cause and found a hurdle out of place, they decided to re-run the race. In the rain! There were no arguments from athletes or coaches. This time Yrjölä recorded 16.6 (only 5 of 33 recorded times were faster than 16 seconds) and was back on track for his record attempt and a gold medal. The rain continued throughout the vault, helping no one. Only 4 of 30 vaulters cleared more than 3.30m (10-10). A farmer by trade, Yrjölä won three events in posting 8053 points, breaking Jim Thorpe's Olympic record. "I did not feel so outstanding breaking Jim Thorpe's record," he would recall years later.

Doherty used 2nd-day skills to top USC high-jumper Stewart and Oklahoma football/basketball star Churchill for the bronze medal. Doherty

Table 6.4 Results of 1928 Olympic Decathlon, Amsterdam

Results		100	lj	sp	hj	400	110H	dis	pv	jav	1500	1912B Total Points	1985 Tables
1. Paavo Yrjölä	FIN	11.8	672	1411	187	53.2	16.6	4209	330	5570	4:44.0	8053 WR	6607
2. Akilles Järvinen	FIN	11.2	687	1364	175	51.4	15.6	3695	330	5558	4:52.4	7932	6645
3. Ken Doherty	USA	11.6	661	1185	180	52.0	15.8	3872	330	5656	4:54.0	7707	6428
4. James Stewart	USA	11.2	661	1304	187	52.8	16.6	4090	330	4807	5:17.0	7624	6310
5. Thomas Churchill	USA	11.6	632	1228	170	52.2	16.8	3819	360	5093	4:55.0	7417	6165
6. Helge Jansson	SWE	11.4	685	1359	187	53.2	16.6	3683	330	4173	5:27.0	7286	6111
7. Ludwig Veseley	AUT	11.6	673	1258	170	52.2	16.6	3546	320	4744	4:47.0	7274	6224
8. Albert Andersson	SWE	12.0	630	1219	175	54.0	15.8	3664	330	4581	4:44.2	7109	6031
9. Henry Lindblad	SWE	12.0	697	1204	170	53.8	17.0	3553	360	4961	5:23.2	7071	5906
10. Wilhelm Ladewig	GER	11.8	673	1096	180	52.4	16.6	3074	310	4610	4:42.0	6881	5964
11. Hugo Barth	GER	12.0	687	1134	165	52.8	16.4	3489	300	5273	5:04.6	6850	5885
12. Tatsuo Toki	JAP	11.6	690	1103	175	54.8	16.8	3401	310	4583	5:10.8	6757	5778
13. Johann Meimer	EST	11.6	643	1120	175	55.0	18.6	3532	300	5688	5:16.2	6733	5636
14. Sven Lundgren	SWE	11.8	650	1076	150	52.4	16.2	3504	330	4571	4:34.8	6727	5878
15. Erwin Huber	GER	11.8	679	1192	160	54.8	16.8	3307	320	4542	4:46.0	6702	5789
16. Martti Tolamo	FIN	12.0	669	1131	170	52.4	18.0	3288	310	4579	4:44.8	6642	5735
17. Barney Berlinger	USA	11.6	597	1305	175	56.2	17.2	3251	360	4827	5:58.6	6619	5499
18. Antoni Cejzik	POL	12.2	592	1211	170	53.0	18.4	3943	290	4396	5:11.4	6356	5415
19. Hermann Lemperle	GER	11.6	650	1296	165	52.8	17.8	3699	nh	4105	4:41.6	6293	5546
20. Stylianos Bernadis	GRE	12.0	637	1103	165	56.6	18.0	3141	330	4448	5:13.8	6149	5270
21. Mattas Farkas	HUN	11.6	662	1178	165	52.4	17.6	3583	300	4313	dnf	6015	5170
22. Yenataro Nakazawa	JAP	12.4	604	1037	175	61.8	18.4	3143	370	4033	5:54.6	5672	4794

23. Gaston Etienne	BEL	13.0	551	965	150	60.2	20.8	2981	320	5485	4:51.4	5256	4577
24. Branko Kallay	YUG	11.6	nm	987	170	57.6	16.8	3224	300	4398	5:50.8	5210	4715
25. Rene Joannes-Powell	BEL	12.2	603	983	150	55.8	16.8	2673	310	3256	5:18.6	5190	4779
26. Gheorghe Czegezi	ROM	11.8	601	945	160	55.6	20.0	2620	300	3185	5:03.8	5081	4658
27. Gerard Noel	BEL	12.4	570	995	170	58.0	19.4	3050	300	3264	dnf	4606	4106
--- O.C. O'Callaghan	IRE	11.8	628	1107	170	56.2	17.8	3169	nh				
--- Howard Ford	GBR	12.8	607	1211	160	59.8	20.6	3282	310				
--- Edouard Médécin	MON	12.0	646	1167	150	53.6	20.0	3071	nh				
--- Adolf Meier	SWI	11.4	689	1215	165	55.0	16.6	3343					
--- Johannes Viljoes	SAF	11.0	685	1017	170	53.0	15.6	2895					
--- J. Haidu	ROM	12.4	574	1051	160	59.4	20.4	3159					
--- Gunnar Fredriksen	NOR	11.8	645	1156	170	55.8							
--- Gunnar Hagen	NOR	12.0	595	1156	175	56.4							
--- George Weightman-Smith	SAF	11.4	626	1054	160								
--- Armas I. Wahlstedt	FIN	11.8	586										
--- Ioan Virgile	ROM	12.4											

Note. There is no explanation why all times end in even digits.

reminds us that conventional decathlon wisdom called for conserving energy during meets. Even coaches insisted on a minimum of training for all track men. Penn coach Lawson Robertson, twice the Olympic coach and fifth in the 1906 Olympic pentathlon, felt that athletes were likely to burn out from overwork. Decathletes in particular were likely to do little or no endurance training for the 400m or 1500m. The Robertson attitude is thought by many to have set United States track back 10 to 20 years.

Los Angeles, 1932

AUGUST 5-6, 14 COMPETITORS, 9 NATIONS

In 1932 economic depression engulfed the world. Worried Americans took handouts and, driven by hunger, stood in soup lines. The Olympic Games were far down on anyone's list of priorities. Money was scarce here and abroad and many nations could not send athletes to the far coast of America. Only 37 nations participated and the decathlon hosted the smallest field ever, 14 starters and 11 finishers.

One spectator was Jim Thorpe, who was now a Los Angeles construction worker. Vice president Charles Curtis, himself part Indian, invited Jim to sit with him. A year earlier Jim had sold the film rights to his life story to MGM and since then had drifted from job to job. Both watched the games' great all-around star. *She* was an 18-year-old Texan, Mildred Didrikson, nicknamed ''Babe'' because she hit a baseball like Babe Ruth. In Los Angeles she broke world records in three of the five women's events, just weeks after having won or tied for six firsts at the women's United States championships. Unfortunately, Babe competed in an era

Figure 6.9. Left to right: Los Angeles medal winners were James Bausch (USA), gold; Akilles Järvinen (Finland), silver; and Wolrad Eberle (Germany), bronze. (From the Official Report of the Organizing Committee of the 10th Olympiad, Los Angeles)

Table 6.5   Results of 1932 Olympic Decathlon, Los Angeles

Results		100	lj	sp	hj	400	110H	dis	pv	jav	1500	Total Points	1985 Tables
1. James Bausch	USA	11.7	695	1532	170	54.2	16.2	4458	400	6191	5:17.0	8462 WR	6735
2. Akilles Järvinen	FIN	11.1	700	1311	175	50.6	15.7	3680	360	6100	4:47.0	8292	6879
3. Wolrad Eberle	GER	11.4	677	1322	165	50.8	16.7	4134	350	5749	4:34.4	8031	6661
4. Wilson Charles	USA	11.2	724	1256	185	51.2	16.2	3871	340	4772	4:39.8	7985	6716
5. Hans-Heinrich Sievert	GER	11.4	697	1450	178	53.6	16.1	4454	320	5391	5:18.0	7941	6515
6. Paavo Yrjölä	FIN	11.8	659	1368	175	52.6	17.0	4077	310	5612	4:37.4	7688	6385
7. Clyde Coffman	USA	11.3	677	1186	170	51.8	17.8	3440	400	4888	4:48.0	7534	6265
8. Robert Tisdall	IRL	11.3	660	1258	165	49.0	15.5	3331	320	4526	4:34.4	7327	6398
9. Erwin Wegner	GER	11.4	641	1170	165	51.6	15.4	3326	310	5383	4:47.8	7179	6189
10. Peter Bacsalmasi	HUN	12.0	671	1190	170	53.8	17.7	4145	350	4859	5:34.6	7001	5788
11. Harry Hart	SAF	11.7	614	1331	165	57.2	15.6	4062	310	5049	5:48.2	6799	5697
-- Janis Dimsa	LAT	11.3	722	1433	178	54.8	16.4	4076	350				
-- Zygmunt Siedlecki	POL	11.6	649	1356	170	53.8	17.0	3905	300				
-- Hector Berra	ARG	11.1	714										

preceding multi-events for women. The 1932 Games were her only Olympics. She was declared a professional shortly thereafter and turned her remarkable talents to golf. The daughter of Norwegian immigrants, Babe once told reporters, "My goal was to be the greatest athlete who ever lived." She and Thorpe were eventually voted the top female and male athletes of the first half of the 20th century.

In the decathlon, Finn Akilles Järvinen was the heavy favorite. Now 26 years old, he had reached the equivalent of 6879 points on the present scoring tables. He broke his own world record in Los Angeles, only to watch, 30 seconds later, upset-minded Jim Bausch cross the 1500m finish line to win the gold medal and set an even newer world mark.

Bausch, a former University of Kansas football star, was fifth after the first day. But he took advantage of splendid performances in the discus,

Figure 6.10. Janis Dimsa of Latvia throws the discus. (From the Official Report of the Organizing Committee of the 10th Olympiad, Los Angeles)

44.58m (146-3), and pole vault, 4.00m (13-1 1/2), to build an insurmountable lead. All the more impressive was his ability to lift a bulky 95 kg (210 lb) frame over the vault crossbar in a day of steel poles. After he cleared 4.00m, officials summoned his University of Kansas coach, Brutus Hamilton, himself an Olympic decathlon silver medalist. They excitedly explained that it looked as if Jim would win the decathlon. "Tell him what to do," they insisted, but Brutus answered, "I don't have to tell him anything. He knows what to do." Bausch then proved it by outthrowing Järvinen in the javelin, which was a surprise because the javelin was the Finn's speciality. In fact, Järvinen's younger brother, Matti, had captured the javelin gold medal 2 days before. Bausch had earned the luxury of trotting the 1500m and he did so.

American Wilson Charles, a Native American from the Kansan Haskell Institute, had led over Latvian Janis Dimsa after the first day. He lost the bronze medal to Wolrad Eberle of Germany in the javelin. Under today's tables their places would have been reversed. Intermediate-hurdle winner Robert Tisdall of Ireland placed eighth, setting a national record that stood 40 years.

Berlin, 1936

AUGUST 7-8, 28 COMPETITORS, 17 NATIONS

In 1936, for the first time, the Olympic flame was carried via relay runners from Olympia, Greece. During the opening ceremonies the marvelous airship *Hindenberg* bore the Nazi swastika over Berlin's stadium. The shadow thrown over the Nazi Games did not, however, dim the luster of individual achievement. The triumphs of Jesse Owens were a case in point. So too was the decathlon, which became strictly an American affair. German champion Hans-Heinrich Sievert was injured and did not compete. Glenn Morris, Bob Clark, and Jack Parker all scored lifetime bests in a USA sweep.

Clark led by 200 points after the first two events, but Morris got all but two back at the end of the first day with a 49.4 400 meters. Dead on his feet at the finish, Morris, a little-known intermediate hurdler from Denver, bested his heat by nearly 3 seconds, a huge margin. Conditions were appalling on the 2nd day. But the cold and rain did not stop Morris, who took the lead for good in the 110m hurdles (14.9).

With an event remaining and the gold medal assured, it was announced that Morris, a 24-year-old automobile salesman, needed to run 4:32.0 or

Figure 6.11. Left to right: Robert Clark, Glenn Morris, and Jack Parker. (From the Official Report of the Organizing Committee of the 11th Olympiad, Berlin)

Table 6.6 Results of 1936 Olympic Decathlon, Berlin

Results		100	lj	sp	hj	400	110H	dis	pv	jav	1500	1934 Total Points	1985 Tables
1. Glenn Morris	USA	11.1	697	1410	185	49.4	14.9	4302	350	5452	4:33.2	7900 WR	7254
2. Robert Clark	USA	10.9	762	1268	180	50.0	15.7	3939	370	5112	4:44.4	7601	7063
3. Jack Parker	USA	11.4	735	1352	180	53.3	15.0	3911	350	5646	5:07.8	7275	6760
4. Erwin Huber	GER	11.5	689	1270	170	52.3	15.8	3546	380	5645	4:35.2	7087	6588
5. Reindert Brasser	HOL	11.6	669	1349	190	51.5	16.2	3945	340	5575	5:06.0	7046	6570
6. Armin Guhl	SWI	11.3	704	1230	180	52.3	15.6	4097	330	5102	4:49.2	7033	6618
7. Olle Bexell	SWE	11.6	668	1354	175	54.9	16.0	3883	370	5707	4:40.4	7024	6558
8. Helmut Bonnet	GER	11.6	666	1350	175	53.7	16.2	3916	360	5815	4:54.0	6939	6489
9. Jerzy Plawczyk	POL	11.6	712	1194	185	54.0	16.4	3830	370	5426	5:04.0	6871	6446
10. Edvard Natvig	NOR	12.1	655	1289	185	56.3	16.1	3960	370	5836	5:05.0	6759	6453
11. Aulis Reinikka	FIN	12.1	632	1274	170	52.5	16.5	3861	390	5080	4:32.4	6755	6342
12. Péter Bácsalmási	HUN	12.1	678	1177	175	53.1	18.4	3964	390	5590	5:30.6	6395	5979
13. Fritz Dällenbach	SWI	11.9	636	1159	170	53.6	16.3	3318	360	5239	4:48.0	6311	6030
14. Lyuben Doitchev	BUL	11.5	635	1226	170	54.1	16.3	3825	370	4813	5:34.2	6307	5940
15. Oswaldo Wenzel	CHI	12.2	625	1243	165	55.3	18.2	3711	320	5493	4:34.6	6058	5798
16. Josef Klein	CZE	11.6	622	1099	155	55.3	17.3	3588	310	5172	4:49.6	5853	5636
17. Maurice Boulanger	BEL	12.4	585	992	160	55.1	19.2	2520	330	4343	4:35.0	5097	5020
-- Leif Dahlgren	SWE	11.6	665	1263	175	51.2	16.0	3806	330	4774			
-- Zoltan Csanyi	HUN	11.6	642	1400	160	54.5	17.0	3586	370	4870			
-- Willy Bührer	SWI	11.8	648	1325	175	54.5	16.6	3643	330	4310			
-- Franz Sterzl	AUS	11.7	652	1098	175	53.3	16.5	3533	320				
-- Emil Binet	BEL	11.4	655	826	165	52.2	16.0	2687					

-- Martti Topelius-Tolamo	FIN	11.5	684	1268	175	51.2	16.6	3436
-- Akilles Järvinen	FIN	11.4	669	1353	175	50.7		
-- Janis Dimsa	LAT	11.9	636	1366	170			
-- Erwin Reimer	CHI	12.0	592					
-- Chang, Sing-Chow	CHN	12.2	628					
-- Karl Vilmundarson	ICE	12.6	562					

faster in the 1500m to break his own global standard. That was 16 seconds faster than he had ever run. He ran himself into exhaustion; when he crossed the line in 4:33.2, there was much disappointment in the Berlin darkness. But a scoring error was discovered. Morris had in fact broken the record after all.

German hopeful Erwin Huber moved from 10th after the first day to finish a respectable fourth. Interestingly, he would become a leading decathlon coach and the mentor of Wolfgang Bergman, the current West German national coach who monitors both Jürgen Hingsen and Siegfried Wentz.

Morris's record score lasted 14 years, almost a record itself for longevity. World War II forced the cancellation of both the 1940 and 1944 Games.

Figure 6.12. Glenn Morris, 1936 gold medalist, throws the javelin. (From the Official Report of the Organizing Committee of the 11th Olympiad, Berlin)

London, 1948

AUGUST 5-6, 35 COMPETITORS, 20 NATIONS

Contested in the cold rain under long, drawn-out conditions, the London decathlon took on Hollywood proportions. It was only the third 10-eventer for a 17-year-old high school product from Tulare, California, Robert Bruce Mathias. That Mathias won was remarkable in itself. That he won against numerous veterans made the victory even more noteworthy.

Mathias's high school coach suggested that Bob take up the decathlon. Bob learned quickly and qualified for the Olympic team. His inexperience cost him a big throw in the shot (a foul for walking out the front of the circle) and some anxious moments in the high jump. He missed twice at an early and low height. Hearing spectators shout ''Come on Tulare'' relaxed him and he finally cleared the crossbar. He then cleared several higher heights to win the event at 1.86m (6-1 1/4). But after day one, Bob stood third behind the Argentine soldier Enrique Kistenmacher and France's hefty Ignace Heinrich.

Conditions at Wembley Stadium were appalling on the 2nd day. Thirty athletes, large by Olympic standards, remained and were split into two

Figure 6.13.   Left to right: France's Ignace Heinrich, American Floyd Simmons, and gold medal winner Bob Mathias. (From the Official Report of the Organizing Committee of the 14th Olympiad, London)

Table 6.7 Results of 1948 Olympic Decathlon, London

Results		100	lj	sp	hj	400	110H	dis	pv	jav	1500	1934 Total Points	1985 Tables
1. Robert Mathias	USA	11.2	661	1304	186	51.7	15.7	4400	350	5032	5:11.0	7139	6628
2. Ignace Heinrich	FRA	11.3	689	1285	186	51.6	15.6	4094	320	4098	4:43.8	6974	6559
3. Floyd Simmons	USA	11.2	672	1280	186	51.9	15.2	3273	340	5199	4:58.0	6950	6531
4. Enrique Kistenmacher	ARG	10.9	708	1267	170	50.5	16.3	4111	320	4506	4:49.6	6929	6542
5. Erik Peter Andersson	SWE	11.6	659	1266	175	52.0	15.9	3607	360	5104	4:34.0	6877	6486
6. Peter Mullins	AUS	11.2	664	1275	183	53.2	15.2	3394	340	5132	5:17.6	6739	6334
7. Per Axil Eriksson	SWE	11.9	680	1196	180	52.5	16.2	3491	330	5670	4:35.8	6731	6382
8. Irv Mondschein	USA	11.3	681	1274	183	51.6	16.6	3874	350	3681	4:49.8	6715	6357
9. Edward Adamczyk	POL	11.7	708	1320	175	52.5	15.8	3911	340	4370	5:01.4	6712	6336
10. Godtfred Holmvang	NOR	12.1	675	1217	170	52.9	16.4	3811	340	5366	4:28.6	6663	6324
11. Per Stavem	NOR	12.0	670	1389	180	56.0	16.4	4106	320	5279	5:07.4	6552	6153
12. Orn Clausen	ICE	11.1	654	1287	180	54.7	16.0	3634	320	4416	5:00.7	6444	6146
13. Yrjo Makela	FIN	11.9	620	1310	180	53.4	17.5	3612	320	6255	4:58.0	6421	6101
14. Pierre Sprecher	FRA	11.9	638	1222	160	51.8	16.7	3702	300	5879	4:34.0	6401	6136
15. Kjell Tannander	SWE	11.6	658	1250	186	54.5	16.4	3650	320	4365	5:04.8	6325	6017
16. Waclaw Kuzmicki	POL	12.0	656	1234	170	54.3	17.6	3806	320	4734	4:41.8	6153	5898
17. Hannes Sonck	FIN	11.9	671	1183	175	55.2	16.8	3471	340	4824	5:01.8	6142	5883
18. Davoin Marcelja	YUG	12.1	605	1219	170	54.4	17.5	3944	330	5534	4:55.2	6141	5851
19. Witold Gerutto	POL	12.1	590	1453	170	55.4	17.0	4180	300	5106	5:17.8	6106	5756
20. Hercules Ascune	URU	11.6	640	1087	186	52.7	17.1	3662	320	3831	5:09.9	6026	5776
21. Hernan Figueroa	CHI	11.6	642	1217	170	54.3	16.5	3298	340	4305	5:06.4	6026	5786
22. Jacques Cretaine	FRA	11.6	642	1078	165	54.8	17.3	3890	340	4326	5:20.4	5829	5604

23. Fritz Nussbaum	SWI	11.9	634	1102	160	53.6	16.5	3354	330	4613	5:02.6	5808	5640
24. Mario Recordon	CHI	11.8	608	1145	170	53.9	15.8	3377	280	3806	4:54.8	5730	5582
25. Lionel J. Fournier	CAN	11.6	651	1042	165	54.5	17.4	3231	320	4239	5:12.4	5590	5453
26. Albert Dayer	BEL	12.0	582	1245	165	57.1	19.5	4154	300	4871	5:01.2	5586	5348
27. Oskar Gerber	SWI	11.9	596	1161	160	54.8	16.8	3432	320	4244	5:10.8	5558	5403
28. Ezz el Din Mukhtar	EGY	11.8	551	1102	150	54.8	17.9	3654	235	4459	5:08.4	5031	5000
--- Baldev Singh	IND	11.8	663	1005	170	57.1	16.1	2963					
--- Josef Seger	LIE	12.3	594	940	165	55.7	18.7	2860					
--- Ed Julve Ciriaco	PER	11.6	666	1303	165	53.5							
--- Oto Rebula	YUG	11.6	653	1155	160	55.3							
--- Rene Kremer	LUX	11.5	625	1167	160	56.5							
--- Gebhard Buchel	LIE	12.7	555	1036	140								
--- Armin Scheurer	SWI	12.5											

Figure 6.14. American Irv Mondschein (left) and Enrique Kistenmacher of Argentina battle in the 1500 meters. (From the Official Report of the Organizing Committee of the 14th Olympiad, London)

sections. Bob drew the second section and spent most of the rainy day huddled under a blanket on the infield. The last three events were conducted in darkness, with flashlights used on the vault crossbar and javelin take-off.

Amidst the general confusion of the 2nd day, Bob lost a big throw in the discus when his marker was knocked over. He was finally credited with 44.00m (144-4), losing perhaps several feet. By the time he dragged his body across the 1500 finish line (10:40 p.m.!), he had become the youngest men's track and field winner in the history of the modern Games. When asked how he intended to celebrate his win, Bob replied, "I'll start shaving, I guess."

Only 45 points separated second, third, and fourth places. American Floyd Simmons lost the silver medal when the gutty Heinrich bettered him by 15 seconds in the last event. Three-time AAU champ Irving "Moon" Mondschein placed eighth. Scores were generally lower than the prewar marks.

MATHIAS REMEMBERS THAT FIRST OLYMPIC YEAR

Bob Mathias, who won the 1948 Olympics at 17 and repeated with a world record in 1952, recalls his introduction to the decathlon:

My first year in high school, my freshman year, I went out for the shot and discus because my older brother threw the shot and discus. My second year I decided to try for the hurdles. They were fun to do so I went out for the low hurdles and high hurdles. My junior year I decided to do a little high jumping, and long jumping, plus the other events. So when I was 17 and a senior I was learning the shot and discus, the high and low hurdles, once in a while I would run in a relay, I would also high jump and long jump. So I was running all over the track, trying all these different events.

About three months before I graduated from high school, when I was 17 years old, I had not heard the word "decathlon." I simply didn't know what decathlon meant. So one day my coach, Virgil Jackson, came up to me on the track at Tulare High and said, "Bob, you're going to graduate in a couple of months and after you graduate you might want to get involved and do something to keep busy, and you might want to be in this decathlon meet down at Los Angeles." I said, "Well, that's great, coach, it sounds like fun. I'd like to try it, but just one question. What is a decathlon?"

Well, my coach didn't even know what the 10 events were at that time. He said, "Well, I'll find out what they are." He did find out what the 10 events were, but we had problems. In high school they threw a 12 pound shot instead of the college or Olympic shot, and a smaller discus. The javelin was not allowed in high school in California so we had to borrow one from a college. The high school hurdles were three inches lower. And I didn't find a pole big enough to hold me, strong enough. So we had big problems just getting started on these 10 events. Well, anyway, I did train the month and I did go to Los Angeles, and somehow I won my first decathlon meet, and believe me, I was scared to death the first time. It was really the first time I was out of Tulare, let alone in a big city like Los Angeles, and competing against college athletes.

I arrived back in Tulare and my good coach had another smart idea. He said, "Bob, why don't you go back to New Jersey and be in the national decathlon meet?" The year was 1948, an Olympic year, which meant the first three places would qualify for the Olympic Games. Well, I didn't have enough money, so the people in my home town raised enough money to fly me and my coach to New Jersey. Well of course this time I was really scared to death, the first time out of California to meet the best people we had in the United States. Well somehow I was lucky again and I placed first, which qualified me for the Olympic Games in London. So three weeks later I was on a great big boat sailing to London for the Olympics. Well, this time I was really scared, I really didn't know what was happening, but somehow I was lucky again and I won the decathlon in London. And to be frank with you, my marks were not that outstanding. I had great competition, but I was lucky to win that meet.

In that first meet Bob scored 7094 on the '34 tables (6609 on the current tables). He did 7224 (6713) at the AAU-Olympic Trials and 7139 (6628) in the Olympics, in terrible conditions.

Note. From *The Decathlon Book* (p. 47) by Frank Zarnowski and Bert Nelson, 1976, Emitsburg, MD: DECA. Copyright 1975 by Frank Zarnowski. Reprinted with permission.

Helsinki, 1952

JULY 25-26, 28 COMPETITORS, 16 NATIONS

It had been 40 years since Czar Nicholas dispatched a team to the 1912 Olympic Games in Stockholm. After one revolution and two world wars, Russians, representing the Soviet Union, rejoined the Olympic family. But Soviet officials offended the Finns even before the games began when they prohibited the Olympic flame to pass through Estonia on its journey from Olympia to Helsinki. And an application from East Germany was turned down by the IOC, which recognized only West Germany. No matter. The political background made little difference to Bob Mathias, now a mature, 21-year-old Stanford student. Mathias now stood 1.91m (6-3) and weighed 93 kg (205 lb). In between 1948 and 1952 he had won the Sullivan Award, become an outstanding Stanford fullback, and twice broken the world decathlon record. He won the decathlon by the largest margin in Olympic history, destroying a deep field.

In Helsinki, with far better weather conditions than in London, Bob had a 352-point lead after the first day and won four events outright, including all three throws. On his way to a third world record, Mathias had trouble only in the javelin, his first two efforts falling far short of

Figure 6.15. Left to right: Floyd Simmons, Bob Mathias, and Milt Campbell celebrate the sweep of the Helsinki decathlon. (Courtesy of *Track and Field News*)

Table 6.8   Results of 1952 Olympic Decathlon, Helsinki

Results		100	lj	sp	hj	400	110H	dis	pv	jav	1500	1950 Total Points	1985 Tables
1. Robert Mathias	USA	10.9	698	1530	190	50.2	14.7	4689	400	5921	4:50.8	7887 WR	7580
2. Milt Campbell	USA	10.7	674	1389	185	50.9	14.5	4050	330	5454	5:07.2	6975	6948
3. Floyd Simmons	USA	11.5	706	1318	192	51.1	15.0	3777	360	5469	4:53.4	6788	6903
4. Valdimir Volkov	SOV	11.4	709	1262	175	51.2	15.8	3804	380	5668	4:33.2	6674	6868
5. Josef Hipp	GER	11.4	685	1326	175	51.3	16.1	4584	350	5414	4:57.2	6449	6705
6. Göran Widenfeldt	SWE	11.4	676	1161	194	51.3	16.1	3953	350	4936	4:38.6	6388	6661
7. Kjell Tannander	SWE	11.4	690	1297	185	52.6	15.8	3930	350	5279	4:57.2	6308	6607
8. Friedel Schirmer	GER	11.7	637	1269	180	50.5	16.0	3701	350	5400	4:47.6	6118	6464
9. Geoffrey Elliott	GBR	11.4	644	1240	175	53.0	15.7	3422	410	4956	5:03.6	6044	6353
10. Sergei Kuznetsov	SOV	11.4	709	1171	165	52.8	16.4	4103	360	4318	4:42.0	5937	6347
11. Hughes Frayer	FRA	11.6	680	1236	165	51.3	15.4	4002	340	4131	5:14.4	5772	6168
12. Brigido Iriarte	VEN	11.6	706	1166	160	53.1	16.6	3823	340	5555	4:49.8	5770	6249
13. Olli Reikko	FIN	11.3	666	1185	170	50.3	18.8	3072	350	5141	4:28.0	5725	6170
14. Eeles E. Landström	FIN	12.0	670	1175	175	56.7	17.1	3451	420	5761	5:01.0	5694	6123
15. Oto Rebula	YUG	11.7	664	1290	165	54.3	16.0	3855	340	5139	5:01.8	5648	6135
16. Fernando Fernandes	POR	11.5	652	1120	170	51.2	15.8	3427	300	4355	4:37.0	5604	6088
17. Hernan Figueroa	CHI	11.7	638	1287	160	52.8	16.4	3808	350	5122	4:58.2	5592	6087
18. Max Wehrli	SWI	11.8	648	1273	160	54.7	16.4	3681	380	5108	4:58.6	5561	6053
19. Robert Adams	CAN	11.8	622	1201	175	55.2	16.6	4245	370	4483	4:57.0	5530	6034
20. Hektor Roman Selva	PUR	11.7	647	1156	165	52.7	16.4	3298	340	4980	5:14.4	5264	5834
21. Reinaldo Oliver	PUR	11.9	615	1022	170	53.4	16.7	2995	350	5668	4:51.8	5228	5817
---. Erkki Hautamäki	FIN	12.1	637	1219	170	53.9	16.3	3720	340	5357	dnr		

---	Ignace Heinrich	FRA	11.5	710	1283	188	51.0	16.0
---	George Breitman	FRA	13.8	543	928	150	63.9
---	Carlos Vera	CHI	11.1	696	952	175
---	Photios Kosmas	GRE	11.5	620
---	Pyotr Kochevnikov	SOV	11.4	580
---	Patrick Leane	AUS	11.9	522

Note. The following fully automatic times were taken in Helsinki. But the above recorded manual times were official: Mathias 11.08, 50.38, 14.91, 4:51.11; Campbell 10.78, 50.96, 14.67, 5:07.60; Simmons 11.52, 51.22, 15.26, 4:53.70; Volkov 11.49, 51.28, 16.11, 4:33.25; Hipp 11.46, 51.43, 16.24, 4:57.32; Widenfeldt 11.53, 51.55, 16.32, 4:38.84; Tannander 11.59, 52.71, 16.03, 4:57.64; Schirmer 11.68, 50.67, 16.28, 4:47.95; Elliott 11.45, 53.12, 15.88, 5:03.88; Kuznetsov 11.56, 53.00, 16.74, 4:42.22; Frayer 11.61, 51.61, 15.65, 5:14.40; Iriarte 11.66, 53.27, ?, 4:49.98; Reikko 11.43, 50.33, 19.19, 4:28.01; Landström 12.10, 56.88, ?, 5:00.96; Rebula 11.72, 54.46, 16.40, 5:01.93; Fernandes 11.54, 51.23, 16.08, 4:37.32; Figueroa 11.73, 52.96, 16.66, 4:58.61; Wehrli 11.93, 54.92, 16.74, 4:58.10; Adams 11.95, 55.43, 16.81, 4:57.25; Selva 11.70, 52.78, 16.66, 5:14.58; Oliver 11.89, 53.62, ?, 4:52.20; Hautamäki 12.22, 54.17, 16.50, --; Heinrich 11.61, 51.12, ?, --; Breitman 13.70, 64.13, --, --; Vera 11.28, --, --; Kochevnikov 11.53, --, --, --; Kosmas 11.60, --, --, --; Leane 11.82, --, --, --.(? = not known; timer did not work for Heat 2)

his potential. The story goes that his Stanford coach, Jack Weierhauser, convinced a group of American fans to chant, "Oh Bob, hey you, don't forget to follow through." Bob got the message down on the field and followed through with the best effort of the meet, 59.21m (194-3). Bob then ran a personal best in the 1500m to set a new world mark. Afterward, he immediately retired. As he had in 1948, Bob claimed he would not do the decathlon again. This time he meant it.

The Helsinki Games saw the last American sweep of the medal places. New Jersey schoolboy Milton Campbell garnered the silver, and Floyd Simmons captured his second bronze. The top European, France's Ignace Heinrich, retired after six events with an injury. His expected battle with Campbell never materialized. Army Lieutenant Vladimir Volkov, the first Russian, was fourth. Sweden's Kjell Tannander placed seventh and fathered two future Olympic heptathletes (Annette and Kristine) several years later. German Freidel Schirmer, later to be one of the event's most renowned coaches, was eighth.

Figure 6.16.   Bob Mathias ends his decathlon career with a lifetime best 1500 meters and a third world record score. (OWPP Wire Photo/Courtesy of *Track and Field News*)

Melbourne, 1956

NOVEMBER 29-30, 15 COMPETITORS, 8 NATIONS

The 1956 Olympics in Melbourne, Australia, were held in late autumn, opening on November 22. It was the first time the games were held in the Southern Hemisphere, causing a change in training schedule for the decathletes.

The fact that only 15 decathletes competed in Melbourne (necessitating heats of two!) did not diminish the glamour of Milt Campbell's feats. World-record holder Rafer Johnson, due to a knee injury, was not at his best, but it is doubtful he could have handled Campbell on the occasion. Milt, a 22-year-old sailor, amassed history's second highest score up to that time. A hurdler who would run a 13.4 a year later, the 1.91m (6-3), 95-kg (210 lb) Campbell never trailed and had a shot at the world record after seven events. His 2nd day included an eye-opening 14.0 hurdles for 1124 points. But a subpar vault, one and one-half feet below his best, cost him a chance at Johnson's world record.

Campbell remembers his surprise in the 1500m when at the bell he heard a voice behind him say, "Come on big boy, it's time to run. You can do better than this. Come on, it's time to run." The voice belonged to

Figure 6.17.   Left to right: Rafer Johnson, Milt Campbell, and Vasily Kuznyet-sov display their Olympic medals. (From the Official Report of the Organizing Committee of the 16th Olympiad, Melbourne)

Table 6.9   Results of 1956 Olympic Decathlon, Melbourne

Results		100	lj	sp	hj	400	110H	dis	pv	jav	1500	1950 Total Points	1985 Tables
1. Milt Campbell	USA	10.8	733	1476	189	48.8	14.0	4498	340	5708	4:50.6	7937	7565
2. Rafer Johnson	USA	10.9	734	1448	183	49.3	15.1	4217	390	6027	4:54.2	7587	7422
3. Vasiliy Kuznyetsov	SOV	11.2	704	1449	175	50.2	14.9	4433	395	6513	4:53.8	7465	7330
4. Uno Palu	SOV	11.5	665	1339	189	50.8	15.4	4038	360	6159	4:35.6	6930	7028
5. Martin Lauer	GDR	11.1	683	1286	183	48.2	14.7	3938	310	5066	4:43.8	6853	6910
6. Walter Meier	GDR	11.3	680	1299	186	49.3	16.1	3759	370	4797	4:20.6	6773	6910
7. Torbjörn Lassenius	FIN	11.8	662	1345	170	50.8	15.9	4136	380	5933	4:36.2	6565	6782
8. Yang Chuan-Kwang	TAI	11.2	690	1156	195	51.3	15.0	3392	330	5788	5:00.8	6521	6697
9. Pat Leane	AUS	11.4	678	1326	186	51.0	16.4	3885	350	5882	4:56.8	6427	6693
10. John Cann	AUS	10.9	656	1218	170	49.4	15.6	3878	270	5788	4:49.2	6278	6544
11. Ian Bruce	AUS	11.7	661	1230	183	51.3	15.9	3661	340	5138	4:50.4	6025	6406
12. Reze Farabi	IRN	12.1	625	1131	170	52.3	17.4	2872	330	4115	4:24.8	5103	5709
--- Bob Richards	USA	11.7	638	1251	175	52.3	16.8	3776	445	4410	dnr		
--- Yuriy Kutyenko	SOV	11.6	663	1446	nh	50.5	15.8	4756	410	nm			
--- Walter Herssens	BEL	11.8	655	1112	180								

Note. The following fully automatic times were taken in Melbourne. But the above recorded manual times were official: Campbell 10.91, 48.83, 14.12, 4:50.68; Johnson 10.99, 49.49, 15.29, 4:54.24; Kuznetsov 11.36, 50.24, 15.25, 4:54.10; Palu 11.66, 50.82, 15.58, 4:35.74; Lauer 11.29, 48.35, 14.97, 4:44.03; Meier 11.48, 49.41, 16.29, 4:20.63; Lassenius 11.99, 50.89, 16.03, 4:36.28; Yang 11.29, 51.37, 15.20, 5:00.97; Leane 11.54, 51.10, 16.59, 4:56.97; Cann 11.06, 49.41, 15.85, 4:49.31; Bruce 11.83, 51.35, 16.18, 4:50.60; Farabi 12.28, 52.26, 17.60, 4:24.88; Richards 11.82, 52.42, 16.97; Kutyenko 11.69, 50.67, 16.05; Herssens 12.04.

Australian decathlete Ian Bruce, who encouraged and paced Campbell during the last lap. Passing runners, they sprinted for the tape as Bruce implored, "Let's pick it up, come on, pick it up." Campbell made an instant friend. Later he would say with emotion, "Here was a guy I'm competing against who wanted to see me win as much as I wanted to win. It was tremendous." Milt's final score was a new Olympic record.

Johnson held on to a solid second, whereas Soviet Vasiliy Kuznyetsov won the first of two bronze medals.

Three other world-record holders competed. The "Vaulting Vicar," Bob Richards, made it through nine events. He won vault golds in both 1952 and 1956. Martin Lauer was fifth. The German was still a generalist who would become the world-record specialist in the high hurdles. And C.K. Yang of Taiwan would hold the world decathlon record in 1963.

At 22, Campbell began a brief professional football career, but he never neared achieving an athletic feat to equal what he'd accomplished in Melbourne. Despite a superlative performance over decathletes who themselves would break the world record a total of seven times, Campbell today remains a forgotten champion.

Figure 6.18. Milt Campbell in the javelin. (From the Official Report of the Organizing Committee of the 16th Olympiad, Melbourne)

Rome, 1960

SEPTEMBER 5-6, 30 COMPETITORS, 20 NATIONS

ABC paid over a million dollars for the rights to broadcast the Rome Olympics to Americans. They got their money's worth in the decathlon alone, for those who saw UCLA teammates Rafer Johnson and C.K. Yang struggle in Rome's darkness will never forget. Johnson, who had set his third world mark at the United States Olympic Trials, was not expected to have an easy time with either Vasiliy Kuznyetsov of Russia or with Yang. But Kuznyetsov was not at his 1959 form, leaving the two Bruins to contest for the gold medal during a 2-day moratorium on their friendship.

Rafer led Yang by 55 points after the first day, despite C.K. besting him in four of five events. Johnson's tremendous point swing in the shot put kept him in the lead. A heavy rainstorm had left the Estadico Olympico infield a sea of mud before the high jump, dragging the meet into darkness. The pair went head-to-head only in the 400m, with C.K. 2 meters in front at the finish.

Figure 6.19.   Rafer Johnson in the long jump. (From the Zarnowski collection)

Table 6.10   Results of 1960 Olympic Decathlon, Rome

Results		100	lj	sp	hj	400	110H	dis	pv	jav	1500	1950/52 Total Points	1985 Tables
1. Rafer Johnson	USA	10.9	735	1582	185	48.3	15.3	4849	410	6976	4:49.7	8392 OR	7901
2. Yang Chuan-Kwang	TAI	10.7	746	1333	190	48.1	14.6	3983	430	6822	4:48.5	8334	7820
3. Vasiliy Kuznyetsov	SOV	11.1	696	1446	175	50.2	15.0	5052	390	7120	4:53.8	7809	7527
4. Yuriy Kutyenko	SOV	11.4	693	1397	180	51.1	15.6	4563	420	7144	4:44.2	7567	7401
5. Evert Kamerbeek	HOL	11.3	721	1376	180	51.1	14.9	4431	380	5749	4:43.6	7236	7212
6. Franco Sar	ITA	11.4	669	1389	180	51.3	14.7	4958	380	5574	4:49.2	7195	7140
7. Markus Kahma	FIN	11.5	693	1455	175	50.5	15.9	4493	360	6050	4:22.8	7112	7161
8. Klaus Grogorenz	GDR	10.8	693	1242	173	48.0	16.9	4012	370	6081	4:27.0	7032	7078
9. Joze Brodnik	YUG	11.6	691	1230	180	51.0	15.7	3766	410	6530	4:37.7	6918	7005
10. Manfred Bock	GER	11.4	679	1203	185	50.5	16.1	3769	390	6363	4:27.6	6894	7005
11. Fritz Vogelsang	SWI	11.3	694	1178	170	50.0	15.3	3703	400	5261	4:27.7	6767	6881
12. Seppo Suutari	FIN	11.1	694	1496	183	51.8	15.6	3794	350	5986	5:04.8	6751	6876
13. Luciano Paccagnella	ITA	11.8	673	1418	180	54.3	15.7	4567	360	4860	4:55.4	6283	6565
14. Holm Bjoergvin	ICE	11.8	693	1358	175	51.8	16.2	3950	330	5745	4:40.6	6261	6600
15. Herman Timme	HOL	11.3	693	1319	183	51.2	15.7	3908	330	5174	5:21.4	6206	6501
16. Walter Meier	GER	11.3	nm	1368	183	49.5	16.0	3918	370	4733	4:30.6	6000	6116
17. Hans Muchitsch	AUT	11.5	714	1177	180	51.3	15.8	3179	320	3844	4:23.3	5950	6361
18. Leopold Marien	BEL	11.5	662	1144	175	50.5	15.5	3428	330	4471	4:40.0	5919	6303
19. Juriz Laipenieks	CHI	11.6	688	1265	165	53.2	17.1	4049	330	6144	4:57.5	5865	6313
20. Hector Thomas	VEN	11.1	681	1342	175	54.1	16.9	4077	320	5115	5:25.2	5753	6187
21. Rodolfo Mijares	MEX	11.3	620	1059	165	50.5	17.3	3755	340	4336	4:49.3	5413	5939
22. George Stulac	CAN	12.0	592	1274	170	53.0	18.4	3735	360	5040	4:59.6	5198	5786

(Cont.)

Table 6.10   (Continued)

Results		100	lj	sp	hj	400	110H	dis	pv	jav	1500	1950/52 Total Points	1985 Tables
23. Pan Epitropoulos	GRE	11.7	623	1206	173	53.6	18.1	3468	nh	5066	4:55.0	4737	5365
-- Yuriy Dyachkov	SOV	11.6	712	1322	185	50.7	15.3	3787	380				
-- Phil Mulkey	USA	11.5	687	1410	183	52.2	18.1	3412					
-- Randhawa Gurbachan Singh	IND	11.6	687	1135	190	52.0	16.4						
-- Mirko Kolnik	YUG	11.2	693	1310	170	53.9							
-- Alois Buchel	LIE	11.5	654	979	173								
-- Julio Santos	POR	12.0	632	1085	165								
-- Dave Edstrom	USA	11.4	639	1359									

Note. Although manual times were official, the following fully automatic times were taken in Rome for the 100 meters and 110 meter hurdles. There are no photos available for the 400 or 1500 meters, probably because of poor lighting. Johnson 11.07, 15.46; Yang 10.88, 14.80; Kuznyetsov 11.25, 15.15; Kamerbeek 11.49, 15.03; Sar 11.51, 14.88; Kahma 11.69, 16.05; Grogorenz 10.95, 16.98; Brodnik 11.74, 15.79; Bock 11.53, 16.27; Vogelsang 11.45, 15.44; Suutari 11.24, 15.70; Paccagnella 11.93, 15.98; Bjorgvin 11.89, 16.37; Timme 11.43, 15.88; Meier 11.45, 16.11; Muchitsch 11.66, 15.99; Marien 11.63, 15.66; Laipenieks 11.73, 17.22; Thomas 11.22, 17.01; Mijares 11.45, 17.45; Stulac 12.13, 18.57; Epitropoulos 11.76, 18.25; Dyachkov 11.69, 15.45; Mulkey 11.56, 18.25; Singh 11.78, 16.55; Kolnik 11.29; Buchel 11.66; Santos 12.15; Edstrom 11.54.

On the 2nd day, Rafer faltered in the hurdles and lost the lead. He soon regained it with a big effort in the discus and never trailed again. But it was ever so close. With only the 1500m left, Johnson led by 67 points. If Yang could best his teammate by 10 seconds, the gold medal was his. His lifetime best was 18 seconds better.

Sitting in the stands, Ducky Drake, coach of both men, knew exactly how the race would be run. Johnson dogged Yang's every step and C.K. could never pull away, finishing just 4 meters in front. Both wobbled and fell against each other for support. Johnson won by a scant 58 points. Yang beat Johnson in 7 of the 10 battles but lost the decathlon war. Rafer's throwing events were superior enough to offset Yang's victories in the other events. Italian spectators chanted, ''Give them both the gold medal, give them both the gold medal.''

Americans Phil Mulkey (seven events) and Dave Edstrom (three events) were both injured and failed to finish. Johnson's 8392 points (converted to 7901 on the current tables) was an Olympic record.

Figure 6.20. Yang in the decathlon shot put. (From the Official Report of the Organizing Committee of the 17th Olympiad, Rome)

Tokyo, 1964

OCTOBER 19-20, 22 COMPETITORS, 14 NATIONS

The ancient Greek games began in 776 B.C., about a century before the birth of the Japanese Empire. To help celebrate the empire's 2600th anniversary, the Japanese had been awarded the 1940 Olympic Games. However, because of World War II, it wasn't until 1964 that Japan's capital played host. Emperor Hirohito opened the games with Oriental splendor, marking the first time the Olympics were held in Asia.

The United States had not lost an Olympic decathlon since 1928, but they were not expected to provide a contender in Tokyo. Surprisingly, however, Paul Herman, a graduate of Santa Barbara's Westmont College, was in the hunt. The gold medal heir apparent was Taiwan's C.K. Yang, who had broken the world record (first over 9000 points) a year earlier. But the late release of new tables relegated Yang to a mere contender. The event was won by a balding, 24-year-old German physical education student, Willi Holdorf, who relied on his running skills.

At the end of day one, Holdorf led countryman Hans-Joachim Walde by 16 points and Estonian Rein Aun by 23. After nine events, Willi had

Figure 6.21.   Willi Holdorf (right) edges Rein Aun in the 100 meters. Bill Gairdner is between them. (From the Official Report of the Organizing Committee of the 18th Olympiad, Tokyo)

Table 6.11   Results of 1964 Olympic Decathlon, Tokyo

Results		100	lj	sp	hj	400	110H	dis	pv	jav	1500	1962 Total Points	1985 Tables
1. Willi Holdorf	GER	10.7	700	1495	184	48.2	15.0	4605	420	5737	4:34.3	7887	7726
2. Rein Aun	SOV	10.9	722	1382	193	48.8	15.9	4419	420	5906	4:22.3	7842	7677
3. Hans-Joachim Walde	GER	11.0	721	1445	196	49.5	15.3	4315	410	6290	4:37.0	7809	7666
4. Paul Herman	USA	11.2	697	1389	187	49.2	15.2	4415	435	6335	4:25.4	7787	7651
5. Yang Chuan-Kwang	TAI	11.0	680	1323	181	49.0	14.7	3959	460	6815	4:48.4	7650	7539
6. Horst Beyer	GER	11.2	702	1432	190	49.8	15.2	4517	380	5817	4:23.6	7647	7488
7. Vasiliy Kuznyetsov	SOV	10.9	698	1406	170	49.5	14.9	4381	440	6787	5:02.5	7569	7454
8. Mikhail Storochenko	SOV	11.0	722	1637	184	53.6	15.0	4320	400	5910	5:00.7	7464	7307
9. Russ Hodge	USA	11.0	675	1493	175	49.6	16.0	4464	370	5021	4:24.9	7325	7130
10. Dick Emberger	USA	11.2	672	1180	190	49.1	14.9	3532	370	5754	4:19.3	7292	7126
11. William Gairdner	CAN	11.2	640	1338	170	49.2	15.4	4291	340	5972	4:24.5	7147	6989
12. Valbjörn Thorlaksson	ICE	11.1	643	1310	181	50.1	15.6	3970	440	5619	5:00.6	7135	6958
13. Franco Sar	ITA	11.3	631	1360	175	52.2	14.8	4746	420	5359	5:08.4	7054	6885
14. Alois Buchel	LIE	11.3	681	1216	181	49.7	17.5	3719	400	4490	4:28.6	6849	6628
15. Shosuke Suzuki	JAP	11.1	653	1135	170	50.8	16.5	3524	425	5188	4:28.1	6838	6654
16. Gerry Moro	CAN	11.6	620	1262	170	52.0	16.8	4090	460	4663	4:38.8	6716	6540
17. Koech Kiprop	KEN	11.7	650	1055	187	52.8	15.1	3307	405	5554	4:41.6	6707	6556
18. Dramane Sereme	MAI	11.1	651	1103	160	51.2	16.4	2924	260	4846	4:51.5	5917	5804
--- Werner Duttweiler	SWI	11.3	694	1380	193	50.5	15.9	3266	nh				
--- Hector Thomas	VEN	10.7	700	1242	175	51.4	16.7	3843					
--- Evert Kamerbeek	HOL	11.3	656	1440	170	52.0							
--- Ar-Min Wu	TAI	11.7	590	1067									

stretched it to 60 over Walde, 137 over Aun, and 160 over Herman. The 1500, however, was one of Aun's strongest events and he made Holdorf pay dearly for his victory. Holdorf held a 17-second lead over Aun, whose lifetime best was 30 seconds better. Holdorf's coach, Friedel Schirmer, purposely misled him, telling Holdorf he had only a dozen seconds to spare. Aun sprinted off at the gun, making a terrific effort to leave the Germans far behind. He finished in 4:22.2. Only Herman could stay close, finishing 3 seconds back. Holdorf, pushing himself hard to stay within 12 seconds of the Russian, nearly collapsed 40m from the finish. But he held on to clock 4:34.3, *exactly* 12 seconds back. Walde's 4:37.0 was enough to hold off Herman for the bronze medal. It was the closest four-man finish in Olympic history. C.K. Yang was a disappointed fifth.

Two other American military men, Russ Hodge (Air Force) and Dick Emberger (Marines), were 9th and 10th, respectively.

Figure 6.22.   Aun helps Holdorf off the track after the 1500 meters. (From the Official Report of the Organizing Committee of the 18th Olympiad, Tokyo)

Mexico City, 1968

OCTOBER 18-19, 33 COMPETITORS, 20 NATIONS

The selection of Mexico City, with its 1 1/2-mile altitude, as a site for the Olympic Games was widely criticized. The thin air so far above sea level was a concern especially for endurance specialists. The dismay of visiting delegations was compounded by student unrest that exploded into full-fledged violence in the Mexico City streets 10 days before the opening ceremonies. More than 30 students were killed in riots and 100 more were injured. Three hundred were jailed.

Amid the turmoil, West German decathlon coach Friedel Schirmer received his just reward. He watched three of his prize pupils, American Bill Toomey, Hans-Joachim Walde, and Kurt Bendlin, all collect medals. Toomey, a 29-year-old English teacher from California, held a commanding lead over the field on the first day. His marks included a spectacular

Figure 6.23. Left to right: Hans-Joachim Walde, Bill Toomey, and Kurt Bendlin. All three medalists were coached by Friedel Schirmer. (From the Official Report of the Organizing Committee of the 19th Olympiad, Mexico City)

Table 6.12 Results of 1968 Olympic Decathlon, Mexico City

Results		100	lj	sp	hj	400	110H	dis	pv	jav	1500	1962 Total Points	1985 Tables
1. Bill Toomey	USA	10.4	787	1375	195	45.6	14.9	4368	420	6220	4:57.1	8193 OR	8158
2. Hans-Joachim Walde	GER	10.9	764	1513	201	49.0	14.8	4354	430	7162	4:58.5	8111	8120
3. Kurt Bendlin	GER	10.7	756	1474	180	48.3	15.0	4678	460	7542	5:09.8	8064	8096
4. Nikolay Avilov	SOV	10.9	764	1341	207	49.9	14.5	4664	410	6012	5:00.8	7909	7884
5. Joachim Kirst	GDR	10.5	761	1643	198	50.2	15.6	4689	415	5702	5:20.1	7861	7791
6. Tom Waddell	USA	11.3	747	1445	201	51.2	15.3	4373	450	6370	5:04.5	7720	7694
7. Rick Sloan	USA	11.2	672	1407	210	51.0	15.5	4558	485	4990	4:44.0	7692	7553
8. Steen Smidt-Jensen	DEN	10.9	717	1303	195	50.2	14.9	4107	485	4680	4:41.3	7648	7507
9. Eduard De Noorlander	HOL	11.1	690	1389	195	50.5	14.5	4170	420	5022	4:37.8	7554	7380
10. Manfred Tiedtke	GDR	10.9	746	1577	195	50.0	14.7	4031	430	5184	5:33.4	7551	7387
11. Lennart Hedmark	SWE	11.1	729	1408	189	51.3	14.9	4296	410	6290	5:11.0	7481	7339
12. Walter Diessl	AUT	10.7	742	1432	183	51.6	14.7	4223	425	5538	5:19.7	7465	7302
13. Clive Longe	GBR	10.9	686	1510	170	49.3	15.5	4760	400	5930	5:18.8	7338	7175
14. Janis Lanka	SOV	10.9	715	1531	180	49.9	14.8	4990	380	5976	dnf	7227	6938
15. Wu A-Min	TAI	11.3	740	1208	180	52.2	14.8	4025	435	6010	5:08.9	7209	7081
16. Spas Dyurov	BUL	10.9	740	1399	189	50.2	15.1	4090	360	4704	5:15.5	7173	6992
17. Roger Lespagnard	BEL	11.1	694	1259	195	50.2	15.8	3774	420	4746	4:57.0	7125	6932
18. Urs Trautmann	SWI	11.2	696	1516	195	63.9	14.9	4620	410	5632	5:13.6	7044	6850
19. Franz Biedermann	LIE	11.5	630	1094	170	51.4	15.5	3067	390	4492	4:47.9	6323	6160
20. Don Vélez	NIC	11.5	663	1060	165	53.1	16.2	3643	340	4894	5:46.1	5943	5757
-- Gert Herunter	AUT	10.5	675	1393	183	49.7	15.0	4038					
-- Hansruedi Kunz	SWI	11.0	654	1367	165	49.1	15.7	4018					

Charlemagne Anyamah	FRA	11.2	603	1400	180	50.9	15.3	3988
Roberto Carmona	MEX	10.9	692	1437	170	50.5		
Valbjörn Thorlaksson	ICE	11.1	676	1259	170	53.2		
Rein Aun	SOV	10.8	740	1475	180			
Herbert Wessel	GDR	10.8	739	1370	186			
Ho Menh Phoc	VIE	11.9	616	1193	170			
Horst Mandl	AUT	11.2	704	1334				
Domin. Rakotoralahy	MAD	11.5	662					
Werner von Moltke	GER	11.1	614					
Werner Duttweiler	SWI	11.2	531					
Chen, Chuan-Show	TAI	10.8						

Note. At the 1968 Olympic Games times were obtained direct from the photo finish, but the timing devices were adjusted to start after a delay of 0.05 seconds following the firing of the pistol. That result was then rounded (4 and down, 5 and up) to conform to the 1/10 second scoring tables. For example, Bill Toomey's 400 meters of 45.68 showed as 45.63 and was rounded down to 45.6. Toomey 10.41, 45.68, 14.95, 4:57.18; Walde 10.97, 49.03, 14.87, 4:58.60; Bendlin 10.75, 48.38, 15.06, 5:09.85; Avilov 10.95, 49.93, 14.58, 5:00.84; Kirst 10.58, 50.25, 15.68, 5:20.16; Waddell 11.33, 51.25, 15.39, 5:04.52; Sloan 11.28, 51.05, 15.51, 4:44.02; Smidt-Jensen 11.00, 50.22, 14.96, 4:31.36; De Noorlander 11.19, 50.57, 14.53, 4:37.81; Tiedtke 10.96, 50.01, 14.80, 5:33.43; Hedmark 11.18, 51.36, 14.99, 5:11.02; Diessl 10.80, 51.67, 14.77, 5:19.71; Longe 10.96, 49.37, 15.55, 5:18.87; Lanka 10.95, 49.92, 14.82, dnf; Wu 11.32, 52.31, 14.82, 5:08.93; Dyurov 10.95, 50.28, 15.17, 5:15.58; Lespagnard 11.12, 50.29, 15.84, 4:57.06; Trautmann 11.26, 63.48, 14.99, 5:13.62; Biedermann 11.56, 51.45, 15.59, 4:47.82; Vélez 11.54, 53.16, 16.24, 5:46.16. Non-finishers: Herunter 10.53, 49.72, 15.07; Kunz 11.04, 49.17, 15.76; Anyamah 11.30, 50.92, 15.34; Wessel 10.85, 53.48; Carmona 10.99, 50.59; Chen 10.84, 50.91; Thorlaksson 11.12, 53.22; Aun 10.84, dnf; Ho 11.99; Mandl 11.30; Rakotoralahy 11.59; von Moltke 11.15; Duttweiler 11.27.

10.4 100m, an impressive 7.87m (25-10) long jump, and an unheard-of 45.6 400m, still the best ever run in a decathlon. His 4499 first-day score was also a best ever.

But for Toomey the 2nd day was totally different. The weather was so hot he drank several gallons of water, which produced a case of "turista." To top things off, Mexican officials misplaced his vaulting pole. Bill found the pole in a shed some distance from the track, but he returned so unsettled that he missed twice at 3.60m (11-0 3/4), his opening height. Up in the stands, family and friends watched the unfolding disaster. Bill's mother covered her face, unable to watch. Jim, a younger brother, was so nervous he left the stands. On his final approach, Bill sprinted toward the pit, then pulled up and stopped. "Pressure," he said. "For the first time in my life I felt the country was expecting something." Bill then realized he had but 30 seconds to jump. He started over, sped down the runway, planted the pole, and sailed up and over the bar. The cheer that followed brought Jim Toomey back into the stands. And Bill's mother took her hands away from her eyes. Bill later said, "If I had missed it would be like dying."

Bill didn't die, but the Germans were gaining. Big javs by Bendlin (75.42m/247-5) and Walde (71.62m/235-0) closed the gap to 56 and 69 points respectively, which meant the West Germans would have to beat

Figure 6.24.   West German Hans-Joachim Walde, silver medalist. (Courtesy of *Track and Field News*)

Bill in the 1500m by anything from 50 to 80m, depending on how slow the race was. Toomey paced himself and led most of the early going, as all athletes suffered from the heat and altitude. Bendlin drifted away on the last lap, but Walde made an effort to win. He couldn't shake Bill, however, who kicked by him in the homestretch. As Bill crossed the finish line he flashed "V" victory signs with both hands. His 8193 points was a new Olympic record. Soviet teenager Nikolay Avilov was a sound fourth. East German Joachim Kirst had faded to fifth. Americans Tom Waddell and Rick Sloan were solid at sixth and seventh.

In the stands, Toomey's mother was greeted by Schirmer. "Your boy is the greatest in the world."

Munich, 1972

SEPTEMBER 7-8, 33 COMPETITORS, 19 NATIONS

On the morning of September 5, 1972, eight militant Arabs, calling themselves Black September terrorists, climbed the fence surrounding the Olympic village in Munich, made their way to where the Israeli Olympic team was quartered, gunned down two Israeli athletes, and took another nine as hostages. For 23 hours the world watched the painful drama, which ended in the deaths of all the main characters. Despite marvelous preparations by the hosts, the violence is all that most guests would remember about the Munich Olympics.

Unyielding to the criminal pressure Avery Brundage, president of the IOC for one more Olympics, postponed all events for September 6. The Olympic Games resumed the following morning. The decathlon was the first event.

Soviet lawyer Nikolay Avilov was supreme in a total runaway victory. Scoring nine personal bests and equaling a 10th, he ended with a world record of 8454 points. Others thought to have a chance faded quickly. Swedish veteran Lennart Hedmark, troubled by a foot injury, withdrew

Figure 6.25.   Soviets Leonid Litvenyenko (left) and Nikolay Avilov (right) were the silver and gold medalists in Munich. (Don Chadez/From the Zarnowski collection)

Table 6.13 Results of 1972 Olympic Decathlon, Munich

Results		100	lj	sp	hj	400	110H	dis	pv	jav	1500	1962/71 Total Points	1985 Tables
1. Nikolay Avilov	SOV	11.00	768	1436	212	48.45	14.31	4698	455	6166	4:22.8	8454 WR	8466
2. Leonid Litvenyenko	SOV	11.13	681	1418	189	48.40	15.03	4784	440	5894	4:05.9	8035	7970
3. Ryszard Katus	POL	10.89	709	1439	192	49.11	14.41	4300	450	5996	4:31.9	7984	7936
4. Jeff Bennett	USA	10.73	726	1282	186	46.25	15.58	3658	480	5748	4:12.2	7974	7920
5. Stefan Schreyer	GDR	10.82	744	1502	192	49.51	15.00	4508	440	6070	4:48.2	7950	7907
6. Freddy Herbrand	BEL	11.00	730	1391	204	49.78	14.87	4712	440	5042	4:27.7	7947	7897
7. Steen Smidt-Jensen	DEN	11.07	695	1335	201	50.13	14.65	4480	480	5524	4:24.7	7947	7908
8. Tadeusz Janczenko	POL	10.64	728	1445	204	49.06	16.89	4526	450	6380	5:01.5	7861	7791
9. Josep Zeilbauer	AUT	10.97	716	1349	201	48.77	15.13	4084	430	6446	4:58.2	7741	7694
10. Bruce Jenner	USA	11.35	653	1356	192	49.49	15.59	4224	455	6602	4:18.9	7722	7671
11. Regis Ghesquiere	BEL	11.45	721	1432	189	49.13	15.68	4556	380	6088	4:19.4	7677	7611
12. Yves LeRoy	FRA	10.94	732	1390	180	48.73	15.34	4404	450	6166	4:58.9	7675	7633
13. Boris Ivanov	SOV	11.24	659	1447	192	50.18	14.76	4158	430	6484	4:37.4	7657	7606
14. Regis Lespagnard	BEL	11.27	701	1292	201	49.51	15.84	3786	460	5060	4:28.7	7519	7441
15. Barry King	GBR	11.32	706	1529	189	50.05	16.61	4606	390	5774	4:38.6	7468	7382
16. Radu Gavrilas	ROM	11.57	690	1265	201	50.90	15.13	4052	440	5716	4:43.1	7417	7357
17. Chauhan V. Singh	IND	11.35	692	1442	180	49.89	15.01	4518	370	5634	4:38.6	7378	7306
18. Jean-Pierre Schoebel	FRA	11.11	689	1379	160	49.23	15.30	4114	420	5754	4:38.8	7273	7217
19. Heinz Born	SWI	11.35	692	1306	198	50.01	15.39	3934	400	4872	4:47.9	7217	7121
20. Jozsef Bakai	HUN	11.08	716	1584	189	50.88	16.50	5146	400	5218	dnf	7071	6831
21. Jeff Bannister	USA	11.09	720	1421	186	46.79	(32.00)	4200	400	5698	4:15.8	7022	6870
22. Wilfred Mwalawanda	MAD	11.95	568	1227	165	52.68	18.54	3882	330	7128	4:37.4	6227	6154

(Cont.)

Table 6.13 (Continued)

Results		100	lj	sp	hj	400	110H	dis	pv	jav	1500	1962/71 Total Points	1985 Tables
Peter Gabbett	GBR	10.65	719	1359	186	46.10	15.47	4558	350				
Ryszard Skowronek	POL	10.78	742	1424	198	48.08	15.74	3366					
Rudolf Mangish	SWI	10.79	694	1227	189	47.59	15.71	3692					
Luis Asturias Flores	GUA	11.59	651	1178	175	50.97	17.44	3564					
Clive Brooks	BAR	11.10	681	1171	175	49.75	16.37	nm					
Gerry Moro	CAN	11.49	691	1399	186	52.02	16.28						
Joachim Kirst	GDR	11.12	759	1609	210	48.90	dnf						
Hans Joachim Walde	GER	11.11	716	1457	192								
Lennart Hedmark	SWE	11.53	689	1443									
Hans-Joachim Perk	GER	11.34	682	1334									
Horst Beyer	GER	11.64	651	1442									

Note. Bannister's hurdle time is an obvious timing and scoring error that has never been corrected.

after three events. Two-time European champion Joachim Kirst, who led after the first day, fell in the hurdles and was done. American Olympic Trials winner Jeff Bannister was in the next lane to Kirst and fell also after the third hurdle. In the next lane, Pole Tad Janczenko slowed dramatically. Unaware of the chaos behind him, Avilov finished first with a 14.31 clocking and suddenly found himself with a huge overall lead.

Throughout the 2nd day there was only the world record to beat. Holding his side during the 1500, Avilov slowed at times but plowed through in 4:22.8 to up Bill Toomey's global standard by 37 digits. Toomey, watching from his ABC telecasting platform, was the first on the field to congratulate the Russian. Leningrad soldier Leonid Litvenyenko moved from eighth place to the silver medal by posting a 4:05.9, the best ever in Olympic decathlon annals. Pole Ryszard Katus, having the benefit of knowing how fast to run in an earlier heat, barely edged American Jeff Bennett for the bronze medal. Most observers felt Bennett was shortchanged, as he had won his 1500 heat easily in 4:12.1 and was denied the chance to run against his top competitors.

Even more curious was the placing of Bannister. He had finished the hurdle race after falling but was "disqualified" on the scoreboard. He was then listed in the official results as running 32.0 for no points, despite

Figure 6.26. Jeff Bennett leads Jeff Bannister in the 1500 meters. (E.D. Lacey/Courtesy of *Track and Field News*)

having finished some 10 seconds faster! A solid 10th was young Bruce Jenner, who climbed up the 2nd day from 23rd position.

The decathlon award ceremony was an ironic moment in sports history, as it was held the very evening Jews celebrate the new year. Sundown, September 8, 1972, ushered in the Hebrew year 5733. Observers of Rosh Hashanah both mourned the slaughter of 11 Israeli athletes and officials and applauded the victory of Nikolay Avilov, a Soviet Jew.

Montreal, 1976

JULY 29-30, 28 COMPETITORS, 17 NATIONS

From the time Montreal was selected as the site for the 1976 Olympic Games, controversy reigned. Spiraling construction costs, labor disputes, and strikes rendered preparations chaotic.

A week before the games the Canadians refused to allow Nationalist China to compete under its own name, suggesting they call themselves Taiwan. The Nationalist Chinese team, including coach C.K. Yang, returned home. And several days before the games opened two dozen African countries boycotted to protest the IOC's refusal to ban New Zealand after the latter's rugby team toured South Africa. Remembering Munich, a 16,000-man militia protected the Olympic village with the tightest security before or since.

The Olympics were marred by incidents of cheating, attempted collusion, and talk of "blood doping." By the time Queen Elizabeth II officially

Figure 6.27. Fred Samara (right) congratulates Bruce Jenner on a new world record. (Don Chadez/Courtesy of *Track and Field News*)

Table 6.14   Results of 1976 Olympic Decathlon, Montreal

Results		100	lj	sp	hj	400	110H	dis	pv	jav	1500	1962/71 Total Points	1985 Tables
1. Bruce Jenner	USA	10.94	722	1535	203	47.51	14.84	5004	480	6852	4:12.61	8618 WR	8634
2. Guido Kratschmer	GER	10.66	739	1474	203	48.19	14.58	4570	460	6632	4:29.09	8411	8416
3. Nikolay Avilov	SOV	11.23	752	1481	214	48.16	14.20	4560	445	6228	4:26.26	8369	8403
4. Raimo Pihl	SWE	10.93	699	1555	200	47.97	15.81	4430	440	7734	4:28.76	8218	8216
5. Ryszard Skowronek	POL	11.02	726	1374	191	47.91	14.75	4534	480	6222	4:29.89	8113	8099
6. Siegfried Stark	GDR	11.35	698	1508	191	49.14	15.65	4548	465	7418	4:24.93	8048	8051
7. Leonid Litvenyenko	SOV	11.12	692	1420	191	48.44	14.71	4626	460	5366	4:11.41	8025	7963
8. Lennart Hedmark	SWE	11.36	709	1500	191	49.80	14.79	4642	430	7858	4:44.28	7974	8002
9. Alexandr Grebenyuk	SOV	11.10	653	1469	197	49.21	15.05	4716	400	6842	4:39.62	7803	7759
10. Claus Marek	GER	10.81	723	1342	191	47.12	15.19	3840	430	5232	4:27.84	7767	7683
11. Johannes Lahti	FIN	10.89	728	1366	200	49.34	15.31	3852	420	6172	4:45.90	7711	7650
12. Ryszard Katus	POL	11.06	704	1348	184	49.87	14.51	4228	450	5754	4:47.00	7616	7568
13. Ludek Pernica	CZE	11.40	697	1358	194	50.37	15.07	4022	440	5526	4:22.30	7602	7535
14. Phillipe Bobin	FRA	11.07	714	1412	191	49.79	14.96	3984	490	5074	4:59.65	7580	7532
15. Fred Samara	USA	10.85	708	1300	184	50.07	14.87	4054	430	5360	4:40.21	7504	7430
16. Georg Werthner	AUT	11.31	714	1349	188	50.08	15.26	3558	410	6408	4:27.43	7493	7443
17. Gilles Gemise-Fareau	FRA	11.15	674	1210	194	50.09	14.89	4012	460	5204	4:31.81	7486	7423
18. Daley Thompson	GBR	10.79	719	1310	191	48.15	15.98	3636	420	4518	4:29.55	7434	7330
19. Roger Lespagnard	BEL	11.21	693	1324	194	48.99	15.67	3864	420	4640	4:36.67	7322	7221
20. Runald Backmun	SWE	11.02	695	1354	188	50.66	15.62	4240	400	5814	4:57.28	7319	7229
21. Eberhard Stroot	GER	10.75	738	1348	188	47.61	15.23	3982	nh	6510	4:27.48	7063	7102
22. Tito Steiner	ARG	11.37	673	1385	184	50.30	15.82	4026	380	4974	4:43.16	7052	6942

23. Fred Dixon	USA	10.94	691	1444	203	48.38	18.11	4582	nh	5596	4:38.49	6754	6808
-- Josef Zeilbauer	AUT	11.08	727	1491	203	48.94	14.87	4426	nh				
-- Regis Ghesquiere	BEL	11.59	699	1415	191	50.32	15.69	4064					
-- Elias Sveinsson	ICE	11.51	637	1394	194	51.77	16.19						
-- Eltjo Schutter	HOL	11.17	712	1174	180								
-- Heikki Leppanen	FIN	11.71	648										

opened the games on July 17, everything that could go wrong for the Canadians did go wrong. It was the first Summer Olympics ever in which the host nation failed to win a gold medal.

It took a 26-year-old Californian named Bruce Jenner to let some sunshine in on the 1976 Games. Early in 1975, Jenner had worked up a slogan for his scoring goals: "Eighty-five in '75, eighty-six in '76." He had set the world record in 1975, and Montreal was to be a showdown with the defending champ, a more muscular and mustachioed Nikolay Avilov, back for his third Olympics.

"As I walked from the training track to the main stadium I felt that it was my destiny to win," Jenner would say later. "Everything in my whole life pointed me toward winning the gold medal." From the first event it was obvious Jenner was on a roll. He hoped to be within 200 points of the leaders after the first day, as his best events were the final four. But at the end of five events he found himself only 35 points behind West German Guido Kratschmer and 17 behind Avilov.

Bruce ran a conservative hurdles (recalling Fred Dixon's fall in an earlier

Figure 6.28. Bruce Jenner in the decathlon shot put. (Don Chadez/Courtesy of *Track and Field News*)

heat and Jeff Bannister's problems 4 years earlier), then tried too hard in the discus, but still managed to win the event. He took the lead for good in the pole vault and actually cleared the opening height of 4.30m (14-1 1/4) in an empty stadium. Morning patrons had been cleared and afternoon ticket holders were still waiting outside when Bruce cleared the bar. From that moment, victory was assured.

As Jenner rested on the infield, Russian Leonid Litvenyenko patted him on the shoulder and said, "Bruce, you are going to be Olympic champion." "Thanks," replied Bruce. Litvenyenko stared at Jenner a few moments and then asked, "Bruce, you going to be millionaire?" Jenner just laughed.

With only the 1500m remaining, the question was not whether Jenner would up the world record again, but by how much. Unlike most decathletes, he actually looked forward to running the event.

At the urging of his father, I went to trackside and yelled at Bruce, "Do you know what you need?" A simple nod told me he had already checked the tables and knew what he needed to clock a new world-record score. He ran the first part of the race conservatively. At the bell, he picked up the pace and blasted the last 400m in 61 seconds, recording another lifetime best with a time of 4:12.61 and posting 8618 points, a new world record. All legendary stuff. Someone shoved an American flag in his hand right after the finish. The crowd roared with delight as he circled the track in a victory lap. He then embraced his wife Christie, reminding her, "We did it. We did it together."

The battle for second went virtually unnoticed. Kratschmer was the beneficiary of a lenient javelin judge who ruled an apparently flat throw (which wouldn't count) fair. Kratschmer then stayed close enough to Avilov in the 1500m to win the silver medal by 42 points. Raimo Pihl of Sweden (and former NCAA champ from Brigham Young) was fourth. Americans Fred Samara and Fred Dixon (no-height in pole vault) suffered subpar efforts in placing 15th and 23rd. All but unnoticed, except by Jenner (who recalled, "That guy asked a lot of questions"), was a British teenager, Daley Thompson, who finished 18th.

Moscow, 1980

JULY 25-26, 21 COMPETITORS, 12 NATIONS

United States President Jimmy Carter, who could find no other way to protest the 1979 Soviet invasion of Afghanistan, used his athletes as a line of defense and boycotted the Moscow Games. Carter and his chief counsel, Lloyd Cutler, made it clear that the United States Olympic Committee was to stay home and used extensive arm-twisting to convince other nations to support the boycott. Carter threatened to revoke the passport of any athlete who tried to travel to the Soviet Union. The British team members made their own choices, and most decided to go to Moscow.

Without West German Guido Kratschmer, the new world-record holder, and Pan American champion Bob Coffman, Britain's Daley Thompson was not seriously challenged. It is doubtful that either could have tackled Thompson, whose strong marks of 10.62, 8.00m (26-3), 48.01,

Figure 6.29. Britain's Daley Thompson in the long jump. (Mark Shearman/Courtesy of *Track and Field News*)

Table 6.15 Results of 1980 Olympic Decathlon, Moscow

Results		100	lj	sp	hj	400	110H	dis	pv	jav	1500	1962/77 Total Points	1985 Tables
1. Daley Thompson	GBR	10.62	800	1518	208	48.01	14.47	4224	470	6416	4:39.9	8495	8522
2. Yuriy Kutsenko	SOV	11.19	774	1450	208	48.67	15.04	3986	490	6808	4:22.6	8331	8369
3. Sergei Zhelanov	SOV	11.40	760	1417	218	49.27	14.83	4280	460	5730	4:27.5	8135	8135
4. Georg Werthner	AUT	11.44	727	1345	203	49.26	15.08	3814	485	7366	4:23.4	8050	8084
5. Josef Zeilbauer	AUT	11.29	714	1531	203	50.91	14.80	4400	450	6486	4:30.6	8007	7989
6. Dariusz Ludwig	POL	11.35	751	1332	208	50.55	15.38	4582	480	5838	4:29.7	7978	7972
7. Atanas Adonov	BUL	11.38	686	1559	200	50.36	14.83	4762	470	5354	4:29.2	7927	7887
8. Steffen Grummt	GDR	11.35	686	1615	194	49.39	14.82	4856	430	5524	4:30.2	7892	7840
9. Esa Jokinen	FIN	11.40	727	1412	206	49.06	15.62	4048	420	6738	4:34.4	7826	7793
10. Janusz Szczerkowski	POL	11.22	738	1406	200	49.64	14.57	4474	490	4522	4:44.9	7822	7794
11. Johannes Lahti	FIN	11.32	720	1428	203	50.06	15.14	4244	460	5694	4:44.0	7765	7725
12. Stefan Nicklaus	SWI	11.17	693	1429	197	49.74	14.96	4218	430	6654	4:44.9	7762	7721
13. Peter Hadfield	AUS	11.04	736	1334	185	48.40	15.18	4508	440	5612	4:44.7	7709	7658
14. Razvigor Jankov	BUL	11.26	661	1628	185	50.37	15.69	4802	460	5812	4:51.2	7624	7572
15. Brad McStravick	GBR	10.97	674	1353	191	48.80	15.23	2946	430	5798	4:31.0	7616	7337
16. Columba Blango	SLE	11.40	640	1000	185	53.48	15.45	2308	nh	3620	5:22.9	5080	5214
--- Miro Ronac	PER	11.88	672	1260	191	52.45	17.19	4642	440	5634			
--- Valery Kachanov	SOV	11.22	765	1470	208	48.67	14.40	4602	nh				
--- Allesandro Brogini	ITA	11.41	733	1302	206	50.97	15.21	3954	nh				
--- Rainer Pottel	GDR	11.16	nm	1432									
--- Siegfried Stark	GDR	11.27	700										

and 14.47 illustrate the importance of speed on the scoring tables. His world-record pace was thwarted on the 2nd day by rain and low temperatures.

Thompson had a massive lead after nine events, but because the world record was beyond reach he decided to run the 1500 just fast enough to win the overall title. Seeing his aunt and friends in the crowd, he waved to them. He finished 10th in the 1500, but it made no difference. The gold medal was his. "I wanted to enjoy it, to have it for myself. And besides, this wasn't my last decathlon. It wasn't my last Olympics. If it had been, I'd have run faster."

Daley's nearest rival, Valeriy Kachanov, pulled a calf muscle in the vault and had to withdraw. Soviet teammates Yuriy Kutsenko and Sergei Zhelanov, whose 2.18m (7-1 3/4) high jump helped, captured the silver and bronze medals. Young Austrian Georg Werthner used a 73.66m (241-8) javelin to boost his chances. The Linz lawyer finished fourth, 43 points ahead of countryman Josef Zeilbauer.

The Soviet fans, who had not been friendly to foreign athletes, gave the gregarious Thompson a standing ovation when he finished the 1500m. Daley's last duty to Olympic protocol carried into the wee hours of the morning. As each athlete must be tested for drugs, a urine specimen is necessary at the completion of the meet. As Daley drank very little during

Figure 6.30.   Daley Thompson celebrates a gold medal performance. He is flanked by Sergei Zhelanov and Yuriy Kutsenko. (Courtesy of Pressen Bild)

the 2nd day, it was nearly 3 in the morning before he'd had enough liquids to give a urine sample. Only then was he released from doping control. "It's three o'clock in the morning and they let me out. The whole town is dead. The first time in 5 years I want to go out, right, and everybody's asleep," he lamented.

At about the same time as the Olympics, the Carter administration offered a sad alternative meet in Philadelphia for boycotting countries. Coffman won the "Freedom Games" decathlon, as neither Kratschmer nor young teammate Jürgen Hingsen finished.

After 1980, many of America's top decathletes retired rather than wait another 4 years for an Olympic chance. Missing the Olympics was a major setback for American decathlon fortunes. We have yet to recover.

Los Angeles, 1984

AUGUST 8-9, 26 COMPETITORS, 18 NATIONS

The 1984 Los Angeles Olympics marked the third successive Games in which a significant number of nations declined to participate for political reasons. This time the Soviet Union led most of its Eastern Bloc allies out, obviously intending to embarrass Americans for their 1980 boycott.

On the field, under 2 days of perfect weather, Daley Thompson did it again. West German Jürgen Hingsen, the world-record holder, had a good meet, but the 90,000 spectators had the feeling that whatever Hingsen did wouldn't matter—Daley would do one better. Event after event, Daley seemed supreme. The only disappointment was that he failed by a single point (later reversed) to break the world standard. His record versus the "German Hercules" ran to 7-0.

Daley blasted the first two events with marks of 10.44 and 8.01m (26-3 1/4). By the end of the first day, he led Hingsen by 114 points and another West German, Siegfried Wentz, by 301. Guido Kratschmer and young Frenchman William Motti were further back. On the 2nd day, there was high drama in the discus. The competition's first toss had the crowd buzzing. Motti, 20, tossed 50.92m (167-1), the best by any Olympic finisher.

Figure 6.31.   Daley Thompson leads American Jim Wooding in the 1500 meters. (Diane Johnson/Courtesy of *Track and Field News*)

Table 6.16 Results of 1984 Olympic Decathlon, Los Angeles

Results		100	lj	sp	hj	400	110H	dis	pv	jav	1500	1962/77 Total Points	1985 Tables
1. Daley Thompson	GBR	10.44	801	1572	203	46.97	14.33	4656	500	6524	4:35.00	8798	8847
2. Jürgen Hingsen	GER	10.91	780	1587	212	47.69	14.29	5082	450	6044	4:22.60	8673	8695
3. Siegfried Wentz	GER	10.99	711	1587	209	47.78	14.35	4660	450	6768	4:33.96	8412	8416
4. Guido Kratschmer	GER	10.80	740	1593	194	49.25	14.66	4728	490	6940	4:47.99	8326	8357
5. William Motti	FRA	11.28	745	1442	206	48.13	14.71	5092	450	6376	4:35.15	8266	8278
6. John Crist	USA	11.33	698	1405	206	48.45	15.01	4618	480	6188	4:23.78	8130	8115
7. Jim Wooding	USA	11.04	701	1390	197	47.62	14.57	4738	460	5720	4:28.31	8091	8054
8. Dave Steen	CAN	11.20	741	1257	204	48.09	15.39	4404	480	5692	4:17.70	8047	8034
9. Dr. Georg Werthner	AUT	11.41	696	1380	194	49.44	15.36	4118	470	7696	4:16.41	8012	8028
10. Michele Ruefenacht	SWI	10.72	696	1386	200	48.63	14.57	4530	430	5510	4:39.47	7924	7855
11. Brad McStravick	GBR	10.92	682	1338	194	48.68	15.01	4554	430	6154	4:25.15	7890	7830
12. Tim Bright	USA	11.22	675	1380	200	48.87	14.52	4174	540	5366	4:49.27	7862	7862
13. Patrick Vetterli	SWI	11.44	713	1388	203	49.83	15.14	4382	450	6466	4:55.06	7739	7717
14. Peter Hadfield	AUS	11.15	713	1368	176	48.50	15.05	4336	450	5522	4:25.90	7683	7633
15. Weng Kangqiang	PRC	11.28	730	1245	188	50.52	15.21	3874	460	6972	4:34.10	7662	7662
16. Guu Jin-Shoei	TPE	11.42	689	1276	203	50.59	14.91	3970	490	6236	4:50.75	7629	7614
17. Trond Skramstad	NOR	11.20	718	1420	185	49.25	15.08	4002	450	5494	4:43.02	7579	7522
18. Doug Fernandez	VEN	11.59	674	1312	188	49.83	16.05	4352	440	6712	4:23.96	7553	7505
19. Lee Fu-An	TPE	10.98	700	1302	203	49.67	15.49	3710	450	5496	4:45.87	7541	7471
20. Colin Boreham	GBR	11.46	690	1351	197	50.19	15.48	4410	420	5266	4:32.50	7485	7400
21. Menssar Saleh	QAT	11.51	662	1154	188	52.04	16.20	3626	360	4502	4:35.64	6589	6504
22. Claudio Escaunza	PAR	11.66	651	1410	182	53.06	17.51	4776	400	6416	dnf	6546	6290

(Cont.)

Table 6.16   (Continued)

Results		100	lj	sp	hj	400	110H	dis	pv	jav	1500	1962/77 Total Points	1985 Tables
23. Fidel Solorzano	ECU	11.15	699	1009	194	49.24	16.22	3354	310	4866	5:07.38	6519	6439
24. Angel Diaz-Granillo	GUA	11.54	648	962	191	52.08	16.02	2868	330	4796	4:26.11	6342	6272
25. Vivian Coralie	MRI	11.37	584	979	182	51.28	16.39	3292	300	4158	4:26.26	6084	6008
26. Albert Miller	FIJ	11.48	632	1307	191	50.22	15.36	3846	nh				

Hingsen's second throw traveled almost as far, 50.82m (166-8), a lifetime best. The pressure was on Daley, who had two awful throws. When he stepped into the ring for the third time he had lost his overall lead and trailed Hingsen by 68 points. Never hesitating, he went for it, and although the throw was low, it had terrific force. The measurement of 46.56m (152-9) was a decathlon personal record and Daley led by 32 points. He never looked back. After vaulting 5.00m (16-4 3/4), he needed only 4:34.8 in the final event to break Hingsen's world record. Daley labored on the second and third lap, then sauntered down the homestretch, breaking the beam at 4:35.0 and missing Hingsen's mark by one point. Eighteen months later the IAAF reread his hurdle photo and awarded one more point. When the tables changed a year later he assumed the world record. He clowned his way through postmeet interviews but turned serious when asked why he hadn't sprinted the last few meters to break the world record. "Hey, all I wanted to do was win. At the end of the day it's how badly *I* want that is going to get me those extra points, not a million people cheering for me."

Figure 6.32. France's William Motti in the ring and on the screen in Los Angeles. (Frank Zarnowski)

The presence of East German, Soviet, and Polish decathletes would not have affected the medals. Germans Hingsen, Wentz, and Kratschmer placed second, third, and fourth. Motti, a freshman at Mount Saint Mary's College, placed fifth with a collegiate record 8266 points. Americans John Crist, Jim Wooding, and Tim Bright were back at sixth, seventh, and twelfth.

Thompson became only the second two-time Olympic winner. High marks went to Sam Adams, the meet director, and low marks to Ernst and Winney (the official scorer of the 1984 Olympics), who gave new meaning to scoring problems.

Seoul, 1988

SEPTEMBER 28-29, 39 COMPETITORS, 26 NATIONS

On the day before the Seoul decathlon the IOC Medical Commission announced that Canadian sprinter Ben Johnson would be stripped of his Olympic 100m gold medal and world record. Traces of anabolic steroids had been found in his system. Johnson was track's first male gold medalist to be removed from the Olympic record books since Jim Thorpe three quarters of a century before. Unfortunately it is this event that most will recall about the Seoul Games, which returned to the Orient after two dozen years.

Seoul marked a changing of the decathlon guard. History's top five scorers were entered. But the veterans fared poorly—only two of them finished and neither medaled.

All eyes focused on Daley Thompson, in his fourth Olympic try. Aware that no one had ever won three Olympic golds Daley indicated a desire

Figure 6.33.   Daley Thompson admires the shirt of surprise bronze medalist Dave Steen (left) of Canada. (All Sport Photography)

Table 6.17   Results of 1988 Olympic Decathlon, Seoul

Results		100	lj	sp	hj	400	110H	dis	pv	jav	1500	Total Points
1. Christian Schenk	GDR	11.25	743	1548	227	48.90	15.13	4928	470	6132	4:28.95	8488
2. Torsten Voss	GDR	10.87	745	1497	197	47.71	14.46	4436	510	6176	4:33.02	8399
3. Dave Steen	CAN	11.18	744	1420	197	48.29	14.81	4366	520	6416	4:23.20	8328
4. Daley Thompson	GBR	10.62	738	1502	203	49.06	14.72	4480	490	6404	4:45.11	8306
5. Christian Plaziat	FRA	10.83	762	1358	212	48.34	14.18	4306	490	5218	4:34.07	8272
6. Alain Blondel	FRA	11.02	743	1292	197	47.44	14.40	4120	520	5746	4:16.64	8268
7. Tim Bright	USA	11.18	705	1412	206	49.34	14.39	4168	570	6160	4:51.20	8216
8. Robert De Wit	HOL	11.05	695	1534	200	48.21	14.36	4132	480	6300	4:25.86	8189
9. Dave Johnson	USA	11.15	712	1452	203	49.15	14.66	4236	490	6646	4:29.62	8180
10. Pavel Tarnovetskiy	SOV	11.23	728	1525	197	48.60	14.76	4802	520	5948	4:52.24	8167
11. Petri Keskitalo	FIN	10.94	756	1534	197	49.94	14.25	4186	480	6664	4:55.89	8143
12. Beat Gaehwiler	SWI	11.18	734	1448	194	49.02	15.11	4246	470	6584	4:16.74	8114
13. Dezso Szabo	HUN	11.02	729	1292	206	48.23	14.96	3954	500	5680	4:17.85	8093
14. Mike Smith	CAN	10.99	737	1361	197	47.83	14.70	4388	430	6654	4:28.97	8083
15. Simon Shirley	AUS	11.03	745	1420	197	48.84	15.44	4168	470	6400	4:27.48	8036
16. Simon Poelman	NZL	11.09	708	1451	203	49.89	14.78	4320	490	5718	4:28.54	8021
17. Mikael Olander	SWE	11.46	675	1607	200	51.28	16.06	5066	480	7280	5:02.42	7869
18. Uwe Freimuth	GDR	11.57	700	1560	194	49.84	15.04	4666	490	6020	4:46.04	7860
19. Lars Warming	DEN	11.07	704	1341	194	47.97	14.49	4038	480	5150	4:22.41	7859
20. Roman Hraban	TCH	10.89	707	1584	179	49.68	14.94	4532	490	6048	5:06.68	7781
21. Georg Werthner	AUT	11.52	736	1393	194	49.99	15.64	3882	460	6704	4:26.42	7753
22. Christian Gugler	SWI	11.49	702	1380	203	50.60	15.22	3908	470	6092	4:21.93	7745

23. Antonio Penalver	SPA	11.38	708	1431	200	50.24	14.97	4634	440	5568	4:32.68	7743
24. Alex Kruger	GBR	11.30	697	1323	215	49.98	15.38	3872	460	5434	4:37.84	7623
25. Lee, Fu-An	TPE	11.00	723	1315	203	49.73	14.96	3806	450	5282	4:45.57	7579
26. Santiago Mellado	ESA	11.33	683	1163	206	48.37	15.39	3752	460	5542	4:30.07	7517
27. Severin Moser	SWI	11.10	698	1269	185	48.63	15.13	3804	470	4952	4:21.90	7502
28. Veroslav Valenta	TCH	11.51	701	1417	194	51.16	15.18	4584	460	5628	5:03.17	7442
29. Carlos O'Connell	IRE	11.26	690	1241	188	48.24	15.61	3802	440	5268	4:32.06	7310
30. Greg Richards	GBR	11.50	709	1294	182	49.27	15.56	4232	450	5350	4:53.85	7237
31. Gong, Guohua	CHN	11.43	622	1398	191	51.25	15.88	4618	460	5784	4:54.99	7231
32. Albert Miller	FIJ	11.47	643	1233	194	50.30	15.00	3872	400	5726	4:53.72	7016
33. Lee, Kwang-Ik	KOR	11.57	719	1027	191	50.71	16.20	3436	410	5494	4:29.98	6917
34. Danbar Kunwar	NEP	12.12	583	971	170	52.32	17.05	2710	280	3910	4:41.24	5339
--- Walter Kulvet	SOV	11.31	714	1529	200	50.62	withdrew					
--- Gary Kinder	USA	11.31	700	1489	197	51.79	withdrew					
--- Fidel Solorzano	ECU	11.01	679	1176	188	withdrew						
--- Alexander Apaitchev	SOV	dnf, withdrew										
--- Jürgen Hingsen	GER	dsq*, withdrew										

*Disqualified for 3 false starts in 100 meters.

to compete just for fun. But those close to him knew he wanted a medal. Despite eroding skills and questionable conditioning, he gave a terrific account, going all out on 30-year-old legs and 12-year-old vaulting poles. The poles didn't last, and the legs could only carry him to a fourth-place finish, just missing a medal.

Other vets fared worse. Twenty-eight-year-old Siggi Wentz never made it to the starting line. He suffered a groin pull and left Seoul even before Ben Johnson did. Teammate Jürgen Hingsen foolishly tried to beat the 100m gun and made Olympic history as the first to be disqualified for three false starts. No amount of pleading helped, and a jury denied his appeal for reinstatement. Soviet Alexandr Apaitchev took but two steps in the 100m race and retreated to the tunnel. And East German Uwe Freimuth was well off his form, placing 18th.

But Freimuth's East German teammates were hotter than *kimchi*, the local fermented cabbage dish with toxic levels of garlic and hot pepper. Twenty-three-year-old Christian Schenk plastered an enormous field of 39 starters, the most ever, while recording four PRs and equaling another to put away the gold medal. He took the lead for good in the high jump, where his 2.27m (7-5 1/4) tied the world decathlon best. The 1987 world champ, Torsten Voss, himself weakened by a leg injury, hung on for the silver medal. Schenk's 8488 was a lifetime best, 89 more than Voss.

All the drama focused on the bronze medal. A snapped vaulting pole on his opening height left Thompson limping. He went on to clear 4.90m (16-3/4) and clung to third. Schenk and Voss had solidified their holds on the gold and silver medals, but only 120 points (less than 20 seconds in the 1500m) separated third through eighth places after nine events. The best bets to dislodge him belonged to American Tim Bright and Soviet vet Pavel Tarnovetsky. Bright's world decathlon best of 5.70m (18-8 1/4) vaulted him into fourth place, just 53 points behind Daley. And Tarnovetsky had 1500m skills. Also on the chase were Finn Petri Keskitalo, Frenchman Christian Plaziat, and Canadian longshot Dave Steen. Bright never made the effort, and everyone but Steen faded after the first lap. It was obvious that the final medal belonged to Thompson (no one had ever won three Olympic medals) if he could just stay about 20 seconds behind Steen. And vice versa. With a gutsy last lap the University of Toronto grad pounded out a 4:23.20. Daley, with his groin heavily taped, could clock only 4:45.11. Steen had moved from eighth to third in less than 5 minutes. "I won't believe it till I see it on the scoreboard," he told NBC newsman Dave Sims. Moments later he believed.

The Seoul decathlon was beset by poor attendance, naive scheduling, and stubborn officiating. All contributed to lower-than-normal scores. And Seoul ushered in a new cast of major decathlon players. But for Daley Thompson there was some satisfaction. He had completed a fourth Olympic decathlon, although the distinction of being the first to do so belonged

Figure 6.34.   Christian Schenk celebrates his gold medal performance. (All Sport Photography)

to steady Austrian Georg Werthner, who had run in the previous 1500m heat. Thompson had met decathlon's ultimate challenge. Even without a medal, at age 30 he had been competitive. And he had endured. And after all, Barcelona, and a fifth Olympic try, would be but 4 years away.

Paris, 1900

A pentathlon, listed on the program, was not contested.

St. Louis, 1904

TRIATHLON, JULY 1-2, 118 COMPETITORS, 4 NATIONS

The event was part of a combined gymnastics and track and field competition known as "turning" or "turnverein gymnastics." It was popular in pockets of the United States and had its origin in 19th-century Germany. One hundred and eighteen (yes, 118!) athletes competed from four nations. Max Emmerich, representing the Indianapolis YMCA, was the victor.

Table 6.18   Results of 1904 Olympic Triathlon, St. Louis

Results		lj		sp		100 yd	Score
1. Max Emmerich	USA	657+	(21-7)	981	(32-2 1/4)	10.6	35.7 pts
2. John Grieb	USA	615	(20-2 1/4)	1023+	(33-7)	11.0	34.0 pts
3. William Merz	USA	606+	(19-10 3/4)	947	(31-1)	10.8	33.9 pts
4. George Mayer	USA	551	(18-1)	1115	(36-7)	11.4	32.4 pts
5. John Bissinger	USA	561	(18-4 3/4)	999	(32-9 1/2)	11.4	30.8 pts
6. Phillip Kassel	USA	585	(19-2 1/4)	877+	(28-9 1/2)	11.2	30.1 pts
7. Christian Busch	GER	576	(18-10 3/4)	953+	(31-3 1/2)	11.6	30.0 pts
7. Fred Schmind	USA	591	(19-4 3/4)	920	(30-2 1/4)	11.6	30.0 pts

Note. The events were measured imperially.

ALL-AROUND, JULY 4, 7 COMPETITORS, 2 NATIONS

The all-around was popular in the United States and was a forerunner of the decathlon. The 1904 competition in St. Louis was actually the national AAU championships. The AAU had developed straight-line scoring tables. In the 100-yard dash and hurdles, only the time of the winner was taken. Points for other finishers were derived by estimating the number of feet each runner was behind at the finish and applying a set of differential points per foot.

Ellery Clark was the defending AAU champ, whereas Adam Gunn of the Buffalo YMCA had won in 1901 and 1902. Penn's Truxtun Hare was one of football's all-time greats in the 19th century. All fell to Irish weightman Tom Kiely, 35, who was offered a free trip if he would represent Great Britain. He refused, paid his own way, and won the championship for his native Ireland. Max Emmerich, triathlon winner 2 days before, pulled up in the 100 yards. All events were measured imperially (Table 6.19).

Athens, 1906

PENTATHLUM (LATER CALLED PENTATHLON), APRIL 25-27, 26 COMPETITORS, 12 NATIONS

Modeled after the ancient Greek pentathlon, the pentathlum's five events were the standing long jump, Greek-style discus throw, javelin throw, stade (192m), and Greco-Roman wrestling. The event was not uncommon in parts of Scandinavia in the early 1890s. American Martin Sheridan was an easy favorite, but he injured a knee during earlier events. After finishing third in the standing long jump, he withdrew.

Now it was anyone's contest. The giant Hungarian Istvan Mudin looked like a possible winner because the event put a premium on strength. His running and jumping reduced his chances and in the end Sweden's Hjalmar Mellander won with consistency, placing no worse than seventh in any event (Table 6.20).

Stockholm, 1912

PENTATHLON, JULY 7, 26 COMPETITORS, 11 NATIONS

Scored on the basis of 1 point for first, 2 for second, and so on, Jim Thorpe scored 7! Enough said. His score on the current tables would be a respectable 3371. Norway's Ferdinand Bie was far superior to the rest of the pack and was content to jog the 1500m, placing last, but he finished second overall, ahead of American James Donahue.

American Avery Brundage did not finish the 1500m, but results awarded him the seven points for last place and a total of 31, for sixth overall (Table 6.21).

Antwerp, 1920

PENTATHLON, AUGUST 6, 19 COMPETITORS, 8 NATIONS

Finn Eero Lehtonen won easily over American Everett Bradley, who dropped off 30 seconds in the last event. Finns Hugo Lahtinen and Ossian Nylund competed, but their entries were protested by other nations (Table 6.22).

Paris 1924

PENTATHLON, JULY 7, 30 COMPETITORS, 17 NATIONS

Eero Lehtonen won his second title, but it was not decided until he edged Hungarian Elemer Somfay in the 1500m. The meet's highlight was a surprising world record of 7.765m (25-5 3/5) by American Robert LeGendre in the long jump. But he was inconsistent and placed third overall.

Had Somfay run 1 1/2 seconds faster or Lehtonen 1 1/2 seconds slower in the 1500 they would have tied at 15 points apiece and the decathlon tables would have been used to break the tie. Ironically, LeGendre had more (decathlon) points than either, potentially setting up the silliest scoring situation ever. Luckily, the event was dropped from the Olympic program (Table 6.23).

Table 6.19   Results of 1904 Olympic All-Around, St. Louis

		100yd	sp	hj	880w	ham	pv	120H	56wt	lj	mile	Points
1. Thomas Kiely	IRE	11.2	35-6	5-0	4:20.0	120-7	9-0	c18.3	29-3	19-6	5:51.0	6036
2. Adam Gunn	USA	c11.2	40-1	5-5	4:13.0	103-0	9-9	c17.9	23-8 1/2	18-2	5:45.0	5907
3. Truxtun Hare	USA	10.8	39-8	5-0	4:20.0	119-0	8-0	c18.3	24-10 3/4	19-11	5:40.0	5813
4. John Holloway	IRE	c10.9	32-10	5-6	3:59.0	90-3	9-6	c18.4	19-7 1/2	18-2	5:40.0	5273
5. Ellery Clark	USA	11.0	33-8	5-4	4:11.0	95-6	nh	withdrew				2778
6. John Grieb	USA	c11.2	34-7	5-4	4:49.0	nm	nh	withdrew				2199
7. Max Emmerich	USA	dnf										--

c = approximate.

Table 6.20   Results of the 1906 Olympic Pentathlon, Athens

Place			s l j	discus	jav	stade	GRW	Points
1	Hjalmer Mellander	SWE	7	5 (12)	5 (17)	4 (21)	3	24
2	István Mudin	HUN	6	1 (7) 3264	9 (16)	8 (24)	1	25
3	Erik Lemming	SWE	15	2 (17) 3129	1 (18)	7 (25)	4	29
4	Uno Haggman (Tuomela)	FIN	18	9 (27)	2 (29)	3 (32)	2	34
5	Lawson Robertson	USA	1 2955	17 (18)	11 (29)	1 (30)	6	36
6	Knut Lindberg	SWE	16	11 (27)	3 (30)	2 (32)	5	37
7	Edward Srchibald	CAN	10	13 (23)	4 (27)	6 (33)	–	
8	Julius Wagner	SWI	8	6 (14)	18 (32)	5 (37)	–	
9	Theodor Scheidl (Petit)	AUT	2 2900	10 (12)	21 (33)	–	–	
10	Gyorgy Luntzer	HUN	24	4 (28)	6 (34)	–	–	
11	Christos Parsalis	GRE	12	14 (26)	10 (36)	–	–	
T12	Arthur Mallwitz	GER	4	20 (24)	14 (38)	–	–	
	Miroslav Sustera	BOHa	23	3 (26) 2843	12 (38)	–	–	
T14	Wilhelm Ritzenhoff	GER	17	8 (25)	16 (41)	–	–	
	Frantisek Soucek	TCH	20	15 (35)	6 (41)	–	–	
16	Wilhelm Dorr	GER	22	7 (29)	15 (44)	–	–	
T17	Carl Kaltenbach	GER	18	12 (30)	17 (47)	–	–	
	Heikki Ahlman	FIN	21	18 (39)	8 (47)	–	–	
19	Emilio Brambilla	ITA	5	21 (26)	22 (48)	–	–	
20	Henri Baur	AUT	11	16 (27)	24 (51)	–	–	
21	Daniel Sullivan	USA	9	22 (31)	23 (54)	–	–	
T22	Gustav Krojer	AUT	12	24 (36)	20 (56)	–	–	

24	Pál Vargha	HUN	24	19 (43)	13 (56)	--	--
	Franz Solar	AUT	26	23 (49)	19 (68)	--	--
dnf	Martin Sheridan	USA	3 2855	withdrew	--	--	--
dnf	André Désfarges	FRA	12	withdrew	--	--	--

Note. s l j = standing long jump; stade = @ 192m race; GRW = Greco-Roman wrestling.
aRepresenting Bohemia, now part of Czechoslovakia.

Table 6.21   Results of the 1912 Olympic Pentathlon, Stockholm

		lj	jav	200	dis	1500	Points	1985 Tables
1. Jim Thorpe	USA	707 (1)	4671 (3)	22.9 (1)	3557 (1)	4:44.8 (1)	7	3371
2. Ferdinand Bie	NOR	685 (2)	4645 (4)	23.5 (7)	3179 (4)	5:07.8 (6)	21	3047
3. James Donahue	USA	683 (3)	3828 (16)	23.0 (2)	2964 (11)	4:51.0 (3)	29	3024
4. Frank Lukeman	CAN	645 (8)	3602 (19)	23.2 (5)	3376 (3)	5:00.2 (5)	29	2913
5. James Menaul	USA	640 (11)	3583 (20)	23.0 (2)	3138 (6)	4:49.6 (2)	30	2933
6. Avery Brundage	USA	658 (4)	4285 (9)	24.2 (15)	3472 (2)	dnf (7)	31	2411
7. Hugo Wieslander	SWE	627 (14)	4956 (1)	24.1 (14)	3074 (7)	4:53.1 (4)	32	2982
8. Inge Lindholm	SWE	632 (12)	4194 (12)	23.5 (7)	3047 (8)	(30 pts after 4 events)		
9. Gösta Holmér	SWE	602 (20)	4546 (5)	24.0 (11)	3178 (5)	(30 pts after 4 events)		
10. Oscar Lemming	SWE	655 (5)	4951 (2)	24.6 (18)	2764 (12)	(31 pts after 4 events)		
11. Nils Fjästad	SWE	643 (10)	4015 (15)	23.6 (9)	3043 (9)	(32 pts after 4 events)		
12. Eemil Kukkola	FIN	619 (17)	4443 (6)	24.0 (11)	2997 (10)	(35 pts after 4 events)		
13. Otto Bäurle	GER	652 (7)	3429 (22)	23.6 (9)	(38 pts after 3 events)			
14. Einar Nilsson	SWE	623 (15)	4367 (8)	24.3 (16)	(39 pts after 3 events)			
15. Erik Kugelberg	SWE	645 (8)	4202 (11)	24.9 (21)	(40 pts after 3 events)			
16. Charles Lomberg	SWE	653 (6)	3715 (17)	24.4 (17)	(40 pts after 3 events)			
17. Pierre Faillot	FRA	629 (13)	3346 (24)	23.2 (5)	(42 pts after 3 events)			
18. Hugo Ericson	SWE	558 (26)	4374 (7)	24.0 (11)	(44 pts after 3 events)			
19. John Eller	USA	617 (18)	3336 (25)	23.1 (4)	(47 pts after 3 events)			
20. Julius Wagner	SWI	622 (16)	4231 (13)	25.3 (23)	(52 pts after 3 events)			
21. Gustav Krojer	AUT	610 (19)	3889 (15)	24.7 (20)	(54 pts after 3 events)			
22. Georges André	FRA	598 (21)	3483 (21)	24.6 (18)	(60 pts after 3 events)			

23. Megerdich Megerian	TUR	559 (25)	3687 (18)	26.4 (24)	(67 pts after 3 events)
24. Alfredo Pagani	ITA	586 (23)	3423 (23)	25.2 (22)	(68 pts after 3 events)
— Karl von Halt	GER	(22/24) ?	4275 (10)	dnf	
— Alexander Abraham	GER	(22/24) ?			
or Josef Weitzer	GER		(26) ?		

Note. Place in individual events is in parentheses. The tie for third place was broken by using the decathlon tables: Donahue 3475.865; Lukeman 3396.975.

Table 6.22   Results of 1920 Olympic Pentathlon, Antwerp

		lj	jav	200	dis	1500	Points	1985 Tables
1. Eero Lehtonen	FIN	6635 (2)	5467 (2)	23.0 (1)	3464 (7)	4:40.2 (2)	14	3383
2. Everett Bradley	USA	661 (3)	4916 (8)	23.0 (1)	3678 (6)	5:10.0 (6)	24	3165
3. Hugo Lahtinen	FIN	659 (4)	5425 (3)	23.6 (5)	3112 (13)	4:36.0 (1)	26	3270
4. Robert LeGendre	USA	6505 (5)	4460 (11)	23.0 (1)	3739 (4)	4:46.0 (5)	26	3224
5. Helge Lövland	NOR	632 (7)	5313 (4)	24.0 (10)	3951 (2)	4:45.8 (4)	27	3262
6. Brutus Hamilton	USA	686 (1)	4836 (10)	23.4 (4)	3713 (5)	5:12.8 (7)	27	3165
7. Robert Olsson	SWE	627 (9)	4368 (12)	23.6 (5)	3980 (1)	4:42.8 (3)	30	3174
8. Alexandr Klumberg	EST	625 (10)	6076 (1)	25.3 (15)	3862 (3)	(29 pts after 4 events)		
9. Erik Gyllenstolpe	SWE	6415 (6)	4988 (7)	24.2 (12)	3350(10)	(35 pts after 4 events)		
10. Evert Nilsson	SWE	620 (12)	5085 (5)	24.2 (12)	3462(8)	(37 pts after 4 events)		
11. Carl Enok Svensson	SWE	5895 (14)	5043 (6)	23.8 (7)	3215(11)	(38 pts after 4 events)		
12. Robert Dunne	USA	5595 (18)	4152 (13)	23.8 (7)	3428(9)	(44 pts after 4 events)		
13. Ossian Nylund	FIN	6285 (8)	4865 (9)	25.2 (14)	2697(13)	(46 pts after 4 events)		
14. Ole Reidstad	NOR	6095 (13)	3899 (15)	23.9 (9)	3198d(12)	(48 pts after 4 events)		
15. Edouard Médécin	MON	621 (11)	-- (16)	24.0 (10)	(37 pts after 3 events)			
16. Constant Roumbesis	GRE	589 (15)	-- (17)	25.8 (15)	(47 pts after 3 events)			
17. And. Demetriades	GRE	5655 (17)	-- (18)	29.0 (16)	(51 pts after 3 events)			
Hironin Masuda	JAP	451 (19)	3982 (14)					
Jonni Myrra	FIN	580 (16)						

Note. Normally, the top 12 advance after 3 events and the top 6 after 4 events. Because there was a protest over Lahtinen and Nylund, 14 and 7 advanced. If ties resulted after five events (a la Lahtinen and LeGendre), the decathlon tables were used to break the tie, thus: Lahtinen 3576.305; LeGendre 3533.14. The same process was used to separate Hamilton and Lövland, who 2 weeks later contested history's closest Olympic decathlon finish.

Table 6.23   Results of the 1924 Olympic Pentathlon, Paris

		lj	jav	200	dis	1500	Points	1985 Tables
1.	Eero Lehtonen	FIN	668 (7)	5093 (4)	23.0 (1)	4044 (1)	4:47.1 (1)	14	3414
2.	Elemer Somfay	HUN	677 (5)	5207 (2)	23.4 (5)	3776 (2)	4:48.4 (2)	16	3352
3.	Robert LeGendre	USA	7765 (1)	4804 (9)	23.0 (1)	3676 (4)	4:52.6 (3)	18	3525
4.	Leo Leino	FIN	672 (6)	5412 (1)	23.2 (4)	3362 (8)	4:55.4 (4)	23	3265
5.	Morton Kaer	USA	696 (2)	5020 (5)	23.0 (1)	3270 (10)	5:38.6 (6)	24	3135
6.	Hugo Lahtinen	FIN	6895 (3)	4866 (7)	23.6 (7)	3608 (5)	4:55.6 (5)	27	3234
7.	Brutus Hamilton	USA	683 (4)	4896 (8)	24.4 (18)	3770 (3)	(24 pts after 4 events)		
8.	Goran Unger	SWE	655 (8)	4845 (10)	23.8 (8)	3511 (6)	(30 pts after 4 events)		
9.	Evert Nilsson	SWE	640 (13)	5117 (4)	25.0 (21)	3345 (9)	(35 pts after 4 events)		
10.	Denis V. Duigan	AUS	6545 (9)	4560 (16)	23.8 (8)	2726 (11)	(39 pts after 4 events)		
11.	Martin Mølster	NOR	620 (19)	4791 (12)	24.2 (15)	3469 (7)	(39 pts after 4 events)		
12.	J. Clifford Argue	USA	646 (11)	4184 (20)	23.4 (5)	withdrew	(36 pts after 3 events)		
13.	David G. Slack	GBR	643 (12)	3418 (28)	23.8 (8)	(48 pts after 3 events)			
14.	Lucien Courtejaire	FRA	629 (16)	4758 (13)	24.6 (20)	(49 pts after 3 events)			
15.	Adolfo Contoli	ITA	599 (23)	4298 (18)	23.8 (8)	(49 pts after 3 events)			
16.	R. Veil	FRA	592 (25)	4258 (19)	23.8 (8)	(52 pts after 3 events)			
17.	Edouard Médécin	MON	649 (10)	3243 (29)	24.0 (13)	(52 pts after 3 events)			
18.	Harry J.M. deKeijser	HOL	619 (20)	4407 (17)	24.2 (15)	(52 pts after 3 events)			
19.	Josse Ruth	BEL	638 (14)	3678 (26)	24.2 (15)	(55 pts after 3 events)			
20.	Albino Pighi	ITA	626 (17)	3982 (23)	25.0 (21)	(61 pts after 3 events)			
21.	Seiichi Ueda	JPN	605 (22)	4747 (15)	25.4 (25)	(62 pts after 3 events)			
22.	Constant Bucher	SWI	617 (21)	3895 (24)	24.4 (18)	(63 pts after 3 events)			

(Cont.)

Table 6.23   (Continued)

		lj	jav	200	dis	1500	Points	1985 Tables
23. Bertil Fastén	SWE	598 (24)	4758 (13)	25.8 (26)	(63 pts after 3 events)			
25. Aleksandar Spalic	YUG	632 (15)	3100 (30)	25.0 (21)	(66 pts after 3 events)			
26. Antonin Svoboda	CZE	537 (28)	3788 (25)	24.0 (13)	(66 pts after 3 events)			
27. Fred Zinner	BEL	588 (26)	4045 (22)	25.2 (24)	(72 pts after 3 events)			
28. Arthur Percy Spark	GBR	529 (30)	4119 (21)	27.0 (28)	(79 pts after 3 events)			
29. Stylianos Benadis	GRE	5345 (29)	3558 (27)	26.2 (27)	(83 pts after 3 events)			
30. Iivari Yrjölä	FIN	625 (18)	5172 (3)	withdrew	(21 pts after 2 events)			
31. Georgios Zacharopoulos	GRE	5485 (27)	4900 (7)	withdrew	(34 pts after 2 events)			

Note. Ten additional athletes were entered, but did not participate: J. Polesc, AUS; E. Weilheim, AUS; H. Wolkmar, AUS; D. Carabatis, GRE; S.M. Cator, HAI; C. Butti, ITA; A. Palmieri, ITA; O. Gulli, NOR; F. Fuhrherr, CZE; and J. Svoboda, CZE.

OLYMPIC TRIVIA

Olympic decathletes are exceptional men. Although much is known of their performances on the track, much less is known about them outside the event. Did you know, for example, that two decathlon champions married Olympic medalists? It's so. Bill Toomey, 1968 champion, wed Mary Rand, England's 1964 Olympic long-jump queen. And the 1972 champ, Nikolay Avilov, married the 1968 high-jump bronze medalist, Valentina Kozyr of the Soviet Union.

This section relays additional trivia concerning Olympic decathletes.

Record Breakers and Medal Winners

Until recently, the Olympic decathlon has been dominated by United States athletes. Americans have won 10 of the 17 contests, placing second five times and third four times. That's 19 medals to 32 for the rest of the world. The Soviet Union has eight medals (1 gold, 3 silver, 4 bronze), West Germany six (1-2-3), Finland three (1-2-0), and Sweden three (0-1-2). East Germany now has a gold and a silver. Britain claims two golds and Norway one. France and Taiwan have silvers. Estonia, Germany, Canada and Poland claim bronzes. The United States has 28 men who have placed in the first six. There have been 390 Olympic decathlon competitors in 16 games. Fifty-three were Americans.

The only repeat winners are Bob Mathias, 1948 and 1952, and Daley Thompson, 1980 and 1984. All three of the 1952 medalists are on the select list of medal repeaters. Milt Campbell was second in 1952 and first in 1956, whereas Floyd Simmons was third in both 1948 and 1952. Rafer Johnson was second in 1956 and won in 1960; Akilles Jarvinen of Finland was second in 1928 and 1932; Nikolay Avilov won in 1972 and was third 4 years later; Vasiliy Kuznyetsov of the Soviet Union was third in both 1956 and 1960; and Hans-Joachim Walde of West Germany was third in 1964 (representing the combined Germanies) and second in 1968.

There have been three medal sweeps. Sweden did it first in the inaugural competition in 1912, taking 1-2-3 after Jim Thorpe was disqualified. The United States took all the medals in 1936 and 1952.

The world record was broken in 9 of the 17 Olympics—by Thorpe in 1912, Harold Osborn in 1924, Paavo Yrjölä of Finland in 1928, Jim Bausch in 1932, Glenn Morris in 1936, Bob Mathias in 1952, Nikolay Avilov in 1972, Bruce Jenner in 1976, and Daley Thompson, belatedly, in 1984. Needing a 4:34.80 or faster in the 1500m in Los Angeles, Thompson ran 4:35.00 and missed tying the world record by one point. New tables were due to go in effect the following year and his performances added up to a new world mark. But the IAAF did not recognize it until later, when the photo of the finish was rechecked and Daley's time in the hurdles was adjusted, which tied him for the world mark under the old tables and gave him the world record under the new. Understand?

Favored for fifth in the 1956 decathlon, Yuriy Kutyenko of Russia blew it by no-heighting in the high jump and three-fouling in the javelin. Only two world-record holders (official IAAF) have never won an Olympic medal—Hans-Heinrich Sievert, whose best was fifth in 1932, and Russ Hodge, ninth in 1964. Of the seven winners who did not score world marks in the Olympics, four did it elsewhere—Helge Lövland of Norway, the 1920 champ; Mathias, who won in 1948 without a record; Johnson, who set three world standards before the 1960 Games; Bill Toomey, who got his world mark the year after his Olympic triumph; and Thompson, who set four world records but won in 1980 without one. Of all the Olympic titlists only Milt Campbell; Germany's Willi Holdorf, the 1964 king; and current champ Christian Schenk failed to claim the world records in their careers. Schenk is still very active, winning the Seoul crown at 23. Campbell came close, winning the 1956 Games with the second highest total ever.

Coaches

Three of the early medalists went on to become internationally known coaches. Gösta Holmér of Sweden placed third in 1912 and fourth in 1920 and was a top middle-distance coach in the 1940s and 1950s, popularizing the Fartlek training system. Brutus Hamilton, second in 1920, led the University of California for nearly 30 years and was the 1952 Olympic coach. Ken Doherty, third in 1928, coached at Michigan and Penn and became America's most successful writer on track technique.

Margin of Victory

Mathias's 912 point margin in 1952 was the biggest victory gap ever, followed by Thorpe's 688 in 1912 and Avilov's 419 in 1972. The smallest margin was in 1920, when Lövland edged Hamilton by 32 points. Holdorf won by only 45 in 1964, and Johnson had only 58 points to spare in 1960. The closest fight for a medal occurred in 1972, when Jeff Bennett lost third place to Ryszard Katus by 10 points. Only 37 points separated third from sixth in that one. There were only 22 points between second and third in 1924 and between third and fourth in 1948 and 1988.

Hollywood Decathletes

Several decathlon champs have starred in movies after their careers. Thorpe appeared in *Battling with Buffalo Bill* in 1931; Glenn Morris starred with Eleanor Holm in a 1938 film, *Tarzan's Revenge*; Bob Mathias and his wife Melba played their own parts in 1954 in *The Bob Mathias Story*; Rafer Johnson appeared with Frank Sinatra in *None But the Brave* in 1965; and Bruce Jenner was a mainstay in a 1980's forgettable film *Can't Stop the Music*.

Veterans

The 1988 Games in Seoul had the biggest field on record. Thirty-nine started, one more than the 1928 field in Amsterdam.

Under the 1985 tables only 36 have scored over 8000 points in Olympic competition. Six are Americans: Toomey, Jenner, John Crist, Jim Wooding, Tim Bright, and Dave Johnson. Only Daley Thompson has scored over 8000 on three occasions (1980-84-88). Four others have scored over 8000 twice: Nikolay Avilov, 1972 and 1976, Guido Kratschmer 1976 and 1984, Georg Werthner 1980 and 1984, and Dave Steen, 1984 and 1988. Only two have ever completed four Olympic decathlons and a handful more have even attempted three:

Four

Georg Werthner	Austria	1976-1980-1984-1988
Daley Thompson	Britain	1976-1980-1984-1988

Three

Rene Joannes-Powell	Belgium	1920-1924-1928
Paavo Yrjölä	Finland	1924-1928-1932
Akilles Järvinen	Finland	1928-1932-1936
C.K. Yang	Taiwan	1956-1960-1964
Vasiliy Kuznyetsov	USSR	1956-1960-1964
Hans-Joachim Walde	West Germany	1964-1968-1972
Roger Lespagnard	Belgium	1968-1972-1976
Lennard Hedmark	Sweden	1968-1972-1976
Nikolay Avilov	USSR	1968-1972-1976
Josef Zeilbauer	Austria	1972-1976-1980

Other Events

Who won an Olympic decathlon and another event in the same Olympics? Two men. Jim Thorpe, who set world records in both the decathlon and the pentathlon in 1912, and Harold Osborn, the 1924 decathlon champion and high-jump titlist. No other has ever come close. Thorpe also was fourth in the high jump and seventh

Table 6.24 Olympic Highlights . . . . . . Lowlights

Event	Best Olympic Mark			Worst Olympic Mark		
100m	10.41	Bill Toomey, USA	1968	13.8a	George Breitman, FRA	1952
Long Jump	8.01m (26-3 1/2)	Daley Thompson, GBR	1984	5.22m (17-1 1/2)	Patrick Leane, AUS	1952
Shot Put	16.43m (53-11)	Joachim Kirst, GDR	1968	8.13m (26-8 1/4)	Noguchi Gensabulo, JAP	1920
High Jump	2.27m (7-5 1/2)	Christian Schenk, GDR	1988	1.40m (4-7)b	Arthur Percy Spark, GBR	1924
					Gebhard Buchel, LIE	1948
400m	45.68	Bill Toomey, USA	1968	63.9	Urs Trautman, SWI	1968
110m Hurdles	14.12	Milt Campbell, USA	1956	20.8	Gaston Etienne, BEL	1928
Discus	51.46m (168-10)c	Jozsef Bakai, HUN	1972	21.88m (71-9 1/2)	Edouard Armand, HAI	1924
	50.92m (167-1)	William Motti, FRA	1984			
Pole vault	5.70m (18-8 1/4)	Tim Bright, USA	1988	2.30m (7-6 1/2)d	Tokushige Noto, JAP	1924
Javelin	78.58m (257-10)	Lennart Hedmark, SWE	1976	11.64m (38-2 1/4)	Edouard Armand, HAI	1924
1500m	4:05.9	Leonid Litvenyenko, SOV	1972	5:58.6	Barney Berlinger, USA	1928

aJürgen Hingsen, FRG disqualified in 100m in 1988 for three false starts. bSeveral athletes have no-heighted in the high jump. cBakai did not finish all 10 events. dA total of 14 athletes have no-heighted in pole vault.

in the long jump and played on the United States Olympic baseball team.

How many American decathletes have competed in another Olympic event? Ten. Besides Thorpe and Osborn, Harold Babcock was in the 1912 vault, Avery Brundage was in the 1912 discus and pentathlon, Bob Clark was in the 1936 long jump, James Donahue in the 1912 pentathlon, Brutus Hamilton in both the 1920 and the 1924 pentathlon, Eugene Mercer in the 1912 long jump, George Philbrook in the 1912 shot and discus, and Bob Richards was in the vault in three Olympics—1948, 1952, and 1956. Richards, the 1956 vault champ, was twelfth in the decathlon. Martin Lauer of Germany was fifth in 1956's decathlon and fourth in the highs.

Olympic decathletes have been successful in the pentathlon, the seldom-contested five-eventer. Bests on record have been achieved by Thorpe, Lövland, Yrjölä, and Toomey of the Olympic champs, and by other such noted decathletes as Hans-Heinrich Sievert, Yuriy Kutyenko, Vasiliy Kuznyetsov, Kurt Bendlin, and Rein Aun.

NFL Olympians

A few Olympic champions have been successful at football. Jim Thorpe was a founding president of the National Football League and played for a variety of teams from 1919 through 1925, notably the Canton Bulldogs and the New York Giants. Jim Bausch was a back in 1933 for both the Cincinnati Reds (football!) and the Chicago Cardinals. Glenn Morris tried his luck with the 1940 Detroit Lions as a running back. Milt Campbell appeared as a back with the 1957 Cleveland Browns after a limited performance in the Canadian Football League. And Bob Mathias played in the 1953 Rose Bowl for Stanford.

Quotable Olympic Quotes

"Thanks, king." Jim Thorpe replying to the king of Sweden, who had just told the 1912 decathlon winner he was the world's greatest athlete.

"Congratulations. Mr. Thorpe is the highest form of citizen." President William Howard Taft, on hearing of Thorpe's Olympic victories. (Interestingly, Thorpe and other Indians were not United States citizens but wards of the state. Only later did they receive American citizenship.)

"No more decathlon, Dad, ever again. I never worked so long and so hard for anything in all my life." Seventeen-year-old Bob Mathias after his win in 1948.

"I was very tired but victory obliterates fatigue. I never want to go through that again, never. This is my last one and you can print that." Rafer Johnson, 1960, who, unlike Mathias, never competed again.

"I don't have to tell him anything. He knows what to do." Brutus Hamilton, after officials and friends realized that Jim Bausch might win the 1932 Games and encouraged Brutus to give him some advice.

"I'm not the greatest athlete in the world. Bob Hayes is. I never thought of myself in that sense." Willi Holdorf, after winning in 1964.

"I almost had a heart attack. I missed twice at the opening height because I didn't have my own pole. They were locked in a room and no one could find the keys. That almost cost me a medal." Bill Toomey, surviving a close win in 1968.

"In 1976 I think I will be able to improve all 10 events . . . I would prefer to have all the events in one day . . . the 400 and 1500 are my most difficult events. If they were not included I could start a decathlon every day." Nikolay Avilov, after winning in 1972 with a world record 8454, in which he scored 9 personal bests and equaled the 10th.

"Congratulations. We did it together, Chrystie, we did it." Bruce Jenner to his wife, after setting a world record of 8618 points and winning the gold in Montreal in 1976.

"If there was any way, any chance of going, I'd just like to go." Bob Coffman, after winning the 1980 Olympic Trials in Eugene but being blocked from Moscow by the boycott.

"Thanks L.A., for a great Games and A Great Time. . . . But what about the T.V. coverage?" The T-shirt that Daley Thompson wore during his victory lap after his 1984 win in Los Angeles.

"I'm going to Disney World." Daley Thompson after finishing fourth in the 1988 Seoul games when asked what would be next in his career.

"While in no way wishing to detract from the merits of the present day decathlon champions, one feels that much progress can still be achieved. The reluctance of great natural talents to embark on the big venture with singleness of purpose may explain the relatively slow advancement of records." Roberto Quercetani in his *World History of Track*, 1964, p. 322.

(Author's note: Perhaps, but we've come a long way.)

7

Scoring Tables

Since 1911, six sets of scoring tables have been used to score decathlon meets. A short summary of each follows. The IAAF "Scoring Tables for Men's and Women's Combined Event Competitions" (1985), also provides a historical summary. But in that 25-page summary and explanation of the scoring tables are at least 130 errors and misleading statements. All the inaccuracies are embarrassing for multi-event people who must use the information. This section is an attempt to provide a more reliable, albeit shorter, history of scoring tables.

History of Decathlon Scoring Tables

At least six nations experimented with scoring tables before the 1912 Olympic Games. The AAU of the United States provided a linear table to score the all-around in 1893 (not 1884!). The Danes, Finns, Swedes, Norwegians, and Germans all developed performance linear tables. World or national records were normally used as a reference.

1912A Tables

The Swedish Olympic Organizing Committee prepared a set of tables for the newly approved decathlon event to be staged in Stockholm. It was performance linear, with 1000 points awarded for the Olympic record as of 1908. Despite what some people think, these tables were not based on earlier Malmo (Sweden) tables. The 1912A tables used fractional point scores, at times extending the tables to three decimal places so that every possible performance in each event had a unique score. The use of fractions made the event needlessly confusing and complex.

Example: Distance

in javelin	40.27m	40.28m	40.29m	40.30m	40.31m
Point score	599.600	599.875	600.150	600.425	600.700

1912B Tables

The 1912 tables were used for the Stockholm Games. By 1915, they had been adjusted by Americans to take into account the 1912 Olympic records. The new tables were performance linear with a new reference point. They are often referred to as the 1920 tables. They were formally accepted by the IAAF in 1921 and were used for four Olympic Games (1920, 1924, 1928, 1932). The new tables resulted in subtracting 661.895 points from all normal 1912 scores.

1934 Tables

All fractional points were dropped in this Finnish version. The tables were performance progressive, based on subjective judgments, and contained a range of 0 to 1150 points. They were approved at the 1934 IAAF Congress and used until 1952.

1950/52 Tables

The 1946 IAAF Congress appointed a committee to revise the 1934 tables. The result was, again, a highly performance-progressive table, with 1500 points listed at the top. Yet the tables could be extended considerably higher in some events. The base of these tables was statistical rather than subjective. The changes from 1950 to 1952 were marginal, resulting from incorrect calculations of the earlier version. There were severe criticisms of this version, even in the early 1950s. So progressive were the tables that twice (by Rafer Johnson and C.K. Yang) the world record was bettered after nine events!

1962/72/77 Tables

A working party under the direction of Axel Jorbeck undertook the preparation of a new set of tables. Jorbeck used the principles of Dr. Karl Ulbrich of Austria. By using velocity for both races and field events and by deciding the top and bottom performance by analyzing an enormous collection of performance data, he came up with a velocity-linear scoring function. For running events, this resulted in a function that was ever-so-slightly performance progressive through the normal range of decathlon performances—virtually a straight line. For field events, the function, when scaled to performance, was slightly regressive through the normal range of decathlon performances. These major advantages made the tables work for almost 20 years. Like earlier tables, they took into consideration changes in the technical nature of events.

In 1971, the IAAF adjusted the tables slightly to score the 100m and 110m hurdles to the 1/100th-second. In 1977, the IAAF again adjusted for 1/100th-second timing for the 400m.

Despite minor complaints (including some by this author), the Ulbrich tables were the fairest in the history of the decathlon, having both a scientific basis and statistical performance references.

Most complaints about the 1962 tables concerned the timing of their introduction, which was just before the 1964 Olympic Games. Athletes did not have enough time to adjust their training. As previously mentioned, the timing of the implementation of the 1962 tables probably cost C.K. Yang a medal.

1985 Tables

The IAAF organized a working committee in 1982 under the direction of Dr. Viktor Trkal of Czechoslovakia to oversee the development of a new set of tables. The new tables were passed in August of 1984 and went into effect on April 1, 1985. They provide several positive steps in decathlon scoring, but on the whole prove to be less reliable than their 1962 counterpart. To date, the IAAF has issued neither a mathematical nor a statistical explanation for the 1985 scoring tables. They appear to have no scientific basis.

The current IAAF scoring table booklet offers no clue in defining the new tables. To compound the problem, the booklet demonstrates little understanding of scoring table theory, appears to be nonobjective, and has proven to be unreliable. The tables and the current booklet constitute a step backward for the event.

Be that as it may, the 1985 tables are official and have provided one positive aspect for scoring. They include both automatic (1/100th-second) and manual (1/10th-second) tables for the 100m, 110m hurdles, 400m, and 200m (for men's pentathlon, although these are reversed and mislabeled *men* for *women*). A conversion factor has been added so that, in effect, all scores are treated as if they were automatic. This is a blessing for statisticians.

Table 7.1   Summary of All Official Decathlon Scoring Tables

Table	In force	Type of table	At the top of the table — Points scored	Reference	Comments
1912A	1911-1919	A	1000	Olympic record	Swedish
1912B	1920-1934	A	1000	Olympic record	Adjusted 1912A
1934	1935-1952	B	1360	Judgment	Finnish
1950/52	1953-1964	B	1500	Performance curve	Swedish/Finnish
1962[a]	1964-1984	C	1200	Performances	Dr. Karl Ulbrich
1985	1985-present	B	Varies?	Unknown	Auto & manual

Note. A = a performance-linear table. B = a performance-progressive table. C = a velocity-linear table (i.e., running is performance progressive and field events are performance regressive, but only slightly, so the normal range is linear).
[a]The 1962 tables were adjusted twice (in 1970 and 1971) for automatic timing.

Table 7.2   1000 Points On All Decathlon Tables

	1912A	1912B	1934	1950	1962	1985
100	10.8	10.6	10.5	10.78	10.25	10.39
lj	7.48	7.605	7.70	7.58	7.90	7.76
sp	14.80	15.34	15.70	16.00	18.75	18.40
hj	1.90	1.93	1.97	1.97	2.17	2.21
400	48.4	48.2	48.0	48.15	46.00	46.17
110H	15.0	15.0	14.6	14.35	13.70	13.80
dis	41.46	45.22	49.00	51.20	57.50	56.18
pv	3.71	3.95	4.20	4.42	4.78	5.29
jav	54.83	61.01	69.98	70.40	81.00	77.20
1500	4:03.4	3:56.8	3:54.0	3:55.0	3:40.2	3:53.79

How to Score a Decathlon

The sole purpose of the tables (Figure 7.1) is to score decathlons. The events are ordered in the tables in the same order they are contested, 100m first, long jump second, etc. Each page contains five columns, with the performance on the left and the point value on the right of each column. The minimum score for each event is 1 point. The maximum score varies from 1399 (discus & javelin) to 1223 (100m).

I suggest that athletes, meet directors, coaches, and fans obtain a copy of *The Little Gold Book* (Figure 7.2) which contains abbreviated decathlon scoring tables as well as metric conversions. You'll find it very helpful (also available from *Track and Field News*).

Directions

1. All times are listed in seconds and 1/100th-seconds for 100m, 400m, 110m hurdles, and 200m (pentathlon). The 1500m tables list minutes, seconds, and 1/100th of seconds. The first four events also have a *separate* table for 1/10th-seconds for when events are timed manually.

2. All the heights and distances are listed in meters and fractions of meters. For example, 45.26 is 45 meters and 26 centimeters. In the case of the shot put, discus, and javelin, every possible distance is not given.

3. If the appropriate distance is not listed, the next poorest (lower numbers) distance is correct for scoring. For example, for a shot put of 16.31 the next poorest performance should be consulted and the athlete awarded 870 points. Longer throws are measured only to the least even centimeter and only even centimeters are listed in the tables. For example, even if the tape reads 43.33m, the throw must be recorded as 43.32 and 732 points awarded in the discus throw.

4. If the appropriate time is not listed, the next poorer (higher numbers) time is correct for scoring. For example, a 4:30.18 1500m is awarded 685 points, the next poorer time listed. Remember, never award points for a performance the athlete did not achieve.

5. The shot put and three jumps are measured to the least whole centimeter. For example, if the height of the high-jump bar is 1.955m, the official height is 1.95m. A score of 758 points is correct. Interpolation is never allowed.

Timing

Unfortunately, the rules on timing and scoring are not self-explanatory in any of the three major rule books (IAAF, TAC, NCAA). For each event

Men　　　　Putting the Shot-Lance

Metres	Points	Metres	Points	Metres	Points	Metres
18.38	999	17.58	949	16.77	899	15.96
18.37	998	17.56	948	16.75	898	15.94
18.35	997	17.55	947	16.74	897	15.93
18.33	996	17.53	946	16.72	896	15.91
18.32	995	17.51	945	16.71	895	15.00
18.30	994	17.50	944	16.69	894	14.98
18.29	993	17.48	943	16.67	893	14.96
18.27	992	17.46	942	16.66	892	14.95
18.25	991	17.45	941	16.64	891	14.93
18.24	990	17.43	940	16.62	890	14.92
18.22	989	17.42	939	16.61	889	14.90
18.21	988	17.40	938	16.59	888	14.88
18.19	987	17.38	937	16.58	887	14.87
18.17	986	17.37	936	16.56	886	14.85
18.16	985	17.35	935	16.54	885	14.84
18.14	984	17.34	934	16.53	884	14.82
18.13	983	17.32	933	16.51	883	14.80
18.11	982	17.30	932	16.49	882	14.79
18.09	981	17.29	931	16.48	881	14.77
18.08	980	17.27	930	16.46	880	14.75
18.06	979	17.25	929	16.45	879	14.74
18.04	978	17.24	928	16.43	878	14.72
18.03	977	17.22	927	16.41	877	14.71
18.01	976	17.21	926	16.40	876	14.69
18.00	975	17.19	925	16.38	875	14.67
17.98	974	17.17	924	16.37	874	14.66
17.96	973	17.16	923	16.35	873	14.64
17.95	972	17.14	922	16.33	872	14.63
17.93	971	17.13	921	16.32	871	14.61
17.92	970	17.11	920	16.30	870	14.59
17.90	969	17.09	919	16.28	869	14.58
17.88	968	17.08	918	16.27	868	14.56
17.87	967	17.06	917	16.25	867	14.55
17.85	966	17.04	916	16.24	866	14.53
17.84	965	17.03	915	16.22	865	14.51
17.82	964	17.01	914	16.20	864	14.50
17.80	963	17.00	913	16.19	863	14.48
17.79	962	16.98	912	16.17	862	14.46
17.77	961	16.96	911	16.15	861	14.45
17.75	960	16.95	910	16.14	860	14.43
17.74	959	16.93	909	16.12	859	14.42
17.72	958	16.92	908	16.11	858	14.40
17.71	957	16.90	907	16.09	857	14.38
17.69	956	16.88	906	16.07	856	14.37
17.67	955	16.87	905	16.06	855	14.35
17.66	954	16.85	904	16.04	854	14.34
17.64	953	16.83	903	16.03	853	14.32
17.63	952	16.82	902	16.01	852	14.30
17.61	951	16.80	901	15.99	851	14.29
17.59	950	16.79	900	15.98	850	14.27

Figure 7.1.　Sample decathlon scoring table (IAAF).

DECATHLON

Javelin

210-0	60.72	749	199-2	57.40	699	188-4
209-10	60.66	748	199-0	57.32	698	188-1
209-8	60.58	747	198-9	57.26	697	187-10
209-5	60.52	746	198-7	57.18	696	198-7
209-3	60.46	745	198-4	57.12	695	187-5
209-0	60.38	744	198-1	57.06	694	187-2
208-10	60.32	743	197-11	56.98	693	186-11
208-7	60.26	742	197-8	56.92	692	186-9
208-4	60.18	741	197-5	56.86	691	186-6
208-2	60.12	740	197-3	56.78	690	186-3
208-11	60.06	739	197-0	56.72	689	186-1
208-8	59.98	738	196-9	56.66	688	185-11
208-6	59.92	737	196-7	56.58	687	185-7
208-3	59.86	736	196-5	56.52	686	185-5
207-0	59.78	735	196-1	56.46	685	185-3
207-10	59.72	734	195-11	56.38	684	185-0
207-7	59.66	733	195-9	56.32	683	184-9
207-4	59.58	732	195-6	56.26	682	184-7
206-2	59.52	731	195-3	56.18	681	184-4
206-0	59.46	730	195-1	56.12	680	184-1
205-8	59.38	729	194-10	56.06	679	183-11
205-6	59.32	728	194-7	55.98	687	183-8
205-4	59.26	727	194-5	55.92	677	183-5
205-1	59.18	726	194-2	55.86	676	183-3
204-10	59.12	725	193-11	55.78	675	183-0
204-8	59.06	724	193-9	55.72	674	182-10
204-5	58.98	723	193-6	55.66	673	182-7
204-3	58.92	722	193-4	55.58	672	182-4
204-0	58.86	721	193-1	55.52	671	182-2
203-10	58.78	720	192-10	55.46	670	181-11
203-7	58.72	719	192-8	55.38	669	181-8
203-4	58.66	718	192-5	55.32	668	181-6
203-2	58.60	717	192-3	55.26	667	181-3
202-11	58.52	716	192-0	55.18	666	181-0
202-8	58.46	715	191-9	55.12	665	180-10
202-6	58.40	714	191-7	55.04	664	180-7
202-3	58.32	713	191-4	54.98	663	180-4
202-0	58.26	712	191-2	54.92	662	180-2
201-10	58.20	711	190-11	54.84	661	179-11
201-9	58.12	710	190-8	54.78	660	179-9

Figure 7.2. Sample decathlon scoring table (Little Gold Book).

there are two acceptable systems of time-keeping. First, *hand timing* (or manual timing) is shown by recording times to 1/10th of a second by using a stopwatch (traditional or digital). In the case of digital watches that record to 1/100th of a second, the times must be rounded up before consulting the tables. For example, a digital stopwatch reading 11.03 must be rounded up to 11.1 and 786 points awarded. Second, fully automatic electrical timing records times to the 1/100 of a second. In these cases, the 1/100 tables should be consulted. Only fully automatic electrical timing is now acceptable for world records. A problem occasionally arises when a fully automatic timing device breaks down. It is now acceptable (IAAF rules as of 1987) to use back-up manual 1/10th times for an event in which the auto timing breaks down and return to 1/100th timing for the remaining running events. The old rule implied (it was never fully explained) that when automatic timing broke down the entire meet had to be rescored on manual (1/10th) tables. Now it's clear that if one heat does not produce 1/100th times, the event is recorded using manual times to 1/10th of a second. All running events that follow return to auto timing.

My preference would be to use automatic timing whenever it is available, perhaps in some but not all of the heats of one event. I believe that doing so would be ultimately fairer. But this is my personal belief and not the rule. The rule is to use manual times for only the event in which automatic timing breaks down, then to return to automatic timing for the remainder of the events.

The current tables have a built-in adjustment between manual and fully automatic times. For the 100m, 110m hurdles, and 200m, the adjustment is .24 seconds. The adjustment is .14 seconds for the 400m. Thus, an athlete who runs an 11.2 manually timed race in the 100m receives 765 points—the same number of points an athlete receives for running 11.44 with a fully automatic timing device. For the 1500m no correction is necessary if the event is manually timed. For example, if the 1500m is timed in 4:43.0, the time is recorded as if it were automatic (4:43.00) and 662 points are awarded. In the event of digital manual times (e.g., 4:55.05), the mark must first be rounded up to 4:55.1 before the tables are consulted. A score of 588 points is awarded, not 589. This process is not adequately explained in any of the existing rulebooks.

Who Wins?

The winner is the competitor who has scored the highest number of points in all events, awarded on the basis of the IAAF scoring tables.

What About Ties?

In a tie the winner is the competitor who has received the higher points in a majority of events. He does not necessarily have to have won a majority of events, only to have received the higher points in the majority of events. This is a mistake in the IAAF and TAC rules that should be corrected in the future. If the tie remains unresolved, the winner is the athlete who has the highest number of points in any one of the events. This procedure applies to any place in the competition. If a tie exists after this point, it is left a tie under IAAF and TAC rules. Under existing NCAA rules, ties are not broken in any situation.

Disqualifications

Any athlete disqualified from an event (e.g., false starts, running outside of lanes, etc.) receives no points for that event but is allowed to continue in the competition.

Attempts and DNFs

Athletes must make an attempt in each event in order to continue and obtain an official place and score. Many athletes attempt the 1500m by taking a few steps, then not finishing. They are awarded zero points for that event but, having attempted all 10 events, count in the final places and receive an official score.

The "One Point for Trying" Rule

It has been the practice at several major American decathlon meets to award one point for "trying" to any athlete who cleared no height, had no fair throw, was disqualified for a running violation, or otherwise came up with a blank. There is no such rule and the practice should be discontinued.

Scoring Team Decathlon Meets

Team decathlons are popular in the United States and Europe (Cups). They are contests between nations, clubs, schools, or whatever. Usually three to eight members constitute a team. Cumulative scores at the end of all events determine the winning team. An example of a five-man team score might be 37,998 to 36,543. Bring your adding machine.

Organization of Scoring

It is important to use a system that minimizes the chances of error. Check and double-check all computations. Pocket calculators are very useful. Some can even be programmed with the current tables. Scoring errors occur frequently. They are born of faulty equipment and programs, ignorance, variation in rules, and just plain bad math. I suggest that you use a scoring sheet, of which I've supplied an example (Figure 7.3). A scoring sheet is arranged with vertical additions, and scores after each event are maintained. It is a simple operation. An additional step toward accuracy is to enter points and cumulative points in a different color ink from the performances. You don't have to be a CPA to score a decathlon meet, but you do have to be careful.

The Scorer

Scoring decathlon meets can be a tricky business. It should be done by someone who is comfortable with figures and who has the time to check and recheck the calculations without distraction. The scorer should provide the current scoring tables and the conversion tables (and perhaps a bottle of aspirin!). Neither the meet announcer nor the meet director should be asked to handle the official scoring.

How to Foul Up a Decathlon Score

How many ways are there to foul up a decathlon score? More than a dozen. All of them contribute to the difficulty of presenting accurate scores.

Many of today's decathlon scores are incorrectly reported. I check many 7000+ scores annually, whether they are from newspaper clippings or meet directors themselves. As errors are discovered, it is necessary to return to the source. Sometimes sources are not helpful, or officials cannot be contacted, or records have not been kept. Sometimes the party contacted is not interested enough to reply. A few years back, a meet director

DECATHLON SCORE SHEET

Meet _____

Date _____

FIRST DAY June 8, 1987, Mason-Dixon Open Decathlon   Start Time_____ Finish Time ____

Name	1. Carlos O'Connell	2. John Perry	3. Steve Long	4.	5.	6.	Name
Team / Event	Mount St. Marys	U of Maryland	Mount TC				Team / Event
100 Meters	10.7	11.0	10.9				Time
	874 1	808 3	830 2				Points
Long Jump	7.25	7.00	6.38				Metric
	23-9 1.2	22-11 3/4	20-11 1/4				Ft - In
	874	814	670				Points
Score: 2 Events	1748 1	1622 2	1500 3				Score 2 Events
Shot Put	12.30	12.21	11.36				Metric
	40-4 1/4	40-3/4	37-3 1/4				Ft. In.
	625	619	568				Points
Score: 3 Events	2373 1	2241 2	2068 3				Score 3 Events
High Jump	1.86	1.92	1.89				Metric
	6-1 1/2	6-3 1/2	6-2 1/4				Ft. In.
	679	731	705				Points
Score: 4 Events	3052 1	2972 2	2773 3				Score 4 Events
400 Meters	48.8	53.0	52.0				Time
	864	676	719				Points
First Day Score	3916	3648	3492				First Day
Place	1	2	3				Place

Figure 7.3. Decathlon score sheet.

left with the scores in his back pocket and has not been heard from since. Finally, there are times when there is just no explanation for errors.

Computers have helped in recent years, but even with computerized scoring, as in the 1984 Los Angeles Olympic Games, there is no guarantee of accuracy. When it was discovered in Los Angeles that the official computer program gave incorrect points for a few of the marks, the entire scoring procedure was done by hand. The following are among the causes of wrong scores.

Simple Mistakes

- The incorrect number of points are awarded.
- Someone has added wrong.
- A mistake has been made in copying or typing.
- The scorer failed to award the *lower* number of points when the exact performance was not listed in the tables (e.g., shot, discus, javelin, or 1500m).
- Incorrect running tables have been used. There are 1/100 and 1/10 tables for the 100m, 200m (pentathlon), 400m, and 110m hurdles. An 11.30 is not 11.3.

Inaccuracies Born of Ignorance

- Sometimes officials award one point for "trying" to an athlete who has cleared no height or received three fouls. This is just plain wrong.
- Sometimes ties are not broken because officials do not know the tie-breaking rules.
- Using digital manual stopwatches results in times to the 1/100 second. These times should be rounded up and the manual tables (1/10 second) consulted.
- Some scorers deliberately add .14 to all manual 1500m times. This is not the rule.

Errors by Field Officials

- Someone on the field is mistaken for another and the wrong athlete is awarded someone else's points. This occurs even in the Olympics.
- The times are misread from the auto-timed photo. Even the recorder has to be careful. Does "fifty . . . one . . . nine" mean 50.19 or 51.90?
- Officials unfamiliar with the metric system often call out measurements that go misreported. I once heard a javelin official call "fifty . . . two." Could he mean 52.00m? 50.20m? 50.02m? It turned out to be the latter.

Faulty Equipment

- A two-sided tape (metric and imperial) with the zero mark at different places has caused problems at more than one NCAA meet.
- Sometimes officials do not use metric tapes as called for in the rules. The errors are compounded by converting feet and inches to meters, which is necessary since the scoring tables are in meters only.
- At times, outstanding distances are remeasured for a decathlon event record. This is usually done with a steel tape, resulting in a longer throw by a few centimeters and a one-point scoring change. This procedure is incorrect and the throw should be scored as originally measured (or the steel tape should be used to measure everyone's throw).

Our Job is Further Complicated

- One kind of error comes from interpolation, especially in the high jump. Interpolation is not allowed and heights should be measured to the whole centimeter, not beyond. A measured jump of 2.005m should be recorded and scored as 2.00m
- Stubbornness of statisticians who reread photos. A misread of a photo by a *T & FN* statistician a few years back caused headaches when he refused to admit the error and foolishly continued to report an incorrect score. Fortunately, cooler heads prevailed and the national federation accepted the original score upon review of the photos, all of which were correctly read in the first place. At times, the statistician must be ignored.
- Sometimes only scores are reported without the individual marks. Should they be counted?

So what can be done to improve the situation? A metric tape should always be used. Rules should be followed, of course. Extreme care must be made in conversions, reading off performances or points, listing scores, and adding. Calculators and computers help. So does common sense.

WHO IS THE WINNER? TWO TRICKY PROBLEMS

Given the current status of decathlon rules, there is the possibility, although it is unlikely, that two silly scoring situations could develop. Assume in the initial case that two athletes, both with fully automatic performances throughout, end up with very close final scores. It goes without saying the fully automatic performances are preferred. They are fairer. But perhaps a malfunction of an unrelated heat of a previous race forces that event to be rescored using manual times. The official winner would have fewer points than his competitor using the fairest method available. An NCAA championship came within an eyelash of this happening. Can you see why? Imagine having to explain to an athlete or coach that he lost even though he scored more points on the fairest method available for both.

In the second case, it is possible under the existing IAAF tie-breaking rule, that when a tie results the athlete who has actually won more events than his competitor can lose. The problem is in the wording "won" versus "awarded more points." Do you understand why?

Let's hope that the rule makers take action on these anomalies in the near future. If they ever occur, they will be embarrassing to explain to athletes and coaches and impossible to explain to the public.

Where to Obtain Scoring Tables and Additional Information

The present IAAF scoring tables for the decathlon have been in effect since April 1, 1985. The scoring tables, officially called "Scoring Tables for Men's and Women's Combined Events Competitions, 1985 edition," are 112 pages. Eighty-four pages of tables comprise the body of the booklet. There is also an introduction that includes a brief history of combined events and the evolution of scoring tables. As mentioned, this section is embarrassingly inaccurate and should be avoided by true observers of the event. The booklet does include an excellent section called "How to Use the Tables." The appendix includes a list of current and world records. Some of the marks are misscored or out of order and half a dozen are missing! But the tables themselves are accurate. An earlier version listing the men's 200m on the women's side and vice versa has been corrected.

The tables (without the introduction and appendix) are included in the current *NCAA Track & Field Rulebook*. This is a big step forward because NCAA decathlon rules are found earlier in the book. The IAAF has never published a set of tables with decathlon rules.

The tables are available from these sources:

Track and Field News, Box 296, Los Altos, CA 94022

International Amateur Athletic Federation, 3 Hans Crescent, Knightsbridge, London SWIX OLN England

NCAA Track & Field Rules, NCAA Publishing Dept., P.O. Box 1906, Mission, KS 66201

I have also suggested that athletes, coaches, meet directors, and fans obtain a copy of *The Little Gold Book* from *Track and Field News*. It contains abbreviated scoring tables as well as metric conversions. It is necessary to have the official tables since *TLGB* does not contain all marks. But you'll find it very helpful.

IAAF rulebooks are also available from *Track and Field News* and the IAAF. The Athletics Congress/USA rulebook is available from the Book Order Department, TAC/USA, Box 140, Indianapolis, IN 46206.

Appendix A

Decathlon Records

The chapter includes a variety of decathlon records. It includes world and United States ranking of decathletes by *Track and Field News* from 1947 to the present. It lists winners of major competitions and illustrates how the world and American records have progressed from the early days of the century. All-time world, American, and collegiate lists are included. There is a record-by-event section, as well as blurbs on reaching point levels and the best nonwinning scores. For fun, a miscellaneous record section is added.

Finally, the record section closes with a comparison of *relative* decathlon scores over the years. The results can be used to start the age-old argument, Who was the greatest athlete of all time?

What Is the Best Decathlon Performance Ever?

What is the world's best decathlon score? Is it simply the current world record? Perhaps. Perhaps not. Certainly for short periods of time the world decathlon record gives us a legitimate basis of comparison for multi-event performances. The scores are valuable.

But over decades or more the world record under the current table may not be comparable to scores of earlier eras. Many things change over the years. Equipment, facilities, shoes, tracks, training techniques, even rules alter over time. Decathlon scores, computed on the same tables, whether they are the 1912A or 1985 tables, are not comparable. For example, one cannot compare a 15.6 in the 110mH in 1912, run on a cinder track over heavy wooden barriers, to a similar mark 75 years later. Nor can one compare a 4.00m pole vault in 1932, when steel poles were used and landings were made in sand, to vaulting 4.00m today, when fiberglass poles are used and landings are on foam rubber. But a 15.6 or 4.00m are scored the same no matter when they are made.

It is helpful to use individual world records to evaluate decathlon scores. One method is to calculate what score the world-record holders of individual events would have achieved on the current (1985) tables. This score is then compared to the decathlon score to get a *relative*, not an absolute, mark. For example, Rafer Johnson scored 7981 points (on the 1985 tables) in 1960. The world records of 1960 would have scored 10,494. Johnson's relative score of .7605 (dividing 7981 by 10,494) can be interpreted as 76.05% of the existing world records. Johnson's relative score can be compared to relative scores of other eras. This technique was first used by Elchanan A. Bar-Lev.

The system of calculation is not complicated. The world record refers to the official world record that stood or was set in the month of the decathlon performance. All altitude-made world records were removed.

Every world best is evaluated. Many of the world decathlon bests were not considered so at the time, but were found to be better than others after a switch to new tables. Many marks were never ratified by the IAAF. I have evaluated 60 decathlon marks, the 56 world bests (see progression of world record section), and the career mark of four other greats (Campbell, Holdorf, Schenk and Watson) who never set a world record. A similar procedure is used to evaluate several early American All-Around performances.

From the results we learn several things. First, Jim Thorpe dominated his competition and even today he stands atop a list of all-time decathlon greats. His score of .7794 is unsurpassed. Second, it is obvious that Thompson's world record isn't the best-ever relative decathlon score; on the contrary, it stands 39th overall. Third, the gap between performances and world-record level was narrowed in the late 1920s through the 1950s and was expanded again afterward. Unfortunately, this is a simplistic method and does not take into consideration the effect of steroids on throwing events.

Dr. Georg Werthner of Austria is the first ever to complete four Olympic decathlons. (From the Zarnowski collection)

Table A.1   World Rankings, 1947-1987

By *Track and Field News*, based on (a) honors won, (b) win-loss record, and (c) sequence of marks. Tables used: 1934 (for 1947-51); 1950/52 (for 1952-63); 1962/71/77 (for 1964-84); 1985 (for 1985-87).

1947
1. Vladimir Volkov, SOV	7159
2. Heino Lipp, SOV	7097
3. Erik Andersson, SWE	7045
4. Enrique Kistenmacher, ARG	7011
5. Al Lawrence, USA	6973
6. Mario Recordion, CHI	6886
7. Sergey Kuznetsov, SOV	6806
8. Celso Doria, BRA	6886
9. Per Eriksson, SWE	6730
10. Irv Mondschein, USA	6715

1948
1. Heino Lipp, SOV	7780
2. Bob Mathias, USA	7224
3. Ignace Heinrich, FRA	6974
4. Floyd Simmons, USA	7054
5. Enrique Kistenmacher, ARG	6929
6. Vladimir Volkov, SOV	7229
7. Petr Denisenko, SOV	7016
8. Irv Mondschein, USA	7101
9. Erik Andersson, SWE	6877
10. Al Lawrence, USA	6841

1949
1. Bob Mathias, USA	7556
2. Heino Lipp, SOV	7539
3. Orn Clausen, ICE	7259
4. Ignace Heinrich, FRA	7271
5. Petr Denisenko, SOV	7287
6. Irv Mondschein, USA	7191
7. Vladimir Volkov, SOV	7173
8. Miroslav Moravec, CZE	7071
9. Armin Scheurer, SWI	7033
10. Enrique Kistenmacher, ARG	6854

1950
1. Bob Mathias, USA	8042
2. Bill Albans, USA	7361
3. Ignace Heinrich, FRA	7364
4. Heino Lipp, SOV	7319
5. Orn Clausen, ICE	7297
6. Kjell Tannander, SWE	7175
7. Jim McConnell, USA	7120
8. Otey Scruggs, USA	7102
9. Petr Denisenko, SOV	7116
10. Brayton Norton, USA	7083

1951
1. Bob Richards, USA	7834
2. Ignace Heinrich, FRA	7476
3. Orn Clausen, ICE	7453
4. Floyd Simmons, USA	7361
5. Otey Scruggs, USA	7178
6. Bill Miller, USA	7174
7. Kjell Tannander, SWE	7110
8. Vladimir Volkov, SOV	7106
9. Petr Denisenko, SOV	7023
10. Brayton Norton, USA	6997

1952
1. Bob Mathias, USA	7887
2. Milt Campbell, USA	7060
3. Floyd Simmons, USA	6803
4. Bill Albans, USA	6627
5. Bob Richards, USA	6713
6. Vladimir Volkov, SOV	6904
7. Sepp Hipp, GER	6449
8. Göran Widenfeldt, SWE	6501
9. Kjell Tannander, SWE	6308
10. Friedel Schirmer, GER	6470

1953
1. Milt Campbell, USA	7743
2. Bob Richards, USA	7388
3. Vasiliy Kuznyetsov, SOV	7205
4. Heino Lipp, SOV	7187
5. Vladimir Volkov, SOV	7047
6. Bill Miller, USA	6921
7. Petre Zambresteanu, ROM	6901
8. James Cooke, USA	6894
9. Walter Meier, GER	6876
10. Miloslav Moravec, CZE	6846

1954
1. Bob Richards, USA	7315
2. Vasiliy Kuznyetsov, SOV	7292
3. Vladimir Volkov, SOV	6922
4. Boris Stolyarov, SOV	6859
5. Yuriy Kutyenko, SOV	6897
6. Walter Meier, GER	6587
7. Brayton Norton, USA	6459
8. Torbjoern Lassenius, FIN	6424
9. Heinz Oberbeck, GER	6263
10. Miloslav Moravec, CZE	6185

1955

1. Rafer Johnson, USA	7983
2. Vasiliy Kuznyetsov, SOV	7645
3. Bob Richards, USA	7043
4. Bob Lawson, USA	7065
5. Walter Meier, GER	6834
6. Brayton Norton, USA	6825
7. Yuriy Kutyenko, SOV	6708
8. Boris Stolyarov, SOV	6700
9. Kim Bukhantsev, SOV	6546
10. Torbjoern Lassenius, FIN	6509

1956

1. Milt Campbell, USA	7937
2. Rafer Johnson, USA	7755
3. Vasiliy Kuznyetsov, SOV	7733
4. Uno Palu, SOV	7167
5. Martin Lauer, GER	7201
6. Walter Meier, GER	7173
7. Yuriy Kutyenko, SOV	7393
8. Torbjoern Lassenius, FIN	6991
9. Bob Richards, USA	7054
10. Bob Lawson, USA	6889

1957

1. Vasiliy Kuznyetsov, SOV	7379
2. Yuriy Kutyenko, SOV	7294
3. Walter Meier, GER	7193
4. Charles Pratt, USA	7164
5. Walter Tschudi, SWI	7151
6. Dave Edstrom, USA	6981
7. Bob Lawson, USA	6910
8. Jim Klein, USA	6793
9. Igor Ter-Ovanesyan, SOV	6783
10. Rudolf Bogomolov, SOV	6736

1958

1. Rafer Johnson, USA	8302
2. Vasiliy Kuznyetsov, SOV	8042
3. Yang Chuan-Kuang, FOR	7625
4. Dave Edstrom, USA	7736
5. Uno Palu, SOV	7559
6. Yuriy Kutyenko, SOV	7989
7. Walter Meier, GER	7388
8. Phil Mulkey, SOV	7405
9. Igor Ter-Ovanesyan, SOV	7184
10. Markus Kahma, FIN	7137

1959

1. Vasiliy Kuznyetsov, SOV	8357
2. Martin Lauer, GER	7955
3. Yang Chuan-Kuang, FOR	7835
4. Dave Edstrom, USA	7599
5. Yuriy Kutyenko, SOV	7535
6. Walter Tschudi, SWI	7298
7. Eef Kamerbeek, HOL	7103
8. Markus Kahma, FIN	7088
9. Walter Meier, GER	7061
10. Mike Herman, USA	7026

1960

1. Rafer Johnson, USA	8683
2. Yang Chuan-Kwang, FOR	8426
3. Vasiliy Kuznyetsov, SOV	7845
4. Yuriy Kutyenko, SOV	7772
5. Dave Edstrom, USA	8176
6. Phil Mulkey, USA	7652
7. Uno Palu, SOV	7598
8. Eef Kamerbeek, HOL	7236
9. Franco Sar, ITA	7195
10. Jim Klein, USA	7185

1961

1. Yuriy Kutyenko, SOV	8360
2. Phil Mulkey, USA	8709
3. Vasiliy Kuznyetsov, SOV	7918
4. Paul Herman, USA	7800
5. Eef Kamerbeek, HOL	7594
6. Joze Bradnik, YUG	7466
7. Dave Edstrom, USA	7293
8. Mikhail Storochenko, SOV	7257
9. Markus Kahma, FIN	7254
10. Willi Holdorf, GER	7238

1962

1. Yang Chuan-Kwang, FOR	8249
2. Vasiliy Kuznyetsov, SOV	8026
3. Werner Von Moltke, GER	8022
4. Manfred Bock, GER	7893
5. Janis Lusis, SOV	7763
6. Paul Herman, USA	7725
7. Eef Kamerbeek, HOL	7724
8. Willi Holdorf, GER	7667
9. Seppo Suutari, FIN	7544
10. Phil Mulkey, USA	7480

(Cont.)

Table A.1 (Continued)

1963
1. Yang Chuan-Kwang, FOR — 9121
2. Vasiliy Kuznetsov, SOV — 7854
3. Willi Holdorf, GER — 8085
4. Anatoliy Ovseyenko, SOV — 7839
5. Werner Von Moltke, GER — 7856
6. Steve Pauly, USA — 7852
7. Eef Kamerbeek, HOL — 7677
8. Hans-Joachim Walde, GER — 7791
9. Paul Herman, USA — 8061
10. Wolfgang Heise, GER — 7517

1964
1. Willi Holdorf, GER — 7887
2. Rein Aun, SOV — 7842
3. Hans-Joachim Walde, GER — 7852
4. Manfred Bock, GER — 7950
5. Paul Herman, USA — 7787
6. Yang Chuan-Kwang, FOR — 7853
7. Horst Beyer, GER — 7854
8. Vasiliy Kuznyetsov, SOV — 7596
9. Mikhail Storochenko, SOV — 7772
10. Russ Hodge, USA — 7740

1965
1. Mikhail Storochenko, SOV — 7883
2. Kurt Bendlin, GER — 7848
3. Bill Toomey, USA — 7764
4. Russ Hodge, USA — 7682
5. Horst Beyer, GER — 7636
6. Paul Herman, USA — 7600
7. Yuriy Dyachkov, SOV — 7519
8. Rein Aun, SOV — 7556
9. Don Shy, USA — 7486
10. Albert Fantalis, SOV — 7443

1966
1. Bill Toomey, USA — 8234
2. Russ Hodge, USA — 8230
3. Werner von Moltke, GER — 7961
4. Yuriy Dyachkov, SOV — 7836
5. Horst Beyer, GER — 7634
6. Jorg Mattheis, GER — 7614
7. Rein Aun, SOV — 7682
8. Mikhail Storochenko, SOV — 7578
9. Juri Otsmaa, SOV — 7600
10. Max Klauss, GDR — 7446

1967
1. Kurt Bendlin, GER — 8319
2. Bill Toomey, USA — 8044
3. Max Klauss, GDR — 7986
4. Hans-Joachim Walde, GER — 7992
5. Rein Aun, SOV — 7979
6. Manfred Tiedtke, GDR — 7690
7. Horst Beyer, GER — 7712
8. Herbert Wessel, GDR — 7636
9. Jorg Mattheis, GER — 7774
10. Janis Lanka, SOV — 7769

1968
1. Bill Toomey, USA — 8222
2. Hans-Joachim Walde, GER — 8111
3. Kurt Bendlin, GER — 8086
4. Nikolay Avilov, SOV — 7909
5. Joachim Kirst, GDR — 7861
6. Rein Aun, SOV — 8026
7. Manfred Tiedtke, GDR — 7904
8. Herbert Wessel, GDR — 7953
9. Janis Lanka, SOV — 7972
10. Max Klauss, GDR — 7889

1969
1. Bill Toomey, USA — 8417
2. Joachim Kirst, GDR — 8279
3. Herbert Wessel, GDR — 8021
4. Manfred Tiedtke, GDR — 8013
5. Kurt Bendlin, GDR — 8055
6. Vladimir Shcherbatikh, SOV — 8032
7. Viktor Chelnokov, SOV — 7872
8. Nikolay Avilov, SOV — 7945
9. Rudiger Demmig, GDR — 8029
10. Rick Sloan, USA — 8051

1970
1. Joachim Kirst, GDR — 8121
2. Kurt Bendlin, GER — 7932
3. Russ Hodge, USA — 8025
4. Lennart Hedmark, SWE — 8011
5. Rudiger Demmig, GDR — 8130
6. Nikolay Avilov, SOV — 7874
7. Herbert Wessel, GDR — 8003
8. John Warkentin, USA — 8026
9. Jeff Bennett, USA — 8072
10. Manfred Tiedtke, GDR — 7989

1971
1. Joachim Kirst, GDR — 8206
2. Lennart Hedmark, SWE — 8065
3. Hans-Joachim Walde, GER — 8122
4. Kurt Bendlin, GER — 8244
5. Heinz-Ulrich Schulze, GER — 8043
6. Leonid Litvenyenko, SOV — 8044
7. Boris Ivanov, SOV — 8237
8. Rick Wanamaker, USA — 7989
9. Herbert Swoboda, GER — 8008
10. Russ Hodge, USA — 7957

1972
1. Nikolay Avilov, SOV — 8454
2. Leonid Litvenyenko, SOV — 8035
3. Ryszard Katus, POL — 7984
4. Jeff Bennett, USA — 8076
5. Jeff Bannister, USA — 8120
6. Ryszard Skowronek, GDR — 8147
7. Stefan Schreyer, GDR — 7950
8. Tadeusz Janczenko, POL — 8006
9. Steen Smidt-Jensen, DEN — 7947
10. Freddy Herbrand, BEL — 7947

1973
1. Sepp Zeilbauer, AUT — 8135
2. Lennart Hedmark, SWE — 8188
3. Ryszard Skowronek, POL — 8206
4. Yves LeRoy, FRA — 8140
5. Aleksandr Blinyayev, SOV — 8100
6. Jeff Bennett, USA — 8121
7. Toomas Suurvali, SOV — 8018
8. Toomas Berendsen, SOV — 8106
9. Rudolf Ziegert, SOV — 8134
10. Ryszard Katus, POL — 8020

1974
1. Bruce Jenner, USA — 8308
2. Ryszard Skowronek, POL — 8207
3. Yves LeRoy, FRA — 8146
4. Guido Kratschmer, GER — 8132
5. Leonid Litvenyenko, SOV — 8122
6. Ryszard Katus, POL — 7938
7. Jeff Bennett, USA — 7939
8. Fred Samara, USA — 7988
9. Philipp Andres, SWI — 7934
10. Aleksandr Grebenyuk, SOV — 7884

1975
1. Bruce Jenner, USA — 8524
2. Fred Dixon, USA — 8277
3. Nikolay Avilov, SOV — 8229
4. Leonid Litvenyenko, SOV — 8159
5. Ryszard Skowronek, POL — 8185
6. Fred Samara, USA — 8077
7. Ryszard Katus, POL — 8005
8. Steve Gough, USA — 8057
9. Craig Brigham, USA — 8027
10. Sepp Zeilbauer, AUT — 7937

1976
1. Bruce Jenner, USA — 8617
2. Guido Kratschmer, GER — 8411
3. Nikolay Avilov, SOV — 8369
4. Ramio Pihl, SWE — 8218
5. Ryszard Skowronek, POL — 8113
6. Leonid Litvenyenko, SOV — 8249
7. Aleksandr Grebenyuk, SOV — 8468
8. Siegfried Stark, GDR — 8280
9. Sepp Zeilbauer, AUT — 8310
10. Lennart Hedmark, SWE — 7974

1977
1. Fred Dixon, USA — 8393
2. Aleksandr Grebenyuk, SOV — 8478
3. Sepp Zeilbauer, AUT — 8097
4. Daley Thompson, GBR — 8124
5. Rainer Pottel, GDR — 8096
6. Guido Kratschmer, GER — 8086
7. Yves LeRoy, FRA — 8069
8. Nikolay Avilov, SOV — 8053
9. John Warkentin, USA — 8031
10. Valeriy Kachanov, SOV — 8133

1978
1. Guido Kratschmer, GER — 8498
2. Aleksandr Grebenyuk, SOV — 8340
3. Daley Thompson, GBR — 8467w
4. Siegfried Stark, GDR — 8208
5. Sepp Zeilbauer, AUT — 8134
6. Johannes Lahti, FIN — 8109
7. Yuriy Kutsenko, SOV — 8041
8. Rainer Pottel, GDR — 8083
9. Fred Dixon, USA — 8034
10. Roger Kanerva, FIN — 7945

(Cont.)

Table A.1 (Continued)

<u>1979</u>
1.	Bob Coffman, USA	8274
2.	Siegfried Stark, GDR	8287
3.	Guido Kratschmer, GER	8484
4.	Sepp Zeilbauer, AUT	8198
5.	Aleksandr Grebenyuk, SOV	8166
6.	Thierry Dubois, FRA	8161
7.	Konstantin Akhapkin, SOV	8141
8.	Aleksandr Nyevskiy, SOV	8057
9.	Jürgen Hingsen, GER	8240
10.	Tito Steiner, ARG	8124

<u>1980</u>
1.	Daley Thompson, GBR	8622
2.	Guido Kratschmer, GER	8649
3.	Jürgen Hingsen, GER	8407
4.	Yuriy Kutsenko, SOV	8331
5.	Bob Coffman, USA	8184
6.	Sergei Zhelanov, SOV	8196
7.	Sepp Zeilbauer, AUT	8196
8.	Georg Werthner, AUT	8050
9.	Siegfried Stark, GDR	8480
10.	Valeriy Kachanov, SOV	8306

<u>1981</u>
1.	Rainer Pottel, GDR	8311
2.	Jürgen Hingsen, GER	8168
3.	Uwe Freimuth, GDR	8213
4.	Siegfried Wentz, GER	8191
5.	Tito Steiner, ARG	8279w
6.	Sepp Zeilbauer, AUT	8191
7.	Yuriy Kutsenko, SOV	8302
8.	Atanas Andonov, BUL	8220
9.	Guido Kratschmer, GER	8095
10.	Siegfried Stark, GDR	8132

<u>1982</u>
1.	Daley Thompson, GBR	8743
2.	Jürgen Hingsen, GER	8723
3.	Siegfried Stark, GDR	8433
4.	Steffen Grummt, GDR	8274
5.	Grigoriy Degtyarov, SOV	8247
6.	Georg Werthner, AUT	8229
7.	Konstantin Akhapkin, SOV	8458
8.	Siegfried Wentz, GER	8313
9.	Valeriy Kachanov, SOV	8233
10.	Torsten Voss, GDR	8387

<u>1983</u>
1.	Daley Thompson, GBR	8666
2.	Jürgen Hingsen, GER	8779
3.	Siegfried Wentz, GER	8718
4.	Uwe Freimuth, GDR	8501
5.	Grigoriy Degtyarov, SOV	8538
6.	Stephan Niklaus, SWI	8337
7.	Aleksandr Nyevskiy, SOV	8412
8.	Torsten Voss, GDR	8337
9.	Konstantin Akhapkin, SOV	8418
10.	Dave Steen, CAN	8205w

<u>1984</u>
1.	Daley Thompson, GBR	8797
2.	Jürgen Hingsen, GER	8798
3.	Grigoriy Degtyarov, SOV	8652
4.	Alexandr Apaychev, SOV	8643
5.	Uwe Freimuth, GDR	8704
6.	Torsten Voss, GDR	8535
7.	Siegfried Wentz, GER	8482
8.	Igor Sobolevskiy, SOV	8530
9.	Alexandr Nyevskiy, SOV	8476
10.	Guido Kratschmer, GER	8420

<u>1985</u>
1.	Torsten Voss, GDR	8559
2.	Uwe Freimuth, GDR	8504
3.	Aleksandr Nevisky, SOV	8409
4.	Sergeiy Popov, SOV	8206
5.	Dave Steen, CAN	8316w
6.	Christian Schenk, GDR	8163
7.	Siegfried Wentz, GER	8440
8.	Gregoriy Degtyarov, SOV	8206w
9.	Yuriy Kutsenko, SOV	8345
10.	Mike Ramos, USA	8294

<u>1986</u>
1.	Daley Thompson, GBR	8811
2.	Jürgen Hingsen, GER	8730
3.	Siegfried Wentz, GER	8676
4.	Torsten Voss, GDR	8450
5.	Guido Kratschmer, GER	8519
6.	Dave Steen, CAN	8254w
7.	Alexsandr Apaychev, SOV	8244
8.	Uwe Freimuth, GDR	8322
9.	Mike Ramos, USA	8322
10.	Grigoriy Degtyarov, SOV	8322

1987

1. Torsten Voss, GDR	8680	
2. Siegfried Wentz, GER	8645	
3. Pavel Tarnavetskiy, SOV	8375	
4. Christian Plaziat, FRA	8317	
5. Christian Schneck, GDR	8304	
6. Simon Poelman, NZE	8359	
7. Uwe Freimuth, GDR	8220	
8. Alain Blondel, FRA	8228	
9. Aleksandr Nyevskiy, SOV	8304	
10. William Motti, FRA	8327w	

Table A.2   American Rankings, 1947-1987

By *Track and Field News*, based on (a) honors won, (b) win-loss record, (c) sequence of marks. Tables used:1934 (for 1947-51), 1950/52 (for 1952-63), 1962/71/77 (for 1964-84), and 1985 (for 1985-87).

1947
1. Al Lawrence, USC	6973
2. Irv Mondschein, NYPC	6715
3. Lloyd Duff, Ohio State	6705
4. Jerry Shipkey, UCLA	6591
5. Floyd Simmons, NCarolina	6580
6. Jack McEwen, Colorado	6333

1948
1. Bob Mathias, Tulare HS	7224
2. Floyd Simmons, NCarolina	7054
3. Irv Mondschein, NYPC	7101
4. Al Lawrence, unat	6841

1949
1. Bob Mathias, unat	7556
2. Irv Mondschein, NYPC	7191
3. Bill Albans, NCarolina	6715

1950
1. Bob Mathias, Stanford	8042
2. Bill Albans, NCarolina	7361
3. Jim McConnell, Nebraska	7120
4. Otey Scruggs, unat-SB	7102
5. Brayton Norton, Santa Ana	7083

1951
1. Bob Richards, unat	7834
2. Floyd Simmons, LAAC	7361
3. Otey Scruggs, unat-SB	7178
4. Bill Miller, Ariz State	7174
5. Brayton Norton, SDNTC	6997

1952
1. Bob Mathias, Stanford	7887
2. Milt Campbell, Plainfield, NJ	7060
3. Floyd Simmons, LAAC	6803
4. Bill Albans, LAAC	6627
5. Bob Richards, unat	6713

1953
1. Milt Campbell, Plainfield, NJ	7743
2. Bob Richards, unat	7388
3. Bill Miller, USMC	6921
4. Jim Cooke, US Army	6894

1954
1. Bob Richards, LAAC	7315
2. Brayton Norton, Oxydental	6459
3. Aubrey Lewis, KearneyAC	6118
	(Cont.)

Table A.2 (Continued)

1955	
1. Rafer Johnson, UCLA	7983
2. Bob Richards, LAAC	7043
3. Bob Lawson, USC	7065
4. Brayton Norton, LAAC	6825

1956	
1. Milt Campbell, US Navy	7937
2. Rafer Johnson, UCLA	7755
3. Bob Richards, LAAC	7054
4. Bob Lawson, USC	6889
5. Sam Adams, unat	6884

1957	
1. Charles Pratt, US Army	7164
2. Dave Edstrom, Oregon	6981
3. Bob Lawson, unat	6910
4. Jim Klein, Striders	6793

1958	
1. Rafer Johnson, UCLA	8302
2. Dave Edstrom, Oregon	7736
3. Phil Mulkey, unat	7405
4. Charles Pratt, NYPC	6922

1959	
1. Dave Edstrom, Oregon	7599
2. Mike Herman, NYU	7026
3. Phil Mulkey, unat	7257

1960	
1. Rafer Johnson, Striders	8683
2. Dave Edstrom, Oregon	8176
3. Phil Mulkey, unat	7652
4. Jim Klein, SBAC	7185

1961	
1. Phil Mulkey, unat	8709
2. Paul Herman, Westmont	7800
3. Dave Edstrom, EEAA	7293
4. J.D. Martin, Oklahoma	7005

1962	
1. Paul Herman, Westmont	7725
2. Phil Mulkey, unat	7480
3. Steve Pauly, Oregon State	7226
4. J.D. Martin, unat	7101

1963	
1. Steve Pauly, Oregon State	7852
2. Paul Herman, US Army	8061
3. Dick Emberger, USMC	7331
4. J.D. Martin, unat	7333

1964	
1. Paul Herman, Striders	7787
2. Russ Hodge, SCVYV	7740
3. Dick Emberger, Camp Pendleton	7728
4. Don Jeisy, Camp Pendleton	7603
5. Bill Toomey, SCVYV	7615
6. J.D. Martin, unat	7270
7. Don Shy, unat	7242
8. Dave Thoreson, SBAC	7151
9. Jerry Dyes, Abilene Christian	7155
10. Bill Smith, Ohio State	7136

1965	
1. Bill Toomey, Striders	7764
2. Russ Hodge, SCVYV	7682
3. Paul Herman, Striders	7600
4. Don Shy, Long Beach 49ers	7486
5. Bill Smith, Pasadena AA	7156
6. Phil Mulkey, unat	7080
7. Larry Melquiond, SBAC	6875
8. Steve Rogers, Kansas State	7004
9. Harry Winkler, Florida	6783
10. Arvista Kelly, Lincoln	6799

1966	
1. Bill Toomey, Striders	8234
2. Russ Hodge, Foothill JC	8230
3. Dave Thoreson, Athens	7484

1966
4. Don Jeisy, unat 7426
5. Larry Melquiond, SBAC 7284
6. Phil Mulkey, unat 7153
7. Norm Johnston, unat 7034
8. Jeff Bannister, unat 7009
9. Phil Shinnick, Washington AC 7162
10. Alvin Pearman, NY HS 6945

1967
1. Bill Toomey, Striders 8044
2. Dave Thoreson, Striders 7524
3. Bill Smith, Pasadena AA 7341
4. Rick Sloan, UCLA 7869
5. Phil Shinnick, USAF 7307
6. Norm Johnston, Iowa Staters TC 7054
7. Sam Goldberg, Merritt JC 7276
8. Denny Stempel, unat 6856
9. John Warkentin, Fresno State 6843
10. Mike Mattox, Graceland 6841

1968
1. Bill Toomey, Striders 8222
2. Rick Sloan, unat 7800
3. Tom Waddell, Fort MacArthur 7720
4. Jeff Bannister, New Hampshire 7650
5. John Warkentin, Fresno State 7370
6. Jeff Bennett, Okla Christian 7468
7. Dave Buck, Pacific Coast C 7417
8. Norm Johnston, unat 7346
9. Dick Emberger, Athens 7263
10. Larry Melquiond, SanJose State 7187

1969
1. Bill Toomey, Striders 8417
2. Rick Sloan, Striders 8051
3. Jeff Bannister, New Hampshire 7668
4. Jeff Bennett, Okla. Christian 7551
5. John Warkentin, Fresno State 7601
6. Vince Bizzaro, Phil Pioneers 7530

1969
7. Norm Johnston, unat 7438
8. Russ Hodge, Striders 7394
9. John Pannel, Westmont 7159
10. Rory Kenward, Colorado 7299

1970
1. Russ Hodge, Striders 8025
2. John Warkentin, unat 8026
3. Jeff Bennett, Okla. Christian 8072
4. Bill Toomey, Striders 7728
5. Jeff Bannister, unat 7754
6. Steve Gough, Seattle Pacific 7520
7. Dave Thoreson, Striders 7501
8. Rick Wanamaker, Drake 7406
9. John Pannel, unat 7467
10. Norm Johnston, unat 7409

1971
1. Rick Wanamaker, unat 7989
2. Russ Hodge, Striders 7957
3. Jeff Bennett, Fort MacArthur 7934
4. Steve Gough, Falcon TC 7800
5. Tom Waddell, unat 7629
6. George Pannel, Westmont TC 7607
7. Fred Samara, Pennsylvania 7579
8. Gary King, unat 7533
9. Mike Hill, Mount San Antonio C 7515
10. Ray Hupp, Ohio State 7456

1972
1. Jeff Bennett, Fort MacArthur 8076
2. Jeff Bannister, Dec. Club Am 8120
3. Bruce Jenner, Graceland 7846
4. Steve Gough, Falcon TC 7822
5. Andrew Pettes, Oklahoma 7762
6. John Warkentin, Striders 7807
7. Gary Hill, Oklahoma Christian 7584
8. Fred Samara, Pennsylvania 7669
9. Rick Wanamaker, San Diego TC 7602
10. Russ Hodge, DCA 7750

(Cont.)

Table A.2 (Continued)

1973

1. Jeff Bennett, Eagle Track Cl	8121
2. Steve Gough, Club North West	7938
3. Ron Evans, Connecticut	7821
4. Fred Samara, Pennsylvania	7656
5. Bruce Jenner, unat	7770
6. John Warkentin, Striders	7662
7. Roger George, Fresno State	7777
8. Craig Brigham, Oregon	7673
9. Carl Wood, Florida TC	7606
10. Rick Wanamaker, unat	7556

1974

1. Bruce Jenner, unat	8303
2. Jeff Bennett, Eagle TC	7939
3. Fred Samara, NYAC	7988
4. Fred Dixon, Striders	8033
5. John Warkentin, Striders	7969
6. Steve Gough, CNW	7930
7. Roger George, Fresno State	7839
8. Ron Evans, Striders	7938
9. Rick Wanamaker, unat	7689
10. Ray Hupp, Ohio TC	7322

1975

1. Bruce Jenner, SJ Stars	8524
2. Fred Dixon, Striders	8277
3. Fred Samara, NYAC	8077
4. Steve Gough, CNW	8057
5. Craig Brigham, Oregon	8027
6. John Warkentin, Striders	7937
7. Mike Hill, unat	7921
8. Roger George, Striders	7909
9. Bill Hancock, Sn III	7978
10. Jeff Bennett, Eagle TC	7784

1976

1. Bruce Jenner, SJ Stars	8617a
2. Fred Dixon, Striders	8294
3. Fred Samara, NYAC	8004
4. Roger George, Striders	7888a
5. Craig Brigham, Oregon	7898

1976

6. Steve Gough, CNW	7896
7. Bill Hancock, UCTC	7881
8. John Warkentin, unat	7842
9. Jeff Bennett, unat	7756
10. Mike Hill, Colorado TC	7758

1977

1. Fred Dixon, Striders	8393a
2. John Warkentin, unat	8031a
3. Steve Alexander, Hurr TC	8055
4. Roger George, Striders	7833
5. Craig Brigham, Oregon TC	7815a
6. Bob Coffman, Hurr TC	7992
7. Fred Samara, NYAC	7763a
8. Jeff Bennett, unat	7702
9. Mauricio Bardales, UC-Irvine	7641
10. Tony Hale, Fisk	7755

1978

1. Fred Dixon, Striders	8034a
2. Mike Hill, Colorado TC	8004a
3. Bob Coffman, Hurr TC	8137
4. John Warkentin, unat	8011
5. Roger George, AW	8034
6. Mauricio Bardales, UC-Irvine	7974a
7. Al Hamlin, Del River AC	7855
8. Lee Palles, Mississippi State	7917a
9. John Whitson, DC Dashers	7829
10. Jim Howell, Hurr TC	7679a

1979

1. Bob Coffman, Hurr TC	8274a
2. John Crist, Grboro Pacers	8149a
3. John Warkentin, unat	7890
4. John Whitson, SunLand TC	7798a
5. Wes Herbst, Houston	7903a
6. Steve Jacobs, Arizona	7902
7. Fred Samara, NYAC	7761
8. Al Hamlin, Del River AC	8031
9. Mike Hill, Colorado TC	7665a
10. Dannie Jackson, Arizona State	7755

1980		
1. Bob Coffman, Houston Ath	8184
2. Lee Palles, Athlete's Attic	8159
3. Fred Dixon, Striders	8154
4. John Crist, Grboro Pacers	8053
5. Mark Anderson, UCLA	7893
6. Tony Allen-Cooksey, THTC	7941h
7. Al Hamlin, SAME	7895h
8. Jim Howell, Houston Ath	7850
9. Jom Wooding, unat	7855
10. Dannie Jackson, unat	7793

1981
1. Mark Anderson, UCLA — 8171w
2. John Crist, AW — 8005
3. Tony Allen-Cooksey, AW — 7972
4. Dannie Jackson, Arizona State — 7861
5. Jim Howell, Philadelphia PC — 7795
6. Steve Alexander, NYAC — 7787
7. Jim Wooding, Shore AC — 7797
8. Steve Jacobs, unat — 7878h
9. Robert Baker, SAME — 7804
10. Mauricio Bardales, ACA — 7778

1982
1. John Crist, AW — 8129
2. Jim Howell, Phila PC — 8038h
3. Mike Brown UCSB Outreach — 7970h
4. Jim Schnurr, unat — 7850
5. dJim Wooding, Shore AC — 8055h
6. Steve Jacobs, unat — 7928h
7. John Sayre, Southern Illinois — 7660
8. Keith Collins, Washington State — 7691w
9. Mike Ramos, Washington — 7638
10. Lane Maestretti, unat — 7703h

1983
1. Mark Anderson, Wilt's AC — 8250
2. John Crist, AW — 7998
3. Gary Bastien, unat — 7877
4. Tony Allen-Cooksey, AW — 7861

1983
5. Kerry Zimmerman, Indiana — 7810
6. Orville Peterson, Campbell — 7743
7. Mike Ramos, Washington — 7838a
8. Steve Erickson, CNW — 7791
9. Jim Wooding, Shore AC — 7819
10. John Sayre, Southern Illinois — 7838

1984
1. John Crist, AW — 8130
2. Jim Wooding, Shore AC — 8091
3. Tim Bright, AIA — 8098
4. Rob Muzzio, George Mason — 8227
5. Mike Ramos, Washington — 7995
6. Mike Gonzales, USC — 7960
7. Fred Dixon, AIA — 8041
8. Jim Connolly, UCLA — 7771
9. John Sayre, Southern Illinois — 7891
10. Tom Harris, All American TC — 7768

1985
1. Mike Ramos, Puma — 8294
2. John Sayre, UCTC — 8391w
3. Tim Bright, AIA — 8221h
4. Rob Muzzio, GMU — 7968
5. Dave Johnson, Azusa Pacific — 7948
6. Gary Kinder, New Mexico — 7965w
7. Orville Peterson, Camp TC — 8031h
8. Steve Erickson, Washington — 8063w
9. Bart Goodell, Adidas — 7720
10. Steve Odgers, unat — 7575w

1986
1. Mike Ramos, Washington — 8322
2. Dave Johnson, Puma — 8203w
3. Tim Bright, AW — 8302h
4. Chris Branham, LATC — 8159
5. John Sayre, unat — 8076
6. Steve Erickson, Adidas — 8030
7. Tony Allen-Cooksey, AtF — 7930
8. Gary Kinder, Adidas — 7998
(Cont.)

Table A.2 (Continued)

1986

9. Bart Goodell, Adidas	8041
10. Gary Armstrong, unat	8203

Note. DECA, The Decathlon Association
has same first 4 rankings; 5. Erickson,
6. Armstrong, 7. Goodell, 8. Sayre,
9. Kinder, 10. Allen-Cooksey.

1987

1. Tim Bright, AW	8340
2. Rob Muzzio, GMU	8134
3. Gary Kinder, NYAC	8227
4. Jim Connolly, UCLA	8121
5. Keith Robinson, BYU	7967
6. Mike Gonzales, S & STC	7956
7. Sheldon Blockburger, LSU	7964
8. Dave Johnson, NYAC	8045
9. Kris Szabadhegy, US Army	7821
10. Jay Thorson, Puma	7684

Note. DECA, The Decathlon Association, has
the same rankings for first 4; 5. Gonzales,
6. Robinson, 7. Johnson, 8. Blockburger,
9. Szabadhegy, 10. Thorson.

Table A.3 Winners of Major International and National Competitions

Olympic Games champions

	Then-current score	1985 Tables			
1912	8412.955	6649	WR	Jim Thorpe, USA	Stockholm
	7724.495	6044		Hugo Wieslander, SWE	
1920	6804.34	5882		Helge Lövland, NOR	Antwerp
1924	7710.775	6562	WR	Harold Osborn, USA	Paris
1928	8053.29	6667	WR	Paavo Yrjölä, FIN	Amsterdam
1932	8462.23	6814	WR	Jim Bausch, USA	Los Angeles

	Then-current score	1985 Tables			
1936	7900	7341	WR	Glenn Morris, USA	Berlin
1948	7139	6713		Bob Mathias, USA	London
1952	7887	7668	WR	Bob Mathias, USA	Helsinki
1956	7937	7657	OR	Milt Campbell, USA	Melbourne
1960	8392	7990	OR	Rafer Johnson, USA	Rome
1964	7887	7816		Willi Holdorf, GER	Tokyo
1968	8193	8158	OR	Bill Toomey, USA	Mexico City
1972	8454a	8466	WR	Nikolay Avilov, SOV	Munich
1976	8617a	8634	WR	Bruce Jenner, USA	Montreal
1980	8495a	8522		Daley Thompson, GBR	Moscow
1984	8798	8847	WR	Daley Thompson, GBR	Los Angeles
1988	--	8488		Christian Schenk, GDR	Seoul

Note. Thorpe was later disqualified for professionalism and Wieslander named the winner. In 1983 his name was reinstated as "Co-Olympic Champion" by IAAF. WR = world record; OR = Olympic record. The 1912 Olympic Games were scored on 1912A tables; 1920-32 on 1912B tables; 1936-48 on 1934 tables; 1952-60 on 1950 tables; and 1964-72 on 1962 tables. Scores in third column are on 1985 tables.

World championship champions

	Then-current score	1985 Tables		
1983	8666	8714	Daley Thompson, GBR	Helsinki
1987		8680	Torsten Voss, GDR	Rome

European champions

	Then-current score	1985 Tables		
1934	8103.245	6667	Hans-Heinrich Sievert, GER	Torino
1938	7214	6687	Olle Bexell, SWE	Paris
1946	6987	6566	Godtfred Holmvang, NOR	Oslo
1950	7364	6827	Ignace Heinrich, FRA	Brussels
1954	6752	6940	Vasiliy Kuznyetsov, SOV	Bern
1958	7865	7563	Vasiliy Kuznyetsov, SOV	Stockholm
1962	8026	7653	Vasiliy Kuznyetsov, SOV	Belgrade
1966	7740	7664	Werner von Moltke, GER	Budapest

(Cont.)

Table A.3 (Continued)

	Then-current score	1985 Tables		
1969	8041	7978	Joachim Kirst, GDR	Athens
1971	8196	8188	Joachim Kirst, GDR	Helsinki
1974	8207	8230	Ryszard Skowronek, POL	Rome
1978	8340	8335	Alexandr Grebenyuk, SOV	Prague
1982	8743 WR	8744	Daley Thompson, GBR	Athens
1986		8811	Daley Thompson, GBR	Stuttgart

Commonwealth champions

	Then-current score	1985 Tables		
1966	7270	7133	Roy Williams, NZE	Kingston, Jamaica
1970	7492	7420	Geoff Smith, AUS	Edinburgh
1974	7417	7363	Mike Bull, GBR	Christchurch
1978	8467w	8470w	Daley Thompson, GBR	Edmonton
1982	8410	8424	Daley Thompson, GBR	Brisbane
1986		8663	Daley Thompson, GBR	Edinburgh

Note. There were two trials in 1964. The 1920-32 trials were scored on the 1912B tables; 1936-48 on 1934 tables; 1952-60 and first 1964 on 1950 tables; 1964-1984 on 1962 tables. Scores in third column are from 1985 tables. MR = meet record.

United States champions 1915-1988

		1912A Tables	1985
1915	Alma Richards (Intermountain Association)	6858.81	5719

		1912B Tables	1985
1920	Brutus Hamilton (University of Missouri)	7022.9815[a]	5937
1921	Dan Shea (Pastime AC)	5849.338	5181
1922	S.H. Thompson (Princeton University)	6890.23	5869
1923	Harold Osborn (Illinois AC)	7351.89[a]	6247
1924	Anthony Plansky (Pere Marquette K of C)	5901.45	4544
1925	Harold Osborn (2nd win) (Illinois AC)	7706.36[a]	6375

		1912B Tables	1985
1926	Harold Osborn (3rd win) (Illinois AC)	7187.832	6021
1927[d]	Pait Elkins (University of Nebraska)	7574.42	6291
1928[e]	Ken Doherty (Cadillac AC)	7600.52	6345
1929	Ken Doherty (2nd win) (Cadillac AC)	7784.68[a]	6393
1930	Wilson Charles (Haskell Institute)	7313.343	6118
1931	Jess Mortenson (LAAC)	8166.66[a]	6757
1932	James Bausch (Kansas City AC)	8103.25	6431
1933	Barney Berlinger (Penn AC)	7597.19	6158
1934	Bob Clark (San Francisco Olympic Club)	7966.30	6861
1935	Bob Clark (2nd win) (San Francisco Olympic Club)	7929.22	6697

		began to use tables revised in 1934	1985
1936	Glenn Morris (unat, Simla, CO)	7880	7213
1937	no meet held		
1938	Joseph Scott (Western Reserve University)	6486	6087
1939	Joseph Scott (2nd win) (Western Reserve University	6671	6218
1940	William Watson (unat, Ann Arbor, MI)	7523	6905
1941	John Borican (Asbury Park AC)	5666	5596
1942	Bill Terwilliger (unat, DeKalb, IL)	6802	6403
1943	William Watson (2nd win) (Detroit Police AA)	5994	5449
1944	Irv Mondschein (Brooklyn Army Base)	5748	5510
1945	Charles Beaudry (Marquette University)	5886	5910
1946	Irv Mondschein (2nd win) (New York University)	6466	6089
1947	Irv Mondschein (3rd win) (New York Pioneer Club)	6715	6300
1948	Bob Mathias (unat, Tulare, CA)	7227	6713
1949	Bob Mathias (2nd win) (unat, Tulare, CA)	7556	6944
1950	Bob Mathias (3rd win) (unat, Tulare, CA)	8042[b]	7287
1951	Bob Richards (Illinois AC)	7834	6552

		began to use tables revised in 1950	1985
1952	Bob Mathias (4th win) (Stanford University)	7829[c]	7543
1953	Milt Campbell (Plainfield, NJ, High School)	7235	7040
1954	Bob Richards (2nd win) (LAAC)	6501	7125
1955	Bob Richards (3rd win) (LAAC)	6862	6864
1956	Rafer Johnson (UCLA)	7754	7420
1957	Charles Pratt (US Army)	7164	6993
1958	Rafer Johnson (2nd win) (UCLA)	7549	7432
1959	C.K. Yang (UCLA)	7549	7246
1960	Rafer Johnson (3rd win) (S.C. Striders)	8683[b]	7981

(Cont.)

Table A.3 (Continued)

	began to use tables revised in 1950	1985
1961 Paul Herman (US Army)	7142	7160
1962 C.K. Yang (2nd win) (UCLA)	8249	7694
1963 Steve Pauly (Oregon State University)	7852	7541
1964 C. K. Yang (3rd win) (Pasadena AA)	8641	7732

	began to use tables revised in 1962	1985
1965 Bill Toomey (Pasadena AA)	7764	7594
1966 Bill Toomey (2nd win) (S.C. Striders)	8234[c]	8096
1967 Bill Toomey (3rd win) (S.C. Striders)	7880	7761
1968 Bill Toomey (4th win) (S.C. Striders)	8037	7900
1969 Bill Toomey (5th win) (S.C. Striders)	7818	7664
1970 John Warkentin (Fresno State)	8026	7908
1971 Rick Wanamaker (unat, Des Moines, IA)	7989	7879
1972 Jeff Bennett (US Army)	7910	7765
1973 Jeff Bennett (US Army)	8121	8006
1974 Bruce Jenner (unat, San Jose, Stars)	8245[a]	8202
1975 Fred Samara (NYAC)	8061	7912
1976 Bruce Jenner (2nd win) (San Jose, Stars)	8542[b](8444[a])	8459
1977 Fred Dixon (Tobias Striders)	8037	8007
1978 Mike Hill (Colorado TC)	8004	7971
1979 Bob Coffman (Hurricane TC)	8154	8082
1980 Bob Coffman (Houston AC)	8184	8166
1981 John Crist (Athletics West)	8005	7976
1982 John Crist (Athletics West)	8129	8121
1983 Mark Anderson (Wilt's AC)	8152	8142
1984 John Crist (Athletics West)	8102	8126

	began to use tables revised in 1985
1985 John Sayre (University of Chicago TC)	8391w
1986 Dave Johnson (Puma)	8203w
1987 Tim Bright (Athletics West)	8340
1988 Gary Kinder (unat)	8293

[a]Meet record. [b]Meet record and world record. [c]Meet record and world record, not officially approved. [d]Meet held in one day. [e]Meet held in 3 days.

(Cont.)

Azusa Pacific's Dave Johnson won the National TAC championship and the U.S. Olympic Festival in 1986. (Sailer/McManus/Courtesy of *Track and Field News*)

Table A.3 (Continued)

Pan American Games champions

Original score	1985 Tables			
1951	6610 (34)	6261 MR	Hernan Figueros, CHI	Buenos Aires
1955	6994 (50)	6946 MR	Rafer Johnson, USA	Mexico City
1959	7245 (50)	7213 MR	Dave Edstrom, USA	Chicago
1963	7335 (50)	7194 MR	J.D. Martin, USA	San Paulo
1967	8044 (62)	7511	Rick Wanamaker, USA	Cali
1975	8045a(62)	8024 MR	Bruce Jenner, USA	Mexico City
1979	8070a(62)	8015 MR	Bob Coffman, USA	San Juan
1983	7958a(62)	7928	Dave Steen, CAN	Caracas
1987		7649	Mike Gonzales, USA	Indianapolis

(Cont.)

Tim Bright won the 1987 TAC title with 8340 points. (Jeff Johnson/Courtesy of *Track and Field News*)

United States Olympic Trials Winners

	Original score	1985 Tables		
1912	7414.555 WR	5867 MR	J. Austin Menaul	
			(University of Chicago)	Evanston, IL
1920	7022.9815	5937 MR	Brutus Hamilton	
			(University of Missouri)	New York City
1924	7377	6248 MR	Harold Osborn	
			(Illinois AC)	New York City
1928	7600.52	6345 MR	Ken Doherty	
			(Cadillac AC)	Philadelphia
1932	8103.25	6431 MR	Jim Bausch	
			(Kansas City AC)	Evanston
1936	7883	7193 MR	Glenn Morris	
			(Denver AC)	Milwaukee
1948	7224	6713	Bob Mathias	
			(unat, Tulare)	Bloomfield
1952	7829	7543 MR	Bob Mathias	
			(Stanford)	Tulare
1956	7754	7420	Rafer Johnson	
			(UCLA)	Crawfordsville
1960	8683 WR	7981 MR	Rafer Johnson	
			(S.C. Striders)	Eugene
1964	7794	7547	Paul Herman	
			(US Army)	Walnut
	7728	7570	Dick Emberger	
			(US Marine Corps)	Los Angeles
1968	8222	8125 MR	Bill Toomey	
			(S.C. Striders)	S Lake Tahoe
1972	8120	7981	Jeff Bannister	
			(Dec. Club America)	Eugene
1976	8542 WR	8459 MR	Bruce Jenner	
			(San Jose Stars)	Eugene
1980	8184a	8082	Bob Coffman	
			(Houston Athletic)	Eugene
1984	8102a	8126	John Crist	
			(Athletics West)	Los Angeles
1988		8293	Gary Kinder	
			(unat)	Indianapolis

(Cont.)

Table A.3 (Continued)

Sites of United States championships

California 24 times in 11 cities
  San Francisco, 1915, 1925
  San Diego, 1935
  Tulare, 1949, 1950, 1952, 1962
  Santa Barbara, 1951, 1968, 1975, 1981
  Kingsburg, 1957, 1959
  Walnut, 1964, 1979
  Bakersfield, 1965, 1969
  Los Angeles, 1967, 1972, 1984
  South Lake Tahoe, 1970
  Porterville, 1971, 1973
  San Jose, 1987
New Jersey 13 times in 9 cities
  Jersey City, 1921
  Newark, 1922
  West Orange, 1924
  Bridgetown, 1941
  Elizabeth, 1943, 1944
  Bloomfield, 1945, 1946, 1947, 1948
  Plainfield, 1953
  Atlantic City, 1954
  Palmyra, 1958
Indiana 5 times in 3 cities
  Crawfordsville, 1955, 1956
  Bloomington, 1977
  Indianapolis, 1985, 1988
Illinois 4 times in 2 cities
  Chicago, 1923, 1933, 1942
  Evanston, 1932

Pennsylvania 3 times in 2 cities
  Philadelphia, 1926, 1928
  Pittsburgh, 1930
Ohio 3 times in 2 cities
  Cincinnati, 1934
  Cleveland, 1939, 1940
Oregon 4 times in 2 cities
  Eugene, 1960, 1976, 1986
  Corvallis, 1963
New York
  New York City, 1920, 1938
Nebraska
  Lincoln, 1927, 1931
Colorado
  Denver, 1929
Wisconsin
  Milwaukee, 1936
New Mexico
  Albuquerque, 1961
Kansas
  Salina, 1966
Virginia
  Richmond, 1974, 1978
Louisiana
  Baton Rouge, 1982

(Cont.)

Multiple United States champions

5 wins:	Bill Toomey	1965	1966	1967	1968	1969
4 wins:	Bob Mathias	1948	1949	1950	1952	
3 wins:	Harold Osborn	1923	1925	1926		
	Irv Mondschein	1944	1946	1947		
	Bob Richards	1951	1954	1955		
	Rafer Johnson	1956	1958	1960		
	C.K. Yang	1959	1962	1964		
	John Crist	1981	1982	1984		
2 wins:	Ken Doherty	1928	1929			
	Bob Clark	1934	1935			
	Joe Scott	1938	1939			
	William Watson	1940	1943			
	Jeff Bennett	1972	1973			
	Bruce Jenner	1974	1976			

Most consecutive United States titles

5 in a row:	Bill Toomey	1965-69
3 in a row:	Bob Mathias	1948-50
2 in a row:	Harold Osborn	1925-26
	Ken Doherty	1928-29
	Bob Clark	1934-35
	Joe Scott	1938-39
	Irv Mondschein	1946-47
	Bob Richards	1954-55
	Jeff Bennett	1972-73
	John Crist	1981-82

For all following United States championships the original scores are used: 1969 to 1984-1962 tables used. 1985 and later-1985 tables used.

United States Junior Champions 1973-1988

1973	Craig Brigham (Oregon)	7357
1974	Russell Fritts (Tennessee)	6677
1975	Tony Hale (Fisk)	6856
1976	Joe Schneider (St. John's)	7004
1977	Vince Reilly (St. Joe's H.S., NJ)	7057
1978	Gary Bastien (Eastern Mich)	7139a
1979	John Irvine (unat, Phoenix, AZ)	6807a

(Cont.)

Table   A.3   (Continued)

1980	Steve Erickson (Washington H.S.)	7188a
1981	Greg Loisel (Azusa Pacific)	6745
1982	Robert Muzzio (D.C. Striders)	7097a
1983	Kevin McGorty (Westfield, NJ)	7133a
1984	Steve Klassen (Boulder T.C.)	7093a
1985	Derek Huff (Western Illinois)	6941
1986	Gerald Swann (Campbell)	7013
1987	Jeff Mooney (Auburn)	6713
1988	Matt Farmer (UC-Irvine)	7015

NCAA Division I Champions 1970-88

1970	Rick Wanamaker (Drake)	7406
1971	Ray Hupp (Ohio State)	7456
1972	Ron Evans (Connecticut)	7571
1973	Raimo Pihl (Brigham Young)	8079a
1974	Rünald Backman (Brigham Young)	7874
1975	Raimo Pihl (Brigham Young)	8079a
1976	Ed Miller (California)	7443a
1977	Tito Steiner (Brigham Young)	7659
1978	Mauricio Bardales (UC-Irvine)	8007
1979	Tito Steiner (Brigham Young)	7922
1980	Mark Anderson (UCLA)	7893a
1981	Tito Steiner (Brigham Young)	8279aw
1982	Trond Skramstad (Mt St Mary's)	7960a
1983	Kerry Zimmerman (Indiana)	7810a
1984	Robert Muzzio (George Mason)	8227a
1985	Robert Muzzio (George Mason)	7968
1986	Mike Ramos (Washington)	8261
1987	Jim Connolly (UCLA)	8121
1988	Mikael Olander (LSU)	8021

NCAA Division II Champions 1970-88

1970	Steve Gough (Seattle Pacific)	7269
1971	Bill Bakley (Westmont)	7067
1972	Don Albritton (NEMO St.)	6999
1973	Paul Fink (Fullerton St.)	6960
1974	Paul Fink (Fullerton St.)	7067
1975	Barry Stebbins (Mt St Mary's)	7023
1976	Barry Stebbins (Mt St Mary's)	7163
1977	Mauricio Bardales (UC-Irvine)	7621
1978	Tom Delmoor (Mt St Mary's)	7257a
1979	Floyd Scholz (Cent. Conn. St.)	7329a
1980	Gudmund Olsen (Mt St Mary's)	7441a
1981	Gudmund Olsen (Mt St Mary's)	7481a
1982	Trond Skramstad (Mt St Mary's)	7860a
1983	Tim Bright (Abilene Christian Univ.)	7743a
1984	William Motti (Mt St Mary's)	8052a

1985	William Motti (Mt St Mary's)	8090
1986	Robert Ekpete (Mt St Mary's)	7380
1987	Mike Ledsome (Abilene Christian)	7655
1988	John Schwepker (Southeast Missouri St)	7773

NCAA Division III Champions 1974-87

1974	Jim Baum (Ashland)	7030
1975	Mark Lineweaver (Brockport St.)	7101
1976	Tony Hale (Fisk)	7537
1977	Tony Hale (Fisk)	7555
1978	Tony Hale (Fisk)	7359
1979	Paul Trocki (Keene St.)	7163a
1980	Rick Grzeszkowiak (Widener)	7160
1981	Dave Bolton (Washington Univ., MO)	7246
1982	Gary Van Vreede (UW, Stevens Point)	
1983	Doug Porter (Occidental)	7139a
1984	Doug Porter (Occidental)	6760a
1985	Mike Meeter (UW-LaCrosse)	7030
1986	Kip Janvrin (Simpson)	7323
1987	Kip Janvrin (Simpson)	7528
1988	Kip Janvrin (Simpson)	7482

NAIA Champions 1969-88

1969	Jeff Bennett (Oklahoma Christian)	7551
1970	Jeff Bennett (Oklahoma Christian)	7304
1971	Bruce Jenner (Graceland)	7403
1972	Gary Hill (Oklahoma Christian)	7538
1973	Dave Bahr (Graceland)	7011
1974	James Herron (Cameron State, OK)	6939
1975	James Herron (Cameron State, OK)	7083
1976	Bruce Kupersmith (Azusa Pacific)	7173
1977	Bill Waters (Point Loma, CA)	7365
1978	Bill Waters (Point Loma, CA)	7288
1979	Gary Wise (Azusa Pacific)	7461
1980	Gary Wise (Azusa Pacific)	7331
1981	Doug Larson (Whitworth)	7519a
1982	Greg Culp (Arkansas-Montgomery)	7304
1983	Phil Schot (Pacific Lutheran)	7452
1984	Doug Loisel (Azusa Pacific)	7622a
1985	Patrick Gellens (Concordia, NE)	7577
1986	Mark Elliston (Oklahoma Baptist)	7023
1987	Jack Nance (Azusa Pacific)	6923
1988	Jack Nance (Azusa Pacific)	7189

NJCAA Champions 1973-88

1973	Jerry Kelley (Montgomery JC, MD)	6020
1974	Mike Anderson (Brevard JC, NC)	6224
1975	John Cecil (Brevard JC, NC)	6540

(Cont.)

Table A.3 (Continued)

NJCAA Champions 1973-88

1976	Dennis Miller (NE Colorado)	6994
1977	Joel Johnson (Lane CC, OR)	6825
1978	Mike Gardner (Ricks, ID)	7220
1979	Jeff Montpas (Mesa CC)	7048
1980	Craig Branham (Pima CC)	7346a
1981	Conny Silfver (Ricks, ID)	7187
1982	Conny Silfver (Ricks, ID)	7448a
1983	Alan Moore (South Plains)	7530
1984	Peter Lung (Ricks, ID)	7167a
1985	Rusty Hunter (Blinn)	7178w
1986	Ron McPhee (Blinn)	6884
1987	Bengt Jarlsjo (Blinn)	7098
1988	Steve Fritz (Hutchinson)	6990

France's William Motti was a two-time NCAA II champion at Mount Saint Mary's College. (Bill Kamenjar/Courtesy of *Track and Field News*)

Mike Ramos of the University of Washington is the collegiate record holder with a personal best of 8322. (Claus Andersen/Courtesy of *Track and Field News*)

Table A.4 World Record Progression

	Scoring Tables						
1912A	1912B	1934	1950/52	1962/71/77	1985	Originally scored using 1912A tables	Note
6220.965	5559.07	5114	4275	5197	5080	Karl von Halt, GER — 11.4 603 1074 1675 — 55.0 — Munster — 17.4 2931 — 226 4028 — Oct. 15, 1911 5:15.4	1
6903.920	6242.025	5516	4646	5584	5386	Hugo Wieslander, SWE — 11.6 615 1125 167 — 55.6 — Goteberg — 18.2 2974 — 300 4889 — Oct. 15, 1911 4:59.4	1
7414.555	6752.66	6095	5307	6051	5867	J. Austin Menaul, USA — 11.4 606 1270 178 — 53.8 — Evanston — 16.6 3300 — 289 4048 — May 23-24, 1912 4:37.2	2
7099.845	6437.950	5655	4764	5687	5493	Hugo Wieslander, SWE — 12.0 604 1144 165 — 55.6 — Stockholm — 18.0 3629 — 300 4838 — June 5-6, 1912 4:47.2	2
7244.100	6582.205	5787	4895	5792	5583	Hugo Wieslander, SWE — 11.9 628 1232 165 — 54.7 — Stockholm — 17.8 3517 — 320 4635 — June 20-21, 1912 5:02.0	2
8412.955	7751.060	6971	6268	6756	6564	Jim Thorpe, USA — 11.2 679 1289 187 — 52.2 — Stockholm — 15.6 3698 — 325 4570 — July 13-14, 1912 4:40.1	3
7724.495	7062.600	6220	5377	6161	5965	Hugo Wieslander, SWE — 11.8 642 1214 175 — 53.6 — Stockholm (2) — 17.2 3629 — 310 5040 — July 13-15, 1912 4:45.0	
7462.790	6800.89	6167	5652	6124	5969	Waldemar Wickholm, FIN — 11.5 643 1129 174 — 51.9 — Malmo (3) — 16.0 3254 — 290 4363 — July 7-9, 1914 4:41.3	4
7786.920	7125.025	6301	5500	6209	6033	Helge Lövland, NOR — 11.4 657 1203 167 — 54.5 — Oslo (Kristinia) — 16.1 3812 — 306 5161 — July 19-20, 1919 5:01.4	
7880.820	7218.925	6297	5431	6216	5987	Evert Nilsson, SWE — 11.8 633 1144 184 — 55.1 — Stockholm — 18.1 3586 — 345 5177 — July 3-4, 1920 4:36.0	
7853.650	7191.755	6365	5533	6278	6073	Bertil Olsson, SWE — 11.8 671 1165 178 — 54.0 — Stockholm (2) — 17.1 3923 — 330 4320 — July 3-4, 1920 4:37.3	
8025.520	7363.625	6363	5466	6236	6025	Aleksander Klumberg, EST — 11.8 681 1205 175 — 56.6 — Tallinn — 18.1 3869 — 340 5845 — July 3-5, 1920 4:55.3	4

Scoring Tables

1912B	1934	1950/52	1962/ 71/77	1985	Originally scored using 1912B tables	Note
7485.610	6450	5531	6270	6087	Aleksander Klumberg, EST — 12.3 659 1292 175 — 55.0 — 17.0 3964 — 340 6220 5:11.3 — Helsinki, Sept. 16-17, 1922	5
7226.905	6408	5644	6304	6147	Gustaf Strandberg, FIN — 11.7 666 1127 170 — 53.0 — 16.2 3303 — 330 5451 4:41.0 — Goteberg, July 7-8, 1923	4
7350.120	6583	5862	6424	6248	Harold Osborn, USA — 11.5 6555 1145 2955 — 52.9 — 15.6 3364 — 320 4611 4:53.1 — Chicago, Sept. 3, 1923	4
7710.775	6877	6163	6668	6476	Harold Osborn, USA — 11.2 692 1143 197 — 53.2 — 16.0 3451 — 350 4669 4:50.0 — Paris, July 11-12, 1924	
7832.030	6889	6077	6651	6460	Paavo Yrjölä, FIN — 11.8 654 1397 185 — 52.4 — 16.9 3731 — 330 5670 4:41.1 — Viipuri, July 17-18, 1926	
8018.990	7053	6244	6768	6586	Paavo Yrjölä, FIN — 11.7 673 1427 185 — 52.8 — 16.8 4076 — 320 5740 4:41.8 — Helsinki, July 16-17, 1927	
8053.290	7071	6246	6774	6587	Paavo Yrjölä, FIN — 11.8 672 1411 187 — 53.2 — 16.6 4209 — 330 5570 4:44.0 — Amsterdam, Aug. 3-4, 1928	6
7931.500	7080	6379	6815	6645	Akilles Järvinen, FIN — 11.2 687 1364 175 — 51.4 — 15.6 3695 — 330 5558 4:52.4 — Amsterdam, Aug. 3-4, 1928	
8117.30	7197	6432	6869	6700	Paavo Yrjölä, FIN — 11.6 676 1472 185 — 53.2 — 16.1 3966 — 310 5888 4:37.5 — Aalborg, July 9-10, 1930	7, 10
8255.475	7378	6719	7036	6865	Akilles Järvinen, FIN — 11.1 689 1314 180 — 50.0 — 15.4 3647 — 360 5815 4:54.2 — Viipuri, July 19-20, 1930	
8292.480	7378	6707	7038	6879	Akilles Järvinen, FIN — 11.1 700 1311 175 — 50.6 — 15.7 3680 — 360 6100 4:47.0 — Los Angeles (2), Aug. 5-6, 1932	6, 8

(Cont.)

Table A.4 (Continued)

Originally scored using 1912B tables

	1912B	1934	1950/52	1962/ 71/77	1985		Note
	8462.235	7396	6590	6896	6735	James Bausch, USA	
	11.7	695	1532	170	54.2	Los Angeles 16.2 4458 — Aug. 5-6, 1932 400 6191 5:17.0	
	8467.620	7432	6636	6999	6833	Hans-Heinrich Sievert, GER	9
	11.4	709	1455	1825	54.0	Hamburg 16.2 4666 — July 22-23, 1932 340 5958 4:59.8	
	8435.360	7449	6680	7003	6828	Hans-Heinrich Sievert, GER	4
	11.2	678	1531	185	53.8	Koln 15.8 4575 — Aug. 12-13, 1933 330 5832 5:06.0	
	8790.460	7824	7135	7292	7147	Hans-Heinrich Sievert, GER	
	11.1	748	1531	180	52.2	Hamburg 15.8 4723 — July 7-8, 1934 343 5832 4:58.8	

Scoring Tables — Originally scored using 1934 tables

1934	1950/52	1962/71/77	1985	Athlete	100	LJ	SP	HJ	400	Loc	110H	Discus	PV	Jav	1500	Date	Note
7883	7275	7394	7213	Glenn Morris, USA	10.7	686	1445	187	50.7	Milwaukee	14.9	4311	345	5606	4:48.2	June 26-27, 1936	10
7900	7310	7421	7254	Glenn Morris, USA	11.1	697	1410	185	49.4	Berlin	14.9	4302	350	5452	4:33.2	Aug. 7-8, 1936	
8042	7444	7453	7287	Bob Mathias, USA	10.9	709	1448	185	51.0	Tulare	14.7	4462	398	5559	5:05.1	June 29-30, 1950	

Scoring Tables — Originally scored using 1950/52 tables

1950/52	1962/71/77	1985	Athlete	100	LJ	SP	HJ	400	Loc	110H	Discus	PV	Jav	1500	Date	Note
7829	7690	7543	Bob Mathias, USA	10.8	715	1521	189	50.8	Tulare	14.6	4815	375	5909	4:55.3	July 1-2, 1952	11
7887	7731	7580	Bob Mathias, USA	10.9	698	1530	190	50.2	Helsinki	14.7	4689	400	5921	4:50.8	July 25-26, 1952	
		7592		11.08					50.38		14.91				4:51.11		
7985	7758	7608	Rafer Johnson, USA	10.5	749	1380	185	49.7	Kingsburg	14.5	4720	387	5909	5:01.5	June 10-11,1955	
8014	7760	7653	Vasiliy Kuznyetsov, SOV	11.0	730	1449	175	49.1	Krasnodar	14.5	4750	400	6616	4:50.0	May 17-18, 1958	
8302	7896	7789	Rafer Johnson, USA	10.6	717	1469	180	48.2	Moscow	14.9	4906	395	7259	5:05.0	July 27-28,1958	

(Cont.)

Table A.4 (Continued)

Originally scored using 1950/52 tables

Scoring Tables 1950/52	1962/ 71/77	1985		Note
<u>8357</u>	7957	7839	Vasiliy Kuznyetsov, SOV 10.7 735 1468 189 49.2 Moscow 14.7 4994 May 16-17, 1959 420 6506 5:04.6	
<u>8683</u>	8063	7981	Rafer Johnson, USA 10.6 755 1585 178 48.6 Eugene 14.5 5197 July 8-9, 1960 397 7110 5:09.9	
8709	8155	8049	Phil Mulkey, USA 10.7 734 1532 199 51.0 Memphis 14.6 4703 June 16-17, 1961 439 6745 4:43.8	12
<u>9121</u>	8089	8009	C.K. Yang, FOR 10.7 717 1322 192 47.7 Walnut 14.0 4099 April 27-28, 1963 484 7175 5:02.4	13

Originally scored using 1962 tables

Scoring Tables 1962/ 71/77	1985		Note
8234	8096	Bill Toomey, USA 10.3 777 1394 195 47.3 Salina 14.8 4495 July 2-3, 1966 396 6063 4:30.0	14
8219	8082	Bill Toomey, USA 10.5 744 1351 190 46.8 Los Angeles (2) 14.7 4452 July 23-24, 1966 410 6419 4:20.3	8
<u>8230</u>	8119	Russ Hodge, USA 10.5 751 1725 185 48.9 Los Angeles 15.2 5044 July 23-24, 1966 410 6449 4:40.4	14
<u>8319</u>	8234	Kurt Bendlin, GER 10.6 755 1450 184 47.9 Heidelberg 14.8 4631 May 13-14, 1967 410 7485 4:19.4	
<u>8417</u>	8309	Bill Toomey, USA 10.3 776 1438 193 47.1 Los Angeles 14.3 4649 Dec. 10-11, 1969 427 6574 4:39.4	14

Scoring Tables 1962/

Originally scored on 1971 revision (100ths) of 1962 tables

71/77	1985	Name	100m	LJ	SP	HJ	400m	110H	Discus	PV	Javelin	1500m	Place	Date	Note
8454e	8466	Nikolay Avilov, SOV	11.00	768	1436	212	48.45	14.31	4698	455	6166	4:22.82	Munich	Sept. 7-8, 1972	15
8524	8429	Bruce Jenner, USA	10.7	717	1525	201	48.7	14.6	5000	470	6552	4:16.6	Eugene	Aug. 9-10, 1975	15
8538	8456	Bruce Jenner, USA	10.7	719	1404	200	48.6	14.3	5168	460	6928	4:16.4	Eugene	June 25-26, 1976	15, 18
8444e	8454		10.93				48.72	14.57				4:16.60			
8618e	8634	Bruce Jenner, USA	10.94	722	1535	203	47.51	14.84	5004	480	6852	4:12.61	Montreal	July 29-30, 1976	16

with (8542w 8461w)
721w l j (8448we 8459w)

Scoring Tables 1962/

Originally scored on 1977 revision (100ths) of 1962 tables

71/77	1985	Name	100m	LJ	SP	HJ	400m	110H	Discus	PV	Javelin	1500m	Place	Date	Note
8622e	8648	Daley Thompson, GBR	10.50	795	1531	208	46.86	14.31	4434	490	6052	4:25.49	Gotzis	May 22-23, 1980	
8649e	8667	Guido Kratschmer, GER	10.58	780	1547	200	48.04	13.92	4552	460	6650	4:24.15	Bernhausen	June 13-14, 1980	
8704e	8730	Daley Thompson, GBR	10.50	795	1531	208	46.86	14.31	4434	490	6052	4:30.55	Gotzis	May 22-23, 1982	
8723e	8741	Jürgen Hingsen, GER	10.74	785	1600	215	47.65	14.64	4492	460	6310	4:15.13	Ulm	Aug. 14-15, 1982	

(Cont.)

Table A.4 (Continued)

Scoring Tables 1962/71/77	1985	Originally scored on 1977 revision (100ths) of 1962 tables										Note
8743e	8774	Daley Thompson, GBR				Athens				Sept. 7-8, 1982		
		10.51	780	1544	203	47.11	14.39	4548	500	6356	4:23.71	
8779e	8825	Jürgen Hingsen, GER				Bernhausen				June 4-5, 1983		
		10.92	774	1594	215	47.89	14.10	4680	470	6726	4:19.74	
8798e	8832	Jürgen Hingsen, GER				Mannheim				June 8-9, 1984		
		10.70	776	1642	207	48.05	14.07	4936	490	5986	4:19.75	
8798e	8847	Daley Thompson, GBR				Los Angeles				Aug. 8-9, 1984		17
		10.44	801	1572	203	46.97	14.33	4656	500	6524	4:35.00	

Note. All underlined marks were IAAF official world decathlon records.

1. The first modern decathlons (present order of events) were held on the same day. The winners of each are listed because there is no way to determine which contest was completed first and so it is impossible to know who was the first world-record holder. The cities (Goteborg, Sweden and Munster, Germany) are in the same time zone.

2. The mark by American Wienaul was recently uncovered. It was at the 1912 United States Olympic Trials, Midwest region. It exceeds the next two marks by Wieslander that, along with his first mark, have been always considered, until now, world bests.

3. Thorpe won by an overwhelming margin at the 1912 Stockholm Olympic Games. He was awarded the record, but in 1913 he was disqualified for playing professional baseball. The record then passed to Wieslander. Thorpe's record was posthumously reinstated in 1984. Had he not lost the record in 1913 the next 10 listed marks would be unnecessary. But because Thorpe's performance was removed from the record books, numerous other marks have been listed as world records before Yrjölä's 1926 score.

4. The performance by Wickholm was the first of several scores that did not break the world mark under the tables then in use but would have exceeded the world best under a later set of tables. Subsequently, many of these have been listed over the years as world records when newer tables came into force. This occurs in the case of Olsson, Strandberg, Osborn, Järvinen, and Sievert. Actually, using the 1912A tables, Wickholm finished third in the 1914 decathlon in Malmo.

5. The 1922 mark by Klumberg (later Klumberg-Kolmpore) was the first ratified world decathlon record by the IAAF.

6. Järvinen's 1928 performance in Amsterdam was the first of two Olympic performances that would have been world records and worth the gold medal under a later set of tables.

7. Several of Yrjölä's marks were misscored. They are correctly listed here.

8. Järvinen's 1932 Los Angeles score was actually the world record for 30 seconds. Jim Bausch crossed the 1500 finish line 30 seconds later to rebreak the record. It was the first time the world decathlon record was set only to be broken moments later. The same situation occurred to Bill Toomey (who lost to Russ Hodge 20 seconds later) in Los Angeles in 1966.

9. Sievert's 1932 mark in Hamburg was never submitted to the IAAF. Many books list it in the progression of world records incorrectly as 8467.620. It should be listed as 8460.620.

The question dealt with 1/2 cm in the high jump. The IAAF record committee president (Stankovits of Hungary) explained to the German federation that 1/2 cm were not allowed and the score did not better Bausch's mark. The Germans then did not submit the mark for record.

10. The 1930 mark of Yrjölä and first 1936 score for Morris were not submitted to the IAAF because the scores were surpassed soon after they were set.

11. Auto times recently were made available for Mathias's 1952 Olympic win in Helsinki. Thus, a second score under current tables using auto times is given. A second score is also listed for Jenner's 1976 Eugene meet. The hand times were official.

12. Mulkey's 1961 score was never submitted for record. In a number of races, pacers were used. Mulkey was the record chairman for his AAU district and did not submit his own score for ratification.

13. Yang became the first decathlete to have broken the world record after nine events in his 1963 record at the Mount Sac Relays. He also became the first over 9000 points on any table. His expertise with the new fiberglass pole resulted in a new set of tables the following year.

14. Toomey's win in Salina was not ratified. It was never clear why, but most accounts refer to lack of proper equipment in Salina. Thus Hodge's mark 3 weeks later, although four points less, became the official record.

15. The IAAF adjusted the tables (1971 revision) to account for 100th-of-a-second performances in the 100m and 110m hurdles. The 1972 score by Nikolay Avilov at the Munich Olympics was the first auto-scored world record. The rules did not require auto timing and the next two marks by Jenner were accomplished with hand timing.

16. The IAAF adjusted the 1962 tables yet again in 1977 to account for 100th-of-a-second timing in the 400m. This slightly altered many scores. For example, Jenner's original 8618 became 8617 and was carried as such until the tables were changed in 1985. After 1976, the decathlon world record had to be set with auto timing.

(Cont.)

Table A.4 (Continued)

17. The 1984 Olympic performance by Daley Thompson was originally 8797 (14.34 for 110mH), missing the world record by one point. The 1985 tables went into effect on April 1, 1985 and, although Thompson's Los Angeles performance was better than Hingsen's Mannheim score on the new tables, his score was not considered the world record. The IAAF stated that his score "cannot be made one (a record) by a change in the tables." Months later, the IAAF discovered an "error" in the reading of the hurdles photo. His adjusted time of 14.33 gave him one more point and 8798 on the old tables. The IAAF then reversed their position and recognized his 8847 as the new world record. Most other lists recognized his 8846 (then 8847) when it was set.

18. Many early marks were submitted without wind reading for the 100m, long jump, and 110mH. Jenner's 1976 Eugene score was achieved with a 721 wind-aided long jump. His second best jump, a non-wind-aided 719, would give scores of 8538 and 8456. Today a wind exceeding 4 mps negates a score for record purposes.

Table A.5   American Record Progression

The following lists include a progression of the American decathlon record. After Thorpe's disqualification there are several marks listed that are inferior, including the official world record by Osborn. Scores are listed if they surpassed an earlier mark on any table. IAAF records are underlined.

1912A	1912B	1934	50/52	62/71/77	1985	Name (affiliation) Meet, Site	Date
7414.555	6651.860	6095	5307	6051	5867	J. Austin Menaul (Univ. of Chicago) Central OT, Evanston	May 22-23, 1912
8412.955	7751.060	6971	6268	6756	6564	Jim Thorpe (Carlisle) OG, Stockholm	July 13-15, 1912
	6858.81	6324	5193	5742	5993	Alma Richards (Intermountain AA) AAU, San Francisco	Aug. 9-10, 1915

						Date
7022.9815	6185	5377	6140	5937	Brutus Hamilton (Univ. of Missouri) AAU/OT, Travers Island	July 9-10, 1920
7350.120	6583	5862	6426	6247	Harold Osborn (Illinois AC) AAU, Chicago	Sept. 3, 1923
7401.285	6581	5800	6424	6248	Harold Osborn (Illinois AC) OT, Southfield, NY	June 10-11, 1924
<u>7710.775</u>	6877	6163	6668	6476	Harold Osborn (Illinois AC) OG, Paris	July 11-12, 1924
7784.29	6864	6082	6666	6424	Fait Elkins (Nebraska) NYAC Games, Travers Island, NY	June 2-3, 1928
7784.680	6828	6054	6617	6416	J. Kenneth Doherty (Cadillac AC) AAU, Denver	July 5, 1929
7842.450	6873	6024	6529	6329	James Bausch (Kansas STC) Kansas Relays, Lawrence	Apr. 17-18, 1931
8164.655	7275	6525	6925	6750	Jess Mortensen (LAAC) Los Angeles	June 22-23, 1931
8164.225	7271	6573	6957	6761	Jess Mortensen (LAAC) AAU, Lincoln	July 3-4, 1931
<u>8462.235</u>	7396	6590	6896	6735	James Bausch (Kansas City AC) OG, Los Angeles	Aug. 5-6, 1932
7958.100	7157	6537	7002	6861	Robert Clark (San Francisco OC) AAU, Cincinnati	July 3-4, 1934
	7575	6869	7191	7109	Glenn Morris (Denver AC) Kansas Relays, Lawrence	Apr. 17-18, 1936
	7595	7072	7202	7054	Robert Clark (San Francisco OC) AAU-OT, Milwaukee	July 26-27, 1936
	7883	7275	7394	7213	Glenn Morris (Denver AC) AAU-OT, Milwaukee	July 26-27, 1936
	<u>7900</u>	7310	7421	7254	Glenn Morris (Denver AC) OG, Berlin	Aug. 7-8, 1936

(Cont.)

Table A.5 (Continued)

1912A	1912B	1934	50/52	62/71/77	1985	Name (affiliation) / Meet, Site	Date
8042			7444	7453	7287	Bob Mathias (unat, Tulare, Cal.) AAU, Tulare	June 29-30, 1950
			7829	7690	7543	Bob Mathias (Stanford) AAU-OT, Tulare	July 1-2, 1952
			7887	7731	7580 (7592e)	Bob Mathias (Stanford) OG, Helsinki	July 25-26, 1952
			7985	7758	7608	Rafer Johnson (UCLA) Invt., Kingsburg	June 10-11, 1955
			8302	7896	7789	Rafer Johnson (UCLA) vs SOV, Moscow	July 27-28, 1958
			8683	8063	7981	Rafer Johnson (Striders) AAU-OT, Eugene	July 8-9, 1960
			8709	8155	8049	Phil Mulkey (unat) SEAAAU, Memphis	June 16-17, 1961
				8234	8096	Bill Toomey (Striders) AAU, Salina	July 2-3, 1966
				8219	8082	Bill Toomey (Striders) (2) International, L.A.	July 23-24, 1966
				8230	8119	Russ Hodge (Striders) International, L.A.	July 23-24, 1966
				8277	8160	Bill Toomey (Striders) Special-UCLA, L.A.	Oct. 3-4, 1969
				8417	8309	Bill Toomey (Striders) Special-UCLA, L.A.	Dec. 10-11, 1969

8524	8429	Bruce Jenner (San Jose Stars) *vs* SOV/POL, Eugene	Aug. 9-10, 1975
8538	8456	Bruce Jenner (San Jose Stars)	June 24-25, 1976
8444e	8454	OT, Eugene (8542w, 8461w/8448ew, 8459w)	
8618e	8634	Bruce Jenner (San Jose Stars) OG, Montreal	July 29-30, 1976

Notes. All underlined marks were IAAF official world decathlon records. The four scores after Thorpe would have been unnecessary had he not been disqualified and lost his records in 1913. His mark was posthumously reinstated in 1984. Ironically, Osborn's Paris score was the official world record yet not the best American score because of the Thorpe ruling. Elkins score surpassed the listed American record, but his was a practice meet and he was the lone entrant, competing against a specialist in each event. The score was never submitted for record purposes. It is included here for historical accuracy. Several marks would have been American records had a later table been in use (Mortensen and Clark). In two cases American records were set (Clark and Toomey) only to be erased moments later by a better score when opponents (Morris and Hodge) crossed the 1500m finish line. Clark's AR lasted two tenths of a second. Osborn's first mark and that of Doherty were made in one day! See world-record progression notes for many explanations.

With only 5 days' rest between meets, Mount Saint Mary's Trond Skramstad became the only decathlete to win the NCAA I and NCAA II titles in the same year (1982).

Table A.6   All-time World List

The following list includes all performances over 8550 points and all performers over 8220 points world wide as of January 1, 1989. All marks are scored on the current (1985) tables.

8847	Daley Thompson (GBR), 1984	8417	Sergi Zhelanov (SOV), 1984
8832	Jürgen Hingsen (GER), 1984	8415	Dave Steen (CAN), 1988
8825	Hingsen, 1983	8400	Alexandr Grebenyuk (SOV), 1977
8811	Thompson, 1986	8397	Fred Dixon (USA), 1977
8792	Uwe Freimuth (GDR), 1984	8387	Alain Blondel (FRA), 1988
8774	Thompson, 1982	8381w	John Sayre (USA), 1985
8762	Siegfried Wentz (GER), 1983	8375	Pavel Tarnavetskiy (SOV), 1987
8741	Hingsen, 1982	8366	Vadim Podmaryov (SOV), 1985
8730	Thompson, 1982	8362	Thomas Fahner (GDR), 1988
8730	Hingsen, 1986	8359	Simon Poelman (NZE), 1987
8714	Thompson, 1983	8356	Victor Gruzyenkin (SOV), 1984
8709	Alexandr Apaychev (SOV), 1984	8340	Tim Bright (USA), 1987
8698	Grigoriy Degtyarov (SOV), 1984	8334	Rainer Pottel (GDR), 1981
8695	Hingsen, 1984	8334	Stefan Niklaus (SWI), 1983
8680	Torsten Voss (GDR), 1987	8327w	William Motti (FRA), 1987
8676	Wentz, 1986	8326	Andreas Rizzi (GER), 1983
8667	Guido Kratschmer (GER), 1980	8322	Mike Ramos (USA), 1986
8667	Thompson, 1986	8322	Andrey Nazarov (SOV), 1987
8663w	Thompson, 1986	8315	Mikhail Medved (SOV), 1986
8648	Thompson, 1980	8309	Bill Toomey (USA), 1969
8645	Wentz, 1987	8304w	Tito Steiner (ARG), 1981
8634	Bruce Jenner (USA), 1976	8293	Gary Kinder (USA), 1988
8617	Degtyarov, 1984	8289	Veroslav Valenta (TCH), 1988
8616	Freimuth, 1984	8288	Valeriy Kachanov (SOV), 1980
8599	Hingsen, 1983	8282	Alexsandr Shablyenko (SOV), 1980
8597	Freimuth, 1984	8267	Mark Anderson (USA), 1983
8592	Apaychev, 1984	8266	Pedro da Silva (BRA), 1987
8590	Wentz, 1986	8261	Steffen Grummt (GDR), 1982
8580	Degtyarov, 1983	8255	Jens Schulze (GER), 1984
8572	Degtyarov, 1984	8250	Karl-Heinz Fichtner (GER), 1988
8559	Voss, 1985	8248	Bob Coffman (USA), 1979
8551	Freimuth, 1983	8245	Dave Johnson (USA), 1988
(9 performers, 32 performances)		8244	Beat Gahwiler (SWI), 1988
8547	Igor Sobolyevskiy (SOV), 1984	8235	Jorg-Peter Schaperkotter (GDR), 1983
8534	Siegfried Stark (GDR), 1980	8234	Kurt Bendlin (GER), 1967
8519	Yuriy Kutsenko (SOV), 1984	8232	Sven Reintak (SOV), 1986
8512	Christian Plaziat (FRA), 1988	8230	Ryszard Skowronek (POL), 1974
8506	Walter Kulvet (SOV), 1988	8227	Andrei Fomochkin (SOV), 1986
8491	Alexandr Nyevskiy (SOV), 1984	8224	Georg Werthner (AUT), 1982
8488	Christian Schenk (GDR), 1988	8224	Igor Kolovanov (SOV), 1983
8485	Konstantin Akhapkin (SOV), 1982		(60 performers)
8466	Nikolay Avilov (SOV), 1972		
8447	Robert de Wit (HOL), 1988		
8437	Richardas Malakhovskis (SOV), 1988		(Cont.)

Table A.6 (Continued)
All-time United States List

The following list includes all American performances over 8000 points and all performers over 7800 points as of January 1, 1988. All marks are scored on the current (1985) tables.

8634	Bruce Jenner (San Jose Stars), 1976		8119	Russ Hodge (Foothill), 1966
8459	Jenner, 1976		8119	Lee Palles (Athletic Attic), 1980
8429	Jenner, 1976		8115	Crist, 1984
8397	Fred Dixon (Striders), 1977		8113	Dixon, 1980
8381w	John Sayre (UCTC), 1985		8109	Bart Goodell (unat), 1988
8340	Tim Bright (A-W), 1987		8109	Coffman, 1980
8322	Mike Ramos (Washington), 1986		8106	Bright, 1984
8309	Bill Toomey (Striders), 1969		8098	Crist, 1979
8302	Bright, 1986		8096	Toomey, 1966
8294	Ramos, 1985		8086	Crist, 1984
8293	Gary Kinder (unat), 1988		8082	Toomey, 1966
8287	Bright, 1988		8082	Coffman, 1979
8267	Mark Anderson (Wilt's AC), 1983		8076	Shannon Sullivan (USAF), 1988
8261	Ramos, 1986		8076	Sayre, 1986
8248	Bob Coffman (Hurr TC), 1979		8075	Derek Huff (Arizona), 1988
8245	Dave Johnson (NYAC), 1988		8071	Ramos, 1985
8227	Kinder,1987		8068w	Bright, 1985
8225	Ramos, 1988		8063	Steve Erickson (CNW), 1988
8221	Bright, 1985		8063	Erickson, 1985
8211	Jenner, 1974		8061	Muzzio, 1987
8205	Rob Muzzio (GMU), 1984		8054	Jim Wooding (Shore AC), 1984
8203	Gary Armstrong (unat), 1986		8053	Kinder, 1987
8203	Mike Gonzales (S&STC), 1988		8049	Phil Mulkey (unat), 1961
8203w	Johnson, 1986		8045	Johnson, 1987
8202	Jenner, 1974		8045	Gonzales, 1988
	(13 performers, 25 performances)		8041	Goodell, 1986
8184	Dixon, 1976		8039	Kinder, 1987
8166	Coffman, 1980		8038	Wooding, 1984
8163	Jenner, 1975		8037	Toomey, 1969
8163	Ramos, 1985		8035	Toomey, 1969
8160	Toomey, 1969		8031	Orville Peterson (Campbell TC), 1985
8159	Chris Branham (LATC), 1986		8030	Erickson, 1986
8156w	Ramos. 1985		8030	Kinder, 1987
8145	Branham, 1986		8026	Connolly, 1987
8144	Toomey, 1968		8024	Jenner, 1975
8142	Anderson, 1983		8023	Goodell, 1986
8141	Anderson, 1981		8023	Connolly, 1987
8134	Muzzio, 1987		8022	Coffman, 1980
8132	Dixon, 1975		8021	Jenner, 1975
8128	Toomey, 1969		8017	Muzzio, 1987
8127	Jenner, 1974		8015	Coffman, 1979
8125	Toomey, 1968		8013	Branham, 1988
8123	Johnson, 1986		8009	Dixon, 1978
8121	John Crist (A-W), 1982		8007	Dixon, 1977
8121	Jim Connolly (UCLA), 1987		8006	Jeff Bennett (US Army), 1973

8004	Coffman, 1979	7900w	Bruce Reid (LSU), 1988
8004	Dixon, 1984	7899	Jim Howell (Philadelphia PC), 1982
8003	John Warkentin (unat), 1977	7899	Heinz Hinrichs (Track West), 1988
	(27 performers, 92 performances)	7891w	Dan O'Brien (MoscowUSA), 1988
7991	Steve Odgers (Adidas), 1987	7884	Lane Maestretti (Outreach), 1984
7981	Jeff Bannister (Dec/Am), 1972	7881	John Schwepker (SE Missouri St), 1988
7981	Rafer Johnson (Striders), 1960	7880	Rick Wanamaker (unat), 1971
7971	Mike Hill (Colorado TC), 1978	7869	Wes Herbst (Houston), 1979
7969	Mauricio Bardales (UC-Irvine), 1978	7868	Bill Hancock (Southern Illinois), 1975
7967	Keith Robinson (BYU), 1987	7862	Grant Neiderhaus (Puma TC), 1984
7964	Tony Allen-Cooksey (A-W), 1981	7859	Tim Taft (AMCT), 1984
7964	Sheldon Blockberger (LSU), 1987	7847	Gary Bastien (unat), 1983
7959	Fred Samara (NYAC), 1975	7845w	Rusty Hunter (Texas), 1988
7951	Rick Sloan (Striders), 1969	7833	Kevin McGorty (North Carolina), 1988
7948	Steve Gough (CNW), 1975	7830	Steve Jacobs (unat), 1979
7946	Jay Thorson (unat), 1988	7829	Mike Brown (Outreach), 1982
7934	Craig Brigham (Oregon), 1975	7825	Dannie Jackson (Arizona State), 1981
7931	Roger George (A-W), 1978	7821w	Ed Brown (Outreach), 1988
7925	Steve Alexander (Hurricane TC), 1977	7818	John Whitson (Sun TC), 1979
7925	Kris Szabadhegy (US Army), 1988	7812	Greg Culp (ACU), 1984
7911	Al Hamlin (DRAC), 1979		(64 performers)

All-time United States Collegiate List

The following list includes all performances over 8000 points and all performers over 7700 points for United States collegians as of January 1, 1988. All marks are scored on the current (1985) tables.

8322	Mike Ramos (Washington), 1986	8071	Raimo Pihl (BYU), 1975
8306	William Motti (Mt St Mary's), 1985	8063w	Steve Erickson (Washington), 1985
8304w	Tito Steiner (BYU), 1981	8061	Muzzio, 1987
8278	Motti, 1984	8040	Olander, 1988
8261	Ramos, 1986	8036	Simon Shirley (Wash St), 1988
8205	Rob Muzzio (GMU), 1984	8026	Connolly, 1987
8141	Mark Anderson (UCLA), 1981	8023	Motti, 1984
8134	Muzzio, 1987	8023	Connolly, 1987
8126	Mikael Olander (LSU), 1988	8008	C.K. Yang (UCLA), 1963
8121	Jim Connolly (UCLA), 1987		(14 performers, 24 performances)
8119	Russ Hodge (Foothill JC), 1966	7990	Sten Ekberg (SMU), 1986
8105	Steiner, 1979	7969	Mauricio Bardales (UC-Irvine), 1978
8097	Trond Skramstad (Mt St Mary's), 1984	7967	Keith Robinson (BYU), 1987
8090	Motti, 1985	7965w	Gary Kinder (New Mexico), 1985
8075	Derek Huff (Arizona), 1988		(Cont.)

Table A.6 (Continued)

7964	Sheldon Blockberger (LSU), 1987	7812	Greg Culp (ACU), 1984
7956	Mike Gonzales (USC), 1987	7795	Kerry Zimmerman (Indiana), 1983
7952	Jeff Bennett (Okla. Christian), 1970	7788	Rafer Johnson (UCLA), 1958
7948	Dave Johnson (Azusa Pacific), 1985	7778	Roger George (Fresno State), 1974
7942	Patrick Gellens (Concordia, Nb),1985	7746	Dave Edstrom (Oregon), 1960
7934	Craig Brigham (Oregon), 1975	7739w	Mike Ledsome (ACU), 1987
7900w	Bruce Reid (LSU), 1988	7738	Jay Novacek (Wyoming), 1984
7891	John Sayre (Southern Illinois), 1984	7737	Rick Sloan (UCLA), 1967
7881	John Schwepker (SE Missouri St), 1988	7737	Tim Bright (ACU), 1983
7869	Wes Herbst (Houston), 1979	7737	Steffan Bloomstrand (UTEP), 1986
7868	Bill Hancock (Southern Illinois),	7732	Gudmund Olsen (Mt St Mary's), 1982
7845w	Rusty Hunter (Texas), 1988	7731	Ernie White (Campbell), 1985
7842	Lee Palles (Mississippi State), 1978	7709	Robert Ekpete (Mt. St. Mary's), 1985
7842	Conny Silfver (Angelo State), 1984	7708	Fedelis Obikwu (N Carolina St.), 1984
7833	Kevin McGorty (North Carolina), 1988	7708	Chris Branham (Pt Loma), 1985
7830	Steve Jacobs (Arizona), 1979	7703	Knut Gundersen (Mr St Mary's), 1988
7825	Dannie Jackson (Arizona State), 1981		(52 performers)
7816	Runald Backmun (BYU), 1976		

Rex Havery of Des Moines, Iowa, is the only decathlete to complete more than 100 decathlons and is the all-time career point scoring leader. (Don Chadez/From the Zarnowski collection)

Table A.7   Records by Event

Official (IAAF) records are kept only for the total decathlon score. Unofficial marks are kept for the 10 individual events and the first- and second-day scores. The following lists include marks referred to as world records, American records, United States collegiate records, junior college records and high school records. The total score for the first two categories are included, original score in ( ), with 7000 points being a cutoff. Notable marks in decathlon competition but with a total score lower than 7000 are listed in the footnotes. No such delineation was made for the last three categories because these athletes are still developing and may be relatively good decathletes although they have not scored 7000 points.

One stipulation is necessary to set a "record": The athlete must complete the entire decathlon. The primary idea in decathlon competition is to have each (record-setting) performance enhance the final score. The record performances below imply performances in nine other events as well. Wind-aided marks are included. As the new IAAF javelin went into use in 1986, both old and new javelin records are included.

World Records (7000-point minimum)

Event	Mark	Athlete	Location (Score)	Date
100m	10.26	Daley Thompson, GBR	Stuttgart (8811)	Aug. 27, 1986
lj	8.11w (26-7 1/4)	Daley Thompson, GBR	Edmonton (8467w)	Aug. 7, 1978
sp	19.17 (62-10)	Edy Hubacher, SWI	Berne (7405h)	Oct. 4, 1969
hj	2.27 (7-7 1/2)	Rolf Beilschmidt, GDR	Jena (7245h)	Sept. 30, 1977
	2.27 (7-5 1/2)	Christian Schenk, GDR	Seoul (8488)	Sept. 28, 1988
400m	45.68	Bill Toomey, USA	Mexico City (8193)	Oct. 18, 1968
110mH	13.84	Ivan Babij, USAR	Sochi (8209)	May 17, 1987
dis	55.00 (180-5)	Razvigor Jankov, BUL	Sofia (7773)	July 5, 1980
pv	5.70 (18-8 1/4)	Tim Bright, USA	Seoul (8216)	Sept. 29, 1988
jav (old)	81.76 (268-3)	Lennart Hedmark, SWE	Spala (7522)	June 25, 1978
(new)	75.50 (247-8)	Mikail Olander, SWE	Baton Rouge (7940)	June 4, 1987
1500m	3:58.7	Robert Baker, USA	Austin (7583)	Apr. 3, 1980

(Cont.)

Table A.7 (Continued)

World Records (7000-point minimum)

1st day	4677 pts	Daley Thompson, GBR	Los Angeles (8847)	Aug. 9, 1984
2nd day	4324 pts	Alexandr Apaichev, SOV	Neubrandenburg (8709)	June 2, 1984
Total	8847 pts	Daley Thompson, GBR	Los Angeles	Aug. 8-9, 1984

Note. Martin Lauer/GER (1959); Russ Hodge/USA (1970); Bob Coffman/USA (1978); and Eugene Gilkes/GBR (1984) have all run 10.2w 100m. The total score is unknown for Sandor Boros/HUN, whose 83.98 (275-6) is jav best. In 1500m, Paul Cummings/USA ran 3:48.2 (1976).

American Records (7000-point minimum)

100m	10.38	Bob Coffman, Hurricane TC	Walnut (8154)	1979
lj	8.00 (26-3)	Mike Herman, NY Pioneer Club	Eugene (7092)	1960
sp	17.76 (58-3 1/4)	Russ Hodge, Foothill JC	Hamburg (7124)	1966
hj	2.19 (7-2 1/4)	Chris Branham, Pt Loma	Fresno (7708)	1985
400m	45.68	Bill Toomey, Striders	Mexico City (8193)	1968
110mH	13.91	Bob Coffman, Hurricane TC	Quebec City (8274)	1979
	13.6w	Bob Coffman, Hurricane TC	Colorado Sp (8137h)	1978
dis	52.90 (173-7)	Bart Goodell, Adidas	Los Gatos (8041)	1986
pv	5:70 (18-8 1/4)	Tim Bright, Athletics West	Seoul (8216)	1988
jav (new)	74.36 (244-0)	Jim Connolly, UCLA	San Jose (8023)	1987
(old)	78.18 (256-6)	Jim Connolly, UCLA	Pullman (7756)	1984
1500m	3:58.7	Robert Baker, Hi Plains TC	Austin (7583)	1980

1st day	4526	Bill Toomey, Striders	Mexico City (8193)	1968
2nd day	4319	Bruce Jenner, San Jose Stars	Montreal (8618)	1976
Total	8634	Bruce Jenner, San Jose Stars	Montreal (8618)	1976

Note. See above notes for Coffman, Hodge, and Cummings.

United States Collegiate Records

100m	10.3	Bill Foucher, Princeton	Trenton, NJ	1970
	10.3w	Barry Stebbins, Mt. St. Mary's	Emmitsburg, MD	1974
lj	7.99 (26-2 1/2)	Dannie Jackson, Arizona State	Tempe, AZ	1979
sp	17.76 (58-3 1/4)	Russ Hodge, Foothill JC	Hamburg, FRG	1966
hj	2.21 (7-3)	Thomas Eriksson, Lamar	Austin, TX	1985
400m	47.2	Jeff Bennett, Oklahoma Christian	S Lake Tahoe, CA	1970
110mH	13.92	Bob Coffman, USC	Austin, TX	1974
dis	52.68 (172-10)	Thrain Hafsteinsson, Alabama	Lexington, KY	1983
pv	5.40 (17-8 1/2)	Dale Jenkins, ACU	Levelland, TX	1981
jav (new)	75.50 (247-8)	Mikail Olander, LSU	Baton Rouge, LA	1987
(old)	78.18 (256-6)	Jim Connolly, UCLA	Pullman, WA	1984
1500m	4:06.3	Robert Baker, Principia	Austin, TX	1978

(Cont.)

Table A.7 (Continued)

United States Collegiate Records

1st day	4458 pts	William Motti, Mt. St. Mary's	Athis-Mons, FRA	1985
2nd day	4117 pts	Mauricio Bardales, UC-Irvine	Eugene, OR	1978
Total	8322 pts	Mike Ramos, Washington	Los Angeles, CA	1986

Junior College Records

100m	10.3	Russ Hodge, Foothill JC	Salina, KS	1966
lj	7.69 (25-2 3/4)	Russ Hodge, Foothill JC	Salina, KS	1966
sp	17.76 (58-3 1/4)	Russ Hodge, Foothill JC	Hamburg, FRG	1966
hj	2.15 (7-3/4)	Jim Sokolowski, DuPage	Eugene, OR	1979
400m	47.81	Ron McPhee, Blinn	Odessa, TX	1986
110mH	13.9	Don Shy, Mt. Sac JC	Bakersfield, CA	1965
dis	50.44 (165-5)	Russ Hodge, Foothill JC	Los Angeles, CA	1966
pv	4.89 (16-3/4)	Sam Caruthers, San Jose CC	Santa Barbara, CA	1968
jav (old)	78.86 (258-9)	Doug Fernandez, Long Beach CC	Caracas, VEN	1983
1500m	3:59.8	Gary McManus, Diablo Valley	Pleasant Hill, CA	1975
1st day	4341 pts	Russ Hodge, Foothill JC	Salina, KS	1966
2nd day	3823 pts	Doug Fernandez, Long Beach CC	Los Angeles, CA	1984
Total	8119 pts	Russ Hodge, Foothill JC	Los Angeles, CA	1966

High School Records

Event	Mark	Athlete, School	Location	Year
100m	10.5	Milt Campbell, Plainfield HS	Plainfield, NJ	1953
	10.5	Fred Samara, Ft. Hamilton HS	New Brunswick, NJ	1969
lj	7.29 (23-11 1/4)	Leroy Spicer, Albuquerque HS	Albuquerque, NM	1971
sp	15.41 (50-6)	Lance Neubauer, Sehome, Bell	Lacey, WA	1976
hj	2.11 (6-11)	Steve Henson, McPherson, KS	Towson, MD	1986
400m	49.1	Aubrey Lewis, Montclair, NJ	Atlantic City, NJ	1954
110mH	14.3	Milt Campbell, Plainfield HS	Plainfield, NJ	1953
dis	46.10 (151-3)	Craig Brigham, South Eugene HS	Eugene, OR	1972
pv	4.75 (15-7)	Tom Richards, Santa Barbara HS, CA	Los Angeles, CA	1988
jav	68.26 (223-11)	Mark Gubrud, Mt. Vernon, WA	Lacey, WA	1976
1500m	3:58.8	Paul Cummings, Righetti HS	Los Angeles, CA	1971
1st day	3937 pts	Milt Campbell, Plainfield HS	Plainfield, NJ	1953
2nd day	3594 pts	Craig Brigham, South Eugene HS	Eugene, OR	1972
Total	7359 pts	Craig Brigham, South Eugene HS	Eugene, OR	1972

Table A.8   Progression and Places

Reaching the 100-Point Levels

First in the world to reach 100-point levels from 7000 to 8800 points as scored on the 1985 tables.

Over					
7000	Hans-Heinrich Sievert, GER	7147	Club Meet, Hamburg	8790h	1934
7100	Hans-Heinrich Sievert, GER				
7200	Glenn Morris, USA	7254	Olympic Trials, Milwaukee	7880h	1936
7300	Bob Mathias, USA	7543	Olympic Trials, Tulare	7825h	1952
7400	Bob Mathias, USA				
7500	Bob Mathias, USA				
7600	Rafer Johnson, USA	7608	Cent Cal AAU, Kingsburg	7985h	1955
7700	Rafer Johnson, USA	7789	vs USSR, Moscow	8302h	1958
7800	Vasiliy Kuznyetsov, SOV	7839	Club Meet, Moscow	8367h	1959
7900	Rafer Johnson, USA	7981	Olympic Trials, Eugene	8683h	1960
8000	Phil Mulkey, USA	8049	SEAAAU, Memphis	8709h	1961
8100	Russ Hodge, USA	8119	International, LA.	8234h	1966
8200	Kurt Bendlin, GER	8234	Heidelberg	8319h	1967
8300	Bill Toomey, USA	8309	Special, UCLA, Los Angeles	8417h	1969
8400	Nikolay Avilov, SOV	8466	Olympic Games, Munich	8454e	1972
8500	Bruce Jenner, USA	8634	Olympic Games, Montreal	8618e	1976
8600	Bruce Jenner, USA				
8700	Jürgen Hingsen, GER	8723	National champs, Ulm	8741e	1982
8800	Jürgen Hingsen, GER	8825	World champs qual, Bernhausen	8779e	1983
8900	?	?	?		19??

Note. First score listed is score on 1985 tables. Second score is original score. h = hand timing; e = automatic timing

Progression on Any Table

6903.920	(1912A table)	Hugo Wieslander, SWE	Goteberg	1911
7414.555		J. Austin Menaul, USA	Evanston	1912
8412.955		Jim Thorpe, USA	Stockholm	1912
8462.235	(1912B table)	Jim Bausch, USA	Los Angeles	1932
8790.46		Hans-Heinrich Sievert, GER	Hamburg	1934
9121	(1950/52 table)	C.K. Yang, FOR	Walnut	1963

Best Score For Place

2nd	8762	Siegfried Wentz, GER	National champs	Bernhausen	1983
3rd	8676	Siegfried Wentz, GER	European champs	Stuttgart	1986
4th	8469	Uwe Freimuth, GDR	World champs	Helsinki	1983
5th	8356	Viktor Gruzenkin, SOV	National champs	Kiev	1984
6th	8296	Simon Poelman, NZE	World champs	Rome	1987

			Best Score For Place		
7th	8216	Tim Bright, USA	Olympic Games	Seoul	1988
8th	8189	Robert de Wit, HOL	Olympic Games	Seoul	1988
9th	8180	Dave Johnson, USA	Olympic Games	Seoul	1988
10th	8167	Pavel Tarnovetskiy, SOV	Olympic Games	Seoul	1988
11th	8143	Petri Keskitalo, FIN	Olympic Games	Seoul	1988
12th	8114	Beat Gaehwiler, SWI	Olympic Games	Seoul	1988
13th	8093	Dezso Szabo, HUN	Olympic Games	Seoul	1988
14th	8083	Mike Smith, CAN	Olympic Games	Seoul	1988
15th	8036	Simon Shirley, AUS	Olympic Games	Seoul	1988
16th	8021	Simon Poelman, NZL	Olympic Games	Seoul	1988

West German Siegfried Wentz has a P.R. of 8762 points, the fourth-highest score ever. (Horstmuller/Courtesy of *Track and Field News*)

Table A.9   Miscellaneous Records

The following records fall under no other listing.

Junior Records

To establish a Junior record the athlete must remain a teenager throughout the entire year of competition.

WR	8387 pts	Torsten Voss, GDR (b. March 24, 1963)	Erfurt, E.G.	July 6-7, 1982
AR	7638 pts	Keith Robinson, USA-BYU (b. April 29, 1964)	Houston	May 30-31, 1983

Brother Combination   Using Original Score of Best Career Mark.

WR	16,425	Rizzi, GER	Andreas, 8369, 1983	&	Thomas, 8056, 1983
AR	15,321	Dixon, USA	Fred, 8392, 1977	&	Dave, 6929, 1976

Others-Foreign

16,071	Motti, FRA	William, 8327, 1987	&	Eric, 7744, 1979
15,808	Kratschmer, GER	Guido, 8649, 1980	&	Hubert, 7159, 1978
15,594	Kyosola, FIN	Heikki, 7831, 1973	&	Hannu, 7763, 1971
15,491	Anders, SWI	Philip, 7934, 1974	&	Matthias, 7557, 1976
15,344	Werthner, AUT	Georg, 8229, 1982	&	Roland, 7115, 1981
15,277	Kozakiewicz, POL	Wladyslaw, 7683, 1977	&	Eduard, 7594, 1975

Others-USA

15,133	Sayre	John, 8381w, 1985	&	Tom, 6752, 1978
15,043	Stebbins	Bob, 7736, 1984	&	Barry, 7307, 1977
14,871	McGorty	Kevin, 7560, 1986	&	Chris, 7311, 1980
14,775	Novacek	Jay, 7762, 1984	&	Jason, 7013, 1985
14,735	Mondschein	Brian, 7810, 1980	&	Mark, 6925, 1976

Brother-Brother-Brother Combination

WR	21,107	Werthner, AUT	Georg, 8229, 1982	&	Roland, 7115, 1981	&	Ulrich, 5763, 1988
WR	20,688	Kahma, FIN	Markus, 7381, 1961	&	Jorma, 6964, 1963	&	Pentti, 6551, 1965
AR	19,453	Kring, USA	Kenny, 7243, 1971	&	Buddy, 6127, 1977	&	Timmy, 6083, 1978

Brother-Brother-Brother-Brother

| WR | 27,151 | Bredholt, NOR | Arild, 7226, 1978 | & | Ivar, 6825, 1978 | & | Knut, 6637, 1974 | & | John, 6463, 1962 |

Twins Record

| WR | 16,425 | Rizzi, GER | Andreas, 8369, 1983 | & | Thomas, 8056, 1983 |
| AR | 11,841 | Goetz | Dave, 5966, 1982 | & | Dan, 5875, 1988 |

(Cont.)

Table A.9 (Continued)

Father-Son Combination

WR	15,275	Steen, CAN	Don, 6860, 1958	&	Dave, 8415, 1988
AR	14,704	Mondschein, USA	Irv, 6894, 1949	&	Brian, 7810, 1980

Others

ER	15,260	Mandl, AUS	Horst, 7760, 1969	&	Horst Jr., 7500, 1985
	14,883	Skramstad, NOR	Knut-Henrik, 6746, 1963	&	Trond, 8137, 1984
	14,553	Richards, USA	Bob, 7381, 1954	&	Tom, 7172, 1988
	14,548	Mulkey, USA	Phil, 8155, 1961	&	Phil Jr., 6393, 1977
	14,451	Jewlew, SOV	Wiktor, 6772, 1949	&	Wiktor Jr., 7679, 1972
	13,622	Farmer, USA	Dixon, 6607, 1958	&	Matt, 7015, 1988

Father-Son-Son Combination

WR, AR	21,629	Mondschein, USA	Irv, 6894, 1949	&	Brian, 7810, 1980	&	Mark, 6925, 1974
ER	20,756	Werthner, AUT	Helmut, 5412, 1953	&	Georg, 8229, 1982	&	Roland, 7115, 1981
other	20,647	Mulkey, USA	Phil, 8155, 1961	&	Phil Jr., 6393, 1977	&	Tim, 6099, 1974
other	19,650	Hytten, NOR	Svein, 6207, 1967	&	Even, 7110, 1988	&	Iver, 6333, 1987

Women's Record

WR, AR 6192 Harrington, Mary, Fort Collins TC   Fort Collins, CO, Sept. 22-23, 1979
(12.4   547   1054   165   61.3   14.9   2305   199   2485   6:15.8) women's implements & hurdles

30-Minute Decathlon

The 30-minute decathlon was invented by Dave Thoreson, Santa Barbara. All 10 events must be contested in order with the 1500m starting within 30 minutes of the start of the 100m. Scores on 1985 tables.

WR	7029	Jens Schulze, GER				Arnsburg			(7243 = 62)			July 7, 1981			
		(10.4	654	1322	189	52.3	14.9	4026	408	5032	5:01.3)				
AR	6526	John Warkentin, unat				Santa Barbara			(6747 = 62)			Aug. ?,1977			
		(11.2	630	1407	192	58.2	15.3	4604	396	5958	6:00.3)				

One-Hour Decathlon

Similar to above, usually run with two competitors side by side.

WR	7647	Simon Poelman, NZE			Auckland							Feb. 24, 1988	
		(11.71	710	1556	203	51.77	15.40	4294	450	5734	5:09.14)		
ER	6955	Georg Werthner, AUT			Salzburg							Oct. 22, 1988	
		(11.58	680	1360	193	53.97	15.92	3616	445	6002	5:01.03)		
AR	6241	Tim Bright, USA			Auckland							Feb. 24, 1988	
		(11.02	698	1421	209	51.87	15.97	3612	nh	5184	5:36.44)		

(Cont.)

Table A.9 (Continued)

Back-To-Back Decathlons

Two decathlons completed on 4 consecutive days.

WR 14,453 Georg Werthner, AUT   (average = 7226.5) 1975
7131e in Rome Sept. 18-19, 1975 & 7322e in Vienna Sept. 20-21, 1975 (1962 tables)

AR 14,261 Dave Thoreson, USA   (average = 7130.5) 1972
6931 in Santa Barbara May 6-7, 1972 & 7330 in Westwood May 8-9, 1972 (1962 tables)

Career Meets

WR 119 started,   Rex Harvey, USA (Iowa State, USAF, Drake TC, unat)
116 completed   from 1965 to 1988 (b. July 4, 1946)

Career Points

WR 782,141   Rex Harvey, USA (average = 6771)
(for 116 completed meets, 102 on 1962 tables
and 14 on 1985 tables). No one else is close!

Table A.10   Relative Decathlon Scores

		Date	Original score	85 Tables	WR-85 Tables	Relative score
1. Jim Thorpe	USA	7/12	8412.955	6564	8421	.7794
2. Hans-Heinrich Sievert	GER	7/34	8790.460	7147	9380	.7619
3. Bob Mathias	USA	7/52	7887	7580	9965	.7607
4. Rafer Johnson	USA	7/60	8683	7981	10494	.7605
5. Glenn Morris	USA	6/36	7883	7213	9507	.7587
6. Phil Mulkey	USA	6/61	8709	8049	10629	.7573
7. Mathias	USA	7/52	7829	7543	9965	.7569
8. Morris	USA	8/36	7900	7254	9587	.7566
9. Akilles Järvinen	FIN	7/30	8255.475	6865	9082	.7559
10. Vasiliy Kuznyetsov	SOV	5/59	8357	7839	10379	.7553
11. Johnson	USA	7/58	8302	7789	10337	.7535
12. Johnson	USA	6/55	7985	7608	10138	.7504
13. Bruce Jenner	USA	7/76	8618	8634	11614	.7434
14. C.K. Yang	FOR	4/63	9121	8009	10784	.7427
15. Järvinen	FIN	8/32	8292.480	6879	9272	.7419
16. Paavo Yrjölä	FIN	7/27	8018.990	6586	8882	.7415
17. Kuznyetsov	SOV	5/58	8014	7653	10337	.7404
18. Järvinen	FIN	8/28	7931.500	6645	8996	.7387
19. Nikolay Avilov	SOV	9/72	8454	8466	11466	.7384
20. Paavo Yrjölä	FIN	7/30	8117.300	6700	9082	.7377
21. Kurt Bendlin	FRG	5/67	8319	8234	11170	.7372
22. Daley Thompson	GBR	9/82	8743	8774	11922	.7360
23. Harold Osborn	USA	7/24	7710.775	6476	8804	.7355
24. Jürgen Hingsen	FRG	6/83	8779	8825	12014	.7346
25. Thompson	GBR	5/82	8704	8730	11885	.7345
26. Mathias	USA	6/50	8042	7287	9926	.73413
27. Thompson	GBR	5/80	8622	8648	11780	.73412
28. Milt Campbell	USA	11/56	7937	7565	10305	.73410
29. Guido Kratschmer	FRG	6/80	8649	8667	11813	.7337
30. Sievert	GER	7/33	8467.200	6833	9316	.7335
31. Yrjölä	FIN	8/28	8053.29	6517	8996	.7333
32. Hingsen	FRG	8/82	8723	8741	11922	.7332
33. Bill Toomey	USA	12/69	8417	8309	11336	.7330
34. Sievert	GER	8/33	8435.360	6828	9316	.7329
35. Hingsen	FRG	6/84	8798	8832	12065	.7320
36. Jenner	USA	8/75	8524	8429	11539	.7305
37. Russ Hodge	USA	7/66	8230	8119	11133	.7293
38. Jenner	USA	6/76	8542w	8456	11596	.7292
39. Thompson	GBR	8/84	8798	8847	12135	.7290
40. Yrjölä	FIN	7/26	7832.030	6460	8863	.7289
41. Toomey	USA	7/66	8234	8096	11133	.7272
42. Jim Bausch	USA	8/32	8462.235	6735	9272	.7264
43. Toomey	USA	7/66	8219	8082	11133	.7259
44. William Watson	USA	6/40	7523	6904	9684	.7129
45. Osborn	USA	9/23	7350.120	6248	8765	.7128
46. Hugo Wieslander	SWE	7/12	7724.495	5965	8421	.7083
47. Helge Lövland	NOR	7/19	7786.920	6033	8527	.7075
48. Waldemar Wickholm	FIN	7/14	7462.790	5969	8451	.7063
49. Bertil Olsson	SWE	7/20	7853.650	6073	8609	.7054

		Date	Original score	85 Tables	WR-85 Tables	Relative score
50. Gustaf Strandberg	FIN	7/23	7226.905	6147	8718	.7051
51. J. Austin Menaul	USA	5/12	7414.555	5867	8325	.7047
52. Alexandr Klumberg	EST	7/20	8025.520	6025	8609	.6998
53. Willi Holdorf	GER	10/64	7887	7726	11046	.6984
54. Klumberg	EST	9/22	7485.610	6087	8718	.6982
55. Christian Schenk	GDR	9/88	8488	8488	12165	.6977
56. Evert Nilsson	SWE	7/20	7880.820	5987	8609	.6954
57. Wieslander	SWE	6/12	7244.100	5583	8380	.6662
58. Wieslander	SWE	6/12	7099.845	5493	8380	.6555
59. Wieslander	SWE	10/11	6903.920	5386	8233	.6542
60. Karl von Halt	GER	10/11	6220.965	5080	8233	.6170

All- Around

		Date	Original score	85 Tables	WR-85 Tables	Relative score
1. Martin Sheridan	USA	/09	7385	7415	11271	.6579
2. Sheridan	USA	/07	7130	7121 1/2	11019	.6463
3. Sheridan	USA	7/05	6820 1/2	6795 1/2	10948	.6207
4. Malcolm Ford	USA	9/86	5899	4166	6722	.6198

Notes. There have been 56 world decathlon best scores and all have been analyzed above. The scores of three all-time greats, Olympic champs Campbell Holdorf, and Schenk, plus Bill Watson have been added. All four scores for the all-around were world records. The AAU All-Around tables have been used in the same fashion as the 1985 decathlon tables. The all-around was contested in one day, lowering the relative scores.

Appendix B

Modern Olympic Games Competitors

Each Olympic competitor in decathlon, pentathlon, and all-around is listed. In most cases, the athlete's birthdate, height, and weight are given along with his score and the year of the competition. If an athlete did not finish, withdrawing, for example, after four events, this information is conveyed in parentheses: (dnf4). Thanks to Bill Mallon, the world's foremost Olympic researcher, who supplied the list of 460 Olympic competitors.

Olympic Multi-Event Index—Men

Abraham, Alex, GER (Jan. 17, 1886), 1912 decathlon—(dnf4).
Adamczyk, Edward, POL (Nov. 30, 1924; 190/83), 1948 decathlon—9 (6712).
Adams, Robert, CAN (1924), 1952 decathlon—19 (5530).
Ahlman, Henrik Aleksander "Heikki," FIN (1879), 1906 pentathlon—17 (dnf3).

Alslebens, Alfreds, SOV (July 12, 1892), 1912 decathlon—11 (5294.615).
Anderson, Otto Kenneth, USA (Oct. 28, 1901), 1924 decathlon—(dnf2).
Andersson, Albert, SWE (Apr. 25, 1902), 1928 decathlon—8 (7108.435).
Andersson, Erik P., SWE (Dec. 16, 1921), 1948 decathlon—5 (6877).
Andonov, Atanas, BUL (July 16, 1955; 190/85), 1980 decathlon—7 (7927).
André, Georges, FRA (Aug. 13, 1889; 188/74), 1912 decathlon—(dnf7); 1912 pentathlon—(dnf).
Anyamah, Charlemagne, FRA (Jan. 23, 1938; 180/85), 1968 decathlon—(dnf7).
Apaitchev, Alexandr, SOV (Dec. 17, 1961; 188/92), 1988 decathlon—(dnfl).
Archibald, Edward Blake, CAN (Mar. 29, 1884), 1906 pentathlon—7 (dnf4).
Argue, John Clifford, USA (Dec. 2, 1901), 1924 pentathlon—(dnf4).
Armand, Edouard B., HAI, 1924 decathlon—(5207.895).
Ascune, Hercules, URU (1928), 1948 decathlon—20 (6026).
Aun, Rein Yanovich, SOV (Oct 5, 1940; 189/88), 1964 decathlon—2 (7842); 1968 decathlon—(dnf4).
Avilov, Nikolay Viktorovich, SOV (Aug. 6, 1948; 191/90), 1968 decathlon—4 (7909); 1972 decathlon—1 (8454); 1976 decathlon—3 (8369).
Babcock, Harold Stoddard, USA (Dec. 15, 1890; 188/75), 1912 decathlon—(dnf3).
Bácsalmasi, Péter, HUN (Nov. 16, 1908), 1932 decathlon—10 (7001).
Bäckman, Runald, SWE (July 5, 1951; 183/83), 1976 decathlon—20 (7319).
Bakai, Jozsef, HUN (Mar. 13, 1942; 184/90), 1972 decathlon—20 (7071).
Bannister, Jeffrey Granville, USA (Aug. 30, 1945; 191/93), 1972 decathlon—21 (7022).
Barth, Hugo, GER (Nov. 20, 1903), 1928 decathlon—11 (6850.605).
Baur, Henri, AUS (Nov. 14, 1872), 1906 pentathlon—20 (dnf3).
Bäurle, Otto, GER (Feb. 3, 1887), 1912 pentathlon—(dnf3).
Bausch, James Aloysius Bernard, USA (Mar. 28, 1906; 188/95), 1932 decathlon—1 (8462.230).
Benadis, Stylianos, GRE, 1924 pentathlon—(dnf3); 1924 decathlon—24 (5189.160).
Bendlin, Kurt, GER (May 22, 1943; 178/91), 1968 decathlon—3 (8064).
Bennett, Jefferson Taft, USA (Aug. 29, 1948; 173/69), 1972 decathlon—4 (7974).
Berlinger, Bernard Ernst, USA (Mar. 13, 1908; 185/91), 1928 decathlon—17 (6619.375).
Berra, Hector, ARG, 1932 decathlon—(dnf2).
Bexell, Karl Olov "Ollie," SWE (June 14, 1909; 190/84), 1936 decathlon—7 (7024).
Beyer, Horst, GER (Apr. 14, 1945; 196/96), 1964 decathlon—6 (7647); 1972 decathlon—(dnf3).
Bie, R. Ferdinand, NOR (Feb. 16, 1888), 1912 pentathlon—1 (16); 1912 decathlon—(dnf9).

Biedermann, Franz, LIE (May 4, 1946; 182/76), 1968 decathlon—19 (6323).
Binet, Emile, BEL (Jan 27, 1908), 1936 decathlon—(dnf7).
Björgvin, Holm, ICE, 1960 decathlon—14 (6261).
Blango, Columba, SLE (Apr. 23, 1956; 188/70), 1980 decathlon—16 (5080).
Blondel, Alain, FRA (Dec. 7, 1962; 185/76), 1988 decathlon—6 (8268).
Bobin, Philippe, FRA (Jan. 24, 1955; 181/78), 1976 decathlon—14 (7580).
Bock, Manfred, GER (May 28, 1941; 190/91), 1960 decathlon—10 (6894).
Bonnet, Helmut, GER (July 17, 1910), 1936 decathlon—8 (6939).
Boreham, Colin Aubrey Geddes, GBR (Mar. 26, 1954; 188/87), 1984 decathlon—20 (7485).
Born, Heinz, SWI (Apr. 26, 1948; 183/83), 1972 decathlon—19 (7217).
Boulanger, Maurice, BEL (Apr. 13, 1909), 1936 decathlon—17 (5097).
Bradley, Everett Lewis, USA (May 19, 1897), 1920 pentathlon—2 (24).
Brambilla, Emilio, ITA (June 26, 1882), 1906 pentathlon—19 (dnf3).
Brasser, Reindert J., HOL (Nov. 20, 1912; 204/90), 1936 decathlon—5 (7046).
Breitman, Georges, FRA (Mar. 27, 1920), 1952 decathlon—(dnf5).
Bright, Timothy William, USA (July 28, 1960; 188/80), 1984 decathlon—12 (7862), 1988 decathlon—7 (8216).
Brodnik, Joze, YUG (Apr. 26, 1936; 192/88), 1960 decathlon—9 (6918).
Brogini, Alessandro, ITA (Dec. 20, 1958; 182/67), 1980 decathlon—(dnf8).
Brooks, Clifford, BAR (Aug. 19, 1944; 181/80), 1972 decathlon—(dnf7).
Bruce, Ian B., AUS (Jan. 25, 1935), 1956 decathlon—11 (6025).
Brundage, Avery, USA (Sep. 28, 1887; 183/91), 1912 pentathlon—5 (26); 1912 decathlon—(dnf8).
Buchel, Alois, LIE (Apr. 16, 1941; 172/78), 1960 decathlon—(dnf4); 1964 decathlon—14 (6849).
Buchel, Gebhard, LIE, 1948 decathlon—(dnf4).
Bucher, Constant, SWI (1899), 1920 decathlon—10 (5273.280); 1924 pentathlon—(dnf3); 1924 decathlon—15 (5961.592).
Buehrer, Willy, SWI (1910), 1936 decathlon—(dnf9).
Butti, Carlo, ITA (Sep. 1, 1891), 1920 decathlon—(dnf6).
Campbell, Milton Gray, USA (Dec. 9, 1933; 190/94), 1952 decathlon—2 (6975); 1956 decathlon—1 (7937).
Cann, John, AUS (Jan. 15, 1938), 1956 decathlon—10 (6278).
Carmona, Roberto, MEX (Oct. 21, 1943; 186/85), 1968 decathlon—(dnf5).
Cejzik, Antoni, POL (May 15, 1900; 188/84), 1924 decathlon—12 (6319.455); 1928 decathlon—18 (6356.280).
Chang, Sing-Chow, CHN (May 28, 1916), 1936 decathlon—(dnf2).
Charles, Wilson David, Jr., USA (Apr. 4, 1908), 1932 decathlon—4 (7985.000).
Chen, Chuan-Show, TPE (Sep. 9, 1941; 172/72), 1968 decathlon—(dnf1).
Choultz, Aleksandr, SOV (June 26, 1892), 1912 decathlon—11 (6134.470).
Churchill, Thomas Ralph, USA (Feb. 26, 1908), 1928 decathlon—5 (7417.115).

Clark, Ellery Harding, USA (Mar. 13, 1874), 1904 all-around—6 (2778).
Clark, Robert Hyatt, USA (Jan. 28, 1913; 188/84), 1936 decathlon—2 (7601).
Clausen, Orn, ICE (Nov. 8, 1928; 184/83), 1948 decathlon—12 (6444).
Coffman, Clifford Clyde, USA (June 2, 1911; 180/75), 1932 decathlon—7 (7534.410).
Contoli, Adolfo, ITA (Feb. 19, 1898), 1924 pentathlon—(dnf3); 1924 decathlon—11 (6406.882).
Coralie, Vivian, MRI (Mar. 11, 1962; 182/72), 1984 decathlon—25 (6084).
Courtejaire, Lucien, FRA 1924 pentathlon—(dnf3).
Cretaine, Jacques, FRA, 1948 decathlon—22 (5829).
Crist, John Harrison, USA (Aug. 28, 1954; 188/84), 1984 decathlon—6 (8130).
Csanyi, Zoltan, HUN (Dec. 25, 1912), 1936 decathlon—(dnf9).
Czegezi, Gheorghe, ROM, 1928 decathlon—26 (5081.605).
Dahlgren, Leif, SWE (Jan. 6, 1906; 184/79), 1936 decathlon—(dnf9).
Dallenbach, Fritz, SWI (Sep. 25, 1911), 1936 decathlon—13 (6311).
Dayer, Albert, BEL, 1948 decathlon—26 (5586).
De Keijser, Harry, HOL, 1924 decathlon—10 (6509.610).
De Noorlander, Eduard J., HOL (Mar. 10, 1945; 192/91), 1968 decathlon—9 (7554).
Demetriades, Andronidas, GRE, 1920 decathlon—(dnf4).
Desfarges, Andre, FRA, 1906 pentathlon—(dnf1).
De Wit, Robert, HOL (July 7, 1962; 186/93), 1988 decathlon—8 (8189).
Diaz-Granillo, Angele, GUA (Oct. 29, 1961; 179/66), 1984 decathlon—24 (6342).
Diessl, Walter, AUS (Apr. 14, 1943; 195/94), 1968 decathlon—12 (7465).
Dimsa, Janis, LAT (Nov. 1, 1906), 1932 decathlon—(dnf); 1936 decathlon—(dnf4).
Dixon, Frederick, USA (Nov. 5, 1949; 191/84), 1976 decathlon—23 (6754).
Doherty, John Kenneth, USA (May 16, 1905; 185/75), 1928 decathlon—3 (7706.650).
Doichev, Lyuben, BUL (Oct. 26, 1911), 1936 decathlon—14 (6307).
Donahue, James Joseph, USA (Apr. 20, 1885; 172/61), 1912 pentathlon—2 (24); 1912 decathlon—4 (7083.450).
Dörr, Wilhelm, GER (Dec. 7, 1881), 1906 pentathlon—16 (dnf3).
Duigan, Denis V., AUS, 1924 pentathlon—(dnf4); 1924 decathlon—(dnf6).
Dunne, Robert Jerome, USA (Aug. 29, 1899; 185/86), 1920 pentathlon—13 (dnf4).
Duttweiler, Werner, SWI (Nov. 21, 1939; 182/80), 1964 decathlon—(dnf8); 1968 decathlon—(dnf2).
Dyachkov, Yuriy, SOV (July 3, 1940; 196/100), 1960 decathlon—(dnf8).
Dyurov, Spas, BUL (Nov. 28, 1944; 184/93), 1968 decathlon—16 (7173).
Eberle, Wolrad, GER (May 4, 1908; 179/77), 1932 decathlon—3 (8030.805).

Edstrom, David Allan, USA (Sep. 10, 1938; 190/91), 1960 decathlon—(dnf3).

Eller, John J., Jr., USA (Oct. 14, 1884; 175/77), 1912 pentathlon—(ac).

Elliott, Geoffrey Michael, GBR (Apr. 7, 1931; 179/80), 1952 decathlon—9 (6044).

Ellis, Everett Ralph, USA (1891), 1920 decathlon—(dnf8).

Emberger, Richard John, USA (July 3, 1938; 183/77), 1964 decathlon—10 (7292).

Emmerich, Max J., USA, 1904 all-around—(dnf1).

Epitropoulos, Panajotis, GRE (May 28, 1938; 182/74), 1960 decathlon—23 (4737).

Ericsson, Hugo, SWE (Mar. 10, 1886), 1912 pentathlon—(ac).

Eriksson, Per Axel, SWE (Apr. 11, 1925), 1948 decathlon—7 (6731).

Escauriza, Claudio, PAR (May 3, 1958; 179/83), 1984 decathlon—22 (6546).

Etienne, Gaston, BEL, 1928 decathlon—23 (5256.625).

Ever, Valter, EST (Nov. 6, 1902), 1924 decathlon—(dnf5).

Failliot, Pierre, FRA (Feb. 21, 1887), 1912 pentathlon—(ac); 1912 decathlon—(dnf4).

Farabi, Reza, IRN (1933), 1956 decathlon—10 (5103).

Farkas, Matyas, HUN, 1928 decathlon—21 (6015.635).

Fastén, Bertil, SWE (Apr. 1, 1900), 1924 pentathlon—(dnf3); 1924 decathlon—(dnf5).

Ferkovic, Peroslav, YUG, 1924 decathlon—18 (5517.925).

Fernandes, Fernando, POR (1920), 1952 decathlon—16 (5604).

Fernandez, Douglas, VEN (Nov. 22, 1959; 192/90), 1984 decathlon—18 (7553).

Figueroa, Hernan, CHI (Aug. 26, 1927), 1948 decathlon—20 (6026); 1952 decathlon—17 (5592).

Fjästad, Nils, SWE (Feb. 26, 1890), 1912 pentathlon—(ac).

Flores, Luis A., GUA (Oct. 29, 1947; 182/75), 1972 decathlon—(dnf7).

Ford, Howard, GBR (Dec. 18, 1905), 1928 decathlon—(dnf8).

Fournier, Lionel J., CAN, 1948 decathlon—25 (5590).

Frayer, Hugues, FRA (Jan. 30, 1923), 1952 decathlon—11 (5772).

Fredriksen, Gunnar, NOR (Feb. 28, 1907), 1928 decathlon—(dnf5).

Freimuth, Uwe, GDR (Sept. 10, 1961; 191/92), 1988 decathlon—18 (7860).

Frieda, Harry Gaylord, USA (Sep. 11, 1901), 1924 decathlon—8 (6618.300).

Gabbett, Peter John, GBR (Nov. 19, 1941; 183/85), 1972 decathlon—(dnf8).

Gaehwiler, Beat, SUI (Jan. 26, 1965; 186/87), 1988 decathlon—12 (8114).

Gairdner, William Douglas, CAN (Oct. 19, 1940; 180/82), 1964 decathlon—11 (7147).

Gaspar, Duro, YUG, 1924 decathlon—(dnf5).

Gavrilas, Radu, ROM (Apr. 5, 1953; 187/86), 1972 decathlon—16 (7147).

Gemise-Fareau, Gilles, FRA (Aug. 27, 1953; 186/83), 1976 decathlon—17 (7486).

Gensabulo, Noguchi, JAP, 1920 decathlon—12 (3668.630).

Gerber, Oskar, SWI, 1948 decathlon—27 (5558).

Gerspach, Ernst, SWI (Apr. 24, 1897), 1920 decathlon—9 (5947.780); 1924 decathlon—6 (6743.530).

Gerutto, Witold, POL (Oct. 1, 1912; 194/87), 1948 decathlon—19 (6106).

Ghesqiere, Regis, BEL (Jul. 15, 1949; 189/86), 1972 decathlon—11 (7677); 1976 decathlon—(dnf7).

Goelitz, Harry George, USA (Jan. 9, 1894), 1920 decathlon—(dnf9).

Gong, Guohoa, CHN (Jan. 22, 1964; 185/84), 1988 decathlon—31 (7231).

Grebenyuk, Alexandr, SOV (May 2, 1951; 188/91), 1976 decathlon—9 (7803).

Grieb, John, USA, 1904 all-around—6 (2199).

Grogorenz, Klaus, GDR (Apr. 27, 1937; 180/75), 1960 decathlon—8 (7032).

Grummt, Steffen, GDR (Sep. 15, 1959; 190/92), 1980 decathlon—8 (7892).

Gugler, Christian, SUI (Aug. 1, 1960; 186/84), 1988 decathlon—22 (7745).

Guhl, Armin, SWI (Sep. 14, 1907), 1936 decathlon—6 (7033).

Gunn, Adam B., USA, 1904 all-around—2 (5907).

Guu, Jin-Shoei, TAI (Jan. 15, 1960; 180/73), 1984 decathlon—16 (7629).

Gyllenstolpe, Axel-Erik, SWE (Apr. 18, 1894), 1920 pentathlon—9 (dnf4); 1920 decathlon—8 (6331.435).

Hackberg, Wiktor, SWE (Aug. 13, 1891), 1912 decathlon—(dnf3).

Hadfield, Peter, AUS (Jan. 21, 1955; 188/87), 1980 decathlon—13 (7709); 1984 decathlon—14 (7683).

Hagen, Gunnar, NOR (June 11, 1904), 1928 decathlon—(dnf5).

Häggman-Tuomela, Uno, FIN (1882), 1906 pentathlon—4 (34).

Haidu, J., ROM, 1928 decathlon—(dnf7).

Halt, Karl Ritter von, GER (June 2, 1891), 1912 decathlon—8 (6682).

Hamilton, Brutus Kerr, USA (July 19, 1900; 183/80), 1920 pentathlon—6 (27); 1920 decathlon—2 (6771.085); 1924 pentathlon—(dnf4).

Hare, Thomas Truxtun, USA (Oct. 12, 1878; 185/90), 1904 all-around—3 (5813).

Hart, Hendrik Beltsazar "Harry," SAF (Sep. 2, 1905), 1932 decathlon—11 (6799.250).

Hasek, Eduard, CZE (1893), 1920 decathlon—(dnf5).

Hautamäki, Erkki Johannes, FIN (Aug. 28, 1930; 183/81), 1952 decathlon—(dnf9).

Hedmark, Lennart Per-Olof, SWE (May 18, 1944; 195/93), 1968 decathlon—11 (7481); 1972 decathlon—(dnf3); 1976 decathlon—8 (7974).

Heinrich, Ignace, FRA (July 31, 1925; 193/92), 1948 decathlon—2 (6974); 1952 decathlon—(dnf6).

Herbrand, Freddy, BEL (June 1, 1944; 190/88), 1972 decathlon—6 (7947).

Herman, Paul Irvin, USA (Mar. 7, 1941; 188/79), 1964 decathlon—4 (7787).

Herssens, Walter, BEL (Feb. 15, 1930), 1956 decathlon—(dnf4).

Herunter, Gert, AUS (Mar. 9, 1942; 190/85), 1968 decathlon—(dnf7).

Hingsen, Jürgen, FRG (Jan. 25, 1958; 200/100), 1984 decathlon—2 (8673), 1988 decathlon—dnf (disqualified, 3 false starts, 100m).

Hipp, Josef "Sepp," GER (Feb. 13, 1927), 1952 decathlon—5 (6449).

Ho Menh Phoc, VIE (Aug. 26, 1940; 178/75), 1968 decathlon—(dnf4).

Hodge, Russell Arden, USA (Sep. 9, 1939; 190/97), 1964 decathlon—9 (7325).

Holdorf, Willi, GER (Feb. 17, 1940; 182/90), 1964 decathlon—1 (7887).

Holloway, John J., IRE, 1904 all-around—4 (5273).

Holmér, Gustaf Richard Mikäl "Gösta," SWE (Sept. 23, 1891; 185/84), 1912 decathlon—3 (7347.855), 1912 pentathlon—(ac); 1920 decathlon—4 (6532.150).

Holmvang, Godtfred, NOR (Oct. 7, 1917), 1948 decathlon—10 (6663).

Hraban, Roman, TCH (June 28, 1962; 183/78), 1988 decathlon—20 (7781).

Huber, Erwin, GER (Apr. 5, 1907; 180/80), 1928 decathlon—15 (6702.820); 1936 decathlon—4 (7087).

Huusari, Anton "Antti," FIN (July 10, 1898), 1924 decathlon—4 (7005.175).

Iriarte, Brigido, VEN (1922), 1952 decathlon—12 (5770).

Ivanov, Boris, SOV (Sep. 29, 1947; 186/86), 1972 decathlon—13 (7657).

Jacobson, Skotte, SWE (Feb. 24, 1888; 170/63), 1912 decathlon—(dnf4).

Järvinen, Eero Johannes Akilles, FIN (Sep. 19, 1905; 187/84), 1928 decathlon—2 (7931.500); 1932 decathlon—2 (8292.480); 1936 decathlon—(dnf5).

Janczenko, Tadeusz, POL (Jan. 9, 1946; 182/81), 1972 decathlon—8 (7861).

Jankov, Rasvigor, BUL (Apr. 10, 1954; 188/90), 1980 decathlon—14 (7624).

Jansson, Helge, SWE (June 1, 1904), 1924 decathlon—7 (6656.160); 1928 decathlon—6 (7286.285).

Jekkals, Guido, LAT, 1924 decathlon—14 (5981.670).

Jenner, William Bruce, USA (Dec. 28, 1949; 188/88), 1972 decathlon—10 (7722); 1976 decathlon—1 (8617).

Joannes-Powell, René, BEL (Feb. 11, 1896), 1920 decathlon—11 (5091.520); 1928 decathlon—24 (5190.650).

Johansson-Jaale, Paavo Pekka, FIN (Oct. 21, 1895), 1920 decathlon—(dnf5).

Johnson, David, USA (April 7, 1963; 189/86), 1988 decathlon—9 (8180).

Johnson, Rafer Lewis, USA (Aug. 18, 1935; 190/91), 1956 decathlon—2 (7587); 1960 decathlon—1 (8392).

Jokinen, Esa, FIN (Feb. 19, 1958; 192/90), 1980 decathlon—9 (7826).

Julve Ciriaco, Eduardo, PER (Aug. 27, 1923), 1948 decathlon—(dnf5).

Kachanov, Valeriy, SOV (July 12, 1954; 186/74), 1980 decathlon—(dnf8).

Kahma, Markus Jaako, FIN (Oct. 16, 1932; 187/88), 1960 decathlon—7 (7112).

Kallay, Branko, YUG, 1928 decathlon—24 (5210.650).

Kaltenbach, Carl, GER (1883), 1906 pentathlon—17 (dnf3).

Kamerbeek, Evert "Eef," HOL (Mar. 17, 1934; 189/91), 1960 decathlon—5 (7236); 1964 decathlon—(dnf5).

Katus, Ryszard, POL (Mar. 29, 1947; 184/81), 1972 decathlon—3 (7984); 1976 decathlon—12 (7616).

Keskitalo, Petri, FIN (March 10, 1967; 187/87), 1988 decathlon—11 (8143)

Kiely, Thomas Francis, IRE (Aug. 25, 1869), 1904 all-around—1 (6036).

Kinder, Gary, USA (Oct. 25, 1962; 186/90), 1988 decathlon—(dnf5).

King, Barry John, GBR (Apr. 3, 1945; 185/90), 1972 decathlon—15 (7468).

Kiprop, Koech, KEN (1934; 180/87), 1964 decathlon—17 (6707).

Kirst, Joachim, GDR (May 21, 1947; 189/94), 1968 decathlon—5 (7861); 1972 decathlon—(dnf6).

Kistenmacher, Enrique A., ARG (Apr. 8, 1923), 1948 decathlon—4 (6929).

Klein, Josef, CZE (Nov. 12, 1916), 1936 decathlon—16 (5883).

Klumberg-Kolmpere, Aleksandr, EST (June 10, 1899), 1920 decathlon— (dnf8); 1924 decathlon—17 (7329.360).

Kochevnikov, Pyotr, SOV (1927), 1952 decathlon—(dnf2).

Kolnik, Mirko, YUG (July 9, 1936; 180/80), 1960 decathlon—(dnf5).

Kosmas, Photios, GRE (1926), 1952 decathlon—(dnf2).

Kratschmer, Guido, FRG (Jan. 10, 1953; 186/89), 1976 decathlon—2 (8411); 1984 decathlon—4 (8326).

Kremer, René, LUX, 1948 decathlon—(dnf5).

Kröjer, Gustav, AUS (June 30, 1885), 1906 pentathlon—22 (dnf3); 1912 pentathlon—(ac).

Kruger, Alex, GBR (Nov. 18, 1863; 192/85), 1988 decathlon—24 (7623).

Kugelberg, Erik, SWE (Mar. 9, 1891), 1912 pentathlon—(ac); 1912 decathlon—7 (6758.780).

Kukko, Eemil, FIN (May 14, 1888), 1912 pentathlon—(ac).

Kulvet, Walter, SOV (Feb. 19, 1964; 190/91), 1988 decathlon—(dnf5).

Kunwar, Dambar, NEP (, 1959; 168/57), 1988 decathlon—34 (5339).

Kunz, Hansruedi, SWI (May 26, 1945; 182/86), 1968 decathlon—(dnf7).

Kutsenko, Yuriy, SOV (Mar. 5, 1952; 190/95), 1980 decathlon—2 (8331).

Kutyenko, Yuriy, SOV (July 8, 1932; 187/90), 1956 decathlon—(dnf9); 1960 decathlon—4 (7567).

Kuzmicki, Waclaw, POL (Apr. 27, 1921; 182/81), 1948 decathlon—16 (6153).

Kuznetsov, Vasiliy Dmitriyevich, SOV (Feb. 7, 1932; 185/82), 1956 decathlon—3 (7465); 1960 decathlon—3 (7809); 1964 decathlon—7 (7569).

Kuznyetsov, Sergei, SOV (June 2, 1918), 1952 decathlon—10 (5937).

Ladewig, Wilhelm, GER (Oct. 8, 1906), 1928 decathlon—10 (6881.520).

Lahti, Johannes Kristian, FIN (May 29, 1952; 181/81), 1976 decathlon—11 (7711); 1980 decathlon—11 (7765).

Lahtinen, Hugo Jalmari, FIN (Nov. 29, 1891), 1920 decathlon—(dnf3).

Laipenieks, Juriz, CHI (Apr. 9, 1940; 182/85), 1960 decathlon—19 (5865).

Landstroem, Eeles Enok, FIN (Jan. 3, 1932; 186/82), 1952 decathlon—14 (5694).

Langkjär, Svend, DEN (Aug. 23, 1886), 1912 pentathlon—(ac); 1912 decathlon—(dnf3).

Lanka, Janis, SOV (Aug. 3, 1940; 186/86), 1968 decathlon—14 (7227).
Lassenius, Lars Torbjörn, FIN (Aug. 4, 1931; 191/89), 1956 decathlon—7 (6565).
Lauer, Martin, GER (Jan. 2, 1937; 186/76), 1956 decathlon—5 (6853).
Leane, Patrick F., AUS (Jan. 11, 1930), 1952 decathlon—(dnf2); 1956 decathlon—9 (6427).
Lee, Fu-An, TAI (Apr. 6, 1964; 185/74), 1984 decathlon—19 (7541), 1988 decathlon—25 (7579).
Lee, Kwang-Ik, KOR (May 27, 1969; 181/80), 1988 decathlon—33 (6917).
Legat, Manlio, ITA (July 20, 1889), 1912 decathlon—(dnf3).
LeGendre, Robert Lucien, USA (Jan. 7, 1897; 190/89), 1920 pentathlon—4 (26); 1924 pentathlon—3 (18).
Lehtonen, Eero Reino, FIN (Apr. 21, 1898), 1920 pentathlon—1 (14); 1920 decathlon—(dnf5); 1924 pentathlon—1 (14).
Lemming, Eric Valdemar, SWE (Feb. 22, 1880; 190/88), 1906 pentathlon—3 (29); 1912 pentathlon—(ac).
Lemming, Oscar R., SWE (Oct. 11, 1886), 1912 pentathlon—(ac).
Lemperle, Hermann, GER (May 22, 1906), 1928 decathlon—19 (6293.755).
Leppänen, Heikki Olavi, FIN (Aug. 31, 1946; 194/90), 1976 decathlon—(dnf2).
LeRoy, Yves, FRA (Feb. 23, 1951; 192/90), 1972 decathlon—12 (7675).
Lespagnard, Roger, BEL (Oct. 24, 1940; 180/89), 1968 decathlon—17 (7125); 1972 decathlon—14 (7519); 1976 decathlon—19 (7322).
Lindberg, Knut, SWE (Feb. 2, 1882), 1906 pentathlon—6 (37).
Lindblad, Henry, SWE (Feb. 25, 1906; 189/87), 1928 decathlon—9 (7071).
Litvenyenko, Leonid Dmitriyevich, SOV (Jan. 28, 1949; 186/88), 1972 decathlon—2 (8035); 1976 decathlon—7 (8025).
Lomberg, Charles, SWE (Dec. 4, 1886; 182/75), 1912 pentathlon—(ac); 1912 decathlon—2 (7413.510).
Longe, Clive Citreon Olaf, GBR (Feb. 23, 1939; 185/90), 1968 decathlon—13 (7338).
Lövland, Helge, NOR (May 11, 1890), 1920 pentathlon—5 (27); 1920 decathlon—1 (6803.355).
Ludwig, Dariusz, POL (Feb. 25, 1955; 185/84), 1980 decathlon—6 (7978).
Lukeman, Frank L., CAN (1887), 1912 pentathlon—3 (24); 1912 decathlon—(dnf8).
Lundgren, Sven, SWE (July 17, 1901), 1928 decathlon—14 (6727.045).
Luntzer, György, HUN, 1906 pentathlon—10 (dnf3).
Magherian, Megerdich, TUR (Sep. 12, 1892), 1912 pentathlon—(ac); 1912 decathlon—(dnf3).
Mäkelä, Jaakko Yrjö, FIN (Dec. 2, 1926; 185/84), 1948 decathlon—13 (6421).
Mallwitz, Arthur, GER (June 15, 1880), 1906 pentathlon—12 (dnf3).
Mandl, Horst, AUS (Jan. 8, 1936; 187/86), 1968 decathlon—(dnf3).
Mangish, Rudolf, SWI (Dec. 6, 1952; 184/84), 1972 decathlon—(dnf7).
Marcelja, Davorin, YUG (1924), 1948 decathlon—18 (6141).

Marek, Claus, FRG (Apr. 3, 1954; 186/89), 1976 decathlon—10 (7767).

Marien, Leopold, BEL (Mar. 22, 1934; 180/78), 1960 decathlon—18 (5919).

Mathias, Robert Bruce, USA (Nov. 17, 1930; 190/92), 1948 decathlon—1 (7139); 1952 decathlon—1 (7887).

McStravick, Bradley Steven, GBR (May 25, 1956; 184/80), 1980 decathlon—15 (7616); 1984 decathlon—11 (7890).

Médécin, Edouard Gaston, MON (1901), 1924 pentathlon—(dnf3); 1924 decathlon—20 (5347.540); 1928 decathlon—(ac).

Meier, Adolf, SWI (Feb. 12, 1902), 1924 decathlon—(dnf6); 1928 decathlon—(dnf7).

Meier, Walter, GDR (Aug. 3, 1927), 1956 decathlon—5 (6773); 1960 decathlon—16 (6000).

Meimer, Johann, EST (June 29, 1904), 1928 decathlon—(6733.150).

Mellado, Santiago, ESA (April 6, 1963; 172/75), 1988 decathlon—26 (7517).

Mellander, Hjalmar, SWE (Dec. 14, 1880), 1906 pentathlon—1 (24).

Menaul, James Austin, USA (Mar. 26, 1888), 1912 pentathlon—4 (25).

Mercer, Eugene Leroy, USA (Oct. 30, 1888; 180/80), 1912 decathlon—5 (7074.995).

Mijares, Rodolfo, MEX (July 17, 1938; 180/75), 1960 decathlon—21 (5413).

Miller, Albert, FIJ (Dec. 12, 1957; 185/78), 1984 decathlon—(dnf8), 1988 decathlon—32 (7016).

Molster, Martin, NOR (Oct. 11, 1900), 1924 pentathlon—(dnf4).

Moltke, Werner von, FRG (May 24, 1936; 190/90), 1968 decathlon—(dnf2).

Mondschein, Irving "Moon," USA (Feb. 7, 1924; 183/89), 1948 decathlon—8 (6715).

Moro, Guerrino "Gerry," CAN (Apr. 17, 1943; 184/84), 1964 decathlon—16 (6716); 1972 decathlon—(dnf6).

Morris, Glenn Edward, USA (June 18, 1912; 185/84), 1936 decathlon—1 (7900).

Moser, Severin, SUI (Oct. 23, 1962; 186/84), 1988 decathlon—27 (7502).

Motti, William, FRA (July 25, 1964; 198/87), 1984 decathlon—5 (8266).

Muchitsch, Hans, AUS (Sep. 30, 1932; 180/72), 1960 decathlon—17 (5950).

Mudin, Istvan, HUN (Oct. 16, 1881), 1906 pentathlon—2 (25).

Mukhtar, Ezz el Din, EGY, 1948 decathlon—28 (5031).

Mulkey, Philip Roy, USA (Jan. 7, 1934; 178/75), 1960 decathlon—(dnf7).

Mullins, Peter M., AUS, 1948 decathlon—6 (6739).

Mwalawanda, Wilfred, MAL (Dec. 20, 1944; 175/78), 1972 decathlon—22 (6227).

Nakazawa, Yenataro, JAP, 1928 decathlon—22 (5672.175).

Natvig, Edvard, NOR (Aug. 18, 1907), 1936 decathlon—10 (6759).

Neumann, Eugen, EST, 1924 decathlon—16 (5899.105).

Niklaus, Stefan, POL (Apr. 17, 1958; 189/85), 1980 decathlon—12 (7762).

Nikolaidis, Apostolos, GRE, 1920 decathlon—(dnf4).

Nilsson, Einar, SWE (June 8, 1891; 190/92), 1912 pentathlon—(ac); 1912 decathlon—(dnf4).

Nilsson, Evert, SWE (Oct. 22, 1894), 1920 pentathlon—10 (dnf4); 1920 decathlon—5 (6433.530); 1924 pentathlon—(dnf4); 1924 decathlon—(dnf3).
Noel, Gerard, BEL, 1928 decathlon—27 (4606.740).
Norton, Emerson Carlysle, USA (Nov. 16, 1900), 1924 decathlon—2 (7350.895).
Noto, Tokushige, JAP, 1924 decathlon—22 (5248.330).
Nussbaum, Fritz, SWI, 1948 decathlon—23 (5808).
Nylund, Ossian Rudolf, FIN (Apr. 22, 1894), 1920 pentathlon—(dnf4).
O'Callaghan, C., IRE, 1928 decathlon—(ac).
O'Connell, Carlos, IRL (June 21, 1963; 192/86), 1988 decathlon—29 (7310).
Ohlson, Bertil, SWE (Jan. 22, 1899), 1920 pentathlon—7 (30); 1920 decathlon—3 (6580.030).
Olander, Lars Mikael, SWE (June 11, 1963; 188/89), 1988 decathlon—17 (7869).
Oliver, Reinaldo, PUR (Mar. 28, 1932), 1952 decathlon—21 (5228).
Paccagnella, Luciano, ITA (May 18, 1939; 195/85), 1960 decathlon—13 (6283).
Pagani, Alfredo, ITA (Sep. 6, 1887), 1912 pentathlon—(ac); 1912 decathlon—(dnf7).
Palu, Uno, SOV (Feb. 8, 1933; 186/87), 1956 decathlon—4 (6930).
Parker, Jack, USA (Sep. 27, 1915; 188/84), 1936 decathlon—3 (7275).
Parsalis, Christos, GRE, 1906 pentathlon—11 (dnf3).
Penalver, Antonio, ESP (Dec. 1, 1968; 195/86), 1988 decathlon—23 (7743).
Perk, Hans-Joachim, FRG (Sep. 19, 1945; 188/88), 1972 decathlon—(dnf3).
Pernica, Ludek, CZE (Dec. 12, 1949; 189/82), 1976 decathlon—13 (7602).
Philbrook, George Warren, USA (Oct. 10, 1886), 1912 decathlon—(dnf9).
Pighi, Albino, ITA (May 15, 1903), 1924 pentathlon—(dnf3).
Pihl, Raimo, SWE (Oct. 28, 1949; 186/89), 1976 decathlon—4 (8218).
Plawczyk, Jerzy, POL (Apr. 16, 1911; 184/82), 1936 decathlon—9 (6871).
Plaziat, Christian, FRA (Oct. 28, 1963; 190/87), 1988 decathlon—5 (8272).
Poelman, Simon, NZL (May 27, 1963; 187/93), 1988 decathlon—16 (8021).
Pottel, Rainer, GDR (Aug. 29, 1953; 185/82), 1980 decathlon—(dnf3).
Räder, Einar, NOR (Feb. 2, 1896), 1920 decathlon—(dnf9).
Rähn, Elmar, EST (Dec. 3, 1904), 1924 decathlon—21 (5292.760).
Rakotoralahy, Dominique, MAD (Aug. 3, 1944; 168/67), 1968 decathlon—(dnf2).
Randhawa, Gurbachan, IND, 1960 decathlon—(dnf6).
Rebula, Otto, YUG (1921), 1948 decathlon—(dnf5); 1952 decathlon—15 (5648).
Recordon, Mario, CHI, 1948 decathlon—24 (5730).
Reikko, Olli Johannes, FIN (Jan. 10, 1927; 178/75), 1952 decathlon—13 (5725).
Reimer, Erwin, CHI (May 29, 1914), 1936 decathlon—(dnf2).
Reinikka, Aulis, FIN (Oct. 21, 1915), 1936 decathlon—11 (6755).

Reistad, Ole, NOR (June 26, 1898, 1920 pentathlon—14 (dnf4).

Richards, Gregory, GBR (April 25, 1956; 194/92), 1988 decathlon—30 (7237).

Richards, Robert Eugene, USA (Feb. 20, 1926; 178/75), 1956 decathlon—(dnf9).

Ritzenhoff, Wilhelm, GER (1878), 1906 pentathlon—14 (dnf3).

Robertson, Lawson, USA (Sept. 24, 1883), 1906 pentathlon—5 (36).

Röhr, Otto, GER (Nov. 22, 1891; 193/81), 1912 decathlon—(dnf4).

Ronac, Miro, PER (Oct. 10, 1961; 188/85), 1980 decathlon—(dnf9).

Rönström, Gunnar, SWE (Jan. 25, 1884), 1912 decathlon—(dnf4).

Ruefenacht, Michele, SWI (Sep. 15, 1959; 186/87), 1984 decathlon—10 (7924).

Ruth, Josse, BEL, 1924 pentathlon—(dnf3); 1924 decathlon—17 (5866.670).

Saleh, Mensser, QAT (177/75), 1984 decathlon—21 (6589).

Samara, Frederick Ameen, USA (Apr. 6, 1950; 182/79), 1976 decathlon—15 (7504).

Santos, Julio, POR (May 30, 1936; 184/75), 1960 decathlon—(dnf4).

Sar, Franco, ITA (Dec. 21, 1933; 187/88), 1960 decathlon—6 (7195); 1964 decathlon—13 (7054).

Schäffer, Josef, AUS (July 2, 1891), 1912 decathlon—9 (6568.585).

Scheidl, (Petit) Theodor, AUS, 1906 pentathlon—9 (dnf3).

Schenk, Christian, GDR (Feb. 9, 1965; 201/93), 1988 decathlon—1 (8488).

Scheurer, Armin, SWI (Dec. 24, 1917; 184/82), 1948 decathlon—(dnf1).

Schirmer, Friedel, GER (Mar. 20, 1926, 1952 decathlon—8 (6118).

Schoebel, Jean-Pierre, FRA (Mar. 18, 1949; 188/88), 1972 decathlon—18 (7273).

Schreyer, Stefan, GDR (Oct. 23, 1946; 184/84), 1972 decathlon—5 (7950).

Schutter, Eltjo, HOL (June 17, 1953; 191/78), 1976 decathlon—(dnf5).

Seger, Josef, LIE, 1948 decathlon—(dnf7).

Selva, Hector Roman, PUR, 1952 decathlon—20 (5264).

Sempe, Gabriel, FRA (1901), 1924 decathlon—(dnf8).

Sereme, Dramana, MAI (May 23, 1942; 181/80), 1964 decathlon—18 (5917).

Shanahan, William, IRE, 1924 decathlon—19 (5426.680).

Sheridan, Martin Joseph, USA (Mar. 28, 1881; 192/90), 1906 pentathlon—(dnf1).

Shirley, Simon, AUS (Aug. 3, 1966; 190/90), 1988 decathlon—15 (8036).

Siedlecki, Zygmunt, POL (Apr. 4, 1907; 185/82), 1932 decathlon—(dnf8).

Sievert, Hans-Heinrich, GER (Dec. 1, 1909; 188/88), 1932 decathlon—5 (7941.070).

Simmons, Floyd Macon, USA (Apr. 10, 1923; 185/82), 1948 decathlon—3 (6950); 1952 decathlon—3 (6788).

Singh, Baldev, IND, 1948 decathlon—(dnf7).

Singh, Chauhan Vijay, IND (Jan. 21, 1949; 183/78), 1972 decathlon—17 (7378).

Singh, Randhawa Gurbachan, IND (June 6, 1939; 183/71), 1960 decathlon—(dnf5).

Skowronek, Ryszard, POL (May 1, 1949; 183/82), 1972 decathlon—(dnf7); 1976 decathlon—5 (8113).

Skramstad, Trond, NOR (Dec. 6, 1960; 184/85), 1984 decathlon—17 (7579).

Slack, David G., GBR, 1924 pentathlon—(dnf3); 1924 decathlon—25 (5148.105).

Sloan, Richard Donald, USA (Nov. 10, 1946; 178/78), 1968 decathlon—7 (7692).

Smidt-Jensen, Steen, DEN (Jan. 26, 1945; 185/84), 1968 decathlon—8 (7648); 1972 decathlon—7 (7947).

Smith, Michael, CAN (Sep. 16, 1967; 196/97), 1988 decathlon—14 (8083).

Solar, Franz, AUS, 1906 pentathlon—24 (dnf3).

Solorzano, Fidel, ECU (May 26, 1962; 182/78), 1984 decathlon—23 (6519), 1988—decathlon (dfn4).

Somfay, Elemer, HUN (Aug. 28, 1898), 1924 pentathlon—2 (16); 1924 decathlon—(dnf4).

Sonck, Johannes E.E., FIN (Aug. 25, 1919; 189/87), 1948 decathlon—17 (6142).

Soucek, Frantisek, CZE, 1906 pentathlon—14 (dnf3).

Spalic, Aleksandar, YUG, 1924 pentathlon—(dnf3).

Spark, Arthur Percy, GBR (June 4, 1894), 1924 pentathlon—(dnf3); 1924 decathlon—(dnf7).

Sprecher, Pierre, FRA (Nov. 9, 1921), 1948 decathlon—14 (6401).

Stark, Siegfried, GDR (June 12, 1955; 186/87), 1976 decathlon—6 (8048); 1980 decathlon—(dnf2).

Stavem, Per, NOR (Mar. 1, 1926), 1948 decathlon—11 (6552).

Steen, David, CAN (Nov. 14, 1959; 185/79), 1984 decathlon—8 (8047), 1988 decathlon—3 (8328).

Steiner, Tito, ARG (Mar. 1, 1952; 198/89), 1976 decathlon—22 (7052).

Sterzl, Franz, AUS (Nov. 6, 1908), 1936 decathlon—(dnf8).

Stewart, James Daniel, USA (Dec. 6, 1905; 190/82), 1928 decathlon—4 (7624.135).

Storochenko, Mikhail, SOV (Nov. 12, 1937; 182/82), 1964 decathlon—8 (7464).

Stroot, Eberhard, FRG (Mar. 20, 1951; 181/79), 1976 decathlon—21 (7063).

Stulac, George, CAN (Mar. 22, 1934; 170/70), 1960 decathlon—22 (5198).

Sullivan, Daniel Albert, USA, 1906 pentathlon—21 (dnf3).

Sustera, Miroslav, CZE, 1906 pentathlon—12 (dnf3).

Sutherland, Edward, G., SAF (Nov. 9, 1902), 1924 decathlon—5 (6794.145).

Suutari, Seppo Juhani, FIN (Dec. 28, 1940; 178/81), 1960 decathlon—12 (6751).

Suzuki, Shosuke, JAP (Nov. 11, 1936; 179/73), 1964 decathlon—15 (6838).

Sveinsson, Elias, ICE, 1976 decathlon—(dnf6).

Svensson, Carl-Enok, SWE (Nov. 3, 1895), 1920 pentathlon—11 (dnf4).

Svoboda, Antonin, CZE, 1924 pentathlon—(dnf3).

Szabo, Dezso, HUN (Aug. 4, 1967; 184/80), 1988 decathlon—13 (8093).

Szczerkowski, Janusz, POL (May 9, 1954; 190/86), 1980 decathlon—10 (7822).

Tannander, Kjell, SWE (June 25, 1927; 193/86), 1948 decathlon—15 (6325); 1952 decathlon—7 (6308).

Tarnovetskiy, Pavel, SOV (Feb. 22, 1961; 183/88), 1988 decathlon—10 (8167).

Thomas, Hector, VEN (Oct. 10, 1938; 178/80), 1960 decathlon—20 (5753); 1964 decathlon—(dnf7).

Thompson, Enrique R., ARG, 1924 decathlon—13 (6311).

Thompson, Francis Morgan "Daley," GBR (July 30, 1958; 185/86), 1976 decathlon—18 (7434); 1980 decathlon—1 (8495); 1984 decathlon—1 (8798), 1988 decathlon—4 (8306).

Thorlaksson, Valbjörn, ICE (June 9, 1934; 182/75), 1964 decathlon—12 (7135); 1968 decathlon—(dnf5).

Thorpe, James Francis, (né Wa-tho-Huck/Bright Path) USA (May 28, 1888; 183/86), 1912 pentathlon—1 (5); 1912 decathlon—1 (8412.955).

Tiedtke, Manfred, GDR (Sept. 7, 1942; 188/92), 1968 decathlon—10 (7551).

Timme, Herman, HOL (July 27, 1933; 189/86), 1960 decathlon—15 (6206).

Tisdall, Robert M., IRE (May 16, 1907), 1932 decathlon—8 (7327).

Toki, Tatsuo, JAP, 1928 decathlon—12 (6757.605).

Toomey, William Anthony, USA (Jan. 10, 1939; 187/87), 1968 decathlon—1 (8193).

Toomsalu, Ruudi, EST (Apr. 2, 1913), 1936 decathlon— (dnf7).

Topelius-Tolamo, Martti, FIN (Feb. 21, 1907; 184/80), 1928 decathlon—16 (6642.115); 1936 decathlon—(dnf7).

Trautmann, Urs, SWI (Mar. 30, 1940; 186/85), 1968 decathlon—18 (7044).

Ueda, Seiichi, JAP, 1924 pentathlon—(dnf3).

Unger, Göran, SWE (Sep. 29, 1899), 1924 pentathlon—(dnf4).

Valenta, Veroslav, TCH (March, 25, 1965; 198/85), 1988 decathlon—28 (7442).

Vargha, Pal, HUN (1878), 1906 pentathlon—22 (dnf3).

Vélez, Donald, NIC (Jan. 18, 1948; 180/70), 1968 decathlon—20 (5943).

Vera, Carlos, CHL (1928), 1952 decathlon-(dnf).

Vesely, Ludwig, AUS (Aug. 20, 1903), 1928 decathlon—7 (7274.850).

Vetterli, Patrick, SWI (Oct. 6, 1961; 200/100), 1984 decathlon—13 (7739).

Vidal, Eugene Luther, USA (Apr. 13, 1895), 1920 decathlon—7 (6358.570).

Viljoen, Johannes Hendrikus, SAF (Jan. 4, 1905), 1928 decathlon—(dnf).

Vilmundarson, Karl, ICE (Dec. 6, 1910), 1936 decathlon—(dnf2).

Virgile, Ioan, ROM, 1928 decathlon—(dnf1).

Vogelsang, Fritz, SWI (Nov. 17, 1932; 188/80), 1960 decathlon—11 (6767).

Volkov, Valdimir, SOV (Mar. 7, 1921), 1952 decathlon—4 (6674).

Voss, Torsten, GDR (March 24, 1963; 186/88), 1988 decathlon—2 (8399).

Waddell, Thomas Flubacher, USA (Nov. 1, 1937; 187/82), 1968 decathlon—6 (7720).

Wagner, Julius, SWI (Oct. 10, 1882), 1906 pentathlon—8 (dnf4); 1912 pentathlon—(dnf3).

Wahlstedt, Armis I., FIN (Aug. 7, 1905; 178/82), 1928 decathlon—(dnf4).

Waitzer, Josef, GER (May 1, 1884), 1912 decathlon—(dnf3).

Walde, Hans-Joachim, FRG (June 28, 1942; 191/89), 1964 decathlon—3 (7809); 1968 decathlon—2 (8111); 1972 decathlon—(dnf4).

Warming, Lars, DEN (June 21, 1963; 192/85), 1988 decathlon—19 (7859).

Wegner, Erwin, GER (Apr. 5, 1909; 191/80), 1932 decathlon—9 (7179).

Wehrli, Max, SWI (1930), 1952 decathlon—18 (5561).

Weightman-Smith, George C., SAF (1906), 1928 decathlon—(dnf).

Weng, Kang-qiang, CHN (May 4, 1959; 183/78), 1984 decathlon—15 (7662).

Wentz, Siegfried, FRG (Mar. 7, 1960; 193/89), 1984 decathlon—3 (8412).

Wenzel, Oswaldo, CHI (Oct. 25, 1911), 1936 decathlon—15 (6058).

Werthner, Georg, AUS (Apr. 7, 1956; 190/87), 1976 decathlon—16 (7493); 1980 decathlon—4 (8050); 1984 decathlon—9 (8012), 1988 decathlon—21 (7753).

Wessel, Herbert, GBR (Mar. 12, 1944; 181/81), 1968 decathlon—(dnf4).

Wickholm, Waldemar, FIN (Nov. 7, 1890), 1912 decathlon—6 (7058.795); 1920 decathlon—6 (6405.460).

Widenfeldt, Göran, SWE (Aug. 13, 1928; 190/86), 1952 decathlon—6 (6388).

Wieslander, Karl Hugo, SWE (June 11, 1889), 1912 pentathlon—6 (28); 1912 decathlon—1 (7724.495).

Wooding, James Dale, USA (Feb. 6, 1964; 192/91), 1984 decathlon—7 (8091).

Wu, Ah-min, TAI (July 19, 1938; 180/75), 1964 decathlon—(dnf3); 1968 decathlon—15 (7209).

Yang, Chuan-kwang, TAI (July 10, 1933; 180/80), 1956 decathlon—8 (6521); 1960 decathlon—2 (8334); 1964 decathlon—5 (7650).

Yrjölä, Iivari, FIN (Sep. 10, 1899), 1924 pentathlon—(dnf3); 1924 decathlon—(dnf5).

Yrjölä, Paavo Ilmari, FIN (June 18, 1902), 1924 decathlon—9 (6548.525); 1928 decathlon—1 (8053.290); 1932 decathlon—6 (7687.990).

Zacharopoulos, Georgios, GRE, 1924 pentathlon—(dnf3).

Zeilbauer, Josef "Sepp," AUS (Sep. 24, 1952; 192/93), 1972 decathlon—9 (7741); 1976 decathlon—(dnf8); 1980 decathlon—5 (8007).

Zhelanov, Sergei, SOV (June 14, 1957; 189/74), 1980 decathlon—3 (8135).

Zinner, Fred, BEL, 1924 pentathlon—(dnf3).

Notes

KEY TO ABBREVIATIONS

Nations

ARG	Argentina
AUS	Australia
AUT	Austria
BAR	Barbados
BEL	Belgium
BOH	Bohemia
BRA	Brazil
BUL	Bulgaria
CAN	Canada
CHI	Chile
CHN	China (PRC in 1984)
CZE	Czechoslovakia (TCH before 1924 and after 1984)
DEN	Denmark
ECU	Ecuador
EGY	Egypt
ESA	El Salvador
EST	Estonia
FIJ	Fiji Islands
FIN	Finland
FOR	Formosa
FRA	France
FRG	Federal Republic of Germany
GBR	Great Britain & Northern Ireland
GDR	East Germany (German Democratic Republic)
GER	Germany (to 1936) West Germany (1952 to present)
GRE	Greece
GUA	Guatemala
HAI	Haiti
HOL	Holland (Netherlands)
HUN	Hungary
ICE	Iceland
IND	India
IRE	Ireland
IRN	Iran
ITA	Italy
JAP	Japan
KEN	Kenya
KOR	Korea
LAT	Latvia
LIE	Liechtenstein

(Cont.)

KEY TO ABBREVIATIONS (Continued)

LIT   Lithuania
LUX   Luxembourg
MAD   Madagascar
MAI   Mali
MAL   Malawi
MEX   Mexico
MON   Monaco
MOR   Morocco
MRI   Mauritius
NEP   Nepal
NIC   Nicaragua
NOR   Norway
NZE   New Zealand
PAR   Paraguay
PER   Peru
POL   Poland
POR   Portugal
PUR   Puerto Rico
PRC   People's Republic of China
QAT   Qatar
ROM Rumania
RUS   Russia (to 1912)
SAF   South Africa
SLE   Sierra Leone
SOV   Soviet Union
SPA   Spain
SWE   Sweden
SWI   Switzerland
TAI   Taiwan (TPE, Chinese Taipei after 1980)
TUR   Turkey
URU   Uruguay
USA   United States of America
VEN   Venezuela
VIE   Vietnam
YUG   Yugoslavia

AR   American Record
AW   Athletes West
DCA   Decathlon Club of America
dis   discus
dnf   did not finish
dns   did not start
ER   European Record
f   finals
FAT   Fully Automatic Timing

GRW   Greco-Roman wrestling
h   hand (or manual) timing
H   hurdles
h j   high jump
IAAF   International Amateur Athletic Federation
jav   javelin
LAAC   Los Angeles Athletic Club
l b   pounds
l j   long jump
m   meter
mps   meters per second
MR   Meet Record
NAIA   National Association of Intercollegiate Athletics
NCAA   National Collegiate Athletic Association
N4A   National Amateur Athletic Association of America
nh   no height (failed to clear opening height)
nm   no mark (three fouls)
NR   National Record
NYAC   New York Athletic Club
NYPC   New York Pioneer Club
OG   Olympic Games
OR   Olympic Record
OT   Olympic Trials
pv   pole vault
SAME   Sam Adams Multiple Events
SBAC   Santa Barbara Athletic Club
sf   semifinals
s l j standing long jump
sp   shot put
TAC   The Athletics Congress/USA
TC   track club
unat   unattached
w   wind assisted mark
WR   World Record
wt   weight throw
y   yard
yd   yards

Others

a   automatic timing
AA   Athletic Association
AAA   Amateur Athletic Association (British)
AAU   Amateur Athletic Union (USA)
ACA   American Council of Athletes
AIA   Athletes in Action

CONVERSION TABLE: METERS TO IMPERIAL

Meters	Feet	Inches	Meters	Feet	Inches	Meters	Feet	Inches	Meters	Feet	Inches	Meters	Feet	Inches	Meters	Feet	Inches
1.60	5	3	3.70	12	1.75	5.90	19	4.25	10.00	32	9.75	23.00	75	5.5	45.00	147	8
1.65	5	5	3.80	12	5.75	6.00	19	8.25	10.50	34	5.5	24.00	78	9	46.00	150	11
1.70	5	7	3.90	12	9.5	6.10	20	0.25	11.00	36	1.25	25.00	82	0	47.00	154	2
1.75	5	9	4.00	13	1.5	6.20	20	4.25	11.50	37	8.75	26.00	85	4	48.00	157	6
1.80	5	11	4.10	13	5.5	6.30	20	8	12.00	39	4.5	27.00	88	7	49.00	160	9
1.85	6	0.75	4.20	13	9.5	6.40	21	0	12.50	41	0.25	28.00	91	10	50.00	164	0
1.90	6	2.75	4.30	14	1.25	6.50	21	4	13.00	42	8	29.00	95	2	51.00	167	4
1.95	6	4.75	4.40	14	5.25	6.60	21	8	13.50	44	3.5	30.00	98	5	52.00	170	7
2.00	6	6.75	4.50	14	9	6.70	21	11.75	14.00	45	11.25	31.00	101	8	53.00	173	11
2.05	6	8.75	4.60	15	1	6.80	22	3.75	14.50	47	7	32.00	105	0	54.00	177	2
2.10	6	10.75	4.70	15	5	6.90	22	7.75	15.00	49	2.5	33.00	108	3	55.00	180	5
2.15	7	0.75	4.80	15	9	7.00	22	11.75	15.50	50	10.25	34.00	111	6	56.00	183	9
2.20	7	2.75	4.90	16	0.75	7.10	23	3.5	16.00	52	6	35.00	114	10	57.00	187	0
2.25	7	4.5	5.00	16	4.75	7.20	23	7.5	16.50	54	1.75	36.00	118	1	58.00	190	3
2.30	7	6.5	5.10	16	8.75	7.30	23	11.5	17.00	55	9.25	37.00	121	5	59.00	193	7
3.00	9	10.25	5.20	17	0.75	7.40	24	3.5	17.50	57	5	38.00	124	8	60.00	196	10
3.10	10	2	5.30	17	4.5	7.50	24	7.25	18.00	59	0.75	39.00	127	11	61.00	200	1
3.20	10	6	5.40	17	8.5	7.60	24	11.25	18.50	60	8.5	40.00	131	3	62.00	203	5
3.30	10	10	5.50	18	0.5	7.70	25	3.25	19.00	62	4	41.00	134	6	63.00	206	8
3.40	11	2	5.60	18	4.5	7.80	25	7.25	20.00	65	7.5	42.00	137	9	64.00	210	0
3.50	11	5.75	5.70	18	8.25	7.90	25	11	21.00	68	10.75	43.00	141	1	65.00	212	3
3.60	11	9.75	5.80	19	0.25	8.00	26	3	22.00	72	7.25	44.00	144	4	66.00	216	6

HOW TO READ THE CHARTS

Career records

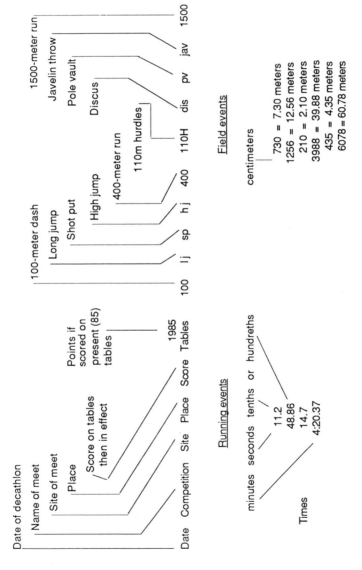

Note. In early sets of scoring tables (1912A and 1912B) decimals were used (e.g., 7726.625). The decimals have been dropped in the column headed "Score".

(Cont.)

HOW TO READ THE CHARTS (Continued)

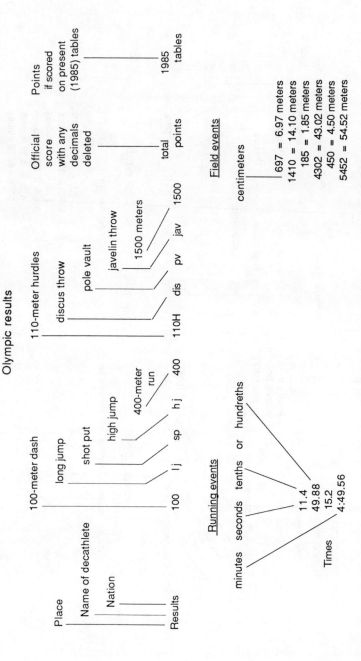

Olympic results

Place
Name of decathlete
Nation
Results

100-meter dash
long jump
shot put
high jump
400-meter run
110-meter hurdles
discus throw
pole vault
javelin throw
1500 meters

100 lj sp hj 400 110H dis pv jav 1500

Official score with any decimals deleted — total points

Points if scored on present (1985) tables — 1985 tables

Field events

centimeters
697 = 6.97 meters
1410 = 14.10 meters
185 = 1.85 meters
4302 = 43.02 meters
450 = 4.50 meters
5452 = 54.52 meters

Running events

minutes seconds tenths or hundreths

11.4
49.88
15.2
4:49.56

Times

Note. Scoring tables in use for 1912 to 1932 Olympic Games included decimals (e.g., 7654.445). The decimals have been dropped from the Olympic result tables. Official scores for individuals can be found in Appendix-B, Modern Olympic Games Competitors.

References

Adams, S. (1975). Decathlon. In F. Zarnowski & B. Nelson (Eds.), *The decathlon book* (p. 93). Emmitsburg, MD: DECA, The Decathlon Association.

Casson, L. (1984, June). The first Olympics: Competing for the greater glory of Zeus. *Smithsonian*, p. 69.

Clark, E. (1911). *Reminiscences of an athlete*. Boston: Houghton-Mifflin.

Doherty, K. (1985). *Track and field omnibook* (4th ed.). Los Altos, CA: Tafnews.

Harris, H.A. (1972). *Sport in Greece and Rome*. Ithaca, NY: Cornell.

International Amateur Athletic Federation. (1985). *Scoring tables for men's and women's combined event competitions*. London: Author.

Knab, R. (1934). *Die Periodoniken* [The all-around victors]. Chicago: Ares Publishers.

Mallon, B. (1985, March). The first tripler. *Fastracks*, p. 9.

Mallon, B. (1985, March). Martin J. Sheridan. *Fastracks*, pp. 11-12.

Mandel, R. (1984). *Sport, a cultural history*. New York: Columbia.

McKay, J. (1973). *My wide world*. New York: Macmillan.

McNab, T. (1971). *Decathlon*. London: British Amateur Athletic Board.

NCAA I track and field championship program. (1977). Champaign, IL: University of Illinois.

Nelson, B. (1969, October). Anatomy of a decathlete. *Track and Field News*, pp. 16-17.

Nelson, B. (1976). Mathias remembers that first Olympic year. In F. Zarnowski & B. Nelson (Eds.), *The decathlon book* (p. 47). Emmitsburg, MD: DECA, The Decathlon Association.

Nelson, B. (Ed.) (1984). *Track and field news' little gold book*. Los Altos, CA: Tafnews.

Nelson, C. (1970). *Track and field: The great ones*. London: Michael Joseph Ltd.

Pariente, R. (1979). *La fabuleuse histoire de l' athletisme* [The fabulous history of athletics]. Paris: Editions ODIC.

Quercetani, R. (1964). *A world history of track and field athletics: 1864-1964*. London: Oxford.

Redmond, G. (1971). *The Caledonian games in nineteenth-century America*. Rutherford, NJ: Fairleigh Dickinson.

Young, D.C. (1984). *The Olympic myth of Greek amateur athletics*. Chicago: Ares Publishers.

For Further Reading

The reader may be interested in additional readings on the decathlon or related topics. The author suggests the following titles.

Ancient Olympics

Andronicos, M. (1983). *Olympia* [The Olympics]. Athens: Ekotike Athenon S.A.

Ebert, J. (1963). *Zum pentathlon der antike* [Concerning the pentathlon of antiquity]. Berlin: Akademie-Verlag.

Harris, H.A. (1972). *Sport in Greece and Rome*. Ithaca, NY: Cornell.

Yalouris, N. (Ed.). (1979). *The eternal Olympics: The art and history of sport*. Athens: Caratzas Brothers.

Young, D. (1984). *The Olympic myth of greek amateur athletics*. Chicago: Ares Publishers.

An Age Without Multi-Events

Burns, F. (1981). *A history of Robert Dover's Olympick games*. Halesowen, Great Britain: Reliance Printing Works.

Redmond, G. (1971). *The Caledonian Games in nineteenth century America*. Rutherford, NJ: Fairleigh Dickinson.

Whitfield, C. (1962). *Robert Dover and the Cotswold Games*. London: Sotheran.

Decathlon History, The Early Years

Newcombe, J. (1975). *The best of the athletic boys*. Garden City, NY: Doubleday.

Pariente, R. (1979). *La fabuleuse histoire de l' athletisme* [The fabulous history of athletics]. Paris: Editions ODIC

Quercetani, R. (1964). *A world history of track and field athletics, 1864-1964*. London: Oxford.

Wheeler, R.W. (1975). *Jim Thorpe, world's greatest athlete*. Norman, OK: University of Oklahoma Press.

Decathlon History, The Modern Era

Jenner, B., & Finch, P. (1977). *Decathlon challenge: Bruce Jenner's story.* Englewood Cliffs, NJ: Prentice-Hall.

Rozin, S. (1983). *Daley Thompson: the subject is winning.* London: Stanley Paul & Company, Ltd.

Olympic Games

The Associated Press and Grollier. (1979). *Pursuit of excellence, the Olympic story.* New York: Franklin Watts.

Mallon, B., & Buchanan, I. (1984). *Quest for gold: the encyclopedia of American olympians.* New York: Leisure Press.

Wallechinsky, D. (1984). *The complete book of the Olympics.* New York: Penguin Books.

Rules and Scoring Tables

IAAF official handbook, 1988/89. (1988). London: International Amateur Athletic Federation.

Nelson, B. (Ed.). (1984). *Track and field news' the little gold book.* Los Altos, CA: Tafnews.

Rico, H. (Ed.). (1988). *1988 competition rules ·for athletics.* Indianapolis: The Athletics Congress/USA.

Scoring Tables for Men's and Women's Combined Events Competitions. (1985). London: International Amateur Athletic Federation.

Simmons, M. (Ed.) (1987). *NCAA track and field/cross-country rules.* Mission, KS: The National Collegiate Athletic Association.

Records

Zarnowski, F., & Hubbard, M. *U.S. decathlon/heptathlon handbook* (annual). Indianapolis: The Athletics Congress/USA.

Track and Field Magazines

Track and Field News Box 296 Los Altos, CA 94022 (monthly)

LeichtAthletik B & W Bartels and Wernitz Sportverlag GmbH Am Eichgarten 15 Postfach 41 05 60 1000 Berlin 41 West Germany (weekly)

Decathlon Newsletters

United States

DECA NEWSLETTER c/o Frank Zarnowski DECA/The Decathlon Association Mount St. Mary's College Emmitsburg, Maryland 21727 U.S.A. (8 issues per year)

Finland

SUL OTTELUT C/O Panu Siltanen Haapasaari 36420 Sahalahti SOUMI (Finland) (4-6 issues per year, in Finnish)

Britain

COMBINED EVENTS CLUB NEWSLETTER c/o Alan Lindop 10 Stanley Grove Baddeley Green' Stoke-on-Trent ST2 7JA England (4-6 issues per year)

Index

Wales, 144
Wallechinsky, David, xiv
Wanamaker, Rick, 4, 115
Warkentin, John, 115, 118
Warner, Glenn "Pop," 40
Warsaw Youth Festival, 79
Washington Park (New York City), 28
Washington State University, 126
Washington, University of, 126, 130
Wa-Tho-Huck (Jim Thorpe), 40
Watson, William, 73, 75-77, 258
Weierhauser, Jack, 184
Weldon, L.D., 61, 125
Wembly Stadium (London), 73, 175
Wentz, Siegfried "Siggi", 4, 129-132,
   137, 174, 214, 218, 222
Werthner, Georg, 129, 144, 212, 223, 237
Western Europe, 21, 24, 154
West Germany (FRG), 3, 7-8, 104, 107,
   111, 125, 129, 131, 179, 235
West Point, New York, 154
Westmont College, 192
Wheaties, 78
Whitson (Whitsun), 25
Wichita, Kansas, 64
Widlund, Ture, xiv
Wieslander, Karl Hugo, 30, 40, 41, 46-
   48, 99-101, 151
Winners, Ancient Olympic Pentathlon,
   17

Wooding, Jim, 4, 130, 218, 237
Worcester Academy (Massachusetts),
   111
World Championships, 129, 131, 138,
   142, 147
World History of Track, 240
World University Games (WUG), 104,
   125, 130, 132
World War I, 42, 154-155
World War II, 69, 154, 174, 192
Wrestling, Greco-Roman, 16

X
Xenophon of Corinth, 20

Y
Yale University, 21
Yang, C.K., 3, 4, 80, 89-90, 95, 96-98,
   103-104, 109, 187-188, 191-192, 194,
   205, 237, 243
Young, David C., 19
Yrjölä, Paavo, 49, 57-59, 60, 66, 162-163,
   235, 237, 239

Z
Zarnowski, Frank, xiv, 240
Zeilbauer, Josef, 212, 237
Zetes, 14
Zeus, 12, 23
Zhelanov, Sergei, 129, 212